D0152876

*Macroeconomic Policy
in a World Economy*

John B. Taylor
STANFORD UNIVERSITY

Macroeconomic Policy in a World Economy

From Econometric Design to Practical Operation

W. W. NORTON & COMPANY
New York   London

The text of this book is composed in Baskerville, with
display type set in Optima.
Composition by Integre Technical Publishing Co., Inc.
Manufacturing by The Maple-Vail Book Manufacturing Group.
Book design by F. Fodet.

Library of Congress Cataloging-in-Publication Data

Taylor, John B.
    Macroeconomic policy in a world economy : from econometric design to prac-
tical operation / John B. Taylor.
        p. cm.
    Includes index.
    1. Economic Policy.   2. International economic relations.   3. Econometrics.
I. Title.
HD87.T39   1993
339.5—dc20   93-16800

ISBN 0-393-96316-0

W. W. Norton & Company, Inc., 500 Fifth Avenue, New York, N.Y. 10110
W. W. Norton & Company Ltd., 10 Coptic Street, London WC1A 1PU

1 2 3 4 5 6 7 8 9 0

To my parents

Contents

List of Figures

List of Tables

Preface

This book deals with some difficult questions of macroeconomics and its practical application to monetary policy, fiscal policy, and international policy. It uses an approach that is an outgrowth of the research that is collectively referred to as the "rational expectations revolution." It is not, of course, the only outgrowth. Real business-cycle models, new classical models, and new Keynesian models are some of the other strands of the rational expectations revolution.[1]

The theoretical ideas and econometric techniques that define the approach have been the subject of much of my research efforts during the 1980s, especially during the years from 1985 to 1988 at Stanford. Although the theoretical and econometric research was essentially complete by the end of 1988, the preparation of this book was interrupted from 1989 to 1991 while I took leave from research and teaching to serve as a member of the President's Council of Economic Advisers. This book is considerably different from the book that would have been published three years ago and that was to focus almost entirely on the *design* of policy rules. As part of my macroeconomic and international economics responsibilities on the council, I had to consider from a practical perspective not only the design of policy rules but also their implementation and operation. Although this experience has increased my confidence in the approach, especially in comparison to the other outgrowths of the rational expectations revolution and to pre–rational expectations macroeconomics, it also convinced me of the importance of research on implementation and operation of policy. In completing the book in 1992, I drew on that experience along with the results from the earlier research.

[1] The research underlying the rational expectations revolution in macroeconomics is perhaps best represented by the collection of papers assembled by Lucas and Sargent (1981). Real business cycle theories are reviewed by McCallum (1989), new classical theories by Sargent (1987a), and new Keynesian theories by Mankiw and Romer (1991).

A significant motivation for this research program has been a conviction that if a new policy approach is genuinely to improve on the Keynesian approach to macroeconomics, it must entail replacements of the traditional Keynesian econometric models that have dominated practical Keynesian policy analysis. "It takes a model to beat a model," is a frequently heard Washington phrase. This is also the view set out by Robert Lucas and Thomas Sargent in their well-known attack on conventional methods of macroeconomic policy evaluation entitled "After Keynesian Macroeconomics" and reprinted in the Lucas and Sargent (1981) collection of readings. They argued,

> The Keynesian Revolution was, in the form in which it succeeded in the United States, a revolution in method. This was not Keynes' (1936) intent, nor is it the view of all of his most eminent followers. Yet if one does not view the revolution in this way, it is impossible to account for some of its most important features.... It is the fact that Keynesian theory lent itself so readily to the formulation of explicit econometric models which accounts for the dominant scientific position it attained by the 1960s. (p. 296)

As I hope becomes clear, the econometric approach presented in this book is fundamentally different from traditional Keynesian econometric approaches.

This book requires an econometric and technical economic background more advanced than the typical undergraduate macroeconomics course. However, the view of macroeconomics presented in this book is quite consistent with that presented in the undergraduate macroeconomics text written by myself and Robert Hall, especially in the emphasis on price-wage rigidities and rational expectations. That text presents very simple, illustrative versions of the more technical and practical models used here. Hence, this book could be titled "A Second Course in Macroeconomics" and could be read by students who would like to learn more about macroeconomic policy evaluation than can be provided at the intermediate undergraduate level. It could be used in first-year graduate courses or by specialists in academia and government who focus on macroeconomics and international finance issues. However, it would be a mistake to advertise this book as a text that attempts to explain all the different types of macroeconomic theories that are now seen in graduate schools. No attempt is made to cover the other outgrowths of the rational expectations revolution.

In developing these ideas and techniques I have been driven by the pragmatic goal of solving practical macroeconomic policy problems. I say this without apology, recognizing that in many cases the resulting econometric models are less elegant and less general than I would have tried to make them were it not for this pragmatic aim. Fortunately, there are ongoing efforts to provide more microfoundations for some of the ideas and techniques. Also fortunately, these efforts have thus far been more supportive than critical of the approach.[2]

---

[2]Phelps (1990) and Stiglitz (1984) summarize the work on microfoundations.

The Research Path

The origins of this book can be traced to my 1979 *Econometrica* paper "Estimation and Control of a Macroeconomic Model under Rational Expectations." That paper represented a prototype model to illustrate the approach and to demonstrate its feasibility. The simplicity of the model enabled me to not only estimate the parameters using rational expectations methods available at the time but also to simulate it and actually compute optimal policy rules. This permitted me to account for policy-induced parameter changes that the Lucas critique pointed out, deal with time-inconsistency issues by examining policy rules, and address some current policy issues by computing inflation-output trade-offs in terms of variances of inflation and real output rather than in terms of their levels. In a short follow-up paper, which I presented at the 1980 American Economics Association annual meeting [Taylor (1981)], I showed that the optimal policy rule could be approximated by a simple rule that embodied a concise principle: macroeconomic policy should not accommodate inflation but should be countercyclical. I have been gratified by the favorable reaction to this early work, and I still think that this basic principle is essentially correct. The model has been replicated many times, used for pedagogical purposes, and cited in debates about the major macroeconomic controversies. But in important respects, such a prototype model did not have the "horsepower" to tackle many practical macroeconomic policy problems.

Three key hurdles had to be crossed before that horsepower could be achieved. First, I had to develop a computationally tractable wage- and price-determination system consistent with the long-run neutrality implied by rational expectations but rich enough to explain wage-price and business-cycle dynamics. This task led me to the simple staggered wage-setting model, hinted at in an appendix to my 1979 *Econometrica* paper, but first published with the kinks worked out in the *Journal of Political Economy* in 1980.[3] That simple uniform-length contract structure needed to be generalized to multiple contract lengths with varying degrees of synchronization before it was able to fit wage data for different countries with a wide variety of wage-setting institutions. That generalization is presented in this book.

Second, rapid rational expectations solution algorithms and estimation techniques that could be applied to large nonlinear systems had to be developed. Stochastic simulations are essential for the macroeconomic policy evaluation approach I was developing, and without fast algorithms, the large number of required replications would be computationally infeasible

---

[3]I first tried to use the formulations of Phelps and Taylor (1977) or Fischer (1977), but I soon found that these would not work empirically: they could not explain the inertia/persistence of either wage-price movements or real output without the imposition of a large amount of ad hoc exogenous serial correlation. I developed the staggered contracts model to explain these dynamics endogenously with plausible, and eventually verifiable, assumptions about the length of wage- and/or price-setting intervals. Phelps (1990) recalls my excitement about the first computer runs, at the Columbia University Computer Center, which provided this verification.

even with supercomputers. Ates Dagli and I (1984) extended the linear symmetric procedures developed by Hansen and Sargent (1981) to linear nonsymmetric systems, which occurred in my models, but it was the non-linear method developed by Ray Fair and myself and published in the 1983 *Econometrica* that turned out to be most useful. That method has since become a workhorse for most large-scale rational expectations models. It is used extensively throughout this book.

Third, international linkages between countries needed to be developed. Empirically speaking, by the late 1970s neither the small open-economy model nor the closed-economy model made any sense for empirical or policy work for the United States. Hence, I decided that a multicountry model was needed and settled on a linkage system with perfect financial capital mobility as in the Mundell-Fleming model and with time-varying risk premia in foreign exchange and capital markets. Developments during the last few years have convinced me that this was a correct decision.

Brief Overview of the Book

The book is organized as follows. In the first chapter I give examples and categorize some of the major policy questions macroeconomists face. I also outline, using very stylized models, a general approach to answering such policy questions. The remaining chapters of the book use that approach to address actual policy issues by using estimated econometric models.

Chapter 2 starts with a linear econometric model of the U.S. economy. In addition to describing the estimation of the parameters of this model, Chapter 2 shows how the model is used for policy evaluation with both stochastic and deterministic simulations.

Chapter 3 describes the equations of a multicountry model of the G-7 countries (Canada, France, Germany, Italy, Japan, the United Kingdom, and the United States). The description focuses on the functional form and parameters of the ninety-eight stochastic equations. Chapter 4 describes the stochastic structure of the model as estimated over the sample period. Chapter 5 explores the effects of one-time changes in the policy instruments in the model.

The last three chapters focus on three modes of policy evaluation that correspond to the categories of questions defined in the opening chapter. Chapter 6 considers general policy-*design* issues, including the classic question of fixed versus flexible exchange rates. Chapter 7 considers *transition* problems, including choosing paths toward fiscal balance and low inflation. Chapter 8 considers the problem of everyday *operation* of policy rules.

Stanford, California
March 1993

Acknowledgments

I am fortunate to have received financial support for this research from the National Science Foundation, the Stanford Center for Economic Policy Research, and the National Bureau of Economic Research.

I am grateful to many colleagues and students who have helped me with this research. Guillermo Calvo, Phillip Cagan, Robert Mundell, and Ned Phelps were colleagues of mine at Columbia when I began to develop this research program. I am grateful to them for their encouragement and their ideas. I am also grateful to Larry Christiano, Ates Dagli, David Papell, and Dawn Rehm for assistance when the research was just beginning. More recently my Stanford macroeconomic colleagues—especially Robert Hall, Bert Hickman, Ronald McKinnon, Tom Sargent, and Joseph Stiglitz— have discussed, challenged, and constructively criticized the work, each from his own perspective. Tamin Bayoumi, Joseph Gagnon, Marcio Garcia, Peter Kleenow, Michael Knetter, Paul Lau, Andrew Levin, Ellen McGrattan, and John Williams all worked as research and programming assistants on the development of the multicountry model at Stanford. I am grateful to Craig Furfine, Jennifer Leland, and John Williams for their assistance in the preparation of the final manuscript.

I have also benefited from helpful comments from colleagues at other universities and research institutions. I am grateful to Robert Lucas for his encouraging comments in publications, seminars, and correspondence. Ray Fair, Ben McCallum, Manfred Neumann, and Ralph Tryon provided constructive written comments on papers that presented preliminary results from the research program. John Helliwell, Ralph Bryant, Dale Henderson, Gerald Holtham, Peter Hooper, Lawrence Klein, Steven Symansky, and Gerald Adams all provided helpful comments on my modeling approach as part of their model-comparison research.

I am also grateful to my colleagues on the Council of Economic Advisers—Michael Boskin and Richard Schmallensee—who, along with me, faced implementation and operation issues in putting forth "systematic and credible" policy principles. And I thank Brian Hall, Andrew Levin, and Brian Madigan for helping to make such a modeling approach work smoothly for policy evaluation at the Council of Economic Advisers.

I

Introduction

1

Macroeconomic Policy Questions and Methods

Monetary policy, fiscal policy, and exchange-rate policy all have powerful effects on the economy. It is not surprising that questions about these macroeconomic policies arise everyday in countries around the world. Sometimes the questions—such as the independence of the central bank, the formation of a currency bloc, or the enforcement of government budget rules—concern the fundamental design of the policy-making institutions. At other times the questions are about implementation of new monetary or fiscal policies—such as how fast to move to a noninflationary monetary policy or how soon to reach a balanced budget. Most frequently the questions concern much shorter-term operational issues, such as whether—in any given week or month—the central bank should be raising or lowering short-term interest rates.

Economists and others—business people, journalists, politicians—are called on, or volunteer, to answer such questions. Of course macroeconomists who work as advisers to the government answer such questions as part of their job. They also have to push their answers through the system until the policy decisions are made. Macroeconomic questions are rarely easy. It seems that the answers are usually either at the cutting edge of economic research—and therefore very controversial—or that there is little research going on and that top research economists are uninterested in the questions. This tends to leave the answering to noneconomists. The questions require quantitative rather than qualitative answers, so that econometric as well as theoretical considerations come into play. Almost always the questions are of great practical importance. Whether the economists' advice is given or not—or taken or not—the resulting policy decisions have profound effects on the performance of the economy.

The purpose of this book is to develop a framework to answer such macroeconomic policy questions. The framework is empirical and can deliver quantitative answers that are usually essential. The framework makes use of modern macroeconomic research, including rational expectations theory, time-consistency analysis, staggered price-setting theories, and new econometric and computer simulation techniques. In fact, the framework *is* modern economic research, and for this reason I think of it as an "interim" approach, recognizing that at least the details—and probably the broad features—of the approach will change as research continues. However, for the present I think that it is a reasonable way to provide "scientific" answers to practical macroeconomic questions. It should not come as a surprise, given its "scientific" aim, that the book is not meant for the casual reader or for the noneconomist. Although it does not dwell on theoretical issues for their own sake, it does require a basic understanding of technical economic and econometric issues.

This chapter develops the overall themes of the book. Section 1.1 outlines three general categories of macroeconomic policy questions. The categories require different modes of policy analysis. I use as examples questions that arose during the early 1990s. Similar questions have arisen before and will undoubtedly arise in the future. The tone of the chapter then shifts abruptly from the practical in Section 1.1 to the technical in Section 1.2, which describes methods used to obtain answers to each category of question. There is no way to avoid this shift, as the technical methods are needed to answer the practical questions, but perhaps the juxtaposition highlights the different levels at which macroeconomists must work. Section 1.3 then uses some stylized examples to illustrate the methods. These same methods are applied to actual policy questions in the remaining chapters of the book as previewed in Section 1.4.

1.1 Policy Rules and Types of Policy Questions

The notion of a policy rule, defined as the systematic response of the policy instruments to the state of the economy, is pervasive in modern macroeconomic research. However, I have found that it is not a common way to think about policy in practice. The distinction between the design of policy rules, the transition to new rules and the operation of policy rules, is meant to help bridge the gap between research and practice. Before explaining this distinction, it is necessary to be precise about the definition of policy rules used in this book.

First, a policy rule is not necessarily a fixed setting for the policy instruments, such as a constant-growth rate rule for the money supply. Feedback rules, in which the money supply responds to changes in unemployment or inflation, are also policy rules. For example, the automatic stabilizers of fiscal policy, such as unemployment compensation and the tax system, can be interpreted as a "policy rule." According to this rule, tax revenues and government expenditures automatically change when the economy expands or contracts. Research on the design of policy rules frequently finds that feedback rules dominate rules with fixed settings for the instruments. This, for example, is the finding of my 1979 *Econometrica* paper. There is little disagreement among macroeconomists that a policy rule should follow this broader interpretation.

Second—and there is more disagreement here—a policy rule need not be a mechanical formula. It can be implemented and operated more informally by policymakers who recognize the general instrument responses that underlie the policy rule and who also recognize that operating the rule requires judgment and cannot be done by computer. This broadens the scope of a policy rule significantly and permits the consideration of issues that would be excluded under the narrower definition. Thus, a policy rule would include a nominal-income rule, in which the central bank takes actions to keep nominal income on target, but it would not include pure discretionary policy. In broadening the definition we need to be careful not to lose the concept entirely. Under pure discretion, the settings for the instruments of policy are determined from scratch each period with no attempt to follow a reasonably well-defined contingency plan for the future. A precise analytical distinction between policy rules and discretion can be drawn from the time-consistency literature. In the time-consistency literature[1] (see Kydland and Prescott [1977], Calvo [1978], or Blanchard and Fischer [1989]), a policy rule is referred to as either the "optimal" or the "precommitted" solution to a dynamic optimization problem. Discretionary policy is referred to as the "inconsistent" or "shortsighted" solution. The advantage of rules over discretion, which the literature amply demonstrates, is one of the reasons why I have focussed on policy rules in this normative-oriented policy research.[2]

Third, if a policy rule is to have any meaning, it must be in place for a reasonably long period of time. For a macroeconomic policy rule, several business cycles would certainly be sufficient, but, for many purposes, several years would do just as well. Policymakers need to make a commitment to stay with the rule if they are to gain the advantages of credibility associated with it. Credibility enhances the performance of an economy under a good policy rule. For example, a credible monetary policy can reduce inflation with less loss of real output. Moreover, if economic analysis is to have much hope of assessing how the economy will perform with a policy rule, some durability of the rule is obviously required. For example, one of our tasks is to calculate how parameters of a reduced-form model change when the parameters of the policy rule change. Such calculations are of little use if the policy rule

---

[1] For an elementary discussion of the concept of time inconsistency in macroeconomics, see Hall and Taylor (1993, 537–543).

[2] It is not the only reason, however. My research on policy rules predates the time-inconsistency literature and goes back to my undergraduate thesis at Princeton in 1968 and my Ph.D. thesis at Stanford in 1973. Arguments made by Friedman (1948), Phillips (1954), and Lucas (1976) as well as rational expectations per se are other reasons to focus on policy rules.

is constantly in flux. On the other hand, a reasonably long period of time does not mean forever. One can easily imagine technological changes, such as, for example, the development of automatic teller machines, affecting the demand for money, which call for revisions in policy rules.

Now consider the three categories of policy issues, namely, those that relate to: (1) appropriate *design* of a policy rule; (2) the *transition* to a new policy rule once it is designed; and (3) the day-to-day *operation* of a policy rule once it is in place.

Design Questions

The first category pertains to the appropriate design of a policy rule. I give two examples of design questions. Both refer to monetary policy. One pertains to international monetary policy and to the exchange-rate system. The other pertains to domestic monetary policy and to the degree of accommodation by the monetary authorities.

Example: International Monetary Reform.   Preparations usually get underway well in advance of the annual economic summit meeting of the leaders of the G-7 countries—Canada, France, Germany, Italy, Japan, the United Kingdom, and the United States. In setting up the agenda for summit meetings in the early 1990s, representatives began to suggest that reform of the international monetary system be placed on the agenda. The emergence of new market economies in Eastern Europe and in the former Soviet Union, as well as the possibility of new roles for the International Monetary Fund (IMF) and the World Bank, have given new impetus to such an agenda. One such reform might be the adoption of a system with greater exchange-rate management, perhaps ultimately tying together the dollar, the yen, and the currencies in the European exchange-rate mechanism in a world fixed exchange-rate system.

Questions to address.   How should the United States and other countries react to such suggestions? Although the eventual answer would involve political and strategic issues, the underlying economic question is straightforward to state: Would it be a net benefit (quantitatively speaking) for the world economy if the dollar, the yen, and the currencies in the European exchange-rate mechanism were tied together in a world fixed exchange-rate system?

Example: Domestic Monetary Policy Accommodation.   In early August 1990, Iraq had just invaded Kuwait. The price of oil rose rapidly, and consumer confidence was dropping. The U.S. economy had been growing slowly since early 1989, partly as a result of a relatively tight monetary policy.

Questions that arose at the time.   How accommodative should monetary policy be to this oil-price shock? That is, by how much, if at all, should the instruments of monetary policy adjust in response to this shock? Is the "rule" that the Federal Reserve System (the Fed) appears to be following appropriate? What about other central banks? Should the issue be raised in the next international policy coordination meeting at the OECD in September? Should diplomatic pressure be applied? How much impact will this have on the performance of the U.S. economy? By how much will inflation rise under alternative circumstances?

Transition Questions

This category of questions involves how, when, or how rapidly to implement a new or modified policy rule. I give three examples of questions in this category. Two involve domestic policy, the other international policy.

Example: A Disinflation Path. There is general agreement among economists that a monetary policy rule should be designed to achieve price stability or near-zero inflation. When inflation persists at a higher rate than desired, whether in double digits as in the United States during the late 1970s or around 5 percent as in the late 1980s, the monetary policy rule must be changed so as to achieve a lower inflation.

Questions to address. How rapidly should the new rule be implemented? How quickly should the rate of inflation be reduced? Is a cold turkey or a gradual reduction more appropriate? How can the adverse effects of disinflation on the economy be minimized?

Example: A Path for Structural Budget-Deficit Reduction. In mid-1990, economic growth in the United States was weak, and economists were beginning to forecast a recession. Also, there was increasing evidence that the U.S. structural budget deficit was no longer declining through the Gramm-Rudman law, and negotiations on a multiyear budget agreement were planned. A key goal in entering the budget negotiations was to reduce the structural budget deficit, ideally to near zero. The intent was to change the "rule" for fiscal policy so that the budget would be balanced at full employment rather than in deficit.

Questions that arose at the time. By *how much* is it appropriate to reduce the Federal budget deficit in the first year of a multiyear agreement? One percent of the GNP? More? Less? Should the focus be on the structural deficit, with the actual deficit permitted to increase if there was a full-blown recession (as there turned out to be)? What would this distinction between structural and actual deficit do to the credibility of the deficit-reduction plan? What should the Fed do in response to a fiscal contraction brought on by a reduction in the federal budget deficit? By *how much* should the Federal funds rate be reduced? Does it matter whether the reduction in the deficit is credible?

Example: International Coordination to Reduce Saving-Investment Gaps.   As part of a series of bilateral talks (called the Structural Impediments Initiative), the government of Japan decided in mid-1990 to shift its fiscal policy stance so as to increase the level of public infrastructure investment as a share of GNP. A ten-year plan was proposed. The goal was to reduce the gap between savings and investment and thereby to reduce the trade surplus in Japan and, it was hoped, to reduce trade frictions between Japan and the United States. In this respect, the goal reflected the accounting identity that the gap between saving and investment equals the trade surplus.

Questions that arose at the time.   By how much is it appropriate to raise public infrastructure investment in the first year of the plan? Does it matter that the Japanese economy is booming and that the Bank of Japan is raising interest rates? Is there any chance that the change would show up in a quantitatively significant effect on the trade surplus in the first year and thereby start to reduce pressures for trade restrictions immediately?

Operational Questions

This category pertains to the day-to-day operation of a policy rule. Suppose that the Fed's policy rule is to raise systematically interest rates when inflation rises or the economy booms and to lower interest rates when inflation falls or the economy slumps. A typical example of how to operate such a rule concerns the interpretation of current developments. Here is an example that pertains to developments in international capital markets.

Example: The Source of a Rise in Long-Term Interest Rates.   In late 1989 and early 1990, long-term interest rates were rising sharply. Two explanations were frequently offered by analysts. (1) Economic unification of East and West Germany was likely and was expected to raise the demand for capital, and/or increase the budget deficit in Germany. Expectations of higher future interest rates in Germany were raising long-term interest rates in Germany and other countries, including the United States. (2) Renewed inflationary pressures were being reflected in higher long-term interest rates.

Questions that arose at the time.   Is the rise in interest rates due to developments in Eastern Europe, and in particular, to the expectation that the budget deficit will soon be increasing in Germany? Or is the increase due to additional pressures on inflation and the expectation of increases in future inflation? If the former is true, then the Fed would be true to the operation of its policy rule if it continued to lower interest rates as it had been planning to do in a weak economy with apparently declining inflationary pressures. Otherwise, it should hold off on further declines in interest rates. Answering such questions is clearly essential for the effective operation of a policy rule.

1.2 Technical Preliminaries: Stochastic Modeling with Rational Expectations

It must be difficult for a noneconomist to imagine how an economist could answer any of these questions without a quantitative framework. Although back-of-the-envelope calculations or textbook diagrams might provide intuition or help explain the answer, they don't tell the economist how to balance off hundreds of interrelated factors that bear on the answer. Moreover, modeling expectations in a reasonably sophisticated way is essential. The questions involve expectations of future interest rates, government spending, exchange rates, and oil prices.

Given the current state of economic knowledge, the most sophisticated quantitative model of expectations is a rational expectations econometric model, and this is the type of model I use in this book to answer these questions. In order to use a rational expectations model, one has to be able to solve it and understand what the solution means. Most rational expectations models that are useful for practical applications are either large or nonlinear or both. Numerical methods are needed to solve them. In order to understand how these methods deliver answers to the policy questions, there is no alternative to studying their technical properties, and this is the objective of this section.

I start with the most elementary of all stochastic rational expectations models: a linear relation between one variable, one expectation, and one stochastic shock. The solution method is one that can be used in different modes to handle the different categories of questions. I consider the solution of this model in some detail. It handles many stylized economic problems. Making analogies with this simple model, I then discuss briefly how one handles larger and nonlinear models.

Linear Models with One Variable

Let y_t be a variable satisfying the relationship

$$y_t = \alpha E_t y_{t+1} + \delta u_t, \tag{1.1}$$

where α and δ are parameters and E_t is the conditional expectation based on all information through period t, including knowledge of the model. The variable u_t is an exogenous shift variable or "shock" to the equation. It is assumed to follow a general linear process with the representation

$$u_t = \sum_{i=0}^{\infty} \theta_i \varepsilon_{t-i}, \tag{1.2}$$

where θ_i, $i = 0, 1, 2, \ldots$, is a sequence of parameters, and where ε_t is a serially uncorrelated random variable with zero mean. Note that ε_{t+i} for

$i \leqslant 0$ is in the information set for making the conditional expectation E_t. The shift variable could represent a policy variable. Alternatively it could represent a stochastic error term as in an econometric equation. In the latter case, δ would normally be set to 1.

The information upon which the expectation in Equation (1.1) is conditioned includes past and current observations on ε_t as well as the values of α, δ, and θ_i. Solving the model means finding a stochastic process for the random variable y_t that satisfies Equation (1.1). The forecasts generated by this process will then be equal to the expectations that appear in the model. In this sense, expectations are consistent with the model, or equivalently, expectations are rational.

The technical discussion will focus on a particular macroeconomic interpretation of Equation (1.1): an elementary macroeconomic model with perfectly flexible prices. This model is of course, far simpler than the econometric models needed to address the questions in Section 1.1. Nevertheless, the technical issues are conceptually the same. There is one policy instrument (the money supply) and one target variable (the price level). For this type of model the real rate of interest and real output are unaffected by monetary policy and thus they can be considered fixed constants. The demand for real-money balances—normally a function of nominal interest rate and real output—is therefore a function of only one variable: the expected inflation rate. If p_t is the log of the price level and m_t is the log of the money supply, then the demand for real money can be represented as

$$m_t - p_t = -\beta(E_t p_{t+1} - p_t), \tag{1.3}$$

where β is a positive coefficient. In other words, the demand for real-money balances depends negatively on the expected rate of inflation, as approximated by the expected first difference of the log of the price level. Equation (1.3) can be written in the form of Equation (1.1) by setting $\alpha = \beta/(1 + \beta)$ and $\delta = 1/(1 + \beta)$ and by letting $y_t = p_t$ and $u_t = m_t$. In this example, the variable u_t represents the supply of money. The money supply is assumed to be generated by the process of Equation (1.2).

The stochastic process for the shock variable u_t is assumed in Equation (1.2) to have a very general form. Any stationary stochastic process can be written this way. If u_t is a policy variable, then one can consider the design of alternative policy rules—as one would do to answer policy-design questions—by specifying different stochastic processes for u_t. For example, one could also have u_t be a function of y_t, which would entail a reinterpretation of the parameters in Equation (1.1).

In both *implementation* and *operation* applications, one is interested in "experiments" in which the policy variable is shifted in a special way and the response of the endogenous variables is examined. In forward-looking rational expectations models, the response depends not only on whether the shift in the policy variable is temporary or permanent but also on whether it is credibly anticipated or unanticipated. For example, the impact of future reductions in the budget deficit discussed in Section 1.1 would depend on whether the reductions were anticipated by the markets. Equation (1.2) can be given a special interpretation to characterize these different experiments, as follows:

Temporary versus permanent shocks. The shock u_t is purely temporary when $\theta_0 = 1$ and $\theta_i = 0$ for $i > 0$. Then any shock u_t is expected to disappear in the period immediately after it has occurred, that is, $E_t u_{t+i} = 0$ for $i > 0$ at every realization u_t. At the other extreme, the shock u_t is permanent when $\theta_i = 1$ for $i \geqslant 0$. Then any shock u_t is expected to remain forever, that is, $E_t u_{t+i} = u_t$ for $i > 0$ at every realization of u_t. By setting $\theta_i = \rho^i$, a range of intermediate-persistence assumptions can be modeled as ρ varies from 0 to 1. For $0 < \rho < 1$ the shock u_t phases out geometrically. In this case u_t can also be interpreted as $u_t = \rho u_{t-1} + \varepsilon_t$, a first-order autoregressive model.

Anticipated versus unanticipated shocks. Time delays between the realization of the shock and its incorporation in the current information set can be introduced by setting $\theta_i = 0$ for values of i up to the length of time of anticipation. For example, we can set $\theta_0 = 0$, $\theta_1 = 1$, $\theta_i = 0$ for $i > 1$, so that $u_t = \varepsilon_{t-1}$. This would characterize a temporary shock that is anticipated one period in advance. In other words, the expectation of u_{t+1} at time t is equal to u_{t+1} because $\varepsilon_t = u_{t+1}$ is in the information set at time t. More generally, a temporary shock anticipated k periods in advance would be represented by $u_t = \varepsilon_{t-k}$. A shock anticipated k periods in advance and that is then expected to phase out gradually would be modeled by setting $\theta_i = 0$ for $i = 1, \ldots, k - 1$ and $\theta_i = \rho^{i-k}$ for $i = k, k + 1, \ldots$, with $0 < \rho < 1$.

Solving the Model: Unanticipated Shocks. In order to find a solution for y_t, we begin by representing y_t in the unrestricted infinite moving average form

$$y_t = \sum_{i=0}^{\infty} \gamma_i \varepsilon_{t-i}. \tag{1.4}$$

Finding a solution for y_t requires determining values for the undetermined coefficients γ_i such that Equations (1.1) and (1.2) are satisfied. Equation (1.4) states that y_t is a general function of all possible events that may potentially influence y_t.

Note that the solution for y_t in Equation (1.4) is a general stationary stochastic process. From Equation (1.4), one can easily compute the variance and the autocovariance function of y_t and thereby study the effects of different policy rules on the stochastic behavior of y_t. That is, one can study the design of policy rules. But one can also use Equation (1.4) to calculate the effect of a one-time unit shock to ε_t, that is, experiment with implementation and operation of policy rules. The dynamic impact of such a shock is simply $dy_{t+s}/d\varepsilon_t = \gamma_s$.

To find the unknown coefficients, substitute for y_t and $E_t y_{t+1}$ in (1.1) by using (1.4) and solve γ_i in terms of α, δ, and θ_i. The conditional expectation $E_t y_{t+1}$ is obtained by leading (1.4) by one period and by taking expectations, making use of the equalities $E_t \varepsilon_{t+i} = 0$ for $i > 0$ and $E_t \varepsilon_{t+i} = \varepsilon_{t+i}$ for $i \leq 0$. The first equality follows from the assumption that ε_t has a zero unconditional mean and is uncorrelated; the second follows from the fact that ε_{t+i} for $i \leq 0$ is in the conditioning set at time t. The conditional expectation is

$$E_t y_{t+1} = \sum_{i=1}^{\infty} \gamma_i \varepsilon_{t-i+1}. \tag{1.5}$$

Substituting (1.2), (1.4), and (1.5) into (1.1) results in

$$\sum_{i=0}^{\infty} \gamma_i \varepsilon_{t-i} = \alpha \sum_{i=1}^{\infty} \gamma_i \varepsilon_{t-i+1} + \delta \sum_{i=0}^{\infty} \theta_i \varepsilon_{t-i}. \tag{1.6}$$

Equating the coefficients of ε_t, ε_{t-1}, ε_{t-2} on both sides of the equality (1.6) results in the set of equations

$$\gamma_i = \alpha \gamma_{i+1} + \delta \theta_i \qquad i = 0, 1, 2, \ldots. \tag{1.7}$$

The first equation in (1.7) for $i = 0$ equates the coefficients of ε_t on both sides of (1.6); the second equation similarly equates the coefficient for ε_{t-1} and so on.

Note that Equation (1.7) is a deterministic difference equation in the γ_i coefficients with θ_i as an exogenous variable. This deterministic difference equation has the same structure as the stochastic difference Equation (1.1). Once Equation (1.7) is solved for the γ_i, the solution for y_t follows immediately from Equation (1.4). Hence, the problem of solving a *stochastic* difference equation with conditional expectations of future variables has been converted into a problem of solving a *deterministic* difference equation.

Consider first the most elementary case where $u_t = \varepsilon_t$. This is the case of unanticipated shocks that are temporary. Then Equation (1.7) can be written

$$\gamma_0 = \alpha \gamma_1 + \delta \tag{1.8}$$

$$\gamma_{i+1} = \frac{1}{\alpha} \gamma_i \qquad i = 1, 2, \ldots. \tag{1.9}$$

From Equation (1.9) all the γ_i for $i > 1$ can be obtained once we have γ_1. However Equation (1.8) gives only one equation in the two unknowns γ_0 and γ_1. Hence, without further information, we cannot determine the γ_i-coefficients uniquely. The number of unknowns is one greater than the number of equations. This indeterminacy is what leads to nonuniqueness in rational expectations models.

If $|\alpha| \leq 1$, then the requirement that y_t is a stationary process will be sufficient to yield a unique solution. To see this, suppose that $\gamma_1 \neq 0$. Since

Equation (1.9) is an unstable difference equation, the γ_i coefficients will explode as i gets large. But then y_t would not be a stationary stochastic process. The only value for γ_1 that will prevent γ_i from exploding is $\gamma_1 = 0$. From Equation (1.9) this in turn implies that $\gamma_i = 0$ for all $i > 1$. From Equation (1.8) we then have that $\gamma_0 = \delta$. Hence, the unique stationary solution is simply $y_t = \delta \varepsilon_t$. In the case of the money-demand Equation (1.3), the price satisfies $p_t = (1 + \beta)^{-1} m_t$.

Using this relationship between the price level and the money supply, the variance of the price level can easily be computed as a function of the variance of the serially uncorrelated money shocks. Thus, the impact of this simple "policy rule" (purely random money shocks) on "macroeconomic performance" can be evaluated, though both are very trivial in this case.

Because $\beta > 0$, a temporary unanticipated increase in the money supply increases the price level by less than the increase in money. This is due to the fact that the log of the price level is expected to decrease to its normal value (zero) next period, thereby generating an expected deflation. The expected deflation increases the demand for money, so that real balances must increase. Hence, the price p_t rises by less than m_t. This is illustrated in Figure 1-1a.

For the more general case where shifts in u_t are expected to phase out gradually, we set $\theta_i = \rho^i$, where $\rho < 1$. Equation (1.7) then becomes

$$\gamma_{i+1} = \frac{1}{\alpha} \gamma_i - \frac{\delta \rho^i}{\alpha} \qquad i = 0, 1, 2, 3, \ldots. \tag{1.10}$$

Again, this is a standard deterministic difference equation. In this more general case, we can obtain the solution γ_i by deriving the solution to the homogeneous part $\gamma_i^{(H)}$ and the particular solution to the nonhomogeneous part $\gamma_i^{(P)}$.

The solution to (1.10) is the sum of the homogeneous solution and of the particular solution $\gamma_i = \gamma_i^{(H)} + \gamma_i^{(P)}$. (See Baumol [1970], for example, for a description of this solution technique for deterministic difference equations.) The homogeneous part is

$$\gamma_{i+1}^{(H)} = \frac{1}{\alpha} \gamma_i^{(H)} \qquad i = 0, 1, 2, \ldots, \tag{1.11}$$

with solution $\gamma_{i+1}^{(H)} = (1/\alpha)^{i+1} \gamma_0^{(H)}$. As in the earlier discussion, if $|\alpha| < 1$, stationarity requires that $\gamma_0^{(H)} = 0$. For any other value of $\gamma_0^{(H)}$ the homogeneous solution will explode. Stationarity therefore implies that $\gamma_i^{(H)} = 0$ for $i = 0, 1, 2, \ldots$.

To find the particular solution, we substitute $\gamma_i^{(P)} = hb^i$ into (1.10) and solve for the unknown coefficients h and b. This gives:

$$b = \rho,$$
$$h = \delta (1 - \alpha \rho)^{-1}. \tag{1.12}$$

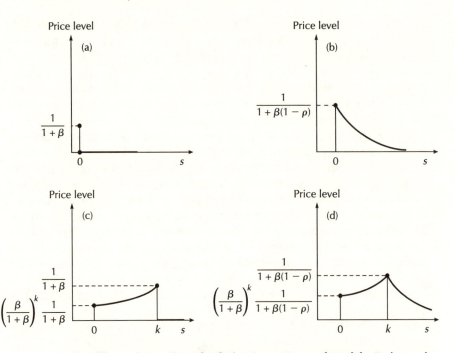

FIGURE 1-1   **The Effects of One-Time Shocks in Money-Demand Models.** Each panel shows the price-level effect. Panel (a) shows the effect of an unanticipated unit increase in m_t that lasts for one period. Panel (b) shows the price-level effect of an unanticipated increase in m_t that is phased out gradually. Panel (c) shows the price-level effect of an anticipated unit increase in m_{t+k} that lasts for one period. The increase is anticipated k periods in advance. Finally, Panel (d) shows the price-level effect of an anticipated unit increase in m_{t+k} that is phased out gradually. The increase is anticipated k periods in advance.

Because the homogeneous solution is identically equal to zero, the sum of the homogeneous and the particular solutions is simply

$$\gamma_i = \frac{\delta\rho^i}{1 - \alpha\rho}, \qquad i = 0, 1, 2, \dots. \tag{1.13}$$

In terms of the representation for y_t this means that

$$y_t = \frac{\delta}{1 - \alpha\rho} \sum_{i=0}^{\infty} \rho^i \varepsilon_{t-i}$$

$$= \frac{\delta}{1 - \alpha\rho} u_t. \tag{1.14}$$

For the simple macroeconomic example, this implies that the price level satisfies

$$p_t = \left(\frac{1}{1 + \beta(1 - \rho)} \right) m_t. \tag{1.15}$$

As in the simpler case, the stochastic properties of the price level can be computed once the value of ρ and hence the stochastic properties of the money supply is known, and the effects of one-time shocks can also be evaluated from these expressions. As long as $\rho < 1$, the increase in the price level will be less than the increase in the money supply. The dynamic impact on p_t of a unit shock to the money supply is shown in Figure 1-1b. The price level increases by less than the increase in the money supply because of the expected deflation that occurs as the price level gradually returns to its equilibrium value of 0. The expected deflation causes an increase in the demand for real-money balances that is satisfied by having the price level rise less than the money supply. For the special case that $\rho = 1$—a permanent increase in the money supply—the price level moves proportionately to money supply as in the simple-quantity theory. In that case, there is no change in the expected rate of inflation since the price level remains at its new level.

If $|\alpha| > 1$, then simply requiring y_t to be a stationary process will not yield a unique solution. In this case, Equation (1.9) is stable, and any value of γ_1 will give a stationary time series. There is a continuum of solutions, and it is necessary to place additional restrictions on the model if one wants to obtain a unique solution for the γ_i. There does not seem to be any completely satisfactory approach to take in this case. One possibility raised by Taylor (1977) is to require that the process for y_t have a minimum variance. An alternative rule for selecting a solution was proposed by McCallum (1983) and is called the "minimum state variable technique." In this case a representation for y_t that involves the smallest number of ε_t terms is chosen, hence giving $y_t = \delta\varepsilon_t$. Fortunately, for the estimated values of the parameters in the empirical models used in this book, this situation never arises.

Solving the Model: Anticipated Shocks. Consider now the case where the shock is anticipated k periods in advance and is purely temporary. That is, $u_t = \varepsilon_{t-k}$, so that $\theta_k = 1$ and $\theta_i = 0$ for $i \neq k$. The difference equations in the unknown parameters can be written as:

$$\gamma_i = \alpha\gamma_{i+1} \qquad i = 0, 1, 2, \ldots, k - 1$$

$$\gamma_{k+1} = \frac{1}{\alpha}\gamma_k - \frac{\delta}{\alpha}$$

$$\gamma_{i+1} = \frac{1}{\alpha}\gamma_i \qquad i = k + 1, k + 2, \ldots. \tag{1.16}$$

The last set of equations in (1.16) is identical in form to Equation (1.9), except that the initial condition is at $k + 1$ rather than at 1. For a stationarity condition we therefore require that $\gamma_{k+1} = 0$. This implies that $\gamma_k = \delta$. The remaining coefficients are $\gamma_i = \delta\alpha^{k-i}$, $i = 0, 1, 2, \ldots, k - 1$. Hence,

$$y_t = \delta[\alpha^k\varepsilon_t + \alpha^{k-1}\varepsilon_{t-1} + \cdots + \alpha\varepsilon_{t-(k-1)} + \varepsilon_{t-k}]. \tag{1.17}$$

In the simple macroeconomic example, when a temporary increase in the money supply is anticipated, the price level "jumps" at the date of announcement and then gradually increases until the money supply *does* increase. This is shown in Figure 1-1c. The eventual increase in the price level is the same as in the unanticipated case.

Finally, we consider the case where the shock is anticipated, but is expected to be permanent or to phase out gradually. Then $\theta_i = 0$ for $i = 1, \ldots, k - 1$ and $\theta_i = \rho^{i-k}$ for $i \geq k$. Equation (1.7) becomes

$$\gamma_i = \alpha\gamma_{i+1} \qquad i = 0, 1, 2, \ldots, k - 1,$$

$$\gamma_{i+1} = \frac{1}{\alpha}\gamma_i - \frac{\delta\rho^{i-k}}{\alpha} \quad i = k, k + 1, \ldots. \tag{1.18}$$

The coefficients can be obtained from (1.18) as in the previous cases. The solution for y_t is

$$y_t = \frac{\delta}{1 - \alpha\rho}(\alpha^k\varepsilon_t + \alpha^{k-1}\varepsilon_{t-1} + \cdots + \alpha\varepsilon_{t-(k-1)} + \varepsilon_{t-k}$$

$$+ \rho\varepsilon_{t-(k-1)} + \rho^2\varepsilon_{t-(k-2)} + \cdots). \tag{1.19}$$

For the simple macroeconomic model, where y_t is the price level, the effect of this type of shock is shown in Figure 1-1d. As before, the anticipation of an increase in the money supply causes the price level to jump. The price level then increases gradually until the increase in money actually occurs. During the period before the actual increase in money, the level of real balances is below equilibrium because of the expected inflation. The initial increase becomes larger as the phase-out parameter ρ gets larger. For the permanent case where $\rho = 1$, the price level eventually increases by the same amount as the money supply.

Linear Models with More than One Variable

The above solution method can be generalized and applied to linear models with many endogenous variables. To see this, first note that the simple model in Equation (1.1) can be generalized into a multivariate linear rational expectations model written as

$$B_0y_t + B_1y_{t-1} + \cdots + B_py_{t-p} + A_1E_ty_{t+1} + \cdots + A_qE_ty_{t+q} = Cu_t, \tag{1.20}$$

where the A_i and B_i are matrices, y_t is a vector of endogenous variables, and u_t is a vector of shocks. Equation (1.20) can be made to look much like Equation (1.1) by writing it as

$$E_t z_{t+1} = A z_t + D u_t \qquad (1.21)$$

by stacking $y_{t+q-1}, y_{t+q-2}, \ldots, y_{t-p}$ into vector z_t. Equation (1.21) can be solved using matrix generalizations of the method used to solve (1.1). In Equation (1.21), z_t is an n-dimensional vector and u_t is an m-dimensional vector of stochastic disturbances. The matrix A is n by n and the matrix D is n by m.

We describe the solution for the case of unanticipated temporary shocks: $u_t = \varepsilon_t$, where ε_t is a serially uncorrelated vector with a zero mean. The solution for z_t can be written in the general form:

$$z_t = \sum_{i=0}^{\infty} \Gamma_i \varepsilon_{t-i}, \qquad (1.22)$$

where the Γ_i values are the n by m matrices of unknown coefficients. Substituting (1.22) into (1.21) and equating the coefficients of the ε_{t-i}, we get

$$\Gamma_1 = A\Gamma_0 + D,$$
$$\Gamma_{i+1} = A\Gamma_i \qquad i = 1, 2, \ldots . \qquad (1.23)$$

Note that these matrix difference equations hold for each column of Γ_i separately, that is,

$$\gamma_1 = A\gamma_0 + d,$$
$$\gamma_{i+1} = A\gamma_i \qquad i = 1, 2, \ldots, \qquad (1.24)$$

where γ_i is any one of the n by 1 column vectors in Γ_i, and where d is the corresponding column of D. Equation (1.24) is a deterministic first-order vector difference equation analogous to the stochastic difference equation in (1.21). The solution for the Γ_i is obtained by solving for each of the columns of Γ_i separately using (1.24).

The analogy from the one-variable case is now clear. There are n equations in the first vector equation of (1.24). In a given application we will know some of the elements of γ_0 but not all of them. Hence, there will generally be more than n unknowns in (1.24). The number of unknowns is $2n - k$, where k is the number of values of γ_0 we know.

To get a unique solution in the general case, we therefore need $(2n - k) - n = n - k$ additional equations. These additional equations can be obtained by requiring that the solution for y_t be stationary or equivalently, in this context, that the γ_i do not explode. If there are exactly $n - k$

distinct roots of A that are greater than 1 in modulus, then we have exactly the number of additional equations necessary for a solution. If there are less than $n - k$ roots, then we have a nonuniqueness problem.

Suppose this root condition for uniqueness is satisfied. Let the $n - k$ roots of A that are greater than 1 in modulus be $\lambda_1, \ldots, \lambda_{n-k}$. Diagonalize A as $H^{-1}\Lambda H = A$. Then the second equation in (1.24) can be written as

$$H\gamma_{i+1} = \Lambda H\gamma_i \qquad i = 1, 2, \ldots. \tag{1.25}$$

$$\begin{pmatrix} H_{11} & H_{12} \\ H_{21} & H_{22} \end{pmatrix} \begin{pmatrix} \gamma_{i+1}^{(1)} \\ \gamma_{i+1}^{(2)} \end{pmatrix} = \begin{pmatrix} \Lambda_1 & 0 \\ 0 & \Lambda_2 \end{pmatrix} \begin{pmatrix} H_{11} & H_{12} \\ H_{21} & H_{22} \end{pmatrix} \begin{pmatrix} \gamma_i^{(1)} \\ \gamma_i^{(2)} \end{pmatrix} \qquad i = 1, 2, \ldots, \tag{1.26}$$

where Λ_1 is a diagonal matrix with all the unstable roots on the diagonal. The γ vectors are partitioned accordingly, and the rows (H_{11}, H_{12}) of H are the characteristic vectors associated with the unstable roots. Thus, for stability we require

$$H_{11}\gamma_1^{(1)} + H_{12}\gamma_1^{(2)} = 0, \tag{1.27}$$

which implies that the solution of the unstable part of the system stays at zero. Equation (1.27) gives the additional $n - k$ equations needed for a solution. Having solved for γ_1 and the unknown elements of γ_0, we then obtain the remaining γ_i coefficients from Equation (1.24).

Alternatively the solution of (1.20) can be obtained directly without forming a large first-order system. By substituting the general solution of y_t into (1.24) and by examining the equation in the Γ_i coefficients, the solution can be obtained by factoring the characteristic polynomial associated with these equations. This approach was used by Hansen and Sargent (1981), where $p = q$ and $B_i = hA_i'$. In that case, the factorization can be shown to be unique by an appeal to the factorization theorems for spectral-density matrices. In general econometric applications, these special properties on the A_i and B_i matrices do not hold. Whiteman (1983) has a proof that a unique factorization exists under conditions analogous to those placed on the roots of A in Equation (1.22). Dagli and Taylor (1984) proposed an iterative method to factor the polynomials in the lag operator in order to obtain a solution. This factorization method is used to solve and estimate the five-equation rational expectations model of the United States using full information maximum likelihood (see Chapter 2).

Nonlinear Models

Unfortunately, many practical rational expectations models are not linear, so that the above methods cannot be used. However, nonlinear solution methods are available and, although computationally different from the above methods, they are conceptually very similar. They can be used to compute the effects of policy in much the same way.

A general nonlinear rational expectations model can be written as

$$f_i(y_t, y_{t-1}, \ldots, y_{t-p}, E_t y_{t+1}, \ldots, E_t y_{t+q}, a_i, x_t) = u_{it} \qquad (1.28)$$

for $i = 1, \ldots, n$, where y_t is an n-dimensional vector of endogenous variables at time t, x_t is a vector of exogenous variables, a_i is a vector of parameters, and u_{it} is a vector of disturbances.

Fair and Taylor (1983) proposed an iterative method—called the extended path method—to solve this type of nonlinear model. Briefly it works as follows. Note that if we knew the expectations of future variables, Equation (1.28) would be easy to solve. It would be a standard system of simultaneous equations that could be solved using some nonlinear method, such as Gauss-Siedel, which is the method used to solve conventional (non-rational expectations) models. The solution would provide values for variables y_t. The extended path method works by guessing and successively updating the guesses of these future variables. For each guess, the model is solved, providing an updated guess. The model is solved again and so on.

To be more specific, first guess values for the expectations $E_t y_{t+j}$ in Equation (1.28) for a particular horizon $j = 1, \ldots, J$. Second, using these values, solve the model to obtain a new solution path for y_{t+j}. Third, replace the initial guess of $E_t y_{t+j}$ with the new solution y_{t+j}. The three steps can then be repeated again and again until the solution path y_{t+j} for $j = 1, \ldots, J$ converges.

However, this solution may depend on the horizon J. To check this, extend the solution path from J to $J + 1$ and repeat the previous sequence of iterations until convergence is reached. If the values of y_{t+j} for this extended horizon ($J + 1$) are within the tolerance range of the values for the J-period horizon, then stop; otherwise, extend the path one more period to $J + 2$ and so on. Because the model is nonlinear, the Gauss-Seidel method is used for each iteration given a guess for the expectation variables.

There are no general proofs available to show that this method works for an arbitrary nonlinear model. When applied to the linear model in Equation (1.1) with $|\alpha| < 1$, the method converges as demonstrated by Fair and Taylor (1983). When $|\alpha| > 1$, the iterations diverge. A convergence proof for the general linear model is not available, but many experiments have indicated that convergence is achieved under the usual assumptions.

The extended path method is fairly easy to use and has become the most common method of solving large nonlinear rational expectations models. It is used extensively in this book to solve the nonlinear multicountry model.

Note that once a solution is obtained, the stochastic properties of y_t can be determined by stochastic simulations: different values for u_{it} on the right-hand side of Equation (1.28) can be drawn from a random-number generator. The means, variances, and covariances of the elements of y_t can then be calculated by averaging across these draws. Moreover, the effects of one-time changes in the instruments are obtained by deterministic simulation, that is, by solving the model for a different path of the exogenous variables. The effects of anticipated and unanticipated changes in the instrument can both be calculated. Hence, although the method is numerical rather than analytical, all the policy simulations conducted with a linear model can be conducted with a nonlinear model.

1.3   The Lucas Critique

Lucas (1976) argued that the parameters of the models conventionally used for policy evaluation—either through model simulation or formal optimal control—would shift when policy changed. The main reason for this shift is that expectations mechanisms are adaptive, or backward looking, in conventional models and thereby unresponsive to those changes in policy that would be expected to change expectations of future events. Hence, the policy-evaluation results using conventional models would be misleading.

The Lucas criticism of conventional policy evaluation has typically been taken as destructive. Yet, implicit in the Lucas criticism is a constructive way to improve on conventional evaluation techniques by modeling economic phenomena in terms of "structural" parameters; by "structural," one simply means invariant with respect to policy intervention. Whether a parameter is invariant or not is partly a matter of a researcher's judgment, of course, so that any attempt to take the Lucas critique seriously by building structural models is subject to a similar critique that the researcher's assumption about which parameters are structural is wrong. This applies even if the only structural parameters are the "deep parameters" of utility functions. If taken to this extreme that no feasible structural modeling is possible, the Lucas critique does indeed become purely destructive and perhaps even stifling. The three examples used by Lucas in his critique were a Friedman-type consumption equation, a Hall-Jorgenson investment equation, and a Phillips curve. None of the examples incorporated the deep parameters of utility functions, although all could clearly benefit—and have benefited— from greater theoretical research. So could the money-demand equation used here for illustration.

Consider the following policy problem, which is based on a model like that of Equation (1.3). Suppose that an econometric policy advisor knows that the demand for money is given by

$$m_t - p_t = -\beta(E_t p_{t+1} - p_t) + u_t. \tag{1.29}$$

Here there are two shocks to the system, the supply of money m_t and the demand for money u_t. Suppose that $u_t = \rho u_{t-1} + \varepsilon_t$ and that in the past the money supply was fixed: $m_t = 0$; suppose that under this fixed money policy, prices were thought to be too volatile. The policy advisor is asked by the Central Bank to advise on how m_t can be used in the future to reduce the fluctuations in the price level. Note that the policy advisor is not asked just what to do today or tomorrow, but what to do for the indefinite future. Advice thus should be given as a contingency rule rather than as a fixed path for the money supply.

The behavior of p_t during the past is

$$p_t = \rho p_{t-1} - \frac{\varepsilon_t}{1 + \beta(1 - \rho)}. \tag{1.30}$$

Conventional policy evaluation might proceed as follows: first, the econometrician would have estimated ρ in the reduced-form relation (1.30) over the sample period. The estimated equation would then serve as a model of expectations to be substituted into (1.31); that is, $E_t p_{t+1} = \rho p_t$ would be substituted into

$$m_t - p_t = -\beta(\rho p_t - p_t) + u_t. \tag{1.31}$$

The conventional econometrician's model of the price level would then be

$$p_t = \frac{m_t - u_t}{1 + \beta(1 - \rho)}. \tag{1.32}$$

Considering a policy rule of the form $m_t = g u_{t-1}$, Equation (1.32) implies

$$\text{Var } p_t = \frac{1}{[1 + \beta(1 - \rho)]^2(1 - \rho^2)} \sigma_\varepsilon^2 [g^2 + 1 - 2g\rho]. \tag{1.33}$$

Equation (1.33) indicates that the best choice for g to minimize fluctuation in p_t is $g = \rho$.

But we know that Equation (1.33) is incorrect if $g \neq 0$. The error was to assume that $E_t p_{t+1} = \rho p_t$ regardless of the choice of policy. This is precisely the point of the Lucas critique. The correct approach would have been to substitute $m_t = g u_{t-1}$ directly into Equation (1.29) and to calculate the stochastic process for p_t. This results in

$$p_t = \frac{-1 - \beta(1 - g)}{(1 + \beta)(1 + \beta(1 - \rho))} u_t + \frac{g}{1 + \beta} u_{t-1}. \tag{1.34}$$

Note how the parameters of Equation (1.34) depend on the parameters of the policy rule. The variance of p_t can thus easily be calculated, and the optimal policy is found by minimizing $\text{Var } p_t$ with respect to g.

This simple policy problem suggests the following approach to macro-policy evaluation: (1) derive a stochastic equilibrium solution that shows how the endogenous variables behave as a function of the parameters of the policy rule; (2) specify a welfare function in terms of the moments of the stochastic equilibrium; and (3) maximize the welfare function across the parameters of the policy rule. In this example, the welfare function is simply Var p.

The Lucas critique can be usefully thought of as a dynamic extension of the critique developed by the Cowles Commission researchers in the late 1940s and early 1950s, which gave rise to the enormous literature on simultaneous equations. At that time it was recognized that reduced forms could not be used for many policy-evaluation questions. Rather, one should model structural relationships. The parameters of the reduced form are, of course, functions of the structural parameters in the standard Cowles Commission setup. The discussion by Marschak (1953), for example, is remarkably similar to the more recent rational expectations critiques; Marschak did not consider expectations variables, and in this sense, the rational expectations critique is a new extension. But earlier analyses like Marschak's were an effort to explain why structural modeling is necessary, and thus they have much in common with more recent research.

1.4   Economic Policy Rules and Shocks in a Stylized Two-Country Model

The previous two sections showed how rational expectations models can be used to calculate the effects of one-time changes in the policy instruments and to evaluate the properties of different policy rules. The primary example, however, has been very simple: a one-policy variable, such as the money supply, and a one-target variable, such as the price level.

To illustrate how the method works in a more meaningful setting, this section examines the effects of policy in a stylized two-country model. The model is similar to that found in an undergraduate textbook model, except that it presents rational expectations and staggered wage setting that generate both short-run fluctuations in the economy and long-run neutrality. In addition, the two countries are linked together by a capital market with perfect capital mobility. In the same way that models used in most undergraduate texts provide a stylized account of how traditional econometric models without rational expectations work, this section provides a stylized account of how the econometric models with rational expectations work. Understanding how the model works will aid greatly in understanding the more complex econometric models introduced later in the book.

Table 1-1 displays the equations of the model and defines the notation. There are two countries: A and B. All the variables except the interest rates and the inflation rates are measured as logarithms, and all variables are deviations from means or secular trends. For example, y is the deviation of the log of real output from secular or potential output. Potential output is assumed to be unaffected by the policy changes considered here, although that assumption could be modified. Equations (1A) through (6A) in Table 1-1 describe country A; Equations (1B) through (6B) describe country B; an

TABLE 1-1   Stylized Two-Country Rational Expectations Model

Country A

$$x_t = (\delta/3)\sum_{i=0}^{2} \hat{w}_{t+i} + [(1 - \delta)/3]\sum_{i=0}^{2} \hat{p}_{t+i} + (\gamma/3)\sum_{i=0}^{2} \hat{y}_{t+i} \tag{1A}$$

$$w_t = \tfrac{1}{3}\sum_{i=0}^{2} x_{t-i} \tag{2A}$$

$$p_t = \theta w_t + (1 - \theta)(e_t + p_t^*) \tag{3A}$$

$$y_t = -dr_t + f(e_t + p_t^* - p_t) + gy_t^* \tag{4A}$$

$$m_t - p_t = -bi_t + ay_t \tag{5A}$$

$$r_t = i_t - \hat{\pi}_t \tag{6A}$$

Capital Mobility Condition

$$i_t = i_t^* + \hat{e}_{t+1} - e_t$$

Country B

$$x_t^* = (\delta^*/3)\sum_{i=0}^{2} \hat{w}_{t+i}^* + [(1 - \delta^*)/3]\sum_{i=0}^{2} \hat{p}_{t+i}^* + (\gamma^*/3)\sum_{i=0}^{2} \hat{y}_{t+i}^* \tag{1B}$$

$$w_t^* = \tfrac{1}{3}\sum_{i=0}^{2} x_{t-i}^* \tag{2B}$$

$$p_t^* = \theta^* w_t^* + (1 - \theta^*)(p_t - e_t) \tag{3B}$$

$$y_t^* = -d^* r_t^* - f^*(e_t + p_t^* - p_t) + g^* y_t \tag{4B}$$

$$m_t^* - p_t^* = -b^* i_t^* + a^* y_t^* \tag{5B}$$

$$r_t^* = i_t^* - \hat{\pi}_t^* \tag{6B}$$

Definition of Variables and Parameter Values

Variables

y_t = real GNP (log)
p_t = price level (log)
i_t = nominal interest rate
r_t = real interest rate
π_t = inflation rate
w_t = nominal wage (log)
m_t = money supply (log)
x_t = contract wage (log)
e_t = exchange rate (log); country A price of country B currency
$\hat{}$ = conditional expectation based on information through period t

Parameter values for simulations

$\delta = 0.5$
$\gamma = 1.0$
$\theta = 0.8$
$d = 1.2$
$f = 0.1$
$g = 0.1$
$b = 4.0$
$a = 1.0$

asterisk denotes the variables of country B. The remaining equation is the condition of perfect capital mobility: the interest rate in country A is equal to the interest rate in country B plus the expected rate of depreciation of the currency of country A. In a Mundell-Fleming model with fixed prices and no expectations, the interest rates are equal. Because the structure in the two countries is the same, we need to describe only the equations in country A.

Equation (1A) is a staggered wage-setting equation much like that used in Taylor (1980). The "contract" wage is denoted by (x). A wage decision is assumed to last for three periods, with only one-third of the wages being negotiated in any one year. The wage set at time t depends on expectations of future wages paid to other workers, expectations of prices, and expectations of future demand conditions as proxied by the deviation of real output from trend. Equation (2A) defines the average wage in the economy as a whole. Equation (3A) is a markup pricing equation; prices of domestic goods are a weighted average of wages and the prices of imported inputs to production measured in domestic currency units. Equations (4A) and (5A) are *IS* and *LM* curves respectively, just like those found in undergraduate texts. The real interest rate differs from the nominal interest rate according to the rationally expected inflation rate as described in Equation (6A).

The Impact of Changes in the Policy Instruments

The Closed Economy.   To give some perspective to the two-country results, first consider the effects of changes in the instruments of monetary and fiscal policy in the *closed* economy described by Equations (1A) through (6A) with $\theta = 1, f = 0$, and $g = 0$. These restrictions correspond to no international linkages. These are the types of experiments one needs to run to find out the properties of this kind of model. As we will see, they are also useful in studying the transition from one policy rule to another. The coexistence of rational expectations and forward-looking, though sticky, prices gives rise to a number of phenomena that are unlike standard models.

Consider separately a money shock and a fiscal shock.[3] The money shock is a 1-percent unanticipated permanent increase in the money supply, and the fiscal shock is a 1-percent unanticipated permanent rightward shift in the *IS* curve (Equation [4A]). The latter shift could be due to a change in government purchases. The results are shown in Figure 1-2. The figure shows the actual values of the variables rather than their logarithms. In Figure 1-2, the fiscal shock is denoted by a dashed line, and the money shock is denoted by a solid line. If only a solid line appears for a particular period, the effects of the money and fiscal shocks are the same. No attempt

[3]The model was solved using the extended path algorithm described in Section 1.2. Alternatively, since the model is linear, it could be solved by the factorization algorithm or by computing the roots explicitly as described in Section 1.2, although for the higher-order models this might not be practical.

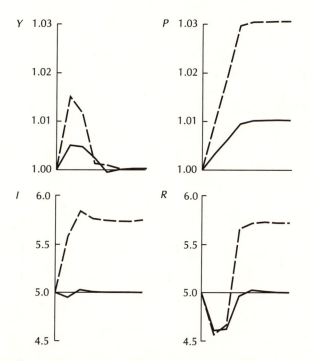

FIGURE 1-2   **Policy Impact in a Closed Economy.** The chart shows the impact of fiscal (dashed line) and monetary (solid line) shocks in a closed economy on real output (*Y*), price level (*P*), nominal interest rate (*I*), and real interest rate (*R*).

has been made to scale the shocks so as to give similar effects for monetary and fiscal policy.

Monetary policy has an expected positive effect on output that dies out as prices rise and real-money balances fall back to where they were at the start. Note that the real interest rate drops more than the nominal rate because of the increase in expected inflation that occurs at the time of the monetary stimulus. For this set of parameters the nominal interest rate hardly drops at all; all the effect of monetary policy shows up in the real interest rate.

Fiscal policy creates a similar dynamic pattern for real output and for the price level. Note, however, that there is a surprising "crowding-in" effect of fiscal policy in the short run as the increase in the expectation of inflation causes a drop in the real interest rate. Eventually the expected rate of inflation declines and the real interest rate rises; in the long run, private spending is completely crowded out by government spending.

Two Countries with a Flexible Exchange Rate.   The effects of monetary and fiscal shocks in the full two-country model are shown in Figure 1-3 when the exchange rate is perfectly flexible. For these simulations the parameters are assumed to be the same in both countries and are given in Table 1-1. In all of

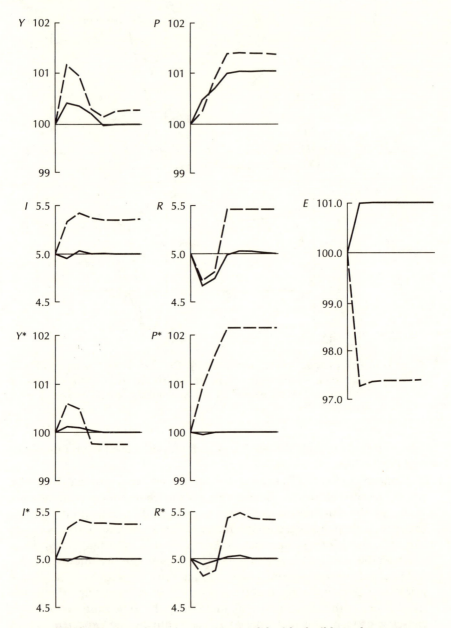

FIGURE 1-3   Policy Impacts in a Two-Country Model with Flexible Exchange Rates. The charts show the effects of fiscal (dashed line) and monetary (solid line) shocks.

these experiments, the policy shock occurs in country A. Later in the book we conduct such experiments in an empirically estimated multicountry model.

The dynamic impact in country A of a fiscal shock is similar to the closed-economy case. The initial impact on real output is only slightly less than in the closed economy, and the effect dies out at about the same rate. There is also an initial drop in the real interest rate, and this is the primary reason for the strong effect of fiscal policy in the flexible exchange-rate regime. As in the fixed-price Mundell-Fleming model, the exchange rate of country A appreciates, so that exports are crowded out by fiscal policy, but the drop in the real interest rate stimulates investment. Note that the long-run output effect of the fiscal shock is slightly positive in country A. This is matched by an equally negative long-run output effect in country B. However, there is an initial positive output effect in country B as the real interest rate first declines before increasing and crowding out investment spending. Fiscal policy has inflationary effects abroad, partly because of the depreciation of the foreign currency.

The effect of an increase in the money supply in country A is also much like that in the closed economy. There is a positive short-run effect on output that diminishes to zero over time. Part of the monetary stimulus comes from a depreciation of the currency of country A, and part comes from the decline in real interest rates. There is no significant overshooting of the exchange rate following the monetary impulse. Unlike in the Mundell-Fleming model, however, the increase in the money supply is not contractionary abroad. A monetary stimulus can have a positive effect abroad because the price level is not fixed; the depreciation of country A's currency reduces prices in country B, and this raises real balances in that country. The real interest rate also declines slightly in country B.

Two Countries with a Fixed Exchange Rate.   For comparison we report in Figure 1-4 the results from similar experiments with fixed exchange rates. For this purpose, the model is altered; the exchange rate becomes an exogenous variable, and the money supply in country B becomes an endogenous variable. The capital-mobility condition is then simply $i_t = i_t^*$. Again the shocks occur in country A. But now country B must give up an independent monetary policy. The money supply in country B must move around in order to keep the exchange rate fixed.

The short-run output effects of fiscal policy with fixed exchange rates are a bit weaker in country A compared with the flexible exchange-rate case. The output effects abroad are strongly negative, even in the short run. There is no short-run decline in the real interest rate in country B, as there was when the exchange rate could adjust. In fact, the real interest rate in country B overshoots its new higher long-run equilibrium value. Note that in order to keep the exchange rate fixed, country B must reduce its money supply. This means that its price level must eventually fall; in the

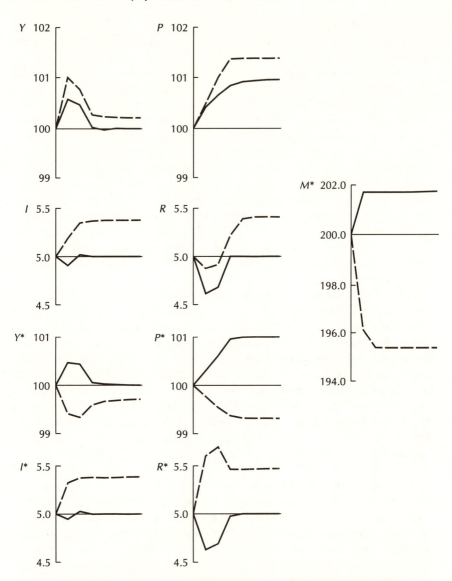

Figure 1-4 Policy Impacts in a Two-Country Model with Fixed Exchange Rates. The charts show the effects of fiscal (dashed line) and monetary (solid line) shocks.

short run there is thus an expected deflation that raises the real interest rate in country B for a time above the long-run equilibrium.

Monetary policy has a larger effect on real output in country A than in the flexible exchange rate case. In the long run, the output effect diminishes, and the price level rises by the same amount as the money supply. The effect of this monetary policy on the other country is much stronger than in the case of flexible exchange rates. In order to keep the exchange rate fixed, the monetary authority in country B must expand its money supply by the same amount as the money increase in country A. This has stimulative effects on real output that duplicate the effects of money in country A.

Effects of Changes in Policy Rules

The problem of designing policy rules can also be illustrated in this stylized model. This is an issue that will be considered empirically in Chapters 2 and 6. There are obviously many alternative policy rules to consider. Besides policy rules for the money supply, one can consider policy rules for interest rates. For example, a nominal interest-rate rule could take the form $i_t = a_i p_t$. A real interest-rate rule could have a similar form $r_t = a_r p_t$. Both of these are different from a money-supply rule of the form $m_t = a_m p_t$. All three are possible characterizations of monetary policy. These rules state that the policy instruments should be changed whenever prices rise above target. Recall that in this model the price target is normalized to zero. The effects of these rules can be calculated by plugging them into the model and by solving the model.

The real interest-rate rule for the single-country model ($\theta = 1$, $f = 0$, $g = 0$) is particularly easy to analyze. Such a rule can be substituted directly into Equation (4A) to obtain an equation involving p_t and y_t (an aggregate-demand equation). Combining this with Equations (1A), (2A), and (3A) gives a simple two-variable model from which stochastic processes for p_t and y_t can be solved. In fact, that model is exactly the same as the simple staggered contract model of Taylor (1980). By varying parameter a_r of the policy rule, the "operating characteristics" of prices and output change. A trade-off between the variance of output and the variance of the price level is traced out.

Consider the variance of output and prices in the two-country world economy under alternative real interest-rate rules. Since there are two countries, we need to specify two such interest-rate rules. Let these be:

$$r_t = a_r p_t,$$
$$r_t^* = a_r^* p_t^*.$$

We can solve and stochastically simulate the two-country model for different values of a_r and a_r^*. Variances calculated for policy rules for four cases in which a_r and a_r^* equal 0.2 and 0.6 are reported in Table 1-2. These calculations are made under the assumption that only supply shocks continually occur in both countries, that these shocks are unanticipated and temporary, and that they are uncorrelated between the countries. In other words, Equations (1A) and (1B) are continuously shocked by serially and contemporaneously uncorrelated random variables.

Table 1-2 indicates that there is relatively little interaction between the policy rules in the two countries. For example, as the home country moves

TABLE 1-2   Output and Price Variability in Two Countries with Alternative Policy Rules

	$\alpha_r^* = 0.6$		$\alpha_r^* = 0.2$	
		0.188 0.147		0.423 0.111
$\alpha_r = 0.6$	0.188 0.147		0.181 0.144	
		0.181 0.144		0.425 0.112
$\alpha_r = 0.2$	0.423 0.111		0.425 0.112	

Key

$$\begin{array}{cc} & \sigma_p^* \\ & \sigma_y^* \\ \sigma_p & \\ \sigma_y & \end{array}$$

from a relatively nonaccommodative interest rate rule to a more accommodative one, its output variability declines, and its price variability increases. But the effect of this move on the other country's variability measure is very small.

An important question is whether these results are also true in more realistic, empirical models. Such a model is developed in Chapter 3 of this book and is used in the remaining chapters to examine this question and many others. But before that we take a first look at econometric policy evaluation in the next chapter.

Reference Notes

The brief discussion of policy rules in Section 1.1 only touches on a very large literature. A useful review of the definition of policy rules, including Friedman's (1948) proposal, and of the rules-versus-discretion debate is found in Fischer's (1990) *Handbook of Monetary Economics* paper. In my view the Kydland and Prescott (1977) work is still the best source on time inconsistency in macroeconomics and is well worth reading; Barro and Gordon (1983) introduced different, perhaps less confusing, terminology for Kydland and Prescott's different solution concepts and also studied reputation as means to maintain the "rules" or the "optimal" solution. The Blanchard and Fischer (1989) text provides a comprehensive review of the Kydland and Prescott models and follow-up models. I am not aware of other work that has explicitly made the distinction between design, transition, and operation of policy rules, though it seems like a natural distinction and is implicit in many discussions. A study of learning during the transition from one policy rule to another is found in Taylor (1975).

The method introduced in Section 1.2 for solving linear rational expectations models is found and explained more fully in my *Handbook of Econometrics* paper (Taylor, 1986). An introduction to dynamic stochastic models needed for this method is provided in Chow (1975) and can now be found in most econometrics texts. Sargent's (1987a) macroeconomics text provides a comprehensive treatment of stochastic difference equations with applications to macroeconomics. Factorization methods for multivariate linear systems and the expended path method are also discussed in the *Handbook* paper (Taylor, 1986). The particular method of undetermined coefficients used in Section 1.2 was the one used by Muth (1961) in his original paper on rational expectations.

The best background reading on the Lucas critique is the original Lucas (1976) paper on the subject. Section 1.3 comes close to illustrating how the critique is dealt with in this book: by plugging alternative rules into model economies, seeing how they work, and informally searching for the optimal rule. More formal methods to find the optimal policy rule in rational expectations models can be found in Taylor (1979), in Hansen, Epple, and Roberds (1985), and in Sargent (1987b).

The stylized two-country model in Section 1.4 was introduced in Carlozzi and Taylor (1985) and in Taylor (1985). References to the two-country Mundell-Fleming model, upon which this model builds, are Mundell (1962) and Fleming (1962). Dornbusch (1976) first introduced rational expectations into a single-country Mundell-Fleming model with capital mobility and focused on the question of exchange rate overshooting, which is slightly evident in Figure 1-3.

2

A First Look at Econometric Policy Evaluation

The models used in the preceding chapter to introduce the methods of policy evaluation are highly stylized. The parameters are assumed rather than estimated, and the shocks to the equations are not empirically based. Hence, they are not of much use for practical policy evaluation. Fully estimated, economywide models that are simple enough to use for illustration are still hard to come by. In this chapter, I examine one such model—a fully estimated rational expectations model for the United States—and I take a first look at econometric policy evaluation.

This model is a useful prelude to the multicountry model introduced in Chapter 3, although in many respects it is still rudimentary. However, for the purposes of illustrating the econometric techniques and the policy methods, a rudimentary model offers important advantages. The model can be kept linear and small. Algebraic formulas rather than numerical solution algorithms can be employed. Systemwide estimation techniques are feasible. The cross-equation constraints, which are the hallmark of the rational expectations approach to policy evaluation, are easy to illustrate algebraically. These constraints become internal to the numerical computations, and hence they are largely invisible in larger, more realistic models.

The single-country model I present in this chapter places considerable emphasis on the institutional detail of wage and price setting. In fact, the wage and price sector looms large and tends to dominate the rest of the model. Wage and price setting is responsible for much of the dynamics in the model. These wage-price dynamics produce cyclical swings in output, employment, and inflation that closely resemble business-cycle fluctuations in the United States. In a typical cyclical pattern, inflation accelerates, government policy becomes restrictive, recession ensues, policy eases, a renewed inflationary boom begins, and so on.

The criterion used for evaluating policy is the size of these recurrent swings of inflation and employment. Good policy rules hold these swings within tolerable limits on the average. An anti-inflation policy, for example, would be judged not only by its forecasted success at bringing down inflation from a historically given high level but also by its ability to prevent renewed cyclical inflationary surges. Similarly, an antirecession policy would be judged not only by its success at stimulating the economy out of a particular recession but also by the attention it pays to expectations and the cyclical workings of the economy to prevent a renewed recession shortly thereafter.

The premise upon which the wage and price sector of this econometric model is based is that forecasts of future inflation rates and business conditions, which figure into wage negotiations, can actually be represented by the forecasts of the model itself. This is, of course, the rational expectations assumption empirically at work. As a technique it is useful if it works better than available alternative techniques. Practical alternative expectations techniques that have been used in traditional econometric models since the 1950s include adaptive expectations mechanisms or subjective "constant adjustment" of expectations equations to make them look more reasonable or perhaps consistent with forecasters' expectations. The view presented here is that the rational expectations technique is empirically more useful than these alternatives. Of course, future research may discover alternative techniques (perhaps with learning behavior incorporated explicitly) that may be superior to those currently available.

The chapter is organized as follows. First, I describe the structure of the model. Second, I develop an estimation technique and describe the estimation of the model over a historical sample period. Third, I use the model for econometric policy evaluation.

2.1 The Structure of the Model

The macroeconomic model describes the behavior of five endogenous variables in the United States: the average wage, the average price, employment, output, and the money supply. Determination of employment, output, and money supply is rather straightforward, given the determination of wages and prices. Hence I begin with the wage-price sector, which also plays an important role in the multicountry model discussed in Chapter 3.

The Determination of Wages and Prices

A difficulty with trying to incorporate wage setting into an empirical model is the reduction of the intricate details of real-world wage data into a manageable framework suitable for aggregate-data analysis without losing those details that make wage setting important. The trick is to find a method of aggregating across individual wage contracts set in the same period for the same length of time and then to determine the behavior of these "contract-wage aggregates." If the method is to capture the interaction between wage contracts negotiated at different dates, then aggregation across wages set at different points in time can only occur at the last stage of analysis, after this interaction has been modeled. The problem becomes more difficult when the individual contract wages are unobservable.

Although very little information is available on implicit or explicit wage contracts in the United States, information published by The Bureau of Labor Statistics (BLS) on the approximately 10 percent of U.S. workers engaged in major collective bargaining gives perspective to the problem. In Chapter 7 I use these data (see Table 7-1) on the number of workers negotiating explicit contracts of different lengths each quarter to calibrate a wage model. For now it is enough to say that the data show that it would be too gross an approximation to assume that contracts in the U.S. economy are all of the same length (as in the stylized model of Chapter 1). Even if we ignore the 90 percent of all workers not represented by major unions— and who probably work under implicit or explicit contracts averaging about one year in duration—the range of contract length is quite wide. On the other hand, abstracting from seasonal influences, the distribution of workers by contract length does not show any systematic pattern or tendency to change over the business cycle. Hence, if one is ultimately interested in describing the behavior of seasonally adjusted data, and if one-year and two-year contracts are more representative of the economy as a whole, then a first approximation would be to assume that the distribution of workers by contract length is homogeneous over time. This approximation results in a major simplification for the aggregation procedures and will be made in the analysis that follows.

To complete the aggregation procedure, three additional approximations need to be made: the variation in average contract wages across contract classes of different lengths is assumed to be negligible relative to the variation in contract wages over time; all wage adjustments are assumed to occur during the quarter in which the contract is negotiated; any indexing that changes the wage contract at regular intervals during the contract period can be approximated as a series of short-term contracts, rather than as one long-term contract. The last approximation is partially a matter of definition and will tend to make our estimated distribution of contract lengths shorter than what a literal reading of the BLS data would indicate. Most indexing in the U.S. economy is found in multiyear contracts. The import of this approximation is that these indexed contracts are comparable to shorter contracts with lengths equal to the indexing review period. It is an approximation because contract-wage adjustments are influenced by a wider range of factors when they are adjusted by renegotiation rather than by indexing.

The starting point for implementing these approximations is the staggered wage-setting model used in Taylor (1980) and used in the model of

Section 1.4 of Chapter 1. In the standard, nonsynchronized version of this model, only a small fraction of workers have their contract wage changed in a given time period. The contract wage is assumed to be set to equal the expected average wage in the economy during the upcoming contract period, plus an amount that depends on expected excess demand in the economy as measured by the deviations of actual output from trend output over the next four quarters. The crucial parameter to estimate in the model is the sensitivity of the wages to this future excess-demand term.

In my 1980 paper, I considered the simple example in which 25 percent of workers change wages each quarter with the wage being set for one year. This example seemed to work well as approximation in that certain general features of the dynamic behavior of wages in the United States could be explained by the model. However, for detailed empirical work, one needs to go beyond this simple example.

Nonsynchronized Wage Setting with Different Contract Lengths

In the more general, but still nonsynchronized version of the model, not all workers are working under contracts that last the same number of quarters (the synchronized version is discussed in Chapter 3). The "contract" wage is determined according to the following equation:

$$
\begin{aligned}
x_t = {} & \pi_0 E w_t + \pi_1 E w_{t+1} + \pi_2 E w_{t+2} + \pi_3 E w_{t+3} \\
& + h(\pi_0 E e_t + \pi_1 E e_{t+1} + \pi_2 E e_{t+2} + \pi_3 E e_{t+3}) + v_t,
\end{aligned}
\tag{2.1}
$$

where x_t is the log of the contract wage, w_t is the log of the average wage, e_t is an index of excess demand in the labor market, and v_t is a disturbance term. The symbol E refers to the conditional-expectation operator based on information through time t. The aggregate wage is given by the equation[1]

$$
w_t = \pi_0 x_t + \pi_1 x_{t-1} + \pi_2 x_{t-2} + \pi_3 x_{t-3}.
\tag{2.2}
$$

Interpreting the π-Coefficients

As described above, in the simple staggered contract model of Taylor (1980), the π-parameters were set to equal .25 with the interpretation that 25 percent of all workers sign contracts each quarter and that each contract lasts four quarters. We now must consider the interpretation of these parameters in the more general case. We seek an interpretation in terms of the

---

[1] For the case where $\pi_i = .25$ the arguments used in Taylor (1980) lead to the weights in Equation (2.1) being identical to those in Equation (2.2). An extension of these arguments can be used in the more general case of the π-weights. However, alternative wage-contract equations can be derived, in which the weights on the future wages and output levels are not the same as the π-weights.

distribution of workers by different lengths of contracts. This interpretation is also used when we consider synchronized contracting. Let

x_{jt} = average contract wage set in quarter t in contracts that are j quarters in length $(j = 1, \ldots, J)$;

n_{jt} = number of workers affected by contract-wage changes in quarter t in contracts that are j quarters in length $(j = 1, \ldots, J)$;

f_{jt} = fraction of workers in quarter t affected by contract-wage changes in contracts that are j quarters in length $(j = 1, \ldots, J)$;

a_{jt} = fraction of workers in the labor force in quarter t who have contracts of length j $(j = 1, \ldots, J)$;

w_t = average wage in the economy in quarter t.

Then, by definition of f_{jt}, a_{jt}, and w_t we have

$$f_{jt} = \frac{n_{jt}}{\sum_{j=1}^{J} n_{jt}} \tag{2.3}$$

$$a_{jt} = \frac{\sum_{s=0}^{j-1} n_{jt-s}}{\sum_{j=1}^{J} \sum_{s=0}^{j-1} n_{jt-s}} \tag{2.4}$$

$$w_t = \frac{\sum_{j=1}^{J} \sum_{s=0}^{j-1} n_{jt-s} x_{jt-s}}{\sum_{j=1}^{J} \sum_{s=0}^{j-1} n_{jt-s}} \tag{2.5}$$

If the distribution of workers by contract length is homogenous over time $(n_{jt} = n_j)$ and if the variation of average contract wages over contracts of different length is negligible $(x_{jt} = x_t)$, then (2.5) reduces to

$$
\begin{aligned}
w_t &= \frac{\sum_{j=1}^{J} \sum_{s=0}^{j-1} n_j x_{t-s}}{\sum_{j=1}^{J} \sum_{s=0}^{j-1} n_j} \\
&= \frac{\sum_{s=0}^{J-1} \sum_{j=s+1}^{J} n_j x_{t-s}}{\sum_{j=1}^{J} j n_j} \\
&= \sum_{s=0}^{J-1} \pi_s x_{t-s},
\end{aligned}
\tag{2.6}
$$

where the π_s are defined as

$$\pi_s = \left(\sum_{j=s}^{J-1} n_{j+1} \right) \left(\sum_{j=1}^{J} j n_j \right)^{-1}. \tag{2.7}$$

Note that the π-weights sum to 1 and are time invariant. Hence the aggregate wage w_t is a moving average of the "index" of contract wages x_t set in the recent past. The π-weights can also be written in terms of the $a_{jt} = a_j$. For example, when $J = 4$,

$$\pi_0 = a_1 + a_2/2 + a_3/3 + a_4/4 \tag{2.8}$$

$$\pi_1 = a_2/2 + a_3/3 + a_4/4 \tag{2.9}$$

$$\pi_2 = a_3/3 + a_4/4 \tag{2.10}$$

$$\pi_3 = a_4/4. \tag{2.11}$$

Some examples are useful for illustrating how the π-weights depend on the distribution of workers across contracts of different lengths. If all contracts are the same length, say four quarters, then $n_1 = n_2 = n_3 = 0$, and $\pi_0 = \pi_1 = \pi_2 = \pi_3 = .25$. This is the type of contract distribution used in the theoretical examination of staggered contracts presented in Taylor (1980). If the distribution of workers across contracts of different lengths in a given quarter is uniform up to four quarter contracts, then $n_1 = n_2 = n_3 = n_4$, and the π-weights decline linearly: $\pi_0 = .4$, $\pi_1 = .3$, $\pi_2 = .2$, and $\pi_3 = .1$. Note that the distribution of workers across contracts can be recovered from the π-weights through the identities

$$(\pi_{i-1} - \pi_i)\pi_0^{-1} = f_i \qquad i = 1, 2, \ldots, J, \quad (\pi_J = 0), \tag{2.12}$$

$$(\pi_{i-1} - \pi_i)i = a_i \qquad i = 1, 2, \ldots, J, \quad (\pi_J = 0). \tag{2.13}$$

The π-weights, and hence this distribution of workers, are part of the economic structure to be estimated. In the estimation we can use assumptions about the a_i to impose constraints on the π_i. For example, we must have that $a_i > 0$ and that a_i sum to 1.

The aggregate wage w_t evolves from the index of contract wages x_t. Since the contracts that constitute this index will prevail for several quarters, workers and firms negotiating a contract wage will be concerned with the labor market conditions expected to prevail during the upcoming contract period. For example, those setting four quarter contracts must forecast labor market conditions four quarters ahead. Moreover, in the process of forecasting future wages, these firms and workers will take account of contracts negotiated in the recent past, as these will be part of the relative wage structure during part of the contract period. Equation (2.1) is a behavioral equation for the determination of the contract-wage index that takes account of these factors.

Some of the important questions about wage and price dynamics can be cast in terms of the parameters in Equation (2.1). The parameter h should be positive. Whether h is large or small is relevant for determining how accommodative policy should be toward price or supply shocks. However, lagged price shocks could enter Equation (2.1) directly to portray catch-up effects. This latter possibility will be considered below when we introduce a stochastic structure to the behavioral equations.

The excess-labor demand variable e in Equation (2.1) will be measured by the unemployment rate (with the sign reversed). Hence, I do not take a logarithmic transformation of e_t. In Equation (2.1), and in the other equations of the model, the constant terms and any trend factors will be omitted since I will be working with detrended data when the model is estimated.

Given the aggregate wage w_t as determined from the contract-wage index x_t, I will assume that prices are determined on the basis of wage and other costs, that is,

$$p_t = \hat{w}_t + \theta_p(L)\, u_{pt}, \tag{2.14}$$

where $\theta_p(L)$ is a lag polynomial and u_{pt} is a serially uncorrelated shock. The term $\theta_p(L)\, u_{pt}$ is a measure of other factors affecting pricing decisions. Our assumption is that the prices that underlie index p_t are relatively free to vary, so that no additional dynamics in the model enter explicitly through staggered price contracts. However, we do model the influence of wages on price decisions as operating with a one period lag; firms forecast their wage costs w_t during the current period and set p_t accordingly. In the empirical work, the error term will be a general stochastic process, so that exogenous serial correlation in the detrended real wage $w_t - p_t$ will be part of the model. Some of the other factors that may affect p_t relative to w_t might be demand conditions, raw material costs, and temporary fluctuations in productivity about trend.

Aggregate Demand and Employment

The remaining parts of the model are rudimentary, especially in comparison with the wage-price sector. An aggregate-demand equation is given by

$$y_t = \alpha_1 (m_t - p_t) + \theta_y(L)\, u_{yt}, \tag{2.15}$$

where y_t is the log of (detrended) real output, and m_t is the log of the (detrended) money supply. As in Equation (1.7), $\theta_y(L)$ is a lag polynomial, and u_{yt} is a serially uncorrelated error. Missing from Equation (2.15) is a measure of the real interest rate that would link this equation explicitly with investment and consumption decisions and with fiscal policy. Also missing are explicit adjustment terms to reflect lags in the impact of monetary policy on real output. Our approach in this "intermediate" model is to think of these factors as part of a general stochastic structure; a better procedure would be to incorporate lagged values of y_t, m_t, and p_t into Equation (2.15), along with measures of the real interest rate. In fact, this is what is done in the model introduced in Chapter 3.

To link the aggregate-demand variable y_t to our measure of labor-market tightness e_t, we will utilize an Okun's law type of relationship with serial correlation to approximate temporary discrepancies or lags. That is,

$$e_t = \alpha_2 y_t + \theta_e(L)\, u_{et}, \tag{2.16}$$

where $\theta_e(L)$ is a polynomial in the lag operator and u_{et} is a serially un-correlated error. Since y_t is the log deviation of output about trend, it will behave like the negative of the percentage output gap. With e_t defined as the negative of the unemployment rate, α_2 should approximately equal the inverse of Okun's law multiplier.

The Monetary Policy Rule

Since fiscal policy is assumed to be incorporated in the error structure of the aggregate-demand equation (2.15), the only tool of aggregate-demand management that is explicitly modeled is monetary policy. Consider feedback reaction functions of the following form:

$$m_t = g_1 \hat{p}_t + g_2 \hat{w}_t + g_3 \hat{y}_t + \theta_m(L) u_{mt}, \tag{2.17}$$

where $\theta_m(L)$ is a polynomial in the lag operator and u_{mt} is serially un-correlated. Equation (2.17) is a feedback rule because all the variables on the right-hand side are predetermined; they are forecasts of conditions in period t given information through the previous period. Coefficient g_3 represents attempts at countercyclical monetary policy; we would expect g_3 to be negative. Coefficients g_1 and g_2 and their sum are measures of how accommodative monetary policy is to price shocks or wage shocks. If $g_1 = g_2 = 0$, then policy is not accommodative at all, whereas if $g_1 < g_2$, then policy is less accommodative to price shocks than to wage shocks. An important policy question is whether it is appropriate to accommodate prices, which tend to be more volatile, but not wages, which are indicators of the underlying inflation rate; the answer depends in part on whether prices enter the wage equation. In order to explore possible variations in g_1 and g_2, it is necessary to estimate these parameters jointly with the rest of the model. It should be emphasized that the form of Equation (2.17) is not derived from a policy-optimization procedure. Later on in Section 2.5, I consider the optimal choice for the g parameters. However, in general, an optimal monetary policy would depend on lagged values of the endogenous variables or on the shocks to the other equations.

Summary of the Equations and the Stochastic Structure

Gathering the above equations together we have

$$
\begin{aligned}
y_t &= \alpha_1(m_t - p_t) + \theta_y(L) u_{yt}; \\
p_t &= \hat{w}_t + \theta_p(L) u_{pt}; \\
m_t &= g_1 \hat{p}_t + g_2 \hat{w}_t + g_3 \hat{y}_t + \theta_m(L) u_{mt}; \\
e_t &= \alpha_2 y_t + \theta_e(L) u_{et}; \\
w_t &= \pi(L) x_t; \\
x_t &= \pi(L^{-1}) \hat{w}_t + h\pi(L^{-1}) e_t + \theta_{xp}(L) u_{pt} + \theta_x(L) u_{xt}.
\end{aligned}
\tag{2.18}
$$

Note that in the contract-wage index equation, I have added an error struc-ture consisting of $\theta_{xp}(L)\,u_{pt}$, which captures catch-up effects from past price shocks to wages, and $\theta_x(L)\,u_{xt}$, which allows for the wage shocks to be serially correlated.

I will assume that the vector $(u_{yt}, u_{pt}, u_{mt}, u_{et}, u_{xt})$ is serially uncorrelated with zero mean and covariance matrix Ω. This correlation assumption does put restrictions on the model despite the fact that I am considering fairly general error processes in each equation via the θ-parameters. I am assum-ing that there is only one cross-effect in the errors (θ_{xp}); the omission of other cross-effects is a constraint.

The parameters of the model are α_1, α_2, h, g_1, g_2, g_3, Ω, and the coef-ficients of the polynomials $\pi(L)$, $\theta_y(L)$, $\theta_p(L)$, $\theta_m(L)$, $\theta_e(L)$, $\theta_{xp}(L)$, $\theta_x(L)$. Hence, the number of parameters depends on the length of the longest contract considered (which determines the order of π) and on the extent of serial correlation. The model offers two simultaneous equations where more than one current endogenous variable appear. Most of the equations contain one-period-ahead rational forecasts of the endogenous variables, but only the contract-wage equation contains multiperiod forecasts. The multicountry model in Chapter 3 considers multiperiod forecasts in other equations. In Section 2.2 I show how the model can be manipulated to obtain a form that can be estimated.

2.2   Solution and Estimation Techniques

In this section I show how the model can be represented as a five-dimensional linear vector autoregressive moving average (VARMA) system with cross-equation constraints. This constrained linear system can then be estimated by full-information maximum-likelihood techniques, which are still not tractable in the larger nonlinear systems described in later chapters. The essence of the rational expectations approach is that the cross-equation constraints must be fully specified when doing policy analy-sis. The maximum-likelihood approach is desirable because the constraint is imposed at the time of estimation and hence tested along with other features of the model.

Solving the Model: Obtaining a Linear Vector Autoregression

The contract-wage equation for x_t involves forecasts of the wage rate w_t and of the labor market demand e_t as far into the future as the length of the longest contract. These forecasts are conditional on all information available through the end of period $t-1$, and can be written as functions of the past shocks to each equation of the model. The solution technique is to solve the equations of the system for the rational forecasts of the wage rate and of the labor-market variable, to substitute these into the contract-wage equation, and finally to determine a reduced form for the contract wage.

First, by taking expectations on both sides of Equation (2.18), the solutions for the forecasts of the labor market variable and of the wage rate can be shown to be

$$\hat{e}_t = -\alpha_2(1 - \alpha_1 g_3)^{-1}[\beta\alpha_1\pi(L)\hat{x}_t - \theta_y(L)\hat{u}_{yt} + \beta_1\alpha_1\theta_p(L)\hat{u}_{pt}$$
$$- \alpha_1\theta_m(L)\hat{u}_{mt}] + \theta_e(L)\hat{u}_{et} \tag{2.19}$$

$$\hat{w}_t = \pi(L)\hat{x}_t, \tag{2.20}$$

where $\beta = 1 - g_1 - g_2$ and $\beta_1 = 1 - g_1$, and where it should be noted that $\hat{u}_{ys} = 0$ for $s > t - 1$ and $\hat{u}_{ys} = u_{ys}$ for $s \leqslant t - 1$ and similarly for the other random shocks.

Substituting Equations (2.19) and (2.20) into the equation for the contract wage x_t and taking expectations results in

$$[1 - (1 - h\gamma\beta\alpha_1)\pi(L^{-1})\pi(L)]\hat{x}_t$$
$$= h\gamma\pi(L^{-1})\theta_y(L)\hat{u}_{yt} - h\gamma\beta_1\alpha_1\pi(L^{-1})\theta_p(L)\hat{u}_{pt}$$
$$+ h\gamma\alpha_1\pi(L^{-1})\theta_m(L)\hat{u}_{mt} + h\pi(L^{-1})\theta_e(L)\hat{u}_{et}$$
$$+ \theta_{xp}(L)\hat{u}_{pt} + \theta_x(L)\hat{u}_{xt}, \tag{2.21}$$

where $\gamma = \alpha_2(1 - \alpha_1 g_3)^{-1}$. Equation (2.21) is a difference equation in the forecast of the contract wage $\hat{x}_{t+s}$ conditional on information through period $t - 1$ with various combinations of the past shocks as forcing variables. To solve the equation, we note its symmetry: the coefficients of L^s and L^{-s} in $\pi(L^{-1})\pi(L)$ are the same. Hence, the lag operator in brackets on the left-hand side of (2.21) can be factored into a form $\lambda R(L)R(L^{-1})$, as explained by Hansen and Sargent (1980). Imposing stability on the system requires that $R(L)$ be chosen so that its roots are outside or on the unit circle. Multiplying both sides of (2.21) through by $[\lambda R(L^{-1})]^{-1}$ and adding u_{xt} to the equation gives

$$R(L)x_t = h\gamma H_y(L)u_{yt} + [H_{xp}(L) - h\gamma\beta_1\alpha_1 H_p(L)]u_{pt}$$
$$+ h\gamma\alpha_1 H_m(L)u_{mt} + hH_e(L)u_{et} + H_x(L)u_{xt} + u_{xt}, \tag{2.22}$$

where

$$H_y(L) = [(\lambda R(L^{-1}))^{-1}\pi(L^{-1})\theta_y(L)]_+$$
$$H_p(L) = [(\lambda R(L^{-1}))^{-1}\pi(L^{-1})\theta_p(L)]_+$$
$$H_m(L) = [(\lambda R(L^{-1}))^{-1}\pi(L^{-1})\theta_m(L)]_+$$
$$H_e(L) = [(\lambda R(L^{-1}))^{-1}\pi(L^{-1})\theta_e(L)]_+$$
$$H_x(L) = [(\lambda R(L^{-1}))^{-1}\theta_x(L)]_+$$
$$H_{xp}(L) = [\lambda(R(L^{-1}))^{-1}\theta_{xp}(L)]_+ \tag{2.23}$$

and the notation $[\ ]_+$ means that only the positive powers of L in the polynomial products are retained.

Equation (2.22) is autoregressive in the contract wage with moving average errors entering from all the equations of the model. Past shocks to aggregate demand enter the equation with positive coefficients (if these shocks are positively correlated), because aggregate-demand shocks are an indicator of low unemployment in the near future that tends to bid up contract wages ($h > 0$). For similar reasons, monetary surprises u_{mt} and employment surprises u_{et} enter the wage equation with positive coefficients. However, the impact of past price shocks on wage determination is ambiguous. We would expect the sum of the coefficients of $H_{xp}(L)$ to be positive, but this catch-up effect may be offset in the reduced form by $h\gamma\beta_1\alpha_1 H_p(L)$, which captures the "anti-inflation" reaction of the monetary authorities to price shocks. If $g_1 = 1$, so that price movements are completely accommodated, then $\beta_1 = 0$ and the "anti-inflation" effect drops out. But if $g_1 < 1$, then price shocks may appear to have a negative effect on wages.

The sensitivity of wages to excess demand h enters into the reduced-form wage equation in several ways. It is one of the determinants of the autoregressive coefficients in $R(L)$ because it appears in the symmetric lag polynomial on the left-hand side of Equation (2.21). Higher values of h will tend to reduce the coefficients of $R(L)$ and make wage changes less persistent. However, h also enters into the serial correlation and cross-serial correlation coefficients in the x_t equation. In these serial correlation expressions, higher values of h will raise the impact of all these shocks on wage behavior. This effect represents the interaction between the forecasts of future labor-market demand (via extrapolations from the model using recent observations) and the impact of demand on wage behavior.

Policy parameters g_1, g_2, and g_3 also enter the equation in several ways. The sum of $g_1 + g_2$ represents the combined accommodation of monetary policy to price and wage shocks. This sum enters the autoregressive coefficients through parameter β. Larger values of $g_1 + g_2$ imply larger autoregressive coefficients and more persistence of wage changes. As mentioned, g_1 produces an effect that g_2 does not: the price-accommodation parameter tends to affect the feedback of prices onto wage determination. Hence, the size of g_1 bears on the impact of price shocks on the wage-price dynamics. But g_1 does not have any unique ability to change the propagation of these price shocks once they are into the dynamics. Both accommodation parameters are equally powerful at changing the propagation properties (i.e., the autoregressive weights). Proposals for policies that are very accommodative toward price shocks, but not toward wage shocks, evidently place emphasis on reducing the propagation effects while ignoring temporary impulse effects.

To complete the solution of the model, we need to substitute the reduced-form contract equation back into the structural equations. First, we compute the average wage w_t, which simply requires us to pass x_t through the moving average operator $\pi(L)$. This results in

$$w_t = -R_1(L)w_t + G_y(L)u_{yt} + G_p(L)u_{pt} + G_m(L)u_{mt}$$
$$+ G_e(L)u_{et} + G_x(L)u_{xt} + u_{xt}, \tag{2.24}$$

where

$$G_y(L) = \pi(L)h\gamma\lambda^{-1}H_y(L)$$
$$G_p(L) = \pi(L)[H_{xp}(L) - h\gamma\beta_1\alpha_1 H_p(L)]$$
$$G_m(L) = \pi(L)[h\gamma\alpha_1\lambda^{-1}H_e(L)]$$
$$G_e(L) = \pi(L)[h\lambda^{-1}H_m(L)]$$
$$G_x(L) = \pi(L)H_x(L)$$
$$R_1(L) = [R(L)]_+.$$

Equation (2.24), along with the equations for y_t, p_t, m_t, and e_t, constitute a system in which only one-period-ahead forecasts of the endogenous variables appear, all with viewpoint date $t - 1$. Using matrix notation, we can write this system as

$$z_t = C_0 z_t + C_1 \hat{z}_t + C(L)z_t + D(L)u_t + u_t, \qquad (2.25)$$

where

$$z_t = (y_t, p_t, m_t, e_t, w_t)'$$
$$u_t = (u_{yt}, u_{pt}, u_{mt}, u_{et}, u_{xt})'$$

and where the relatively sparse C and D matrices are

$$C_0 = \begin{bmatrix} 0 & -\alpha_1 & \alpha_1 & 0 & 0 \\ 0 & 0 & 0 & 0 & 0 \\ 0 & 0 & 0 & 0 & 0 \\ \alpha_2 & 0 & 0 & 0 & 0 \\ 0 & 0 & 0 & 0 & 0 \end{bmatrix}$$

$$C_1 = \begin{bmatrix} 0 & 0 & 0 & 0 & 0 \\ 0 & 0 & 0 & 0 & 1 \\ g_3 & g_1 & 0 & 0 & g_2 \\ 0 & 0 & 0 & 0 & 0 \\ 0 & 0 & 0 & 0 & 0 \end{bmatrix}$$

$$C(L) = \begin{bmatrix} 0 & 0 & 0 & 0 & 0 \\ 0 & 0 & 0 & 0 & 0 \\ 0 & 0 & 0 & 0 & 0 \\ 0 & 0 & 0 & 0 & 0 \\ 0 & 0 & 0 & 0 & -R_1(L) \end{bmatrix}$$

$$D(L) = \begin{bmatrix} \theta_y(L) & 0 & 0 & 0 & 0 \\ 0 & \theta_p(L) & 0 & 0 & 0 \\ 0 & 0 & \theta_m(L) & 0 & 0 \\ 0 & 0 & 0 & \theta_e(L) & 0 \\ G_y(L) & G_p(L) & G_m(L) & G_e(L) & G_x(L) \end{bmatrix}.$$

Substituting for $\hat{z}_t$ by taking expectations on both sides of Equation (2.25) results in

$$
\begin{aligned}
z_t = C_0 z_t &+ (I - C_0)(I - C_0 - C_1)^{-1} C(L) z_t \\
&+ (I - C_0)(I - C_0 - C_1)^{-1} D(L) u_t + u_t
\end{aligned} \tag{2.26}
$$

or

$$
A_0 z_t = A(L) z_t + B(L) u_t, \tag{2.27}
$$

where the matrix A_0 and the matrix polynomials $A(L)$ and $B(L)$ are defined accordingly. This equation system is simultaneous ($C_0 \neq 0$) with an autoregressive moving average (ARMA) structure. The structure is very heavily constrained both because $C(L)$ and $D(L)$ are constrained as discussed and because C_0 and C_1 contain many of the same elements that are in $C(L)$ and $D(L)$.

Maximum-Likelihood Estimation

The system of Equation (2.26) can be estimated with maximum-likelihood techniques using the working assumption that u_t is normally distributed. The concentrated log-likelihood function (given a set of initial conditions) can be written as

$$
\frac{T}{2} \log \left| \sum_{t=1}^{T} u_t u_t' \right| + T \log |I - C_0|, \tag{2.28}
$$

excluding the constant term. This function can be evaluated numerically in terms of the fundamental structural and stochastic parameters introduced in Section 2.1, and hence it can be maximized by using numerical techniques. Tests of the model can be developed using likelihood-ratio tests, and standard errors can be estimated from the matrix of second derivatives of the likelihood function. Because the factorization technique requires finding the roots of polynomials with orders as high as 8, the constrained-likelihood function cannot be represented analytically. Hence, derivatives and second derivatives must be computed numerically.[2] The matrix of second derivatives was computed at the last iteration for the purposes of estimating the variance-covariance matrix of the estimated coefficients.

2.3   Empirical Implementation and Parameter Estimates

Specific empirical measures for the five endogenous variables correspond to the seasonally adjusted real GNP for y, the GNP deflator for p, the compensation per man hour in the private sector for w, the $M1$ definition

---

[2]I had the most success using the Davidon-Fletcher-Powell technique, computing numerical first derivatives during each iteration. See Goldfeld and Quandt (1972) for a description of this numerical technique.

of the money supply for m, and the (inversely scaled) unemployment rate for males between the ages of 25 and 54 for e. This single-country model was originally estimated for the United States over the sample period 1960:1 through 1977:4, and I focus on the same sample period here. (The U.S. part of the multicountry model described in Chapter 3 is estimated with more recent data.) Using the original parameter estimates permits an assessment of the model as a method to evaluate alternative policy proposals to end the high inflation of the late 1970s and early 1980s. For all the variables except e, a logarithmic transformation was used. The logarithmically transformed data were then detrended by a regression on a linear-time trend over the sample period.

In order to limit the number of parameters to be estimated in the stochastic processes describing the shocks to each equation, the general moving average representation for these shocks was restricted. The restrictions were of two types: first, the moving average was truncated after a certain number of lags, and second, the coefficients of the resulting truncated lag were constrained to be functions of a smaller number of parameters than the length of the lag. More specifically, the following parametric forms were assumed for the θ-polynomials describing the stochastic part of the model

$$\theta_y(L) = [1 - \rho_{y1}L - \rho_{y2}L^2]^{-1} \tag{2.29}$$

$$\theta_p(L) = [1 - \rho_p L]^{-1} \tag{2.30}$$

$$\theta_m(L) = [1 - \rho_{m1}L - \rho_{m2}L^2]^{-1} \tag{2.31}$$

$$\theta_e(L) = [1 - \rho_{e1}L]^{-1} \tag{2.32}$$

$$\theta_{xp}(L) = [1 - \rho_{xp}L]^{-1} \tag{2.33}$$

$$\vartheta_x(L) = 1 + \theta_{x1}L + \theta_{x2}L^2 + \theta_{x3}L^3 + \theta_{x4}L^4, \tag{2.34}$$

where the subscripted ρ and θ were treated as unconstrained. The infinite-power series in the lag operator in Equations (2.29) through (2.33) were truncated at the fourth order. We found that some truncation of these polynomials was necessary to keep the order of the moving average parts of the vector model from growing too large. The G-polynomials in Equation (2.24) have orders equal to the maximum contract length plus the order of the corresponding θ-polynomials. (Because of the expectations variables, operation on both sides of the equation by the inverse of the nontruncated θ-polynomials was not useful in reducing the moving average length as is typical in ARMA modeling.) In choosing the parametric form and the truncations in (2.29) through (2.34), the serial correlation matrices of the residuals were examined; when the serial correlation was judged to be too high, the restrictions were loosened.

In addition to restricting the θ-polynomials, I also put constraints on the π-polynomial that describes the distribution of contracts in the economy. For the results reported, I truncated π at the seventh lag, thereby permitting a maximum contract length of eight quarters. The shape of π was also constrained to decline very slowly for short lags and never to take on negative values. (Recall that neither negative nor increasing π-weights makes any economic sense from the point of view of contract distributions.) Operationally, these constraints were imposed by assuming that π_j/π_0 is equal to points on the right-hand side of a normal-density function in which the "standard deviation" parameter was estimated. The hypothesis can be tested by estimating the model with fully unconstrained π-weights and by comparing the value of the likelihood function with that in the constrained case.

With these specifications the system (2.27) becomes a five-dimensional VARMA $(7, 11)$ model with simultaneous relationships among the dependent variables. The ninety elements of the ARMA matrices are functions of eighteen fundamental parameters. The computational steps for evaluating the likelihood function in terms of these parameters are summarized as follows: (1) evaluate $\pi(L)$, $\pi(L^{-1})$, and hence the fourteenth-order symmetric polynomial on the left-hand side of Equation (2.21); (2) factor this polynomial to obtain $R(L)$ in Equation (2.22), use the inverse of $R(L)$ to evaluate the truncated polynomials in (2.23), and thereby obtain the basic G polynomials in the wage equation (2.24); (3) evaluate $(I - C_0)(I - C_0 - C_1)^{-1}$ in Equation (2.26); and (4) compute a time series of vector u_t corresponding to these parameters using Equation (2.26), and from these, compute log-likelihood function (2.28). These function evaluations are then used for computing gradients during the numerical iterations and for computing numerical second-order derivatives for estimating the variance-covariance matrix of the estimated coefficients.

Estimation Results

The estimates of the structural and stochastic shock parameters are given in Table 2-1, along with the ratio of these coefficients to their standard errors as computed from the inverse of the second derivative matrix of the likelihood function. All the structural coefficients have signs and magnitudes that are reasonable. The elasticity of real output with respect to real money balances α_1 corresponds to an income elasticity of money demand of about two-thirds. The estimated elasticity of unemployment with respect to the output gap is .4, which corresponds to an Okun's law multiplier of 2.5. The responsiveness of contract wages to excess demand h is .11, but it is only marginally significantly different from zero. The policy-evaluation procedures, which we report in Section 2.5, are very dependent on h.

The policy parameters g_1, g_2, and g_3 indicate that monetary policy was significantly accommodative during the sample period. The sum of g_1 and g_2, which represents the combined accommodation to wage and price shocks, is .53 with a standard error of .18. (The estimated covariance between the estimates of g_1 and g_2 is $-.019$.) However, the individual accommodation coefficients suggest that it is important to distinguish wages from prices when estimating policy functions. According to these estimates, policy is almost fully accommodative to wages, but it is not at all accommodative to prices.

TABLE 2-1   Maximum-Likelihood Estimates of the
             Structural Parameters

Parameter	Estimate	Asymptotic "t-Ratio"
α_1	1.48	5.5
α_2	.40	11.6
h	.11	1.5
g_1	−.46	3.5
g_2	.99	6.2
g_3	−.11	2.1
δ	2.55	5.4
ρ_{y1}	1.30	14.9
ρ_{y2}	−.50	4.9
ρ_p	.78	3.5
ρ_{m1}	1.37	11.7
ρ_{m2}	−.56	6.2
ρ_e	.66	2.1
θ_{x1}	−.58	4.7
θ_{x2}	.10	1.2
θ_{x3}	.17	1.9
θ_{x4}	.06	.7
θ_{xp}	.69	6.1

Maximum value of the log likelihood: 1284.20.
Sample period: 1961:4–1977:4 (7 observations lost due to lags).
Correlation between actual values and sample period simulations:
y: .972; p: .995; m: .975; e: .977; w: .991.

In fact, price shocks seem to generate a restrictive monetary policy, after taking account of the accommodation to wages. Whether this is optimal or not depends on how price shocks enter into the inflationary dynamics, through both expectations and contract effects. Finally, parameter g_3 indicates a countercyclical reaction of monetary policy. When the economy is expected to move below full employment, monetary policy becomes more stimulative.

The estimate of δ, which constrains the contract distribution weights, is most easily interpreted in terms of the π-weights, which can be computed from δ by using the formula $\pi_j/\pi_o = K_1 \exp(-j^2/\delta)$. From the π-weights, the distribution of contract lengths can be computed using Equations (2.12) and (2.13). This distribution is given in Table 2-2. According to these estimates, contract lengths in the three- to four-quarter range appear to predominate. This corresponds to the general view that most implicit contracts are about one year in length.

The parameters of the stochastic processes that describe the stochastic shocks are generally very significant with the exception of the last three unconstrained parameters of the wage shock. The serial correlation matrices presented in Table 2-3 suggest that some serial correlation remains in the estimated residual vectors. The cross-serial correlation parameter between

TABLE 2-2   Estimated Distribution of Workers by Contract Length

Contract Length in Quarters	Fraction of Workers in Quarter (f_{jt})	Fraction of Workers in Labor Force (a_{jt})
1	.074	.271
2	.190	.251
3	.234	.199
4	.208	.136
5	.146	.079
6	.084	.039
7	.040	.017
8	.023	.006

price shocks and wage shocks is very significant and indicates that past price shocks do feed back into the wage-formation process.

The implied ARMA coefficients for the model are given in Table 2-4, where the constraints we have imposed are evident. Note that these coefficients represent the simultaneous form of the model. The reduced form would be obtained by multiplying through by A_0^{-1} and would have fewer

TABLE 2-3   First- through Fourth-Order Serial Correlation Matrices

$$\Gamma_s = \hat{E}(\hat{u}_t, \hat{u}_{t-s})$$

$$\Gamma_1 = \begin{bmatrix} .13 & -.20 & .11 & .01 & .13 \\ -.11 & .33 & -.07 & -.14 & -.47 \\ .23 & -.06 & .19 & .19 & .05 \\ .02 & -.02 & -.05 & .15 & .18 \\ -.01 & .10 & .13 & .09 & .29 \end{bmatrix}$$

$$\Gamma_2 = \begin{bmatrix} .08 & -.12 & -.22 & -.21 & .04 \\ -.14 & .24 & .17 & -.06 & -.11 \\ -.10 & -.22 & .10 & -.22 & .03 \\ .34 & -.11 & -.09 & .10 & .09 \\ .15 & -.06 & .16 & .07 & .11 \end{bmatrix}$$

$$\Gamma_3 = \begin{bmatrix} .28 & -.19 & .03 & .00 & -.04 \\ .16 & .31 & .09 & -.04 & .12 \\ .02 & -.10 & .17 & -.15 & .13 \\ .47 & -.18 & .16 & .22 & .10 \\ .19 & -.21 & .18 & .07 & .06 \end{bmatrix}$$

$$\Gamma_4 = \begin{bmatrix} .12 & .04 & -.10 & .00 & -.07 \\ -.19 & .41 & .17 & -.02 & .17 \\ .27 & -.20 & .19 & -.00 & .18 \\ .18 & -.10 & -.08 & -.01 & .06 \\ .25 & .01 & .27 & .13 & .17 \end{bmatrix}$$

Note: The order of the elements of these matrices is y, p, m, e, w.

TABLE 2-4 Constrained Simultaneous VARMA Model

$$A_0 y_t = A(L)y_t + B(L)u_t$$

	Lag										
	1	2	3	4	5	6	7	8	9	10	11
A(2, 5)	.359	.230	.131	.066	.028	.010	.003				
A(3, 5)	.216	.138	.079	.034	.017	.006	.002				
A(5, 5)	.359	.230	.131	.066	.028	.010	.003				
B(1, 1)	1.230	1.189	.897	.572							
B(2, 1)	.016	.024	.026	.022	.015	.009	.005	.002	.001	.000	.000
B(2, 2)	1.108	1.123	1.041	.883	.362	.227	.125	.061	.024	.007	.002
B(2, 3)	.025	.040	.043	.036	.025	.015	.008	.004	.001	.000	.000
B(2, 4)	.017	.026	.027	.022	.015	.009	.004	.002	.001	.000	.000
B(2, 5)	.376	.445	.535	.470	.337	.219	.127	.057	.031	.010	.002
B(3, 1)	-.115	-.099	-.007	-.004	-.009	.005	.003	.001	.000	.000	.000
B(3, 2)	.001	.002	.218	.212	.217	.136	.075	.037	.014	.005	.001
B(3, 3)	1.188	1.142	.891	.574	.015	.009	.005	.002	.001	.000	.000
B(3, 4)	.010	.016	.016	.013	.009	.005	.003	.001	.000	.000	.000
B(3, 5)	.226	.267	.321	.282	.202	.131	.076	.034	.019	.006	.001
B(4, 4)	.656	.430	.282	.185							
B(5, 1)	.016	.024	.026	.022	.015	.009	.005	.002	.001	.000	.000
B(5, 2)	.326	.511	.562	.508	.362	.227	.125	.061	.036	.007	.002
B(5, 3)	.025	.040	.043	.036	.025	.015	.008	.004	.001	.000	.000
B(5, 4)	.017	.026	.027	.22	.015	.009	.005	.002	.001	.000	.000
B(5, 5)	.376	.445	.535	.470	.337	.219	.127	.057	.031	.010	.002

Note: Each column represents a matrix coefficient stacked by rows from the matrix polynomial A(L) or B(L). If a component is not listed, then the coefficients corresponding to that component are constrained to zero for all lags. If there is no entry for a listed component, then that coefficient is constrained to zero.

elements constrained to equal zero. For example, some of the reduced-form dynamics in y_t are due to past movements in m_t and p_t. These would be evident in the reduced form but are only implicit in the simultaneous form of the model.

The constraints that the model and the expectations assumptions put on the wage and price dynamics are evident in the second and fifth rows of matrices A and B given in Table 2-4. The second row corresponds to the price dynamics and the fifth row to the wage dynamics. With one important exception, these dynamics are the same. The exception is that $B(2,2) \neq B(5,2)$. The $B(2,2)$ coefficients are partially determined by the impact of non-wage shocks on the pricing process; that is, the influence of the other components of unit costs, such as productivity shifts. The $B(5,2)$ coefficients reflect the impact of these same price shocks on wages.

Note, however, that both $B(2,2)$ and $B(5,2)$, as well as most of the other elements of matrices A and B depend on the policy parameters g_1, g_2, and g_3. As these coefficients change, the coefficients of A and B will change in a predictable way. It is this impact of the policy parameters on the dynamics of the model that will form the basis of the policy-evaluation procedure.

2.4   The Effect of Policy Changes on the Reduced-Form Coefficients

The estimated structural equations of the model are summarized below:

$$y_t = 1.48(m_t - p_t) + u_{yt} + 1.30u_{yt-1} + 1.19u_{yt-2} + .90u_{yt-3} + .57u_{yt-4}$$

$$p_t = \hat{w}_t + u_{pt} + .78u_{pt-1} + .63u_{pt-2} + .48u_{pt-3} + .30u_{pt-4}$$

$$m_t = g_1\hat{p}_t + g_2\hat{w}_t - .11\hat{y}_t + u_{mt} + 1.37u_{mt-1} + 1.36u_{mt-2}$$
$$+ 1.22u_{mt-3} + .96u_{mt-4}$$

$$e_t = .40y_t + u_{et} + .66u_{et-1} + .47u_{et-2} + .33u_{et-3} + .18u_{et-4}$$

$$w_t = .27x_t + .248x_{t-1} + .199x_{t-2} + .137x_{t-3} + .82x_{t-4} + .042x_{t-5}$$
$$+ .019x_{t-6} + .007x_{t-7}$$

$$x_t = .267\hat{w}_t + .248\hat{w}_{t+1} + .199\hat{w}_{t+2} + .137\hat{w}_{t+3} + .082\hat{w}_{t+4} + .042\hat{w}_{t+5}$$
$$+ .019\hat{w}_{t+6} + .007\hat{w}_{t+7} + .029\hat{e}_t + .027\hat{e}_{t+1} + .022\hat{e}_{t+2}$$
$$+ .015\hat{e}_{t+3} + .009\hat{e}_{t+4} + .005\hat{e}_{t+5} + .002\hat{e}_{t+6} + .001\hat{e}_{t+7}$$
$$+ .69u_{pt-1} + .48u_{pt-2} + .35u_{pt-3} + .22u_{pt-4} + u_{xt}$$
$$- .58u_{xt-1} + .10u_{xt-2} + .17u_{xt-3} + .06u_{xt-4}.$$

The estimated values of g_1 and g_2 are $-.46$ and $.99$ respectively. In writing down the model, I do not enter these specific values since I will be concerned with varying these parameters. The policy-evaluation problem concerns how variations in the policy parameter g_1 and g_2 affect the performance of the economy.

As shown in Section 2.2, the model can be reduced to a five-dimensional VARMA model the coefficients of which depend on the policy parameters. The 5×5 matrix A_0 in Equation (2.27) contains structural parameters that are assumed not to depend on the policy parameters. The matrix polynomials $A(L)$ and $B(L)$, which are seventh and eleventh orders respectively, depend explicitly on the policy parameters. The relationship between the reduced form and the policy parameters does not have a closed form but can be evaluated numerically. This is illustrated by comparing Tables 2-4 and 2-5.

Recall that Table 2-4 gives the values of the matrix polynomials $A(L)$ and $B(L)$ when the policy parameters are set to their estimated values along with all the other parameters in the model. These parameter values for $A(L)$ and $B(L)$ are the maximum-likelihood estimates of the ARMA model as constrained by the rational expectations relationships between the equations. As mentioned above, the estimated values of g_1 and g_2 are $-.46$ and $.99$ respectively. When these parameter values are changed, the parameters of $A(L)$ and $B(L)$ will also change. Recall that the Lucas critique for conventional econometric policy evaluation, as explained in Chapter 1, is that parameters of models change when policy changes. The calculations in Table 2-5 show how we have incorporated the Lucas critique into the policy-evaluation procedure. For example, when g_1 is increased from $-.46$ to 0, representing a more accommodative policy, the parameters of $A(L)$ and $B(L)$ shift from those given in Table 2-4 to those given in Table 2-5. Note that most of the 172 parameters in Tables 2-4 and 2-5 change as a result of the shift in the single parameter g_1. The only parameters that do not change are the eight exogenous serial correlation parameters in the output and unemployment equations ($B[1,1]$ and $B[4,4]$). This strong interaction between policy parameters and econometric equations is due to the rational expectations assumption.

Considering first the autoregressive parameters in the wage equation $A(5,5)$, the effect of the more accommodative policy is to raise uniformly these autoregressive weights. The moving average weights in the wage equation are also increased. As one would expect, moving to an easier monetary policy raises the coefficients of the lagged dependent variables in the wage equation and thereby increases the persistence of wages. Because of the markup relationship between wages and prices, the effect of a more accommodative policy on the price dynamics is similar to that of wages.

The $B(3,2)$ parameters measure the impact of price changes on the money supply. These enter not only directly through the forecast of prices but also through the wage forecast in the money-supply rule. The increase in the parameter g_1 has the effect of increasing the response of the money supply to price movements as reflected by the $B(3,2)$ parameters, which are much higher in Table 2-5 than in Table 2-4.

TABLE 2-5   ARMA Parameters with More Accommodative Policy ($g_1 = 0$; $g_2 = .99$)

					Lag						
	1	2	3	4	5	6	7	8	9	10	11
A(2, 5)	.429	.270	.152	.075	.032	.011	.003				
A(3, 5)	.425	.268	.150	.074	.032	.011	.003				
A(5, 5)	.429	.270	.151	.075	.032	.011	.003				
B(1, 1)	1.300	1.189	.897	.572							
B(2, 1)	.018	.028	.029	.025	.017	.010	.005	.003	.001	.000	.000
B(2, 2)	1.170	1.215	1.135	.961	.415	.259	.142	.069	.026	.008	.002
B(2, 3)	.029	.046	.048	.040	.028	.017	.009	.004	.002	.000	.000
B(2, 4)	.020	.029	.030	.025	.017	.010	.005	.002	.001	.000	.000
B(2, 5)	.375	.484	.594	.526	.379	.246	.142	.065	.034	.010	.002
B(3, 1)	-.107	-.086	-.057	-.030	.017	.010	.005	.003	.001	.000	.000
B(3, 2)	.495	.684	.718	.634	.411	.257	.141	.068	.026	.008	.002
B(3, 3)	1.202	1.163	.914	.592	.028	.017	.008	.004	.001	.000	.000
B(3, 4)	.020	.029	.030	.025	.017	.010	.005	.002	.001	.000	.000
B(3, 5)	.372	.480	.588	.520	.375	.244	.141	.064	.034	.011	.002
B(4, 4)	.656	.430	.282	.185							
B(5, 1)	.018	.028	.029	.025	.017	.010	.005	.003	.001	.000	.000
B(5, 2)	.388	.603	.656	.587	.415	.259	.142	.069	.026	.008	.002
B(5, 3)	.029	.046	.048	.040	.028	.017	.009	.004	.002	.000	.000
B(5, 4)	.020	.029	.030	.024	.017	.010	.005	.002	.001	.000	.000
B(5, 5)	.375	.484	.594	.526	.379	.246	.142	.065	.034	.011	.002

2.5   Design of Policy Rules

In the remainder of this chapter, I consider two modes of policy analysis: design of a policy rule and transition to a new policy rule. In this section, I consider the design question and ask how the economy would behave over an extended period of time if different policy rules were in place. The distribution of the endogenous variables indicates how the economy would operate if subject to random shocks with the same variance-covariance structure as those observed during the sample period. Since I have normalized the endogenous variables to have zero means, I focus on the steady-state variance-covariance matrix of the distribution of the endogenous variables in z_t.

Steady-State Covariance Matrix of the Endogenous Variables

From Equation (2.27) we can obtain

$$
\begin{aligned}
z_t &= A_0^{-1}A(L)z_t + A_0^{-1}B(L)u_t \\
&= [I - A_0^{-1}A(L)]^{-1}A_0^{-1}B(L)u_t \\
&= \sum_{i=0}^{\infty} \theta_i u_{t-i},
\end{aligned}
\tag{2.35}
$$

where the matrix series θ_i is a function of A_0, $A(L)$, and $B(L)$ and hence is a function of g_1 and g_2. The steady-state covariance matrix of the vector of endogenous variables z_t is therefore equal to

$$
V(g_1, g_2) = \sum_{i=0}^{\infty} \theta_i \Omega \theta_i',
\tag{2.36}
$$

where Ω is the variance-covariance matrix of the serially uncorrelated shocks u_t. If the system (2.27) is stable, then (2.36) is a convergent series and hence, can be evaluated to within any desired level of accuracy.

We will focus primarily on the diagonal elements of V, the variances of the steady-state distribution of each endogenous variable. Table 2-6 shows these diagonal elements in percentage standard-deviation units. Recall that each variable is measured as a deviation from secular trend; for example, when $g_1 = 0$ and $g_2 = .99$, the case illustrated in Table 2-5, the standard deviation of output around trend is 1.5 percent.

Most of the variation in the policy parameters in Table 2-6 is confined to g_2, with g_1 held to zero. The reason for this is that the *sum* of g_1 and g_2 is quantitatively more important than the individual values. This is illustrated by comparing the results when $g_1 = 0$ and $g_2 = .50$ with $g_1 = -.46$ and $g_2 = .99$. The steady-state distribution is the same in both cases, and the sum $g_1 + g_2$ is close to .5 in both cases. The same results follow from comparing the last two rows in Table 2-6. Evidently, the total degree of accommodation

TABLE 2-6   Effect of Policy Parameters on the Behavior of the Endogenous Variables

g_1	g_2	σ_y	σ_p	σ_m	σ_u	σ_w
.0	.99*	1.5	8.8	8.8	0.5	8.7
.0	.95	1.5	6.0	5.8	0.5	5.8
.0	.90	1.6	5.0	4.6	0.5	4.8
.0	.85	1.7	4.5	4.0	0.6	4.3
.0	.80	1.7	4.1	3.5	0.6	3.9
.0	.75	1.8	3.9	3.2	0.6	3.7
.0	.70	1.9	3.7	3.0	0.7	3.5
.0	.65	2.0	3.6	2.7	0.7	3.3
.0	.60	2.1	3.4	2.5	0.8	3.2
.0	.55	2.2	3.3	2.4	0.8	3.1
.0	.50	2.3	3.2	2.2	0.8	3.0
−.46*	.99*	2.3	3.2	2.2	0.8	3.0
.0	.45	2.4	3.1	2.1	0.9	2.9
.0	.40	2.5	3.1	1.9	0.9	2.8
.0	.35	2.5	3.0	1.8	0.9	2.7
.0	.30	2.6	2.9	1.7	1.0	2.6
.0	.25	2.7	2.9	1.7	1.0	2.6
.0	.20	2.8	2.8	1.6	1.0	2.5
.0	.15	2.9	2.8	1.5	1.1	2.5
.0	.10	3.0	2.7	1.5	1.1	2.4
.0	.05	3.0	2.7	1.4	1.1	2.4
.0	.0	3.1	2.7	1.4	1.2	2.3
−.46*	.50	3.1	2.7	1.4	1.2	2.4

Note: The policy parameters g_1 and g_2 are the elasticities of the money supply with respect to prices and wages respectively, as given by the policy rule. The σ-parameters are the standard deviations (in percent) evaluated at the equilibrium distribution as a function of these policy parameters. The asterisk represents the estimated value of the policy parameter during the sample period.

is more significant in this model than the differential accommodation between prices and wages. This result reflects both the markup assumption we have used for determining prices and the nature of the feedback of prices into the wage equation.

In any case, because only the sum of g_1 and g_2 is quantitatively important, most of the policy comparisons in Table 2-6 consider only variations in g_2. Alternative policies range from almost full accommodation in the top row of Table 2-6 to no accommodation in the last two rows. As policy moves in a less accommodative direction, the variability of real variables, output, and unemployment increases, whereas the variability of the nominal variables, prices, wages, and of the money supply, decreases. The estimated policy ($g_1 = -.46$ and $g_2 = .99$) is halfway between these two extremes.

Focusing on σ_y and σ_p, it is clear that small changes in policy in either direction from the estimated policy, lead to point-for-point changes in output variability and price variability. That is, when the standard deviation of output increases by .1 percent, the standard deviation of prices falls by .1 percent. This may seem paradoxical in the sense that wages and prices are "sticky" in this model, so that changes in money should result in more of a change in output than in prices. The paradox is resolved by noting that the standard deviation of these variables measures their behavior on average over a long period of time. In the short run, wages and prices may be rigid, but in the long run, they adjust. Measures of economic performance, such as the standard deviation in steady-state distribution, combine these two features.

Note that this point-for-point trade-off changes as the policy parameters move away from the estimated policy. At the extreme of a very accommodative policy, reductions in output variability are accompanied by very large increases in price variability. Similarly, at the extreme of nonaccommodation, more price stability is very costly in terms of increased output variability.

Comparison of Policy Rules with Historical Shocks

Comparative policy analysis in econometric models has been traditionally achieved by simulating alternative paths for the policy variables in the reduced form of the model over some historical period. The steady-state covariance matrix presented is conceptually different from such comparisons since it is not restricted to a particular episode. In effect, the performance of the economy is evaluated over some arbitrary period with the shocks generated by the distribution of the residuals in each equation. Here I address the policy-evaluation problem by asking how the economy would have performed in the mid-1970s if alternative policy *rules* had been in operation at the start of the simulation period and had been maintained throughout.

Technically, this is done by simulating the model with the actual estimated shocks in each equation in each time period, but with different policy rules determining the response of the money supply to these shocks. We consider two alternatives to the estimated policy: a more accommodative policy with $g_1 = 0$ and $g_2 = .99$ and a less accommodative policy with $g_1 = 0$ and $g_2 = 0$. These alternative policies correspond to the first and last rows of Table 2-6.

The results of this comparison are presented in Tables 2-7 and 2-8. The inflation effects of the different policies are shown in Table 2-7, while the output effects are shown in Table 2-8. As before, output is measured as a deviation from a secular trend. For each of the policies, a trade-off between higher inflation and higher output levels is evident. (Such a trade-off does not exist in the long run, however. It appears here because only a single episode is considered.) For the estimated policy, the rate of inflation averaged 7.1 percent over the 4 years ending in 1977:4, while output averaged 3.1 percent below normal. The more accommodative policy cuts this output loss to near zero but results in a much higher rate of inflation (8.8 percent), which is accelerating rapidly at the end of the simulation period. The less

TABLE 2-7   Inflation Effects of Alternative Policy Rules, 1973:2–1977:4
(quarterly percent change in the GNP deflator, seasonally
adjusted annual rate)

	Estimated Policy	More Accommodative Policy	Less Accommodative Policy
73:2	7.0	6.0	6.4
73:3	7.4	6.7	6.6
73:4	8.6	8.8	8.4
74:1	8.7	7.9	7.2
74:2	9.8	10.8	10.0
74:3	12.2	11.6	10.0
74:4	13.5	12.8	10.8
75:1	8.5	11.6	8.8
75:2	4.3	7.6	4.3
75:3	7.1	8.8	5.9
75:4	6.6	7.6	4.8
76:1	3.9	5.2	2.9
76:2	4.7	6.4	3.6
76:3	4.5	6.4	3.6
76:4	5.7	7.4	4.4
77:1	6.0	7.8	4.8
77:2	7.7	11.6	6.4
77:3	5.1	7.6	3.9
77:4	5.5	10.4	6.8
4 quarters ending:			
74:4	11.1	10.7	9.5
75:4	6.6	8.9	6.0
76:4	4.7	6.4	3.6
77:4	6.1	9.3	5.4
4 years ending:			
77:4	7.1	8.8	6.1

Note:
For the estimated policy, $\hat{g}_1 = -.46$ and $\hat{g}_2 = .99$.
For the more accommodative policy, $g_1 = 0$ and $g_2 = .99$.
For the less accommodative policy, $g_1 = 0$ and $g_2 = 0$.

accommodative policy increases the output loss and has a corresponding
reduction in the rate of inflation.

The inflation reduction that is associated with the less accommodative
policy as compared with the actual policy, is somewhat more than implied
by many econometric models without rational expectations or without an
explicit model of contracts. A consensus in the late 1970s was that "the cost

TABLE 2-8   Output Effects of Alternative Policy Rules, 1973:2–1977:4 (percent deviation of real GNP from secular trend)

	Estimated Policy	More Accommodative Policy	Less Accommodative Policy
73:2	3.9	2.1	4.0
73:3	3.5	2.0	3.3
73:4	3.2	1.9	2.7
74:1	1.3	0.6	1.0
74:2	0.0	−0.1	−0.4
74:3	−1.5	−0.3	−2.0
74:4	−3.7	−1.7	−4.8
75:1	−6.9	−3.9	−8.7
75:2	−6.3	−2.5	−8.6
75:3	−4.6	−1.4	−7.2
75:4	−4.8	−1.3	−6.7
76:1	−3.4	0.1	−4.8
72:2	−3.3	0.7	−4.8
76:3	−3.5	0.8	−5.3
76:4	−3.8	0.2	−6.2
77:1	−2.9	1.3	−5.4
77:2	−2.3	2.4	−5.2
77:3	−1.7	3.4	−4.9
77:4	−2.5	2.7	−5.8
Average for 4 years ending:			
1977:4	−3.1	0.1	−5.1

Note: See Table 2-7 for the specific parameter values associated with each policy.

of a *1-point* reduction in the basic inflation rate is *10 percent* of a year's GNP" (Okun, 1978). According to the columns of Tables 2-7 and 2-8, if real output averaged 2 percent below the actual performance, inflation would have been about 1 percent lower on average.

Response to Individual Wage Shocks

Insight into how the economic system behaves can be gained by looking at the effects of isolated wage shocks. I focus on temporary unanticipated wage shocks and examine only the output and price responses. The simulation of a single wage shock is performed just as a temporary unanticipated shock, as explained in Chapter 1, Section 1.2.

Table 2-9 shows the response of the system to a temporary wage shock under the same three alternative policy rules examined above. Three general properties of the model and of the policies are worth emphasizing.

Table 2-9   Effect of an Unanticipated Temporary Wage Shock
(shock equals 10 percent in initial quarter, zero thereafter)

Quarter	Estimated Policy		More Accommodative Policy		Less Accommodative Policy	
	y	p	y	p	y	p
0						
1	−4.2	7.0	−1.1	7.7	−8.5	6.7
2	−5.3	9.0	−1.5	10.5	−10.5	8.3
3	−6.6	11.1	−1.9	13.7	−12.8	10.1
4	−7.2	12.1	−2.2	15.6	−13.5	10.6
5	−7.1	12.0	−2.3	16.5	−13.0	10.2
6	−6.9	11.6	−2.4	16.8	−12.1	9.5
7	−6.4	10.8	−2.4	16.9	−10.9	8.5
8	−5.9	9.9	−2.3	16.7	−9.5	7.5
9	−5.4	9.1	−2.3	16.5	−8.5	6.6
10	−4.9	8.3	−2.2	16.3	−7.4	5.8
11	−4.5	7.6	−2.2	16.0	−6.5	5.1
12	−4.1	6.9	−2.2	15.8	−5.7	4.4
13	−3.8	6.3	−2.2	15.6	−5.0	3.9
14	−3.4	5.8	−2.1	15.4	−4.3	3.4
15	−3.1	5.3	−2.1	15.2	−3.8	3.0
16	−2.9	4.9	−2.1	14.9	−3.3	2.6
17	−2.6	4.4	−2.0	14.7	−2.9	2.3
18	−2.4	4.1	−2.0	14.5	−2.6	2.0
19	−2.2	3.7	−2.0	14.3	−2.3	1.8
20	−2.0	3.4	−2.0	14.1	−2.0	1.6
21	−1.8	3.1	−1.9	13.9	−1.7	1.4
22	−1.7	2.8	−1.9	13.8	−1.5	1.2
23	−1.5	2.6	−1.9	13.6	−1.3	1.0
24	−1.4	2.4	−1.8	13.4	−1.2	0.9
25	−1.3	2.2	−1.8	13.2	−1.0	0.8

Note: See Table 2-7 for the specific parameter values associated with each policy. Note that y is the deviation of real GNP from the baseline and p is the deviation of the log of the GNP deflator from the baseline.

First, the gradual impact of a wage shock on both prices and output is evident in Table 2-9. The peak effect of the shock occurs after four quarters for the estimated policy and the less accommodative policy and after seven quarters for the more accommodative policy. This gradual impact is due to the staggered wage contracts: it takes several periods before a shock passes through the several levels of contracts.

Second, note that the persistence of the wage shock depends very heavily on which policy is being used. For the more accommodative policy, the wage shock is still above the peak of the other two policies after twenty-five quarters and is diminishing very slowly. The persistence of the price behavior is mirrored by the output behavior. Although the depth of the downturn is much lower for both the estimated and the less accommodative policies, these downturns do not last as long. Moreover, after twenty quarters, the other two policies "overtake" the less accommodative policy and result in higher output levels.

Finally, Table 2-9 indicates very clearly the difference between the long-run and the short-run effects of policy. These were mentioned as an explanation for the point-for-point trade-off between the standard deviations of output and prices. In the short run, a comparison of the three policies shows how the temporary rigidity of wages implies that output takes the major effect of a tighter monetary policy. The main difference between the three policies in the first several quarters shows up in output rather than in prices. However, in the longer run, most of the difference is found in price behavior rather than in output behavior. Comparing rows 1 and 25 of Table 2-9 shows this effect most dramatically.

2.6   Transition to a New Policy Rule: Disinflation

The policy evaluation presented in the previous section considers how different monetary policy rules influence the deviation of actual prices and output from a trend. In this section, I consider the problem of changing to a less inflationary policy rule and examine the output effects that are associated with such a change.

Consider a situation in which the rate of inflation is viewed as too high, and the objective of monetary policy is to bring this inflation rate to a lower level, to disinflate the economy. Clearly, disinflation requires a reduction in the rate of monetary growth. The important question is how fast this reduction in money growth should be. The "gradualist" proposal is that the reduction in money growth should be slow. One rationale for the gradualist approach is that outstanding contracts, such as the contracts described in the model discussed here, will translate a sudden reduction in money growth into a large loss in output and employment. A gradual reduction in money growth will give some time for contracts to adjust.

The output effects associated with an announced program of monetary disinflation, either gradual or sudden, can be evaluated using the model of this chapter by changing the money-supply rule to the following simple form:

$$m_t = [(1 - L^2)(1 - kL)]^{-1}(1 - k)u_{mt}, \qquad (2.37)$$

where the disturbance term u_{mt} is serially uncorrelated. An announced monetary disinflation (unanticipated before the announcement date) can be characterized by a *particular realization* of the disturbance process u_{mt}. For example, if u_{mt} equals $-.0025$ in quarter $t = 1$ and zero thereafter, then a permanent 1-percent (annual rate) reduction in money growth begins

TABLE 2-10   Inflation and Output Effects of a 1-Percentage Point Reduction in Money Growth (growth at annual rates)

| | Immediate Reduction in Money Growth | | |
Quarter	Money Growth Rate	Inflation Rate	GNP Gap (percent)
0	10.00	10.00	.00
1	9.00	10.00	.37
2	9.00	9.32	.50
3	9.00	9.07	.52
4	9.00	8.93	.50
5	9.00	8.85	.44
6	9.00	8.85	.38
7	9.00	8.86	.33
8	9.00	8.87	.29
9	9.00	8.90	.25
10	9.00	8.91	.21
11	9.00	8.92	.18
12	9.00	8.93	.15

| | Gradual Reduction in Money Growth | | |
Quarter	Money Growth Rate	Inflation Rate	GNP Gap (percent)
0	10.00	10.00	.00
1	9.50	10.00	.19
2	9.25	9.39	.24
3	9.12	9.16	.25
4	9.06	9.03	.24
5	9.03	8.95	.21
6	9.02	8.93	.18
7	9.01	8.94	.15
8	9.01	8.94	.13
9	9.00	8.95	.11
10	9.00	8.96	.09
11	9.00	8.97	.08
12	9.00	8.97	.07

in quarter $t = 1$ and is perfectly anticipated starting at that time. If $k = 0$, then the 1-percent reduction in money growth occurs entirely in the first period. If k is greater than zero, then the reduction is gradual; more specifically, it is phased in geometrically. It may be useful to recall the distinction between the effects of one-time policy shocks and the effects of policy rules emphasized in Section 1.2 of Chapter 1. Here we are considering a one-time shock.

Table 2-10 shows the effects of such a monetary disinflation for values of k equal to 0 and .5. It is assumed that the previous rate of inflation was

10 percent and that all other shocks to the model are set to zero during the disinflation. Hence, the important question about future accommodation is ignored. Suppose that the goal is to reduce the rate of inflation by one percentage point.

When the disinflation is immediate, the output loss is larger than with the gradualist policy. Although the rate of inflation does not reach the new target as quickly under a gradualist path, there is not as much overshoot before the inflation rate settles at the new equilibrium. Overall, the advantages of a gradualist policy as compared to a more sudden change in money growth are clearly illustrated in this comparison. The total output loss associated with the sudden 1-percent disinflation is about 4 1/2 percent of GNP. The gradualist policy cuts this loss in half.

2.7 Model Validation with Policy Analysis

Much has been made of the importance of validating econometric models by evaluating their forecasting accuracy. One looks at how well the model forecasts beyond the sample period over which the model has been estimated. Forecasting is an especially good model-validation tool if the forecasting is done for a period after the date on which the econometrician actually estimates the model. Then there is no way that the econometrician could have peeked at the data to fit the model so as to generate good forecasts.

Although rarely done, policy evaluation is also a good model-validation procedure, especially for models whose purpose is policy analysis rather than pure forecasting. Is the policy analysis of the model more accurate in retrospect than other analyses? If so this would lend support for the model and the approach.

It turns out that such a validation is feasible with the model presented in this chapter. As described above, the simulations of output loss under alternative disinflation paths were performed on the basis of the model estimated with data from the 1960s and 1970s before the disinflation of the early 1980s. The calculations reported in the previous two sections were made before the disinflations of the 1980s and were distributed in unpublished working papers (See Reference Notes at the end of the chapter).

Were the estimates of output loss accurate? How do the estimates compare with the actual experience of disinflation in the 1980s? Are the estimates more accurate than other policy analyses?

The calculations from the rational expectations model suggest that the output loss associated with a sudden disinflation would be around 4 1/2 percent for each percentage-point decline in the inflation rate (see the discussion at the end of Section 2.6). A more gradual disinflation would lower this number. As mentioned, conventional estimates in the late 1970s suggested that the loss would be much greater than this: around 10 percent of a year's GNP for 1-percent inflation reduction is the average estimate summarized by Okun (1978). These conventional estimates come from traditional models without rational expectations. Which output loss ratio is more accurate?

Work backward from the unemployment rate: during the seven years from 1980 through 1986 the difference between the unemployment rate and a 6.5-percent natural unemployment rate summed to 10.2 percent. With an Okun's law coefficient of 2.5, this implies a cumulative output loss of 26 percent. The underlying inflation rate fell from about 10 percent to about 4 percent, or by about 6 percentage points during this period. (The decline was larger than 6 percentage points for the underlying consumer price index (CPI) inflation rate and slightly less for the GNP deflator.) Dividing the output loss (26 percent) by the inflation decline (6 percent) gives an actual output loss ratio of about 4.3 percent. This number is remarkably close to the 4 1/2 number calculated in 1980 with the model presented in this chapter and reported at the end of Section 2.6. It is certainly much closer than the conventional estimates at the time.

Such a comparison of course depends on an assumption that other factors did not affect the relationship between inflation and unemployment. It also depends on an assumption about the natural rate of unemployment and the underlying inflation rate. However, for these calculations, such factors seem unlikely to change the estimates by much. The estimates provide considerable validation of the model and of the approach.

2.8   Policy Summary, Retrospect, and Prospect

The purpose of this chapter has been to illustrate the general econometric policy-evaluation approach by comparing alternative monetary policy rules and disinflation paths in a small econometric business cycle model of the United States. Although many types of policy problems could be addressed within this framework, the analysis has focused primarily on how different degrees of monetary accommodation affect the behavior of real output versus inflation. Since the model contains both rational expectations and an explicit process for the determination of wage contracts, it is especially suited for this type of comparison.

The implications of these simulations can be summarized as follows: (1) changes in the monetary policy rule trace out a trade-off between the variability of output and prices; (2) although more accommodative monetary policy rules do reduce the depth of recessions, they tend to increase their length (the model suggests that five years after a price shock sets off a recession, a less accommodative monetary policy would lead to output levels that are higher than more accommodative policies); and (3) the trade-off between output and inflation, which is implicit in this model, is considerably more favorable (in the sense that smaller output reductions are associated with a given reduction in inflation) than traditional econometric models without rational expectations or explicit wage contracts would have suggested. A comparison of *ex ante* calculations of the costs of disinflation with this model and with what actually happened in the 1980s provides validation for the model.

In commenting on this model in the early 1980s, Robert Lucas said, "We have come a very long way toward restoring seriousness to our discussions of macroeconomic policy, perhaps as far as we can go on the basis of the theory and the evidence we have so far processed" (1981, p. 565). The "very long way" was in comparison to conventional models and reflects the use of rational expectations and the focus on policy rules. The purpose of the rest of this book is to build on this model in ways that were infeasible ten years ago. Development in both economic theory and econometric theory, as well as evidence from two recessions, a major disinflation and a long expansion, have provided a basis for considerable progress, as I think the following chapters show.

Reference Notes

The economywide model of the United States introduced in Section 2.1 is drawn from two of my unpublished papers: "An Econometric Business Cycle Model with Rational Expectations: Some Estimation Results" and "An Econometric Business Cycle Model with Rational Expectations: Policy Evaluation Results," which were circulated and discussed in seminars in the early 1980s. I initially viewed this single-country linear model as an intermediate step between my 1979 *Econometrica* paper and a more general, but more complicated, multicountry model such as the one described in Chapter 3. Because the model is "intermediate," it is a good expositional device for econometric policy-evaluation procedures.

The Davidon-Fletcher-Powell method for maximizing the likelihood function in Section 2.2 was originally introduced in Davidon (1959) and Fletcher and Powell (1963). Fair (1984) provides a good exposition of how this and other methods are used in maximum-likelihood estimation. Wallis (1980) discusses estimation and identification in rational expectations models like the one estimated here. Dawn Rehm's (1982) Columbia University Ph.D. dissertation estimated open economy models for the United States and Germany with more complicated structures than the model in this chapter, although using similar solution and estimation methods.

A derivation and intuitive explanation of the trade-off between the variance of real output and the variance of the price level in Section 2.5 is provided in Taylor (1980).

II

An International Macroeconomic Framework

3

Building a Multicountry Empirical Structure

Using the single-country model of the United States in Chapter 2 as a foundation, this chapter builds a rational expectations econometric model of the G-7 countries: Canada, France, Germany, Italy, Japan, the United Kingdom, and the United States. Central to the multicountry model is a theory of the link between aggregate demand and production based on the staggered wage- and price-setting framework that is also central to the single-country model. Because a significant number of wage decisions are made in the spring and early summer in one of the G-7 countries, Japan, it is necessary to generalize that framework to allow some wages to be set in a synchronized fashion.

The single-country model offers a rudimentary description of aggregate spending and financial markets. Hence, that model cannot be used to evaluate the appropriate mix of fiscal policy and monetary policy or the choice of an exchange-rate policy. These limitations are removed in this chapter. As described below, the multicountry model disaggregates consumption, investment, import, and export decisions and explicitly shows how these depend on estimates of future income prospects, expected sales, real interest rates, and exchange rates. Interest rates and exchange rates are determined in a worldwide capital market in which capital flows freely between countries.

3.1 An Overview: Key Features of the Model

The seven-country model consists of ninety-eight stochastic equations and a number of identities. The parameters of the model are estimated by using quarterly data over a period that includes the worldwide recessions of the

1970s and early 1980s and part of the long expansion that ended in the early 1990s. The variables used in the model are listed in Box 3-1. No attempt is made to review the behavior of the time-series data here, although it should be emphasized that the model was formulated with these data series in mind, and as will be shown below, the equations fit the data very well. An easy-to-use data bank with all the series in the model is available on diskette for use with standard graphing and statistical packages. (See Appendix 1.) This makes it very easy to get a broad overview of the properties of the data in any country, if desired.

On an equations-per-country basis, this is not a large model in comparison with other econometric models, and the structure of the model is fairly easy to understand. Most of the assumptions of the model—financial capital mobility, sticky wages and prices, rational expectations, consumption smoothing, slowly adjusting import prices and import demands—have been discussed widely in the international economics or macroeconomic literature during the last ten years. The model is not a "black box" in which only the builders of the model know what is going on inside. Nevertheless, a rational expectations model with around 100 equations is technically difficult to solve and analyze and therefore, gaining an intuitive understanding of its properties requires a little work.

In attempting to gain such an understanding, it is helpful to stress several key features of the model. These assumptions all have sound economic rationales, although they are still the subject of continuing research and debate.

1. *An explicit microeconomic model of wage setting generates sticky aggregate nominal wages and prices.* As already mentioned, the specific model of nominal-wage determination is the staggered wage-setting model introduced in Chapter 2. Staggered wage-setting equations are estimated for each of the seven countries separately, and the properties of these equations differ from country to country. Wages adjust most quickly in Japan and most slowly in the United States. A significant fraction of wage setting is synchronized in Japan.

In all countries, prices are set as a markup over wage costs and imported input costs; however, the markup varies over time because prices do not adjust instantaneously to changes in either wage costs or other input costs. Moreover, import prices and export prices adjust with a lag to changes in domestic prices and to foreign prices denominated in domestic currency units. Because of these lags (and because of imperfect mobility of real goods and physical capital), purchasing-power parity does not hold in the short run. The lags and the short-run elasticities in these equations differ from country to country. Throughout the model, however, long-run neutrality conditions hold. All real variables are unaffected in the long run—after prices and wages have fully adjusted—by a permanent change in the money supply. There are a total of twenty-eight stochastic equations describing wage and price behavior, and these are discussed in Sections 3.2, 3.3, and 3.4.

Box 3-1   Key Variables in Each Country

Financial Variables

RS   short-term interest rate (the federal funds rate for the United States, the call-money rate for Canada, France, Germany, Japan, and the United Kingdom, and the 6-month treasury bill rate for Italy)

RL   long-term interest rate (long-term government bonds)

RRL   real interest rate (defined as RL less the expected percentage change in the GNP deflator over the next four quarters)

Ei   exchange rates (U.S. cents per unit of foreign currency)
      E1: Canada, E2: France, E3: Germany, E4: Italy, E5: Japan, E6: U.K.

M   money supply (billions of local currency units, M1 definition)

Real GNP (or GDP) and Spending Components

The variables are measured in billions of local currency units; base years are 1982 for the United States, 1981 for Canada, 1970 for France and Italy, 1980 for Germany, Japan, and the United Kingdom.

Y   real GNP (or GDP for France, Italy, and the United Kingdom)
C   consumption (total)
CD   durable consumption
CS   services consumption
CN   nondurables consumption
INS   nonresidential structures investment
INE   nonresidential equipment investment
IR   residential investment
II   inventory investment
IF   fixed investment (total)
IN   nonresidential investment (total)
IR   residential investment (total)
EX   exports in income-expenditure identity
IM   imports in income-expenditure identity
G   government purchases of goods and services

Variables Relating to GNP

YP   permanent income, a weighted sum of Y over eight future quarters
YW   weighted foreign output (of the other six countries)
YT   trend or potential output
T   time trend (T = 1 in 1971:1)
YG   percentage gap between real GNP and trend GNP

Wages and Prices

W   average wage rate
X   "contract" wage rate (constructed from average wage index)
P   GNP (or GDP) deflator
PIM   import-price deflator
PEX   export-price deflator
PW   trade-weighted foreign price (foreign currency units)
EW   trade-weighted exchange rate (foreign currency/domestic currency)
FP   trade-weighted foreign price (domestic currency units)

2. *Both the supply side and the demand side matter: shocks to aggregate demand affect production in the short run; if the shocks do not continue, production eventually returns to a growing long-run aggregate supply identified with potential GNP.* With aggregate wages and prices that are sticky in the short run, changes in monetary policy affect real-money balances and aggregate demand and thereby affect real output and employment. Aggregate demand is disaggregated into consumption (durables, nondurables, and services), investment (residential and nonresidential), exports, imports, and government purchases. Both consumption demand and investment demand are determined according to forward-looking models in which consumers attempt to forecast future income and firms attempt to forecast future sales. The demand for investment and consumer durables is affected by the real interest rate with rational expectations of inflation. Export and import demand respond to both relative price differentials between countries and income. For all components of private demand (consumption, investment, net exports), there are lagged responses to the relevant variables. There are a total of fifty stochastic equations devoted to explaining aggregate demand, and these are discussed in Sections 3.7, 3.8, 3.9, and 3.10.

3. *Financial capital is perfectly mobile across countries, as if there were one world capital market; however, time-varying "risk premia" exist for both foreign exchange and long-term bonds.* In particular, it is assumed that the interest-rate differential between any two countries is equal to the expected rate of depreciation between the two currencies plus a random term that may reflect a risk premium or some other factor affecting exchange rates.[1] The risk premia are modeled and estimated. In policy simulations, they are treated as serially correlated random variables with the same statistical properties as was observed during the sample period. Similarly, the long-term interest rate in each country is assumed to equal the expected average of future short-term interest rates plus a term that reflects a risk premium. This risk-premium term is also treated as a random variable. The monetary authorities in each country are assumed to set the short-term interest rate. They do this according to a "policy rule" that may depend on prices, output, or exchange rates.[2] There are a total of twenty stochastic equations explaining interest rates and exchange rates in the financial sector. These are discussed in Sections 3.5, 3.6, and 3.11.

4. *Expectations are assumed to be rational.* This assumption almost goes without saying, but expectations play a much bigger role in an international model than they do in a single-country model. The rational expectations

---

[1] It should be emphasized that "risk premium" is not the only interpretation of this term. Miller and Williamson (1988) refer to a similar term as a "fad."

[2] This chapter reports the money-demand equation in which the short-term interest rate appears. When solving the model, that equation is either inverted to get a policy rule for the interest rate or another interest-rate rule is used in simulation. Interest-rate targeting may lead to an indeterminate price level in rational expectations models. However, indeterminacy of the price level is avoided as long as the interest-rate rule pins down some nominal variable, as it does for all policy rules considered in this research. See McCallum (1983).

assumption is appropriate for examining issues such as the choice of an international monetary regime, which, one would hope, would remain in place for a relatively long period of time. It should be emphasized, however, that a rational expectations approach does not mean perfect foresight. As described below, all equations of the model undergo stochastic shocks that cannot be fully anticipated as well as expectations of future variables. For example, the investment and consumption equations feature expectations of future prices, incomes, and sales; the wage equations contain expectations of future wages and demand conditions; the term structure relations have expectations of future interest rates. Forecasts of the future are not perfect, and sometimes the errors can be quite large. Nevertheless, over the long run, the errors average out to zero.

Under the rational expectations assumption, these equations must be estimated either with full information methods that take account of the cross-equation restrictions imposed by the full model or with limited information methods. With a model of this size, it is a huge computational task—requiring supercomputing speeds—to obtain full-information estimates. Unlike what we saw in the preceding chapter, the estimation procedures in this chapter are single-equations oriented: they include two-stage least squares, the generalized method of moments, and a maximum-likelihood method in which many equations in the model are approximated by a linear autoregressive system. These estimates are consistent, but in general, they are not efficient. They are not as useful as the full information methods for testing and measuring the goodness of fit of the model.[3]

Although the equations are estimated by using single-equation techniques, once the parameter estimates are obtained, the model is simulated using systemwide solution techniques. This imposes constraints similar to the explicit cross-equation constraints on Chapter 2, although in this computer-intensive nonlinear model, the constraints are less visible. They cannot be written down with algebra.

3.2   Wage Determination: Synchronized and Staggered Wage Setting

Wages are determined in the model according to the staggered wage-setting approach described in Chapter 2. The wage-setting equation (2.1) is repeated below as Equation (3.1) in modified form with a change in notation necessary to represent many variables and countries:

$$LX_i = \pi_{i0}LW_i + \pi_{i1}LW_i(+1) + \pi_{i2}LW_i(+2) + \pi_{i3}LW_i(+3)$$
$$+ \alpha_i(\pi_{i0}YG_i + \pi_{i1}YG_i(+1) + \pi_{i2}YG_i(+2) + \pi_{i3}YG_i(+3)),$$

$$(3.1)$$

---

[3]Recent research reported in Fair and Taylor (1990) is concerned with finding approximate maximum-likelihood estimates that are computationally feasible.

Box 3-2   Ninety-Eight Stochastic Relationships

The subscripts indicate the country (0 = United States, 1 = Canada, 2 = France, 3 = Germany, 4 = Italy, 5 = Japan, and 6 = the United Kingdom). *Expectations* of future variables are indicated by a *positive* number in parentheses. Lagged variables are indicated by a *negative* number in parentheses. An "*L*" indicates a logarithm. The shocks to the equations are assumed to be serially uncorrelated unless otherwise indicated.

Ex Ante Interest-Rate Parity

$$LE_i = LE_i(+1) + .25 * (RS_i - RS) + U_{ei}$$
$$U_{ei} = \rho_e U_{ei}(-1) + V_{ei}$$

Term Structure

$$RL_i = b_{i0} + (1 - b_i)/(1 - b_i^9) \sum_{s=0}^{8} b_i^s RS_i(+s)$$

Consumption

$$CX_i = c_{i0} + c_{i1} CX_i(-1) + c_{i2} YP_i + c_{i3} RRL_i, \text{ where}$$
$CX_i = CD_i, CN_i, CS_i$ for the United States, Canada, France, Japan, and the United Kingdom and
$CX_i = C_i$ for Germany and Italy.

Fixed Investment

$$IX_i = d_{i0} + d_{i1} IX_i(-1) + d_{i2} YP_i + d_{i3} RRL_i, \text{ where}$$
$IX_i = INE_0, INS_0, IR_0$ in the United States ($i = 0$)
$IX_i = IN_i, IR_i$ in France, Japan, and the United Kingdom and
$IX_i = IF_i$ in Canada, Germany, and Italy

Inventory Investment

$$II_i = e_{i0} + e_{i1} II_i(-1) + e_{i2} Y_i + e_{i3} Y_i(-1) + e_{i4} RRL_i$$

---

where LX is the log of the contract wage, LW is the log of the average wage, and YG is the output gap (a measure of excess demand). Consider the notation carefully. A positive number in parenthesis after a variable represents the *expectation* of the variable over that number of periods in the future. For example, $LW(+3)$ is the *expectation* of the log of the average wage *three quarters ahead*. All expectations are conditional on information through the current quarter. Negative numbers in parentheses represent lags. The subscripts indicate each of the seven different countries. Also, *the error term in Equation (3.1) is suppressed in the notation, although it is part of the model.* Only when error terms are serially correlated are they shown explicitly in this chapter. Following Equation (2.2) of Chapter 2, the aggregate wage is given by the equation

$$LW_i = \pi_{i0} LX_i + \pi_{i1} LX_i(-1) + \pi_{i2} LX_i(-2) + \pi_{i3} LX_i(-3).$$

For ease of reference, Box 3-2 summarizes the equations of the model.

Box 3-2 (Continued)

Real Exports

$LEX_i = f_{i0} + f_{i1} LEX_i(-1) + f_{i2}(LPEX_i - LPIM_i) + f_{i3} LYW_i$

Real Imports

$LIM_i = g_{i0} + g_{i1} LIM_i(-1) + g_{i2}(LPIM_i - LP_i) + g_{i3} LY_i$

Wage Determination

$LX_i = \pi_{i0} LW_i + \pi_{i1} LW_i(+1) + \pi_{i2} LW_i(+2) + \pi_{i3} LW_i(+3)$
$\qquad + \alpha_i(\pi_{i0} YG_i + \pi_{i1} YG_i(+1) + \pi_{i2} YG_i(+2) + \pi_{i3} YG_i(+3),$
where
$LW_i = \pi_{i0} LX_i + \pi_{i1} LX_i(-1) + \pi_{i2} LX_i(-2) + \pi_{i3} LX_i(-3)$
(π-weights vary by quarter in Japan)

Aggregate Price

$LP_i = h_{i0} + h_{i1} LP_i(-1) + h_{i2} LW_i + h_{i3} LPIM_i(-1) + h_{i5} T + U_{pi}$
$U_{pi} = \rho_{pi} U_{pi}(-1) + V_{pi}$
with $h_{i1} + h_{i2} + h_{i3} = 1$

Import Price

$LPIM_i = k_{i0} + k_{i1} LPIM_i(-1) + k_{i2} LFP_i + U_{mi}$
$\quad U_{mi} = \rho_{mi} U_{mi}(-1) + V_{mi}$
with $k_{i1} + k_{i2} = 1$

Export Price

$LPEX_i = \beta_{i0} + \beta_{i1} LPEX_i(-1) + \beta_{i2} LP_i + \beta_{i3} LFP_i + \beta_{i4} T + U_{xi}$
$\quad U_{xi} = \rho_{xi} U_{xi}(-1) + V_{xi}$
with $\beta_{i1} + \beta_{i2} + \beta_{i3} = 1$

Money Demand

$L(M_i/P_i) = a_{i0} + a_{i1} L(M_i(-1)/P_i(-1)) + a_{i2} RS_i + a_{i3} LY_i$

Some modification of the π-coefficients is required for the multicountry model because a significant amount of wage setting in Japan is synchronized during the spring quarter when the Shunto (spring wage offensive) occurs. The parameter a_{jt} in Equation (2.4) is the fraction of workers in the labor force in quarter t who have contracts of length j. Thus, a_{4t} measures the fraction of workers who sign contracts four quarters in length (annual contracts). If all contracts are annual and if there is *complete* synchronization of annual wage contracts with *all* wage changes occurring in the second (spring) quarter, then $a_{1t} = a_{2t} = a_{3t} = 0$ for all t and a_{4t} would equal 1 in the second quarter of each year and 0 in the other three quarters. This would imply that the π-weights would have a seasonal pattern: in the second quarter of each year π_0 would equal 1 and $\pi_1 = \pi_2 = \pi_3 = 0$, implying that $LW = LX$ in the second quarter when the wage is changed. In the third quarter, $LW = LX(-1)$, so that $\pi_1 = 1$, with the other π-weights equal to zero. In the fourth quarter, $LW = LX(-2)$, so that $\pi_2 = 1$, with the other π-weights equal to zero. In the first quarter $LW = LX(-3)$, so that $\pi_3 = 1$.

The contract-wage determination Equation (3.1) would have a similar seasonal pattern. In the second quarter, the contract wage $LX = LW + \alpha YG$, which implies that the expected value of YG was equal to zero. Wages would adjust in the second quarter, so that excess demand, as measured by the output gap YG, would be expected to be zero. In this sense, full synchronization would reduce the business-cycle persistence of output fluctuations; in the second quarter of each year, real output would bounce back to the full employment level. Hence, output fluctuations would last at most one year.

Of course, even in the Japanese economy, not all workers have wage adjustments in the second quarter. Some of the annual wage changes in the annual Shunto actually occur in the summer quarter. Moreover, not all annual wage contracts are adjusted as part of the Shunto, and wages for some workers change more frequently than once per year.

To allow for these possibilities, I estimate a seasonal pattern for the a_{4i} in Japan, but I do not impose the assumption that $a_1 = a_2 = 0$. These fractions are assumed to be fixed non-zero constants in each quarter. I assume in the multicountry model that there are no three-quarter contracts ($a_3 = 0$) either in Japan or in the other countries. Making the necessary changes to Equations (2.8) through (2.11), the π-weights are then given by

$$\pi_{0i} = a_1 + a_2/2 + a_{4i-3}$$
$$\pi_{1i} = a_2/2 + a_{4i}$$
$$\pi_{2i} = a_{4i-1}$$
$$\pi_{3i} = a_{4i-2},$$

where the index i runs from the first quarter to the fourth quarter and a_{4i} has a seasonal pattern. For all countries except Japan, I assume that $a_{4i} = a_4$ for all i so that there is no synchronization. The remainder of the π-weights are assumed to be zero in the multicountry model. (Note that in the single-country model of Chapter 2 there are non-zero π-weights for contracts up to eight quarters in length. But for contracts longer than four quarters, the weights are very small.)

The π-weights were estimated with data on average wages in Japan that *excluded* the bonus payments (overtime is included in the wage measure but this is a fairly small percentage on average). If the Shunto is an important element in the overall Japanese economy, then we would expect to estimate a value for a_{42} that is high (though not as high as 1) and a relatively low value for the other a's.

The Estimation Procedure and Results

In Chapter 2, I estimated Equation (2.1) by using full-information maximum likelihood as part of the linear closed-economy model of the United

States. Because of the large size of the multicountry model, a simpler approach is taken here to estimate Equation (3.1).[4] An alternative scaled-down method is used, in which a simple autoregressive model approximates the relationship between wages and demand—the "aggregate-demand" equation—in each country. In other words, rather than estimate an entire aggregate-demand model jointly with the wage equation, a single reduced-form relation between wages and output is estimated jointly with the wage equation. In this reduced form, real GNP as a deviation from trend is assumed to depend on its own two lags and on the deviation of the average wage from a linear trend during the sample period 1973:1–1986:4. (There is a break in the trend as described below.) Several variations on this same autoregressive equation were tried, but the following, relatively simple, time-series model was able to describe the data very well. "Aggregate demand" for each country is given by

$$YG = \beta_1 YG(-1) + \beta_2 YG(-2) + \beta_3 LW(-1)$$

plus a serially uncorrelated disturbance. The parameters of this equation were estimated jointly with Equation (3.1) by using maximum likelihood.[5]

The estimation results for the synchronized case for Japan and the non-synchronized case for the other countries (United States, Canada, France, Germany, Italy, and the United Kingdom) are shown in Tables 3-1, 3-2, and 3-3.[6] Table 3-1 reports the estimates of Equation (3.1) along with the corresponding distribution of workers by contract length. Table 3-2 reports the results for the synchronized estimates in Japan. Table 3-3 reports the results for the autoregressive aggregate-demand equation. The maximum-

---

[4]An even simpler approach—the instrumental variable approach, whereby the four future expected wages and four future expected output terms are replaced by their actual values and two-stage least squares or Hansen's generalized method of moments (GMM) estimator is applied—turned out to give values for the sensitivity parameter that were the wrong sign. In other words, high expected future output would lead to lower wages, a property that neither makes economic sense nor is compatible with the model being stable. Timing of expectations in the staggered wage-setting model is important for the implied behavior of wages. Effectively, average wages today depend on expected past, current, and future wages, with a whole-term structure of viewpoint dates. Replacing the expected values with their actuals—as in the Hansen method—ignores these different viewpoint dates, and it is likely that this is the source of the problem with these limited information methods as applied to this model.

[5]Evaluation of the likelihood function is straightforward once the model is solved. Since the two-equation model is linear in the variables, the model can be solved by using methods like those in Chapter 2. For the estimates reported here, the model was solved by the factorization method of Dagli and Taylor (1984). Because the initial values of the contract wages are unobservable and figure into the calculation of the likelihood function, these values were estimated along with the other coefficients.

[6]The reporting conventions in this table and in all the following tables in this chapter are as follows: SE represents the standard error of the equation, DW is the Durbin-Watson statistic, and sample indicates first and last quarter. Standard errors are reported in parentheses. Fits of the equations are generally very good and unless otherwise indicated, the R^2 for the "non-detrended" variables are above .99.

TABLE 3-1 The Wage Equations

	Canada	France	Germany	Italy	Japan	U.K.	U.S.
α	0.0541	0.0368	0.0393	0.1084	0.2965	0.0528	0.0298
	(.043)	(.012)	(.025)	(.091)	(.111)	(.031)	(.011)
$\pi(0)$	0.4499	0.5117	0.5024	0.4991	*	0.5272	0.3270
$\pi(1)$	0.3173	0.2883	0.2892	0.3009	*	0.2728	0.2744
	(.033)	(.024)	(.029)	(.028)		(.029)	(.015)
$\pi(2)$	0.1164	0.1000	0.1042	0.1000	*	0.1000	0.1993
	(.045)		(.045)				(.013)
$\pi(3)$	0.1164	0.1000	0.1042	0.1000	*	0.1000	0.1993
% annual	46.6	40.0	41.7	40.0	87.5	40.0	79.7
% semi-annual	40.2	37.7	37.0	40.2	0.7	34.6	15.0
% quarter	13.3	22.4	21.3	19.8	11.8	25.4	5.3
SE	.0091	.0083	.0061	.0167	.0157	.0159	.0027
DW	1.9	1.7	2.1	.9	1.9	1.9	1.3
Sample	76.4	71.4	71.4	71.4	71.4	71.4	71.4
	86.4	86.2	86.3	86.3	86.3	86.3	86.4
Target shift	82.4	81.3	77.3	82.3	76.3	81.2	83.1
Initial Conditions							
$LX(-1)$	−0.4684	−1.2406	−0.7687	−1.3675	−0.8793	−1.3188	−0.4541
$LX(-2)$	−0.3628	−1.2491	−0.5475	−1.6123	−1.1033	−1.3935	−0.4031
$LX(-3)$	−0.2811	−1.1870	−0.6528	−1.7719	−1.0157	−1.3128	−0.3821

* Japanese estimates of π's by quarter allowing for synchronization are shown in Table 3-2.
Note: All equations were estimated with maximum likelihood. In France, Italy, and the United Kingdom, the number of annual contracts was constrained to equal 40 percent, which is not significantly different from the unconstrained likelihood for these countries. The target shift is the quarter in which it is assumed that the central banks reduce their "target" for wage inflation. Using the formula that relates the percentage of contracts to the weights, the standard error of the estimated percent annual contracts can be calculated. These standard errors of the percent annual contracts are 5.2 percentage points for the United States, 18.2 percentage points for Canada, and 16.6 percentage points for Germany.

likelihood approach generally gives sensible results for contract-length distributions. The equations fit the data well with relatively small standard errors.[7]

Focusing first on Japan, the estimates indicate that aggregate wages behave as if roughly 88 percent of wage contracts in Japan were adjusted

[7]For France, Italy, and the United Kingdom, the fully unconstrained maximum-likelihood estimates resulted in weights on the contract wages that declined very rapidly and implied an unrealistic distribution of contracts. For these three countries, I chose a contract-wage distribution close to that of Germany and that is not statistically different from the maximum-likelihood estimate for each of the other three countries. This distribution entails 40 percent annual contracts in France, Italy, and the United Kingdom. With this exception, all the other estimates in Tables 3-1, 3-2, and 3-3 are the maximum-likelihood estimates.

TABLE 3-2 Estimated Wage Coefficients for Japan

	Quarter			
	I	*II*	*III*	*IV*
$\pi(0)$	0.1533	0.5414	0.3857	0.2815
$\pi(1)$	0.1633	0.0351	0.4232	0.2675
$\pi(2)$	0.2638	0.1597	0.0314	0.4196
$\pi(3)$	0.4196	0.2638	0.1597	0.0314
% of workers changing wages in quarter (a_{4i})				
	3	42	26	16

annually, 12 percent were adjusted every quarter, and a negligible amount were adjusted every two quarters. The effect of the Shunto shows up clearly in the seasonal π-coefficients, which have the same general form as in the extreme case where all contracts are adjusted in the spring quarter. However, because some workers have more frequent wage adjustment, and because not all annual wage adjustments occur in the spring quarter, the coefficients do not have the exact 0-1 pattern. According to these estimates, aggregate wages in Japan adjust as if 42 percent of workers have their wages changed each spring, 26 percent each summer, 16 percent each fall, and 3 percent each winter. This general pattern is what one would expect from the Shunto system. About 77 percent of workers who have their wages adjusted annually receive the adjustments in the spring or summer quarters.

As already discussed, such synchronization would make aggregate wages appear more flexible in the sense that the aggregate wage would quickly adjust to eliminate excess demand or supply and that cyclical fluctuations would be short-lived. This greater aggregate wage flexibility with synchronization compared with nonsynchronization would occur even if the adjustment parameter α were the same.

Now compare these estimates with those in the other countries where it is assumed that wage setting is nonsynchronized, so that the coefficients do not have a seasonal pattern. The coefficients for the other countries indicate that annual contracts are the most common length of contract. Wages in the United States behave as if about 80 percent of workers have annual contracts. The fraction is smaller in all the other countries except

TABLE 3-3 Auxiliary Autoregressions for Aggregate Demand

The dependent variable is YG. The autoregressions were used to obtain estimates of the wage equation using a maximum-likelihood technique described in the text. The equations are *not* part of the multicountry model.

	Canada	France	Germany	Italy	Japan	U.K.	U.S.
YG(−1)	1.14	1.26	0.64	0.96	1.05	0.80	1.24
YG(−2)	−0.33	−0.33	−0.13	−0.14	−0.25	−0.02	−0.40
LW(−1)	−0.17	−0.03	−0.30	−0.05	−0.06	−0.05	−0.20

Japan. Although we know that some wage contracts, especially in the United States, Canada, and Italy, extend for more than one year, indexing in these longer contracts usually calls for adjustment in the second and third year. They therefore appear like a series of annual contracts.

It is important to note that the adjustment parameter is not the same in the different countries. In particular, the adjustment coefficient in Japan is much greater than in the other countries. As shown in the first row of Table 3-1 the Japanese coefficient is about 6 times greater than the average adjustment coefficient in the other countries. Even if the estimated equations showed no synchronization in Japan, the contract wages would adjust more quickly than in other countries. It appears, therefore, that a significant part of the high aggregate-wage responsiveness in Japan is not due to synchronization per se. Some other factor must be at work. Perhaps the Shunto bargaining process itself makes the individual wage adjustments at each date more responsive to demand and supply conditions. As part of the annual discussions between unions, firms, and the government, the rationale for wage changes given alternative forecasts for the aggregate economy could lead to a more flexible wage-adjustment process.

Note in Table 3-3 that for all the countries, the aggregate-demand equations have a negative coefficient on the average wage. The coefficient is relatively large in the United States, Canada, and Germany and relatively small in France, Italy, Japan, and the United Kingdom. This negative coefficient is important, for it ensures that the two-equation model is stable and has a unique rational expectations solution. It corresponds to the aggregate-demand curve (with the nominal wage rather than the price on the vertical axis) being downward sloping: when the nominal wage rises, real output falls. This negative effect is influenced by monetary policy and reflects how accommodative the central bank is to inflation. High absolute values of this coefficient represent less accommodative policies.

In interpreting these aggregate demand equations, it is important to note that the implicit target rate of wage inflation is assumed to have shifted down in the late 1970s or early 1980s. The exact date is shown in Table 3-1. The date was chosen to match as closely as possible the marked and visible break in the time series for wage inflation in each country. In other words, after the shift in the target rate of wage inflation, it is assumed that the central banks are not willing to tolerate as high a rate of inflation. According to the estimates in Table 3-1, Japan was the first of the seven countries to shift down its implicit inflation target.

3.3   Aggregate-Price Adjustment

Markup pricing underlies the aggregate-price equations. Prices are assumed to be set as a markup over wages and other costs. However, the markup is not a fixed constant. Higher import prices (in domestic currency units) increase the costs of inputs to production and raise the markup over wage costs. It

is through this effect that depreciations of the currency have direct inflationary consequences in the depreciating country, and deflationary effects
abroad. For each country i the price behavior is shown in Equation (3.2).

$$LP_i = h_{i0} + h_{i1}LP_i(-1) + h_{i2}LW_i + h_{i3}LPIM_i(-1) + h_{i5}T + U_{pi}$$
$$U_{pi} = \rho_{pi}U_{pi}(-1) + V_{pi}$$
$$\text{with } h_{i1} + h_{i2} + h_{i3} = 1, \tag{3.2}$$

where LP is the log of the aggregate price, LW is the log of the aggregate
wage, $LPIM$ is the log of the import-price index, and T is a time trend. The
lagged dependent variable is entered to capture slow adjustment of output
prices to changes in costs. The relative importance of this lag and the relative importance of wages and import prices were estimated separately for
each country. Homogeneity conditions were imposed on the price equations, in the sense that a 1-percent increase in both wages and import prices
eventually leads to a 1-percent increase in output prices. (This condition was
imposed during estimation by subtracting the lagged value of the dependent variable from the wage, the import price, and the dependent variable
itself.)[8]

The details of the final estimated aggregate-price equations are shown
in Table 3-4. Positive serial correlation was found in all countries except
Germany and was corrected with a first-order autoregressive process. The
negative coefficient on the time trend primarily reflects secular increases
in the real wage, although trends in the import price may also affect that
coefficient. The coefficient on the time trend is smallest for the United
States, reflecting the poorer performance of real wages in the United States
compared with the other countries. The effect of import prices on domestic
prices is typically positive and significant. The large estimated coefficients
on the lagged output price terms in each equation as well as the serially
correlated errors indicate that there are large and persistent deviations from
fixed markup pricing in practice. Higher wage or input costs translate into
higher prices, but their full effect is not felt immediately. This is important
for the policy analysis of later chapters: these equations imply that temporary
appreciations or depreciations of the currency do not have a large impact
on domestic prices in the short run.

3.4 Import and Export Prices

Imports into each country depend in part on the price of imports relative to
the price of domestically produced goods. Similarly, exports from a country
depend in part on the price of those exports compared with prices of

---

[8]In estimating each equation, the output gap was also entered as a variable. However, the effect
was found to be quite small or insignificant and in the end was omitted from each equation.

TABLE 3-4   Aggregate Price Equations

The dependent variable is the log of the aggregate price *LP*, and the functional form is shown in Equation (3.2). For all countries except Germany, the equation was estimated with a first-order autoregressive error.

Country	Constant	LP(−1)	LW	LPIM(−1)	T	ρ	SE	DW
U.S.	−0.163	0.518	0.455	0.027	−0.016	0.57	0.003	2.1
	(0.039)	(0.089)	(0.091)	(0.007)	(0.007)			
Canada	0.089	0.874	0.100	0.026	−0.034	0.69	0.007	2.4
	(0.046)	(0.071)	(0.071)	(0.017)	(0.024)			
France	0.147	0.862	0.102	0.036	−0.077	0.26	0.006	2.0
	(0.038)	(0.027)	(0.032)	(0.017)	(0.024)			
Germany	0.085	0.848	0.132	0.019	−0.074	—	0.007	2.5
	(0.045)	(0.075)	(0.063)	(0.015)	(0.030)			
Italy	0.210	0.856	0.111	0.033	−0.086	0.33	0.009	2.0
	(0.072)	(0.029)	(0.042)	(0.022)	(0.032)			
Japan	0.033	0.932	0.053	0.015	−0.046	0.85	0.007	2.3
	(0.019)	(0.053)	(0.053)	(0.016)	(0.047)			
U.K.	0.037	0.752	0.160	0.088	−0.072	0.65	0.010	2.2
	(0.010)	(0.067)	(0.072)	(0.029)	(0.033)			

Notes:
1. For Germany and Canada, *LFP*(−1) replaces *LPIM*(−1).
2. The *T*-coefficients are .01 times those shown.
3. The sample is 71.2 to 86.3 for all countries except the United States (86.4) and France (86.2).
4. For Canada, Italy, and Japan, the time-trend coefficient was computed by including the trend in the real wage in the right-hand side wage variable.

competitive goods produced abroad. In order to have a complete model, we therefore need to describe the behavior of export prices and import prices.

Import Prices

Import prices are assumed to be related to an average of foreign prices translated into domestic currency units using the exchange rate. Consider, for example, the price of U.S. imports from Japan. The price of Japanese goods denominated in dollars equals $P_5 E_5$. This price will tend to rise if the price of goods produced in Japan (P_5) rises or if the dollar exchange rate (E_5) depreciates. However, in a multicountry setting we must consider the price of general U.S. imports, not only those from Japan. The appropriate variable is thus a weighted average of foreign prices denominated in dollars, $P_i E_i$ for $i = 1, \ldots, 6$, or in the currency of the other six G-7 countries. We call this weighted average FP_0 for the United States. Similar weighted averages can be computed for other countries. For each country, the theory is that the price of imports into the country PIM_i depends on the weighted average

TABLE 3-5 Import-Price Equations

The dependent variable is the log of the import price (*LPIM*), and the functional form is shown in Equation (3.3).

Country	Constant	LPIM(−1)	LFP	ρ	SE	DW	Sample
U.S.	−0.284	0.894	0.106	0.59	0.023	1.9	71.2
	(0.118)	(0.042)	(0.042)				86.2
Canada	0.296	0.894	0.106	0.74	0.016	2.2	71.2
	(0.008)						86.2
France	1.243	0.318	0.682	0.99	0.026	1.9	71.2
	(0.288)	(0.078)	(0.078)				86.2
Germany	0.422	0.820	0.180	0.83	0.020	2.2	71.2
	(0.160)	(0.069)	(0.069)				86.2
Italy	−1.241	0.581	0.419	0.91	0.027	1.6	71.2
	(0.268)	(0.088)	(0.088)				86.2
Japan	−1.890	0.454	0.546	0.91	0.040	1.5	71.2
	(0.364)	(0.106)	(0.106)				86.2
U.K.	1.655	0.553	0.447	0.92	0.021	1.8	71.2
	(0.204)	(0.055)	(0.055)				86.2

Note: For Canada, the coefficients on *LPIM*(−1) and *LFP* are constrained to be equal to those in the U.S. equation.

of foreign prices in terms of that country's currency FP_i. In the long run, we assume that the effect is one-for-one. Hence, the long-run elasticity of import prices with respect to foreign prices is assumed to be unity. As has been clear in recent years, however, import prices adjust with a long lag to changes in foreign prices, especially when the change is due to exchange-rate movements. This lagged response is captured statistically through the lagged dependent variable in the regressions.[9]

To summarize, the import-price equations have the following log-linear forms for each country:

$$LPIM_i = k_{i0} + k_{i1} LPIM_i(-1) + k_{i2} LFP_i + U_{mi}$$
$$U_{mi} = \rho_{mi} U_{mi}(-1) + V_{mi}$$
$$\text{with } k_{i1} + k_{i2} = 1, \tag{3.3}$$

where $LPIM_i$ is the log of the import price and LFP_i is the log of the foreign price. Note that the long-run elasticity is constrained to be 1.

The details of the estimated import prices are presented in Table 3-5. The lags between changes in exchange rates (which are reflected in *LFP*)

---

[9]Import prices may also be affected by domestic prices, but in preliminary data analysis the effect was small and statistically insignificant and for simplicity was omitted from the final equations.

and changes in import prices seem reasonable though fairly long for the United States, where, for example, a sustained 10-percent depreciation increases import prices by 1 percent in the first quarter, by 3.4 percent after a year, and by 5 percent after two years. The adjustment speed is about the same in Germany, but it is faster in the United Kingdom, France, Italy, and Japan. (The coefficient on the lagged dependent variable for Canada was estimated to be greater than one. To insure stability of the overall model, the coefficient was set equal to that in the United States, which is already fairly close to 1.) The shocks to import prices are highly serially correlated in France. It should be emphasized that for this equation and others, we are faced with the difficulty of effectively distinguishing between serial correlation and autoregressive variables.

Export Prices

The prices of exports from each country are assumed to be related to the average price of goods produced in each country. The rationale is very similar to that for import prices. However, in the case of export prices, we found the effect of prices in the country where the goods were sold to be a significant influence in several countries. This effect was accounted for in the general function form

$$LPEX_i = \beta_{i0} + \beta_{i1} LPEX_i(-1) + \beta_{i2} LP_i + \beta_{i3} LFP_i + \beta_{i4} T + U_{xi}$$
$$U_{xi} = \rho_{xi} U_{xi}(-1) + V_{xi}$$

with $\beta_{i1} + \beta_{i2} + \beta_{i3} = 1$, (3.4)

where *LPEX* is the log of the price of exports, *LP* is the log of the domestic price index, and *LFP* is the log of the foreign price index.

The estimated export-price equations are shown in Table 3-6. For the United States, the lags are slightly shorter than in the case of the import prices, but there is more serial correlation of the errors. The domestic price level is highly significant for the United States and Canada. The foreign price term is not statistically significant for the United States, Canada, or France and was omitted from the final equations. However, foreign prices are important for Japan, Germany, Italy, and the United Kingdom. The finding for the United States reflects the common observation that foreigners price to the large U.S. market and tend to absorb exchange-rate changes more than U.S. firms selling abroad. Note that the size of the foreign price term in Japan is about the same size as the domestic price term (in Italy, it is larger).

3.5   Exchange Rates and Interest Rates

Uncovered interest-rate parity states that the difference between interest rates in each pair of countries is equal to the expected change in the exchange rate between the two countries over the near future. Time-varying

TABLE 3-6 Export-Price Equations

The dependent variable is the log of the price for exports (*LPEX*), and the functional form is shown in Equation (3.4).

Country	Constant	LPEX(−1)	LP	LFP	T	ρ	SE	DW
U.S.	0.122	0.566	0.434	—	−0.265	0.93	0.009	1.8
	(0.050)	(0.098)	(0.098)		(0.104)			
Canada	0.111	0.411	0.589	—	−0.312	0.92	0.015	2.0
	(0.070)	(0.117)	(0.117)		(0.150)			
France	0.011	0.704	0.296	—	−0.058	0.62	0.016	2.1
	(0.014)	(0.117)	(0.117)		(0.034)			
Germany	0.170	0.798	0.143	0.059	−0.069	0.82	0.007	1.8
	(0.068)	(0.087)	(0.091)	(0.026)	(0.032)			
Italy	−1.324	0.275	0.277	0.448	−0.273	0.88	0.020	2.0
	(0.351)	(0.115)	(0.161)	(0.107)	(0.133)			
Japan	−0.918	0.287	0.386	0.327	−0.431	0.88	0.015	1.5
	(0.187)	(0.106)	(0.087)	(0.058)	(0.105)			
U.K.	0.798	0.601	0.221	0.178	−0.309	0.94	0.013	1.8
	(0.162)	(0.101)	(0.099)	(0.040)	(0.158)			

Note:
1. The *T*-coefficients are .01 times those shown.
2. The Sample is 71.1 to 86.2 for all countries.

risk premia and other factors can shift this relation. Such relations, along with possible shifts, are shown in Equation (3.5):

$$LE_i = LE_i(+1) + .25 * (RS_i - RS_0) + U_{ei}$$
$$U_{ei} = \rho_e U_{ei}(-1) + V_{ei}, \tag{3.5}$$

where LE_i is the log of the exchange rate between country i and the United States and $RS_i - RS_0$ is the short-term interest rate differential between each country and the United States. The coefficient .25 occurs because the interest rates are measured at annual rates, and the expected change in the exchange rate is over one-quarter. Coefficients were not estimated, but residuals were computed as described in Chapter 4 to be used in the policy analysis. Recall that the notation indicates that the *expected value* of the log of next quarter's exchange rate appears on the right-hand side. For the seven countries there are a total of six independent exchange-rate pairs and interest-rate differentials. All six of these are written relative to the dollar. For example, the expected change in the yen/dollar exchange rate is equal to the interest-rate differential between the short-term interest rate in Japan and the short-term interest rate in the United States. All other cross-exchange rates—say between the yen and the pound—can be derived from these six pairs.

These equations are the implications of financial capital mobility. Such an assumption seems warranted for most of these countries at this time (though not for Japan and Italy in the 1970s). There are still some restrictions on capital flows, but for most of the countries, covered interest-rate parity holds very closely.

Of course in the sample period, the simple uncovered interest-rate parity equations do not fit perfectly, and the residuals are serially correlated. (The residuals must be computed with measures of the expected exchange rate. As described in Chapter 4, we compute them assuming rational expectations.) The residuals may reflect risk premia or other deviations from pure market efficiency. They may also be due to the use of quarterly averages for the interest rates and the exchange rates and to the assumption that the time interval for the expected change is one quarter. In any case, these residuals should be an important consideration in any policy evaluation that is carried out with the model. As will be described later, these estimated residuals can be used to measure the size of shifts that are likely to continue to occur from time to time in the future. The estimated distribution of these residuals is used for stochastic simulations and policy evaluation.

3.6   Term Structure of Interest Rates

The basic assumption of this model is that the standard rational expectations model of the term structure of interest rates serves as a good approximation to the relationship between short- and long-term interest rates. For simplicity, a simple linear approximation of the term structure used by Shiller (1979) was employed. The numerical parameters of this functional form should be consistent with the data in each country, and this requires that they be estimated econometrically.

The basic linear term structure relationship estimated for each country is of the form:

$$RL_i = b_{i0} + \frac{1 - b_i}{1 - b_i^9} \sum_{s=0}^{8} b_i^s RS_i(+s), \qquad (3.6)$$

where RL is the long-term interest rate, and values of RS represent expected future short-term interest rates. The parameters in Equation (3.6) must be estimated.

The estimation results are shown in Table 3-7. For these equations, the two-stage least squares method was used, where the actual values of RS replace the expected future values. This estimation procedure is consistent, but the standard error of the estimate of b_i is inconsistent because of the serial correlation of the error that arises due to the forecast errors in projecting interest rates. The last eight observations are lost because the actual leads of the short-term interest rate must appear in the equation.

All the results seem plausible with the exception of Italy where coefficient b is negative. Italian capital markets were relatively restricted during the

TABLE 3-7 Term Structure of Interest Rates

The dependent variable is the long-term interest rate RL. The equation was estimated with nonlinear two-stage least squares with instruments $RL(-1)$, $RL(-2)$, $RS(-1)$, $RS(-2)$, $LY(-1)$, $LY(-2)$, $LFP(-1)$, $LFP(-2)$, G.

Country	Constant	b	SE	R^2	DW	Sample
U.S.	−0.005	0.753	0.023	0.47	0.1	71.3
	(0.003)	(0.097)				84.4
Canada	0.011	0.464	0.017	0.78	0.4	71.3
	(0.002)	(0.154)				84.4
France	0.015	0.514	0.014	0.78	0.3	71.3
	(0.002)	(0.087)				84.4
Germany	0.015	0.641	0.018	0.49	0.2	71.3
	(0.002)	(0.084)				84.4
Italy	−0.006	−0.182	0.019	0.82	0.4	71.3
	(0.003)	(0.512)				84.4
Japan	0.004	0.738	0.016	0.37	0.2	71.3
	(0.002)	(0.062)				84.4
U.K.	0.023	0.895	0.029	0.01	0.1	71.3
	(0.004)	(0.133)				84.4

sample period, so perhaps it should not be surprising that the b-coefficient does not reflect the term-structure model. Since this coefficient is insignificantly different from zero, it was set to zero when simulating the model. Perhaps with recent changes in financial markets in Italy, a positive value for b could be obtained for more recent data. The standard errors in these equations are large (for example .023 for the United States, which means 2.3 percentage points). The errors are due either to forecast errors in projecting future interest rates or risk premia. In Chapter 4, we can attempt to separate these two components.

3.7 Consumption Demand

The consumption equations are based on the rational expectations forward-looking model of consumption as discussed, for example, in Hall and Taylor (1991). The forward-looking behavior is captured empirically by constructing a measure of permanent income which depends on rational expectations of actual future income. The consumption equations also include the real interest rate, which depends on the expected rate of inflation. The equations were estimated using the generalized method of moments (GMM) estimator (described in Appendix 3A), which gives consistent estimates of the parameters as well as consistent estimates of the standard errors of the estimates.

The equations are linear in the levels of the variables. For the United States, Canada, France, Japan, and the United Kingdom, consumption was broken down into durables, nondurables, and services. The degree of disaggregation was chosen because durables are more volatile than services and more sensitive to interest rates. Nondurables tend to lie in between on these volatility and sensitivity issues. (No attempt was made to isolate the flow of services on consumer durables.) For Germany and Italy, however, only total consumption was estimated because of data availability in the OECD sources. Overall, seventeen consumption equations were estimated—three for five countries and one for two countries. The general form for the equations is shown in Equation (3.7):

$$CX_i = c_{i0} + c_{i1} CX_i(-1) + c_{i2} YP_i + c_{i3} RRL_i, \qquad (3.7)$$

where CX_i becomes consumer durables CD_i, consumer nondurables CN_i, and consumer services CS_i for the United States, Canada, France, Japan, and the United Kingdom, where CX_i becomes total consumption C_i for Germany and Italy, and where YP is permanent income and RRL is the real interest rate. The permanent-income variable is defined as

$$YP_i = \sum_{s=0}^{8} (.9)^s Y_i(+s).$$

Real output is assumed to be the measure of income in each country. The real interest rate is scaled so that its absolute effect grows with the estimated trend in the real economy to prevent the real interest-rate elasticity from declining as consumption grows. Hence, the real interest-rate variable RRL is the difference between the long-term interest rate and the expected rate of inflation multiplied by the exponentially growing trend. The trend equals 1 at the start of the sample and then grows at the same rate as potential output, that is,

$$RRL_i = (RL_i - LP_i(4) + LP_i) \exp(gT),$$

where g is the growth rate of potential GNP.

The details of the estimated consumption equations and regression statistics are shown in Table 3-8 (durables), Table 3-9 (nondurables), Table 3-10 (services), and Table 3-11 (total consumption for Germany and Italy). The interest-rate semi-elasticities—the percentage change in consumption associated with a percentage-point change in the interest rate—are shown in Appendix 3B. They are highest for durables, ranging as high as 1 in France and Japan. In other words, an increase in the real interest rate of 1 percentage point lowers French and Japanese durable consumption by 1 percent after adjustment lags. The impact is about one-half as large in the United States and Germany. The real interest rate enters significantly in all the consumer durables equations that were estimated, except in the

TABLE 3-8 Durables Consumption

The dependent variable is *CD*. The estimation method is the GMM, and the instruments are *CD*(−1), *Y*(−1), *Y*(−2), *RL*(−1), *LP*(−1), *LP*(−2), *T*, *G*.

Country	Constant	CD(−1)	YP	RRL	SE	R²	DW	Sample
U.S.	−45.4	0.698	0.040	−29.3	8.37	0.95	1.8	71.3
	(23.7)	(0.072)	(0.013)	(41.2)				84.4
Canada	−5.79	0.632	0.047	−7.53	0.79	0.97	2.1	71.3
	(1.56)	(0.054)	(0.008)	(2.74)				84.3
France	−41.6	0.344	0.079	−34.5	1.51	0.98	1.4	71.3
	(5.9)	(0.077)	(0.010)	(9.1)				80.4
Japan	−4279	0.356	0.041	−4098	284.8	0.98	1.6	71.3
	(459)	(0.065)	(0.004)	(636)				84.3
U.K.	−10.2	0.516	0.073	—	1.04	0.72	2.1	71.3
	(3.5)	(0.118)	(0.021)					84.3

United Kingdom and in the total consumption equation estimated for Germany and for Italy. The real interest rate also enters negatively in consumer nondurables in the United States, Canada, and the United Kingdom but was not found to be significant in services consumption. Overall the effect of real interest rates on consumption is an important part of its effect on aggregate demand, though the effect differs widely among the countries.

The permanent-income variable is very significant in all the equations. Recall that this variable includes *current* income and expectations of future income based on information available in the *current* period. Hence, the

TABLE 3-9 Nondurables Consumption in Five Countries

The dependent variable is *CN*. The estimation method is the GMM, and the instruments are *CN*(−1), *Y*(−1), *Y*(−2), *RL*(−1), *LP*(−1), *LP*(−2), *T*, *G*.

Country	Constant	CN(−1)	YP	RRL	SE	R²	DW	Sample
U.S.	63.2	0.508	0.098	−24.8	4.66	0.99	1.4	71.3
	(8.4)	(0.055)	(0.012)	(13.1)				84.4
Canada	3.19	0.899	0.015	−3.27	0.67	0.99	2.2	71.3
	(0.84)	(0.037)	(0.008)	(2.24)				84.3
France	25.09	0.330	0.196	—	2.45	0.99	2.1	71.3
	(4.66)	(0.091)	(0.028)					80.4
Japan	5180	0.822	0.026	—	821.5	0.98	2.5	71.3
	(1,019)	(0.043)	(0.007)					84.3
U.K.	3.44	0.666	0.090	−5.00	0.708	0.95	1.9	71.3
	(1.57)	(0.072)	(0.020)	(2.00)				84.3

TABLE 3-10   Services Consumption in Five Countries

The dependent variable is *CS*. The estimation method is the GMM, and the instruments are $CS(-1)$, $Y(-1)$, $Y(-2)$, $RL(-1)$, $LP(-1)$, $LP(-2)$, T, G.

Country	Constant	CS(−1)	YP	SE	R²	DW	Sample
U.S.	−24.1 (4.4)	0.906 (0.011)	0.038 (0.005)	4.08	0.99	2.7	71.3 84.4
Canada	−1.2 (1.2)	0.912 (0.037)	0.026 (0.012)	0.449	0.99	2.2	71.3 84.3
France	−31.4 (4.9)	0.810 (0.026)	0.076 (0.010)	1.33	0.99	2.8	71.3 80.4
Japan	−1725 (524)	0.692 (0.072)	0.093 (0.020)	809.3	0.99	2.4	71.3 84.3
U.K.	−2.8 (1.0)	0.913 (0.027)	0.032 (0.008)	0.433	0.99	1.8	71.3 84.3

significance of this term is not a contradiction of Hall's (1978) prediction of the forward-looking model that income does not Granger-cause consumption. Note, however, that with the lagged dependent variable, the short-run impact of a change in expected permanent income is smaller than the long-run impact. (See Appendix 3B for the size of the difference.) This could reflect habit persistence or errors in our permanent-income variable. The greater volatility of durables is reflected in the relatively smaller coefficient on the lagged durables consumption compared with lagged services consumption.

3.8   Fixed Investment

Investment demand is assumed to depend on the cost of capital, as measured by the real rate of interest, and on expected future sales. The measure of expected future sales is assumed to have the same form as the measure of expected future income in the consumption equations.

TABLE 3-11   Aggregate Consumption in Germany and Italy

The dependent variable is *C*. The estimation method is the GMM, and the instruments are $C(-1)$, $Y(-1)$, $Y(-2)$, $RL(-1)$, $LP(-1)$, $LP(-2)$, T, G.

Country	Constant	C(−1)	YP	RRL	SE	R²	DW	Sample
Germany	−34.8 (14.7)	0.733 (0.057)	0.177 (0.039)	−95.0 (41.3)	9.19	0.98	2.5	71.3 84.3
Italy	−388 (655)	0.877 (0.037)	0.085 (0.028)	−1204 (609)	260.3	0.99	1.1	71.3 84.3

TABLE 3-12   Nonresidential Equipment Investment in the United States

The dependent variable is *INE*. The estimation method is the GMM, and the instruments are $INE(-1)$, $INE(-2)$, $Y(-1)$, $Y(-2)$, $RL(-1)$, $LP(-1)$, $LP(-2)$, G.

Country	Constant	INE(−1)	YP	RRL	SE	R²	DW	Sample
U.S.	−73.6	0.759	0.043	−98.7	7.05	0.96	1.1	71.3
	(15.3)	(0.052)	(0.007)	(23.6)				84.4

In the United States, fixed investment is disaggregated into three components: nonresidential equipment, nonresidential structures, residential structures. Because of data availability in the OECD publications, less disaggregation occurs in the other countries. Equipment and structures are added to get total nonresidential investment in France, Japan, and the United Kingdom. All three components of investment are added to get fixed investment for Canada, Germany, and Italy. Overall, twelve fixed-investment equations were estimated. The general form for all the fixed-investment equations is as follows:

$$IX_i = d_{i0} + d_{i1} IX_i(-1) + d_{i2} YP_i + d_{i3} RRL_i, \qquad (3.8)$$

where IX_i is the nonresidential equipment (*INE*), the nonresidential structure (*INS*), and the residential structures (*IR*) in the United States, where IX_i is the nonresidential (*IN*) and residential (*IR*) investment in France, Japan, and the United Kingdom, and where IX_i is the total fixed investment (*IF*) in Canada, Germany, and Italy. The variables *YP* and *RL* are as defined for consumption. The equations are linear in the levels of investment. Lagged investment enters the equations, representing either the cost of adjusting capital or the periods of time to build capital. The details of the twelve estimated equations are shown in Tables 3-12 through 3-16. The real interest rate has a negative effect on investment in all the countries and for almost all components of investment. The semi-elasticity is shown in Appendix 3B and ranges as high as 6 for U.S. nonresidential structures. Of the twelve investment equations estimated, only one did not result in a negative coefficient on the real interest rate; for this equation—French total nonresidential investment—the real interest was omitted.

TABLE 3-13   Nonresidential Structures Investment in the United States

The dependent variable is *INS*. The estimation method is the GMM, and the instruments are $INS(-1)$, $INS(-2)$, $Y(-1)$, $Y(-2)$, $RL(-1)$, $LP(-1)$, $LP(-2)$, G.

Country	Constant	INS(−1)	YP	RRL	SE	R²	DW	Sample
U.S.	−16.2	0.963	0.007	−25.0	3.72	0.95	1.2	71.3
	(6.8)	(0.026)	(0.002)	(12.2)				84.4

TABLE 3-14 Total Nonresidential Investment in Three Countries

The dependent variable is *IN*. The estimation method is the GMM, and the instruments are *IN*(−1), *IN*(−2), *Y*(−1), *Y*(−2), *RL*(−1), *LP*(−1), *LP*(−2), *G*.

Country	Constant	IN(−1)	YP	RRL	SE	R²	DW	Sample
France	11.9	0.812	0.020	—	3.10	0.95	1.7	71.3
	(3.6)	(0.045)	(0.007)					84.2
Japan	−4755	0.899	0.041	−13454	538.6	0.99	1.5	71.3
	(454)	(0.046)	(0.007)	(1,060)				84.3
U.K.	1.5	0.726	0.034	−4.0	0.921	0.65	2.1	71.3
	(4.1)	(0.142)	(0.012)	(3.3)				84.3

TABLE 3-15 Residential Investment in Four Countries

The dependent variable is *IR*. The estimation method is the GMM, and the instruments are *IR*(−1), *IR*(−2), *Y*(−1), *Y*(−2), *RL*(−1), *LP*(−1), *LP*(−2), *G*.

Country	Constant	IR(−1)	YP	RRL	SE	R²	DW	Sample
U.S.	−132.0	0.614	0.063	−269.5	9.61	0.87	0.9	74.1
	(32.5)	(0.062)	(0.013)	(62.8)				84.4
France	9.2	0.858	—	−21.5	0.665	0.98	2.2	71.3
	(1.4)	(0.022)		(2.5)				85.2
Japan	2835	0.823	—	−2578	733.9	0.72	2.1	71.3
	(590)	(0.038)		(865)				85.3
U.K.	2.4	0.728	—	−1.33	0.429	0.71	2.0	71.3
	(0.7)	(0.075)		(1.03)				85.3

TABLE 3-16 Total Fixed Investment in Three Countries

The dependent variable is *IF*. The estimation method is the GMM, and the instruments are *IF*(−1), *IF*(−2), *Y*(−1), *Y*(−2), *RL*(−1), *LP*(−1), *LP*(−2), *G*.

Country	Constant	IF(−1)	YP	RRL	SE	R²	DW	Sample
Canada	−2.9	0.933	0.026	−9.70	1.61	0.98	1.4	71.3
	(2.5)	(0.049)	(0.015)	(5.53)				84.3
Germany	−1.3	0.810	0.049	−213.8	10.4	0.74	2.2	71.3
	(13.4)	(0.038)	(0.016)	(80.4)				84.3
Italy	−1128	0.907	0.030	−3016	299.8	0.89	1.1	71.3
	(820)	(0.029)	(0.012)	(848)				84.3

The expected future sales term is significant in most of the equations, having the highest overall impact in the United States and the lowest in France. Over the sample period, there was little trend in the level of residential investment in these countries. Note that *residential* investment in France, Japan, and the United Kingdom showed no systematic relationship to the expected sales variable, and therefore, this term is omitted from the equations.

3.9 Inventory Investment

Inventory investment is assumed to have a different, less forward-looking, functional form than fixed investment. Current sales are assumed to affect the desired level of inventories. Hence, the change in inventories depends on the change in sales—the usual accelerator model. In addition, we considered the effect of real interest rates on inventory investment. The general equation for inventory investment is

$$II_i = e_{i0} + e_{i1}II_i(-1) + e_{i2}Y_i + e_{i3}Y_i(-1) + e_{i4}RRL_i, \tag{3.9}$$

where II is inventory investment, Y is real output, and RRL is again the real interest rate. The lagged dependent variable was included to reflect any adjustment cost. If $e_{i2} > 0$ and $e_{i2} = -e_{i3}$, then only the *change* in real output affects inventory investment.

The estimates are shown in Table 3-17. The real-output terms always enter with opposite signs, suggesting an accelerator model in all countries except Japan. In Japan, the signs are reversed, indicating a buffer stock role of inventories: when sales decline, inventories rise so that production does not fall so much. The real interest rate enters negatively in all the equations.

3.10 Exports and Imports

In each country, exports and imports are measured in real terms in the local currency and correspond to the export and import measures used to compute GNP or GDP by the expenditure approach in the national income accounts. Hence, these flows include not only merchandise trade but also services. For countries for which output is measured by GNP, the service component of exports and imports includes factor payments on nongovernment capital and labor because net factor payments from abroad are part of GNP. For countries for which GDP is the output measure, exports and imports do not include any factor services. Bilateral trade flows between the individual countries in the model were not modeled. In fact, a large part of exports and imports for each of the seven countries involves trade flows with developing countries and other countries not included in the G-7. Recall that the model is not a closed-world model in the sense that all countries or regions in the world are accounted for. Rather, it is an open-economy model of the seven countries as a group.

TABLE 3-17   Inventory Investment

The dependent variable is II. The estimation method is the GMM for all countries except Japan, for which $2SLS$ was used. The instruments are $II(-1)$, $II(-2)$, $Y(-1)$, $Y(-2)$, $RL(-1)$, $LP(-1)$, $LP(-2)$, G.

Country	Constant	$II(-1)$	Y	$Y(-1)$	RRL	SE	R^2	DW
U.S.	−15.4	0.656	0.207	−0.201	−86.3	17.3	0.59	2.1
	(23.6)	(0.047)	(0.083)	(0.084)	(59.2)			
Canada	−8.4	0.715	0.632	−0.605	−24.3	2.7	0.67	2.2
	(3.3)	(0.043)	(0.107)	(0.104)	(7.6)			
France	−0.7	0.699	0.156	−0.151	−45.0	6.8	0.53	1.8
	(13.2)	(0.099)	(0.195)	(0.187)	(21.5)			
Germany	7.7	0.326	0.178	−0.171	−261	13.5	0.30	1.9
	(19.0)	(0.138)	(0.181)	(0.193)	(156)			
Italy	−3462	0.543	0.561	−0.515	−7551	752.0	0.65	1.9
	(1,089)	(0.147)	(0.191)	(0.200)	(2309)			
Japan	−1064	0.296	−0.306	0.323	−16349	1270	0.31	1.6
	(1,559)	(0.129)	(0.139)	(0.141)	(4994)			
U.K.	0.65	0.639	0.034	−0.036	−2.52	2.06	0.45	1.9
	(2.6)	(0.123)	(0.144)	(0.144)	(7.6)			

Note: Sample periods were 71.3 to 85.3 for all countries except the United States (85.4) and France (85.2).

The export and import-demand equations have the following log-linear form:

$$LEX_i = f_{i0} + f_{i1}LEX_i(-1) + f_{i2}(LPEX_i - LPIM_i) + f_{i3}LYW_i \quad (3.10)$$
$$LIM_i = g_{i0} + g_{i1}LIM_i(-1) + g_{i2}(LPIM_i - LP_i) + g_{i3}LY_i, \quad (3.11)$$

where LEX is the log of exports, $LPEX$, $LPIM$, and LP are the price deflators for exports, imports, and output respectively, and LYW is the log of a weighted average of output in the other countries.

The relative price variable for exports is the ratio of export prices PEX to import prices PIM. The ratio of the import price to the domestic price deflator is used in the import equation. Alternative relative price ratios (such as $LPEX$-LP for exports and $LPIM$-$LPEX$ for imports) were tried in the preliminary statistical work. These measures were chosen simply because they gave more plausible and better-fitting equations on average in all the countries.[10]

---

[10]The log ratio LFP-LP was also used for both exports and imports but performed poorly compared to measures that explicitly included export or import prices. The fact that LFP-LP did not work well necessitated the estimation of equations $LPEX$ and $LPIM$ as already discussed in Section 3.4.

TABLE 3-18 Export Demand

The dependent variable is LEX, and the estimation method is OLSQ (ordinary least squares).

Country	Constant	LEX(−1)	LPEX-LPIM	LYW	SE	R^2	DW	Sample
U.S.	−0.70	0.794	−0.151	0.230	0.034	0.98	1.7	71.2
	(0.63)	(0.094)	(0.129)	(0.125)				86.2
Canada	−6.63	0.581	−0.325	1.015	0.033	0.98	2.0	71.2
	(1.34)	(0.088)	(0.104)	(0.205)				86.2
France	−5.69	0.509	−0.376	0.999	0.016	0.99	1.9	71.2
	(0.91)	(0.071)	(0.071)	(0.154)				86.2
Germany	−2.94	0.532	−0.340	0.684	0.024	0.99	2.0	71.2
	(0.66)	(0.080)	(0.103)	(0.129)				86.2
Italy	−1.79	0.704	−0.080	0.595	0.032	0.98	1.8	71.2
	(0.68)	(0.084)	(0.070)	(0.184)				86.2
Japan	−0.82	0.814	−0.153	0.372	0.029	0.99	1.5	71.2
	(0.72)	(0.043)	(0.039)	(0.139)				86.2
U.K.	−6.12	0.131	−0.370	1.129	0.031	0.96	2.1	71.2
	(0.86)	(0.112)	(0.076)	(0.151)				86.2

The demand variable in the import equations is measured by real output. The demand variable in the export equations is a trade-weighted average of real output in the other six countries. In all the equations, the role of the lagged dependent variable is to approximate the slow adjustment of importers and consumers to changes in relative prices.

The details of the estimated equations are listed in Tables 3-18 and 3-19. The equations are all estimated with ordinary least squares. Surprisingly, there appeared to be little relationship between relative prices and import demand in Germany and, hence, this term was omitted from the German import equation. With this exception, the sign of the price variable is negative for all of the export- and import-demand equations. The elasticities (shown in Appendix 3B) vary considerably across the countries. Long-run income elasticities are all greater than 1, reflecting the growing importance of trade during the last twenty years. The significant lagged dependent variable shows, however, that adjustments to either price or income changes occur with a lag.

3.11 Money Demand

Finally we consider the money-demand equation, which is assumed to have the traditional Cagan semi-log form for all countries just like in Chapter 1. The log of real-money demand is assumed to depend on the log of real

TABLE 3-19   Import Demand

The dependent variable is *LIM*, and the estimation method is OLSQ (ordinary least squares).

Country	Constant	LIM(−1)	LPIM-LP	LY	SE	R^2	DW	Sample
U.S.	−7.00	0.440	−0.216	1.275	0.032	0.98	1.7	71.2
	(0.97)	(0.080)	(0.036)	(0.177)				86.4
Canada	−1.48	0.679	−0.100	0.498	0.032	0.98	1.4	71.2
	(0.46)	(0.076)	(0.075)	(0.134)				86.3
France	−3.16	0.688	−0.148	0.698	0.024	0.99	1.6	71.2
	(0.94)	(0.079)	(0.044)	(0.196)				86.2
Germany	−5.39	0.291		1.325	0.024	0.98	2.2	71.2
	(0.81)	(0.100)		(0.191)				86.3
Italy	−7.57	0.414	−0.190	1.177	0.034	0.98	1.5	71.2
	(1.24)	(0.093)	(0.039)	(0.187)				86.3
Japan	−0.35	0.902	−0.081	0.111	0.032	0.97	1.7	71.2
	(0.32)	(0.059)	(0.026)	(0.051)				86.3
U.K.	−2.14	0.651	−0.061	0.657	0.036	0.94	2.0	71.2
	(0.70)	(0.097)	(0.041)	(0.194)				86.3

income, the level of the short-term interest rate, and on the log of lagged real-money balances. Using a common functional form for all countries permits easy comparison across countries and seems to work well as an approximation, although of course there have been large shifts in money demand because of technological and regulatory changes. The equation for money demand is given by

$$L(M_i/P_i) = a_{i0} + a_{i1}L(M_i(-1)/P_i(-1)) + a_{i2}RS_i + a_{i3}LY_i, \qquad (3.12)$$

where M is money supply ($M1$), and where all other variables have been defined previously. Real output is the measure of income or scale variable. Lagged real-money balances appear in the equation to account for slow adjustment. There are no lead variables in these equations. A time trend starting in 1982:1 was added to the U.S. and U.K. equations to capture the effects of regulatory change and financial innovation in the 1980s.

The estimates are shown in Table 3-20. The equations were estimated by two-stage least squares. The only significant sign of serial correlation in these equations is in Italy (but recall that there is a time-trend variable for the United States and United Kingdom). The signs on the interest rates and income variable are all correct and usually statistically significant. The large coefficient on the lagged dependent variable indicates that the short-run elasticities are much smaller than the long-run elasticities (shown in Appendix 3B).

Table 3-20   Money Demand

The dependent variable is *LMP*. The estimation method is two-stage least squares, and the instruments are $LM(-1)$, $LM(-2)$, $LP(-1)$, $LP(-2)$, $LY(-1)$, $LY(-2)$, $RS(-1)$, G. A linear time trend starting in 1982:1 is included in the equations for the United States and the United Kingdom.

Country	Constant	LMP(−1)	RS	LY	SE	R^2	DW	Sample
U.S.	−0.009	0.953	−0.224	0.040	0.009	0.98	1.6	71.3
	(0.413)	(0.036)	(0.055)	(0.031)				86.4
Canada	0.060	0.937	−0.511	0.033	0.019	0.93	2.1	71.3
	(0.225)	(0.039)	(0.106)	(0.026)				86.3
France	0.671	0.683	−0.316	0.167	0.010	0.87	1.7	78.3
	(0.544)	(0.116)	(0.097)	(0.080)				86.2
Germany	−1.241	0.697	−0.646	0.403	0.020	0.98	2.5	71.3
	(0.497)	(0.090)	(0.120)	(0.133)				86.3
Italy	0.289	0.895	−0.387	0.077	0.016	0.93	1.2	71.3
	(0.386)	(0.037)	(0.068)	(0.030)				86.3
Japan	1.107	0.750	−0.479	0.139	0.016	0.99	1.8	71.3
	(0.194)	(0.059)	(0.090)	(0.043)				86.3
U.K.	−0.778	0.916	−0.778	0.212	0.020	0.97	1.9	71.3
	(0.662)	(0.034)	(0.173)	(0.116)				86.2

3.12   Identities and Potential GNP

The remaining equations of the model include several identities and the definition of aggregate supply. The income-expenditure identities are shown below in Equation (3.13), which is a useful summary of the degree of disaggregation of aggregate demand used in each country:

$$Y_0 = CD_0 + CN_0 + CS_0 + INE_0 + INS_0 + IR_0 + II_0 + G_0 + EX_0 - IM_0$$
$$Y_1 = CD_1 + CN_1 + CS_1 + IF_1 + II_1 + G_1 + EX_1 - IM_1$$
$$Y_2 = CD_2 + CN_2 + CS_2 + IN_2 + IR_2 + II_2 + G_2 + EX_2 - IM_2$$
$$Y_3 = C_3 + IF_3 + II_3 + G_3 + EX_3 - IM_3$$
$$Y_4 = C_4 + IF_4 + II_4 + G_4 + EX_4 - IM_4$$
$$Y_5 = CD_5 + CN_5 + CS_5 + IN_5 + IR_5 + II_5 + G_5 + EX_5 - IM_5$$
$$Y_6 = CD_6 + CN_6 + CS_6 + IN_6 + IR_6 + II_6 + G_6 + EX_6 - IM_6.$$

$$(3.13)$$

Many of the equations in the model are estimated in log form, with the main exceptions being consumption and investment. These income-expenditure identities obviously need to be written in linear form. The mixture of linear

---

Box 3-3   Key Identities in Each Country

Income-Expenditure Identities

$Y_0 = CD_0 + CN_0 + CS_0 + INE_0 + INS_0 + IR_0 + II_0 + G_0 + EX_0 - IM_0$

$Y_1 = CD_1 + CN_1 + CS_1 + IF_1 \qquad\qquad + II_1 + G_1 + EX_1 - IM_1$

$Y_2 = CD_2 + CN_2 + CS_2 + IN_2 \qquad + IR_2 + II_2 + G_2 + EX_2 - IM_2$

$Y_3 = C_3 \qquad\qquad + IF_3 \qquad\qquad + II_3 + G_3 + EX_3 - IM_3$

$Y_4 = C_4 \qquad\qquad + IF_4 \qquad\qquad + II_4 + G_4 + EX_4 - IM_4$

$Y_5 = CD_5 + CN_5 + CS_5 + IN_5 \qquad + IR_5 + II_5 + G_5 + EX_5 - IM_5$

$Y_6 = CD_6 + CN_6 + CS_6 + IN_6 \qquad + IR_6 + II_6 + G_6 + EX_6 - IM_6$

Weighted Price of Other Six Countries (foreign currency units)

$LPW_0 = \qquad\qquad .09LP_1 + .18LP_2 + .26LP_3 + .12LP_4 + .19LP_5 + .16LP_6$

$LPW_1 = .27LP_0 \qquad\quad + .14LP_2 + .21LP_3 + .10LP_4 + .15LP_5 + .13LP_6$

$LPW_2 = .29LP_0 + .08LP_1 \qquad\quad + .23LP_3 + .11LP_4 + .16LP_5 + .14LP_6$

$LPW_3 = .31LP_0 + .08LP_1 + .16LP_2 \qquad\quad + .12LP_4 + .18LP_5 + .15LP_6$

$LPW_4 = .28LP_0 + .08LP_1 + .15LP_2 + .22LP_3 \qquad\quad + .16LP_5 + .13LP_6$

$LPW_5 = .29LP_0 + .08LP_1 + .15LP_2 + .23LP_3 + .11LP_4 \qquad\quad + .14LP_6$

$LPW_6 = .28LP_0 + .08LP_1 + .15LP_2 + .23LP_3 + .11LP_4 + .16LP_5$

Weighted Exchange Rate (foreign currency/domestic currency)

$LEW_0 = -.09LE_1 - .18LE_2 - .26LE_3 - .12LE_4 - .19LE_5 - .16LE_6$

$LEW_1 = \quad LE_1 \qquad - .14LE_2 - .21LE_3 - .10LE_4 - .15LE_5 - .13LE_6$

$LEW_2 = -.08LE_1 + LE_2 \qquad - .23LE_3 - .11LE_4 - .16LE_5 - .14LE_6$

$LEW_3 = -.08LE_1 - .16LE_2 + LE_3 \qquad - .12LE_4 - .18LE_5 - .15LE_6$

$LEW_4 = -.08LE_1 - .15LE_2 - .22LE_3 + LE_4 \qquad - .16LE_5 - .13LE_6$

$LEW_5 = -.08LE_1 - .15LE_2 - .23LE_3 - .11LE_4 + LE_5 \qquad - .14LE_6$

$LEW_6 = -.08LE_1 - .15LE_2 - .23LE_3 - .11LE_4 - .16LE_5 + LE_6$

Weighted Price of Other Six Countries (domestic currency units)

$LFP_0 = LPW_0 - LEW_0$

$LFP_1 = LPW_1 - LEW_1$

$LFP_2 = LPW_2 - LEW_2$

$LFP_3 = LPW_3 - LEW_3$

$LFP_4 = LPW_4 - LEW_4$

$LFP_5 = LPW_5 - LEW_5$

$LFP_6 = LPW_6 - LEW_6$

Weighted Output of Other Six Countries

$LYW_0 = \qquad\qquad .09LY_1 + .18LY_2 + .26LY_3 + .12LY_4 + .19LY_5 + .16LY_6$

$LYW_1 = .27LY_0 \qquad\quad + .14LY_2 + .21LY_3 + .10LY_4 + .15LY_5 + .13LY_6$

$LYW_2 = .29LY_0 + .08LY_1 \qquad\quad + .23LY_3 + .11LY_4 + .16LY_5 + .14LY_6$

$LYW_3 = .31LY_0 + .08LY_1 + .16LY_2 \qquad\quad + .12LY_4 + .18LY_5 + .15LY_6$

$LYW_4 = .28LY_0 + .08LY_1 + .15LY_2 + .22LY_3 \qquad\quad + .16LY_5 + .13LY_6$

$LYW_5 = .29LY_0 + .08LY_1 + .15LY_2 + .23LY_3 + .11LY_4 \qquad\quad + .14LY_6$

$LYW_6 = .28LY_0 + .08LY_1 + .15LY_2 + .23LY_3 + .11LY_4 + .16LY_5$

equations and nonlinear equations means that the entire model cannot be reduced to either a log-linear or a linear form.

The remaining identities in the model simply define several weighted averages of other variables. These are shown in Box 3-3. They include the weighted price LPW_i, the weighted foreign price LFP_i, and the weighted output LYW_i in each country. Each of these variables has already been discussed.

Finally, potential output is assumed to be growing exponentially. For the purposes of simulation and structural residual calculation during the sample period, the exponential trend is assumed to be constant and was estimated by regressing the log of real output on a linear trend. The estimated growth rates in percent per year were 2.4 for the United States, 3.2 for Canada, 2.5 for France, 2.0 for Germany, 2.2 for Italy, 4.2 for Japan, and 1.5 for the United Kingdom. No explicit attempt was made in the simulations to change the potential growth rate either exogenously or as a function of policy. The focus of this model is on economic fluctuations around this potential level. Of course, this does not mean that potential output or its growth rate are unaffected by macropolicy. The volatility of inflation surely affects real output, for example. But in order to focus on fluctuations, I abstract from these effects. In my judgment, this abstraction does not detract from the analysis.

3.13   The Whole Model

Equations (3.1) through (3.13), along with the definitions of the weighted averages of prices, exchange rates, and output, define the entire multicountry model. There are a total of ninety-eight estimated stochastic equations: twenty-eight describing wage and price behavior, fifty describing aggregate demand, and twenty describing financial markets. These are summarized in Box 3-2. The estimation of most of these equations required econometric methods to deal with rational expectations that did not exist ten years ago. In addition, there are thirty identities, summarized in Box 3-3, and seven equations defining the long-run growth trend of GNP or GDP.

Although I have not emphasized it, there are a number of remarkable characteristics about these equations. For example, the real interest rate appears to be statistically and quantitatively significant in a large number of equations, including those relating to inventories and durables consumption. The signs of the price variables in the exports, imports, and money-demand equations are correct in virtually every country. Perhaps most remarkable is the fact that essentially the same functional form worked well for all countries.

Although I have presented the estimated stochastic equations, I have not yet described the stochastic disturbances to these equations, which are essential for policy analysis. This requires considering the model as a whole. In the next chapter I discuss how the entire model is put together, solved, and simulated, along with the estimation of the stochastic disturbance structure. In doing so I will rely on the nonlinear extended path method for solving and simulating rational expectation models as described in Chapter 1.

Reference Notes

The chapter makes no attempt to compare the structure of this model with other econometric models, either rational or conventional. Several such comparisons are available in the literature, however. An early version of the multicountry model was presented at the first Brookings Model Comparison Project conference in 1986 and published in Bryant, et al. (1988a). Along with many other things, that useful volume provides a brief comparison of this model with other multicountry models in existence as of that time. Several useful analytic comparisons of this model with conventional models are found in Helliwell, Cockerline, and Lafrance (1990) and Brayton and Marquez (1990), who focus on the financial sector, and in Visco (1991), who focuses on the wage-price sector.

The properties of most of the instrumental variable-estimation techniques used in this chapter are found in any advanced econometrics textbook. The generalized method of moments estimator designed to estimate rational expectations models in time-series applications is derived by Hansen (1982).

Many papers have been written on the estimation of single equations for the components of consumption and investment, inventories, and net exports, examining issues such as real-interest-rate sensitivity, lag structure, and income elasticities. No attempt has been made to compare systematically my equations with these others. Most of the other studies have focused on a single country and have used different data and different functional forms.

Appendix 3A: Estimation and Test Procedures

The generalized method of moments (GMM) estimator and a test of the overidentifying restrictions were programmed in *TSP*. The specific formulas for the estimator and the test are briefly described in this appendix, and a table is presented with the results of the tests of the overidentifying restrictions for the equations of the model.

Each equation of the model can be written in the form

$$y = Z\delta + \varepsilon,$$

where

$y = (T \times 1)$ vector of observations;
$Z = (T \times K)$ matrix of observations;
$\delta = (K \times 1)$ vector of parameters to be estimated;
$\varepsilon = (T \times 1)$ vector of disturbances.

The GMM estimator of δ is given by

$$\hat{\delta} = (Z'W\hat{\Omega}^{-1}W'Z)^{-1}Z'W\hat{\Omega}^{-1}W'y \qquad (1)$$

and an estimate of the covariance matrix of δ is given by

$$\hat{V} = T(Z'W\hat{\Omega}^{-1}W'Z)^{-1}, \qquad (2)$$

where

$W = (T \times q)$ matrix of instrumental variables,
$\hat{\Omega}^{-1} = (q \times q)$ consistent estimate of the optimal weighting matrix.

Actual computation of $\hat{\delta}$ and $\hat{V}$ requires calculation of $\hat{\Omega}^{-1}$.

Sargan's Test of Overidentifying Restrictions
for Consumption and Investment

Dependent Variable	Sargan's Test Statistic	Degrees of Freedom	P Value (%)
CD0	11.23	5	4.71
CN0	9.40	5	9.40
CS0	8.99	6	17.41
CD1	5.32	5	37.82
CN1	10.32	5	6.67
CS1	7.95	6	24.17
CD2	2.89	5	71.64
CN2	4.23	6	64.58
CS2	6.70	6	34.98
C3	9.18	5	10.20
C4	6.60	5	25.20
CD5	1.94	5	85.75
CN5	5.68	6	45.96
CS5	6.47	6	37.28
CD6	9.40	6	15.22
CN6	5.38	5	37.16
CS6	8.10	6	23.10
INE0	7.28	5	20.07
INS0	9.49	5	9.10
IR0	9.47	5	9.18
II0	8.94	4	6.26
IF1	5.64	5	34.31
II1	10.06	4	3.94
IN2	3.57	6	73.42
IR2	1.44	6	96.31
II2	3.99	4	40.73
IF3	4.85	5	43.47
II3	6.90	4	14.13
IF4	9.20	5	10.13
II4	7.79	4	9.95
IN5	5.69	5	33.81
IR5	9.66	6	13.99
II5	3.24	4	51.91
IN6	7.51	5	18.56
IR6	11.43	6	7.59
II6	7.80	4	9.94

Hansen (1982) showed that the optimal GMM estimator of δ (the consistent estimate with the smallest asymptotic variance) is obtained when the weighting matrix is proportional to the inverse of the variance-covariance matrix

$$\Omega \equiv \text{Var}(T^{-1}W'(y - Z\delta))$$

Newey and West (1987) developed a consistent, positive semidefinite estimate of Ω given by

$$\hat{\Omega} = \hat{R}_0 + \sum_{j=1}^{m}\left[1 - \frac{j}{m+1}\right]\left[\hat{R}_j + \hat{R}_j'\right],$$

where

$$\hat{R}_j = \sum_{t=j+1}^{T} w(t)e(t)e(t-j)w(t-j)',$$

and where

$w(t) = (q \times 1)$ vector, the transpose of the tth row of the matrix W,
$e(t) = t$th estimated residual from a two-stage least squares procedure,
$m = $ order of the autocorrelation in the disturbance terms.

Note that both $\hat{R}_j$, and therefore $\hat{\Omega}$, are $q \times q$ matrices. Once $\hat{\Omega}$ is obtained, GMM estimates are produced directly from (1) and (2). As the number of intrumental variables q exceeds the number of explanatory variables K, a Sargan test can be used to test the $(q - K)$ overidentifying restrictions (Hansen, 1982). (See table on p. 100.)

Under the null hypothesis that the $(q - K)$ overidentifying restrictions are not binding, the Sargan statistic Q has a chi-square $(q - K)$ distribution, where Q is defined as

$$Q = \frac{1}{T}(y - Z\hat{\delta})'W\hat{\Omega}^{-1}W'(y - Z\hat{\delta}) \stackrel{A}{\sim} \chi^2_{q-K}.$$

Values for Q for the consumption and investment equations are shown in the following table. These were computed subsequent to the specification and estimation of these equations, and no attempt was made to respecify or change the instruments as a result of these tests. Note that the test fails at the 5-percent level for only two of the thirty-six equations: consumer durables in the United States and inventory investment in Canada.

Appendix 3B: Summary of Elasticities

This appendix gives the long-run and short-run elasticities of money demand, consumption, investment, exports, and imports with respect to the relevant interest rate, income, or price variable. They are compiled directly from the estimated equation presented in Chapter 3. The semi-elasticities with respect to the interest rate were calculated at the last sample point for the dependent variable of consumption and investment.

Semi-Elasticities of Consumption Demand with Respect to the Real Interest Rate

		Short Run	Long Run
U.S.	CD	−0.12	−0.40
	CN	−0.04	−0.08
	CS	0.00	0.00
	C	−0.03	−0.09
Canada	CD1	−0.32	−0.88
	CN1	−0.06	−0.59
	CS1	0.00	0.00
	C1	−0.08	−0.38
France	CD2	−0.63	−0.96
	CN2	0.00	0.00
	CS2	0.00	0.00
	C2	−0.06	−0.09
Germany	C3	−0.15	−0.55
Italy	C4	−0.03	−0.23
Japan	CD5	−0.62	−0.96
	CN5	0.00	0.00
	CS5	0.00	0.00
	C5	−0.05	−0.07
U.K.	CD6	0.00	0.00
	CN6	−0.08	−0.24
	CS6	0.00	0.00
	C6	−0.04	−0.12

Impact of a Change in Permanent Income on Consumption

		Short Run	Long Run
U.S.	CD	0.04	0.13
	CN	0.10	0.20
	CS	0.04	0.41
	C	0.18	0.74
Canada	CD1	0.05	0.13
	CN1	0.01	0.15
	CS1	0.03	0.30
	C1	0.09	0.57
France	CD2	0.08	0.12
	CN2	0.20	0.29
	CS2	0.08	0.40
	C2	0.35	0.81
Germany	C3	0.18	0.66
Italy	C4	0.08	0.69
Japan	CD5	0.04	0.06
	CN5	0.03	0.15
	CS5	0.09	0.30
	C5	0.16	0.51
U.K.	CD6	0.07	0.15
	CN6	0.09	0.27
	CS6	0.03	0.36
	C6	0.19	0.78

Semi-Elasticities of Investment Demand with Respect to the Real Interest Rate

		Short Run	Long Run
U.S.	INE	−0.43	−1.79
	INS	−0.23	−6.24
	IR	−2.10	−5.45
	I	−0.85	−3.83
Canada	IF1	−0.18	−2.74
France	IN2	0.00	0.00
	IR2	−0.62	−4.33
	I2	−0.12	−0.87
Germany	IF3	−0.88	−4.62
Italy	IF4	−0.28	−2.96
Japan	IN5	−0.44	−4.38
	IR5	0.00	0.00
	I5	−0.35	−3.49
U.K.	IN6	−0.13	−0.49
	IR6	0.00	0.00
	I6	−0.11	−0.40

Impact of a Change in Expected Sales on Investments

		Short Run	Long Run
U.S.	INE	0.04	0.18
	INS	0.01	0.19
	IR	0.06	0.16
	I	0.11	0.54
Canada	IF1	0.03	0.38
France	IN2	0.02	0.10
	IR2	0.00	0.00
	I2	0.02	0.10
Germany	IF3	0.05	0.26
Italy	IF4	0.03	0.33
Japan	IN5	0.04	0.40
	IR5	0.00	0.00
	I5	0.04	0.40
U.K.	IN6	0.03	0.12
	IR6	0.00	0.00
	I6	0.03	0.12

Export-Demand Elasticities

		Short Run	Long Run
U.S.	Income	0.23	1.12
	Price	−0.15	−0.73
Canada	Income	1.01	2.42
	Price	−0.32	−0.78
France	Income	1.00	2.03
	Price	−0.38	−0.77
Germany	Income	0.68	1.46
	Price	−0.34	−0.73
Italy	Income	0.59	2.01
	Price	−0.08	−0.27
Japan	Income	0.37	2.00
	Price	−0.15	−0.82
U.K.	Income	1.13	1.30
	Price	−0.37	−0.43

Import-Demand Elasticities

		Short Run	Long Run
U.S.	Income	1.27	2.28
	Price	−0.22	−0.39
Canada	Income	0.50	1.55
	Price	−0.10	−0.31
France	Income	0.70	2.24
	Price	−0.15	−0.47
Germany	Income	1.32	1.87
	Price	0.00	0.00
Italy	Income	1.18	2.01
	Price	−0.19	−0.32
Japan	Income	0.11	1.13
	Price	−0.08	−0.83
U.K.	Income	0.66	1.88
	Price	−0.06	−0.18

Money-Demand Elasticities with Respect to Income and Interest Rate
(semi-elasticity for the interest rate)

		Short Run	Long Run
U.S.	Income	0.04	0.85
	Interest	−0.22	−4.73
Canada	Income	0.03	0.53
	Interest	−0.51	−8.11
France	Income	0.17	0.53
	Interest	−0.32	−0.99
Germany	Income	0.40	1.33
	Interest	−0.65	−2.13
Italy	Income	0.08	0.73
	Interest	−0.39	−3.67
Japan	Income	0.14	0.55
	Interest	−0.48	−1.91
U.K.	Income	0.21	2.52
	Interest	−0.78	−9.24

4

Shocks and Disturbances to the World Economy

It is a fact of life that the world economy is subject to continual disturbances or shocks. Some disturbances are large and noticeable, such as the sudden oil-price increases in 1973 and 1979 or the more recent oil-price rise after Iraq invaded Kuwait in August 1990. These oil-price shocks affected real economic growth and inflation in almost every country throughout the world. Although the 1990 oil-price shock ended quickly after the successful Allied military intervention in Kuwait, the shock probably helped bring the U.S. economy into recession; the first month of recession according to the National Bureau of Economic Research (NBER) was September 1990, one month after the Iraq invasion of Kuwait.

Of course not all disturbances are caused by oil shocks. In the fall of 1991, a different type of shock apparently hit the economy: a marked drop in consumer confidence. Whatever its source, it caused a decline in consumption demand and thereby slowed down the U.S. economy. Money-demand shocks, exchange-rate shocks, and international-portfolio shocks are other noticeable disturbances to the world economy. Numerous times, such shocks have altered the course of different economies.

Many shocks, however, go unnoticed. They may be small, or they may not be understood until well after they occur, if ever. Debate continues, for example, about whether shocks to the money supply, or to tariffs, or to financial intermediaries, or even to consumption demand were the source of the Great Depression of the 1930s.

If macroeconomic policy is to be effective, it must be designed to work well in a world where shocks and disturbances are everyday phenomena. A good policy rule will generally be effective in ironing out shocks and will not add more disturbances to the economy; a bad policy will tend to amplify shocks and may even add disturbances to the system.

In order to design policy systems that deal effectively with shocks, it is necessary to assess their past behavior and project their future behavior. Because shocks are by their nature unanticipated, however, no economic model can project particular paths for future shocks. For example, no reasonable model could make a prediction that there will be an oil-price increase of 50 percent in January 2012. It is only the general properties of these future shocks—for instance, their variances and their covariances—that we can hope to project. But even bits of information about these general properties can greatly improve the reliability of economic policy and should be taken into account when designing economic policy systems.

A physical-design analogy is useful if not taken too far. The design of a policy rule—say an international monetary system—can be compared with the design of an off-road vehicle. The design of such a vehicle—the suspension system, the center of gravity, the ground clearance, the gear ratio, and so on—will depend on the nature of the terrain. Similarly, the design of a macroeconomic policy—the degree of responsiveness of the instruments of policy—depends on the pattern of future economic shocks. A good macroeconomic policy design requires a forecast of the general properties of future shocks but not necessarily a forecast of when and where each individual shock will occur. Individual shocks will, by definition, be unanticipated. Analogously, the design of a good off-road vehicle requires an analysis of the typical terrain, not where each bump is placed on a given trail.

The purpose of this chapter is to try to measure and interpret systematically the shocks that hit the world economy during the 1970s and 1980s and to use this information to project future disturbances for policy-design analysis. I do this by using the model described in Chapter 3. I treat the "residuals" to the equations of that model as measures of the shocks that hit the real world. For example, the residuals in the durable-goods consumption equation in the United States are a measure of the shocks to durables-consumption demand during the sample period. Interpreting the consumption shock is more difficult. In principle it is a reflection of any variable not incorporated in the consumption equation as well as pure randomness. In order to assess the reliability of a policy-design analysis based on such shocks, however, it is essential to have some interpretation or intuitive understanding of the nature of the shocks. Otherwise, the analysis becomes a "black box" in which it is hard to place much confidence and that will have little practical appeal. Moreover, the analysis of the shocks can provide insights into the working of the world economy, which might have implications for this and other research programs.

Systematically studying the shocks is not an easy job for a model of this size. Even though, as I have argued, the ninety-eight individual equations of the model have straightforward theoretical interpretations, there are still ninety-eight different shocks to analyze. I will be working under the assumption that these shocks are serially uncorrelated, but that still leaves a 98 by 98 matrix with 4,851 distinct variances and contemporaneous covariances to describe and analyze.[1] Clearly some effort is required to find a good way to present simply such information, let alone to organize it in a manageable form for discussion.

I begin by describing how the shocks are computed and then go on to summarize the major properties of the variance-covariance matrix of the shocks. To do this I organize the ninety-eight shocks into three groups corresponding to the familiar framework of stylized macroeconomic models. The first group consists of twenty different *financial-market shocks,* which correspond to shocks to the demand for money, to the term structure of interest rates, and to the *ex ante* interest-rate parity relation for exchange rates. The second group consists of fifty different *goods-market shocks,* which correspond to different shocks to the components of consumption, the components of investment, exports, and imports. The third group consists of twenty-eight different *price shocks,* which correspond to shocks to wages, to the markup relations for product prices, export prices, and import prices.

For each of these groups I describe the volatility of the shocks and the correlation between the shocks. As detailed later, I find a significant amount of correlation between shocks in different sectors within the same country as well as significant correlation within some sectors across countries. The volatility of the shocks differs from country to country and from sector to sector.

One obvious point should be emphasized at the outset of this discussion. The correlations between the shocks are just that—correlations—not necessarily causal relations. It is useful to give interpretations to the correlations, and I do that in a number of cases. In some cases, however, the most satisfactory explanation is that there is a missing third factor explaining the behavior of more than one shock.

4.1   Defining and Computing the Shocks

The typical behavioral equation in the multicountry model features endogenous variables, predetermined variables, expectations of future variables, and an additive stochastic shock. It might help to look at Equation (1.28) of Chapter 1 that gave a general algebraic notation for the typical equation. For example, the durable-consumption equation in the United States presents personal consumption of durable goods on the left-hand side and the expectation of future income, the expectation of future inflation, the long-term interest rate, lagged durable consumption, and a stochastic shock on the right-hand side. In some equations—like the consumption equations—the stochastic shock is assumed to be serially uncorrelated. In other equations,

---

[1] As described in Chapter 3, some of the ninety-eight equations are modeled with $AR(1)$ disturbances. In these cases, the characteristics of the serially uncorrelated shock to the disturbances are estimated in this chapter.

the shock is serially correlated and usually modeled according to a first-order autoregressive process, with the shock to that autoregressive process assumed to be serially uncorrelated. It is this serially uncorrelated stochastic shock—whether directly to the equation or indirectly to the autoregressive error process in the equation—that is the subject of this chapter. These shocks are the *structural* residuals to the equations of the model. The task is to compute these residuals and estimate their properties.

Structural residuals for each equation can be computed for the period during which the model was estimated: the first quarter of 1972 through the last quarter of 1986. It would be a matter of simple arithmetic (again, it may help to check out Equation [1.28]) to compute the residuals if the expectation of future variables in each equation were known. In other words, the right-hand side variables could be subtracted from the left-hand side variables, just as the residuals are computed in a simple regression model. However, expectations of future variables are not known and must be computed at each date during the sample period. This can be accomplished by simulating the model dynamically into the future, conditional on data through each sample point. This generates forecasted values for each endogenous variable that can then be used in place of the expectations variable in each equation. In other words, at each of the sixty-eight points in the sample, one solves the model using the extended path method. This ensures that the expectations are rational forecasts in the sense that they are consistent with the model and are based only on information available at the time the forecast is made. Using this procedure, which is straightforward but computer intensive, the conditional forecasts can be computed for every equation in the model. How one treats exogenous variables—that is variables not modeled—is more ambiguous. There are only two exogenous variables in each country in this model—government purchases and the money supply. These were set to their actual values rather than extrapolated with auxiliary equations.

Note that these structural residuals are not the same as the residuals obtained from the instrumental variables-estimation procedure in Chapter 3. Those residuals—used to compute R^2—effectively assume that the forecast variables are equal to the actual future variables. Hence, those residuals include both the forecast errors in projecting the future and the structural equation errors. The procedure used here removes the forecast error from the residuals. Full-information maximum-likelihood (FIML) methods would require that the residuals be computed as in this chapter. FIML estimation has not been used, however, because it is not computationally feasible. This would require thousands of computations of the residuals for each of the sixty-eight sample points; only one computation for each of the sixty-eight sample points is done here.

Figure 4-1 illustrates the structural residual computations with examples from four of the ninety-eight stochastic equations of the model. The four time-series charts in Figure 4-1 each show the structural residual for each equation for the 1972:1 through 1986:4 period: (1) consumer durables in

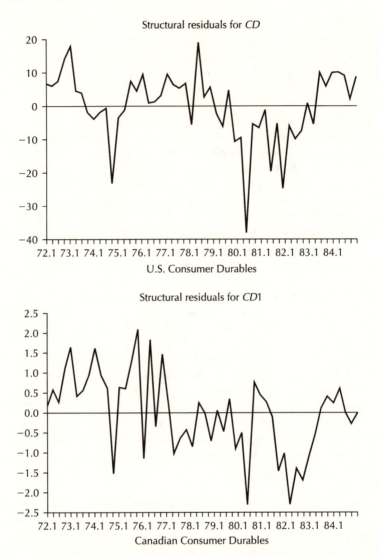

FIGURE 4-1   **Shocks to Consumer Demand and Import Prices (structural residuals from multicountry model).** The correlation coefficient between shocks to consumer durables in the United States and Canada is .51. The correlation coefficient between import price in the United States and Japan is .61. (See Table 4-1 and Table 4-2.)

the United States; (2) consumer durables in Canada; (3) import prices in the United States; and (4) import prices in Japan. As discussed below, there is a relatively high correlation between shocks to import prices in Japan and in the United States, and this correlation is visible in the time-series charts. The charts suggest this is largely due to a simultaneous occurrence of a large

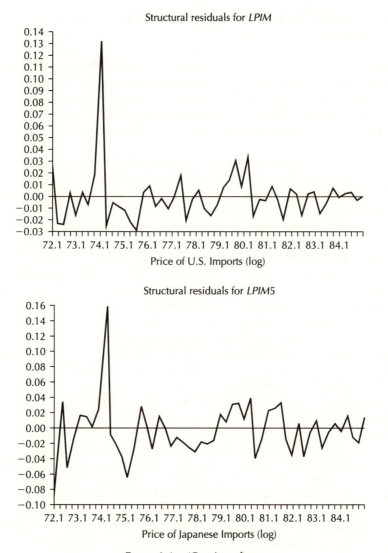

FIGURE **4-1**   *(Continued)*

shock in 1974. This was apparently due to the increase in the price of oil following the war in the Middle East, and it gives an illustration of how price shocks show up in the multicountry model. The time-series charts also show a correlation between shocks to consumer durables in the United States and shocks to consumer durables in Canada. It is interesting to note that much of this correlation appears to be related to a simultaneous occurrence of a shock in 1980 when credit controls were instituted in the United States. The next section examines these and other correlations between the structural residuals more systematically.

4.2   Estimating the Variance-Covariance Matrix and Drawing New Shocks

Consistent estimates of the variance of each of the shocks and the covariance between the shocks in each pair of equations are obtained from the sample moments—the average of the sums of squares and cross-products—of the estimated residuals. Each of these estimates is perfectly well defined and consistent; as the sample size grows, the estimates converge to the true values.

It is straightforward to construct an estimated covariance matrix from these estimates of the variances and covariances, with the variances on the diagonal and the covariances on the off-diagonal. Call this 98 by 98 covariance matrix S. For stochastic simulation, I make the assumption that the 98-dimensional vector of structural residuals is normally distributed with mean vector 0 and covariance matrix S.

In order to determine how the endogenous variables of the multicountry model behave for different policy rules, it is necessary to stochastically simulate the model. For stochastic simulation, shocks from this normal distribution can be created by using a standard random-number generator. The resulting shocks will have the same distribution as the shocks to the equations during the sample period (under the normal and serially uncorrelated distribution assumption). Note that because the shocks are serially uncorrelated, the expectation of future shocks is zero in each equation (their unconditional mean). Of course, the shocks turn out not to be zero when the future periods of the simulation occur. No series of shocks drawn from this distribution will match the pattern during the sample period, but the statistical properties will be the same. Using the off-road vehicle analogy, the properties of the terrain are known, although a particular path is not.

A comparison of this approach with the simpler approach of Chapter 2 is useful. In Chapter 2 the model of the U.S. economy was linear and could be reduced to a linear VARMA. The structural shocks to this model were computed as part of the estimation procedure, and an estimate of the variance-covariance matrix of the shocks was obtained. That covariance matrix was 5 by 5. Given this covariance matrix, the statistical properties of the endogenous variables could be computed analytically *without* stochastic simulation; the variance-covariance matrix of the endogenous variables was a known function of the variance-covariance matrix of the shocks. The multicountry model is not linear, and therefore such a simple analytic computation is not feasible. Hence, we use stochastic simulation and a random-number generator to compute the statistical properties of the endogenous variables. Hence, although computationally different, the methods are conceptually the same.

One important technical issue in this computation procedure should be noted. Because the sample size (68) is less than the dimensions of the covariance matrix (98 by 98), the estimated covariance matrix is singular—that is, there is perfect contemporaneous correlation among some linear combinations of the estimated residuals. In other words, the normal distribution that is generated randomly is singular.

Using the Actual Shocks Again

Recall that in several experiments reported in Chapter 2, the actual residuals were used rather than the new residuals drawn from the estimated normal distribution. That same procedure is possible for the multicountry model, and the advantages and disadvantages are similar. An advantage is that nonnormalities—such as large outliers—can be taken into account if they are important during the sample period. A disadvantage is that there are only sixty-eight shocks to work with.

Dealing with Changes in the Stochastic Structure

One disadvantage of using estimated residuals (whether the actual estimates or randomly generated ones) for policy design is that it implicitly assumes that the properties of the disturbances in the future will be like those in the past, but this is a disadvantage for any empirical analysis based on actual data. This disadvantage can be dealt with by sensitivity analysis, changing the disturbances slightly and observing whether the results change. For example, one might suspect that the shocks to the exchange-rate equations (the "risk-premium terms") might be reduced significantly if exchange rates were fixed. To test whether the results are sensitive to such a change, the simulations could be conducted with and without the risk-premium shocks. This approach is followed in Chapter 6, which explores policy design.

4.3   Which Shocks Are Big and Which Are Correlated?

Table 4-1 shows the standard deviations of the errors to each equation (the square roots of the diagonal elements of the covariance matrix). The equations are usually labeled by the variable on the left-hand side of the equations. One exception is the shock to short-term interest rates that is computed from an inverted money-demand equation. For those equations that are not estimated in logs, I also report the ratio of the standard deviation of the shock to the mean of the right-hand side variable in order to control the large difference in the average size of the residuals. Hence, each standard deviation is stated in units roughly proportional to the average value of the variable on the left-hand side of the equation in question.

Table 4-2 shows the correlation matrix in several blocks (the elements below the main diagonal are grouped as shown on the first page of Table 4-2). In reading the correlation matrix, note that I have omitted the decimal point of each correlation and show only the first two digits to the right of the decimal. The first entry of 28 thus indicates that the correlation between the

TABLE 4-1   Standard Deviations of the Shocks to the Equations

Variable Name*	Standard Deviation of Shock	Variable Name	Standard Deviation of Shock	Variable Name	Standard Deviation of Shock	Standard Deviation/ Mean
RS	0.041	LX	0.006	CD	10.38	0.042
RS1	0.036	LX1	0.069	CN	10.58	0.014
RS2	0.107	LX2	0.016	CS	5.46	0.006
RS3	0.032	LX3	0.010	CD1	1.00	0.040
RS4	0.040	LX4	0.057	CN1	0.68	0.009
RS5	0.033	LX5	0.054	CS1	0.49	0.006
RS6	0.026	LX6	0.022	CD2	3.75	0.058
LE1	0.037	LP	0.003	CN2	6.92	0.020
LE2	0.088	LP1	0.008	CS2	2.65	0.011
LE3	0.101	LP2	0.006	C3	10.35	0.013
LE4	0.076	LP3	0.007	C4	335.70	0.007
LE5	0.083	LP4	0.021	CD5	393.59	0.053
LE6	0.067	LP5	0.009	CN5	843.51	0.014
RL	0.020	LP6	0.010	CS5	872.27	0.014
RL1	0.018	LPIM	0.023	CD6	1.09	0.083
RL2	0.031	LPIM1	0.016	CN6	0.79	0.011
RL3	0.015	LPIM2	0.025	CS6	0.45	0.009
RL4	0.019	LPIM3	0.019	INE	9.07	0.041
RL5	0.022	LPIM4	0.025	INS	3.84	0.031
RL6	0.025	LPIM5	0.034	IR	17.58	0.119
LEX	0.029	LPIM6	0.020	II	17.22	0.971
LEX1	0.033	LPEX	0.009	IF1	1.75	0.026
LEX2	0.014	LPEX1	0.015	II1	2.95	1.305
LEX3	0.023	LPEX2	0.016	IN2	3.03	0.018
LEX4	0.033	LPEX3	0.007	IR2	1.07	0.018
LEX5	0.028	LPEX4	0.020	II2	6.80	0.553
LEX6	0.030	LPEX5	0.014	IF3	12.52	0.041
LIM	0.032	LPEX6	0.011	II3	12.94	1.847
LIM1	0.032			IF4	377.38	0.027
LIM2	0.024			II4	819.64	0.773
LIM3	0.022			IN5	897.65	0.026
LIM4	0.033			IR5	786.28	0.051
LIM5	0.028			II5	1462.42	0.812
LIM6	0.037			IN6	0.96	0.029
				IR6	0.43	0.049
				II6	2.04	3.623

*The definitions of the variable names are summarized in Box 3-1 (see p. 69).

shocks to the short-term interest-rate equation in Canada and the shocks to the short-term interest-rate equation in the United States is .28. The lower left-hand entry of −9 says that the correlation between shocks to inventory investment in the United Kingdom and the short-term interest-rate equation in the United States is −.09.

Financial-Sector Shocks

This group includes shocks to short-term interest rates (money-demand shocks), shocks to long-term interest rates (term-structure shocks), and shocks to exchange rates (*ex ante* interest-rate parity shocks).

The short-term interest-rate shocks have large standard deviations compared with the other equations. Recall that the short-term interest-rate equations were derived by first estimating a money-demand equation with the short-term interest rate on the right-hand side, and subsequently by inverting the equation to put the interest rate on the left-hand side. Hence, the shocks to short-term interest rates are directly related to velocity shocks that appear to be large in this model. Moreover, the estimated short-run interest-rate elasticity in the money-demand equations is very low. Hence, the inversion of the equation gives an even larger interest-rate variance—the inverse of a very low interest-rate elasticity multiplies the money-demand residual. Estimating the equation with the interest rate on the left-hand side might give a smaller variance. However, the size of these variances does not affect the policy analysis of later chapters. The policy rules we examine in this book do not rely on these equations, so that the large variance of the shocks does not affect the policy-design results. In other words, the monetary policy rules analyzed are interest-rate rules rather than money-supply rules. Since these interest-rate rules replace the money-demand equations in the simulations, the short-term interest-rate shocks do not enter the analysis.

The long-term interest-rate equations have shocks with smaller variances than for the short-term interest rates. Recall that these are simply shocks to the term-structure equations. A positive shock will steepen the yield curve. The standard deviation of these shocks is generally around 2 or 3 percentage points and thus not insignificant. This represents deviations from the simple efficient model of the term structure and might be due to risk premia or other factors (including measurement error). Under the risk-premia interpretation, the risk premia are time varying and stochastic.

The shocks to the exchange-rate equations are important for the international policy analysis. These shocks are fairly large—with a standard deviation ranging from a relatively low 4 percent for the U.S. dollar/Canadian dollar exchange rate to around 10 percent for the U.S. dollar/deutsche mark exchange rate—but perhaps not surprisingly large given the behavior of exchange rates during the sample period. These standard deviations measure the size of the departure from *ex ante* interest-rate parity. They may be thought of as risk premia. If so, then the risk-premia shocks to *ex ante* interest-rate parity are generally larger than the risk-premia shocks to the

(continued on p. 130)

Table 4-2A Correlation Matrix of Errors to the Equations

	RS U.S.	RS Can.	RS Fra.	RS Ger.	RS It.	RS Jap.	RS U.K.	LE Can.	LE Fra.	LE Ger.	LE It.	LE Jap.	LE U.K.	RL U.S.	RL Can.	RL Fra.	RL Ger.	RL It.	RL Jap.	RL U.K.
RS																				
Can.	28																			
Fra.	19	−6																		
Ger.	9	4	14																	
It.	14	6	30	−4																
Jap.	16	7	7	−0	2															
U.K.	12	−7	−4	20	25	−2														
LE																				
Can.	33	−24	−26	−38	−18	9	−14													
Fra.	−4	24	19	23	30	7	1	−60												
Ger.	−14	14	27	−6	23	11	−17	−47	79											
It.	−10	18	−29	2	−3	−2	−1	−10	39	41										
Jap.	−2	15	23	11	30	1	−9	−39	80	73	40									
U.K.	16	20	14	9	−1	0	3	−8	25	26	55	17								
RL																				
U.S.	4	−8	1	−2	7	−17	18	−3	−20	−40	−21	−14	−32							
Can.	11	−36	−30	1	−34	−9	3	40	−32	−37	23	−18	−2	42						
Fra.	24	19	28	14	16	−18	18	−25	34	1	−16	21	15	29	−13					
Ger.	3	3	−40	−32	−24	6	0	39	−32	−23	38	−21	2	29	51	−18				
It.	28	17	35	15	23	−12	16	−28	32	1	−1	21	13	44	11	73	−5			
Jap.	16	15	−26	9	5	−4	29	10	−11	−30	51	−2	14	39	38	2	53	21		
U.K.	−22	−12	−50	−20	−16	−5	−12	30	−34	−6	37	−9	−9	−8	26	−65	49	−61	33	
Consumption																				
U.S. *D*	9	11	−23	−11	27	−8	−5	21	1	−18	12	20	−27	32	20	5	29	14	39	14
N	11	−3	−19	−7	17	−1	6	22	−4	−19	35	16	−17	39	41	−3	45	14	64	18
S	25	18	−15	−7	12	8	−1	15	−2	−9	28	6	−4	32	31	−7	45	8	42	20
Can. *D*	7	12	−49	−7	−6	3	−18	44	−14	−22	19	4	−15	−13	14	−28	25	−29	29	35
N	−11	−5	−25	16	−18	−2	11	15	−10	−18	6	2	−15	1	6	−12	5	−22	12	23
S	2	10	7	1	7	12	−21	18	−15	−2	−6	−1	−13	−6	−1	−38	2	−33	3	11

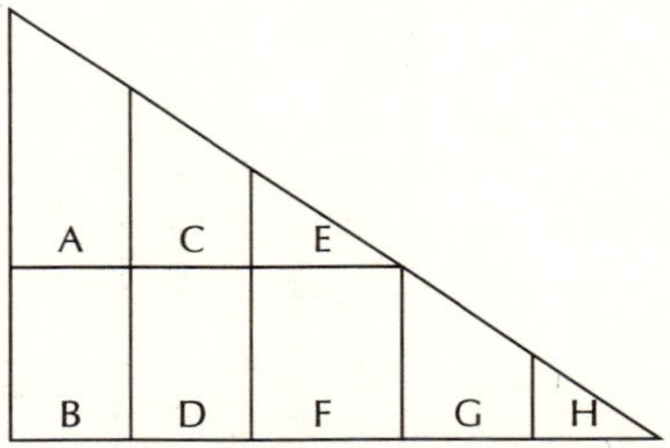

Location of Parts of Correlation Matrix

Consumption (Continued)

	RS							LE							RL						
	U.S.	Can.	Fra.	Ger.	It.	Jap.	U.K.	U.S.	Can.	Fra.	Ger.	It.	Jap.	U.K.	U.S.	Can.	Fra.	Ger.	It.	Jap.	U.K.
Fra. D	42	−12	−29	−12	−8	17	24	58	−50		−53	−6	−38	−14	29	53	−17	45	−7	46	29
N	8	−12	−50	−13	−14	7	11	63	−53		−51	25	−31	−15	16	55	−39	62	−27	59	58
S	3	−9	−38	−15	−14	9	−17	45	−43		−47	14	−17	−27	25	47	−29	55	−17	45	40
Ger.	25	8	−20	8	−9	10	23	18	15	−8		42	7	22	−8	23	−2	26	2	48	7
It.	24	−4	20	−10	25	10	36	8	7	−20	−27		−7	−12	8	−10	39	−28	39	5	−54
Jap. D	−4	−8	−20	−9	7	24	10	5	17	4	40	10		10	−6	9	−13	24	8	40	4
N	−9	18	−11	−12	5	8	6	−11	33	24	33	15		11	−8	−14	3	18	5	17	−9
S	3	10	16	3	13	19	−28	−7	24	28	28	20		26	−16	−13	4	4	23	−7	−21
U.K. D	24	−14	3	1	−8	24	−5	27	−19	−32	−9	−14	−23		31	30	13	25	14	32	−11
N	19	−10	10	3	9	10	4	31	5	−8	15	15	3		10	17	25	14	21	33	−11
S	33	6	13	0	−3	7	−1	27	−15	−27	6	−17	23		19	24	31	18	39	33	−22

Investment

	RS							LE							RL						
	U.S.	Can.	Fra.	Ger.	It.	Jap.	U.K.	U.S.	Can.	Fra.	Ger.	It.	Jap.	U.K.	U.S.	Can.	Fra.	Ger.	It.	Jap.	U.K.
U.S. NE	4	−6	−12	−16	19	−9	−2		27	−9	−24	11	19	−17	14	10	6	13	11	37	16
NS	15	10	9	−19	34	8	13		12	−2	−16	4	6	1	2	−20	6	−5	14	34	4
R	17	2	−29	−10	19	−11	7		39	−24	−40	26	−1	−17	38	41	−7	49	9	69	34
I	−29	−25	13	−16	−2	−29	16		4	−21	−15	−23	−3	−18	−4	−12	2	−11	−2	6	10
Can. F	31	15	−19	19	7	6	−9	25		4	−10	19	6	22	−40	−5	−11	−8	−20	19	9
I	−11	−14	−12	−20	−9	9	17	28		−44	−21	11	−35	0	−17	5	−28	35	−27	24	38
Fra. N	25	12	−4	−4	19	13	8	14	2		−19	−2	−5	2	12	−3	12	−3	5	19	−11
R	37	−8	−13	1	−21	1	12	56	−54		−54	−13	−38	−4	−5	21	−15	19	−15	33	16
F	8	−22	5	−17	−9	−4	21	32	−17		−12	−15	−16	8	15	20	8	−7	−1	−10	−14
I	38	−1	−11	8	−14	20	5	41	−33		−52	−9	−37	−5	9	26	4	17	7	36	−6
Ger. F	−3	−12	−14	−6	−3	−1	11	19	−17	−14		−1	−19	−19	−35	−13	−19	−1	−24	5	−3
I	30	−11	−8	−7	13	−5	23	46	−32	−48		−20	−23	−1	4	10	−2	−5	−9	16	−14
It. F	21	−28	−25	−5	−18	15	−1	45	−38	−33	5		−24	22	11	53	−39	18	−27	18	28
I	1	3	−29	−9	−5	3	19	17	−11	−24	48		−7	7	3	27	−17	30	0	65	16
Jap. N	−0	−7	7	34	19	16	16	−13	5	−18	20	9		21	21	11	9	3	15	45	6
R	9	−12	−25	−1	−6	3	1	27	−25	−27	27	2		25	−6	21	−16	22	−12	44	30
I	−10	−32	0	4	7	−0	−4	22	−13	−19	−4	−20		17	24	27	−16	22	−12	18	4
U.K. N	3	−11	−0	−6	24	18	3	9	25	−6	24	15	−1		24	11	3	4	19	22	1
R	−9	−2	−4	4	19	4	0	−0	−2	−38	−2	−23	17		15	27	0	24	4	45	30
I	−9	−2	−8	−25	7	−6	−3	8	−20	−23	−1	−6	17		−1	−8	−3	−1	−6	5	6

TABLE 4-2B   Correlation Matrix of the Errors

LEX

	RS							LE							RL						
	U.S.	Can.	Fra.	Ger.	It.	Jap.	U.K.	U.S.	Can.	Fra.	Ger.	It.	Jap.	U.K.	U.S.	Can.	Fra.	Ger.	It.	Jap.	U.K.
U.S.	-6	7	6	-14	25	3	13	10	-1	-3	16	-3	21	-23	-23	-23	-2	-21	2	23	-4
Can.	13	-4	1	-2	-9	-16	0	17	-9	-26	-29	9	-22	-5	3	-5	11	-9	-4	-4	-5
Fra.	17	-19	19	10	18	12	0	7	9	-1	-1	17	-17	-14	19	5	-1	13	16	18	-2
Ger.	-0	-45	-7	-15	-16	8	12	35	-21	-20	-17	-4	-35	6	13	21	-11	16	-19	3	28
It.	-6	24	-6	-8	22	5	29	-16	15	9	8	7	-38	-10	4	-24	5	12	9	8	7
Jap.	2	-18	19	-20	5	-18	-8	26	-52	-32	-40	-37	8	-12	4	-14	-13	2	-14	-4	14
U.K.	-4	8	2	-10	9	33	-13	-10	30	25	8	12	-33	-33	-5	-14	-4	-8	-2	-18	-4

LIM

	RS							LE							RL						
	U.S.	Can.	Fra.	Ger.	It.	Jap.	U.K.	U.S.	Can.	Fra.	Ger.	It.	Jap.	U.K.	U.S.	Can.	Fra.	Ger.	It.	Jap.	U.K.
U.S.	-34	-8	2	-34	12	-10	-9	6	-27	-0	-7	-21	-5	-21	-13	-24	-31	10	-31	-14	29
Can.	-3	-1	-7	1	4	4	-8	18	5	-1	3	14	-6	14	-49	-27	-12	-10	-23	1	7
Fra.	16	-9	4	-28	-0	1	11	47	-38	-31	-36	-35	-14	-35	11	-9	-3	-2	-20	-6	5
Ger.	4	10	-2	26	-12	9	16	-21	21	-7	-6	-6	6	-6	10	-15	14	1	20	2	-21
It.	11	-6	-8	-3	27	2	31	17	-4	-7	1	-2	-10	-29	0	-1	-14	-6	-8	12	9
Jap.	-11	-23	11	-1	13	-3	34	9	-35	-35	-29	-29	-12	-27	-3	-22	-10	-24	-4	8	-0
U.K.	-2	-8	9	-23	-6	13	-2	21	-38	-28	-25	-27	-33	-33	10	1	-21	12	-0	4	7

LX

	RS							LE							RL						
	U.S.	Can.	Fra.	Ger.	It.	Jap.	U.K.	U.S.	Can.	Fra.	Ger.	It.	Jap.	U.K.	U.S.	Can.	Fra.	Ger.	It.	Jap.	U.K.
U.S.	5	15	-12	-16	-1	-18	11	14	-13	-15	26	0	6	-15	11	11	3	31	2	33	19
Can.	11	-10	-6	6	-15	-31	5	35	-48	-47	-13	-54	7	-47	19	20	13	11	9	10	-6
Fra.	12	-15	-18	-5	-38	-1	4	49	-54	-49	-23	-35	-22	-49	10	42	-17	29	-11	3	13
Ger.	17	-7	-30	-14	-24	9	7	43	-21	-19	22	-6	19	-19	-12	30	-16	23	-18	21	19
It.	11	9	38	9	-5	0	-6	-21	10	-5	-66	-5	-26	49	22	-21	37	-39	33	-53	-71
Jap.	-11	10	29	-6	3	13	-31	-27	25	49	-2	20	9	3	-34	-43	-10	-8	-13	-46	-8
U.K.	-21	-10	5	-7	-2	1	9	-15	-1	3	2	-15	1	1	-14	1	-1	20	-2	-14	-4

LP

	RS							LE							RL						
	U.S.	Can.	Fra.	Ger.	It.	Jap.	U.K.	U.S.	Can.	Fra.	Ger.	It.	Jap.	U.K.	U.S.	Can.	Fra.	Ger.	It.	Jap.	U.K.
U.S.	−48	−4	−31	12	1	−6	1	1	−10	2	−2	11	−1	−7	−34	−15	−25	−10	−27	−6	20
Can.	1	−20	−26	−12	−2	16	11	11	33	−23	−16	21	−11	1	−22	24	−40	20	−31	29	45
Fra.	8	−14	−7	3	−18	−5	10	10	19	1	−5	7	−6	16	−22	13	−3	−7	−4	−1	−14
Ger.	−7	−10	−6	−29	−11	−5	−13	−13	20	−21	−21	2	−21	12	−11	10	−6	4	−8	−3	3
It.	−2	−20	−41	−10	−18	12	13	13	48	−36	−24	44	−15	16	−14	39	−51	48	−48	48	61
Jap.	−3	−19	−15	−24	1	−22	25	25	32	−36	−34	15	−19	5	12	31	−8	8	−4	45	23
U.K.	13	28	20	−11	−17	15	−53	−53	4	11	19	14	1	36	−16	−13	2	3	17	−11	−24

LP/M

	RS							LE							RL						
	U.S.	Can.	Fra.	Ger.	It.	Jap.	U.K.	U.S.	Can.	Fra.	Ger.	It.	Jap.	U.K.	U.S.	Can.	Fra.	Ger.	It.	Jap.	U.K.
U.S.	19	−19	11	2	12	4	−1	22	−17	−14	−19	−19	−19	7	−14	−8	−3	−21	−12	−14	4
Can.	5	10	−5	−13	−18	−15	−16	20	−21	0	10	10	−4	11	−31	−11	−27	5	−22	−1	31
Fra.	6	−18	−3	−8	8	27	8	21	10	14	7	7	13	−12	−35	−8	−26	0	−26	10	18
Ger.	8	13	−5	−44	11	10	−5	5	7	18	7	13	13	−3	−10	−15	−4	3	−4	−2	7
It.	2	−8	−6	0	28	13	19	8	−12	−8	−15	−5	−5	−23	−25	−28	−9	−17	−11	−14	2
Jap.	30	4	14	8	20	17	4	11	9	8	−22	17	17	−17	−32	−31	−4	−32	−7	−4	−6
U.K.	7	−13	5	5	12	13	20	8	−3	3	−8	−3	−3	−1	−31	−13	−10	−25	−15	−4	7

LPEX

	RS							LE							RL						
	U.S.	Can.	Fra.	Ger.	It.	Jap.	U.K.	U.S.	Can.	Fra.	Ger.	It.	Jap.	U.K.	U.S.	Can.	Fra.	Ger.	It.	Jap.	U.K.
U.S.	2	−11	15	14	26	6	2	2	28	30	3	3	32	1	−37	−12	−8	−29	−15	−22	−4
Can.	4	−6	8	−4	−5	−6	−13	2	3	14	9	9	14	18	−28	−11	−11	−21	−2	0	1
Fra.	16	2	18	−20	18	16	1	5	2	16	−10	−10	16	17	−23	−29	−9	−14	−15	−35	−1
Ger.	21	6	14	−17	26	21	10	12	−10	7	−21	−21	7	−16	−24	−34	0	−25	−8	−14	2
It.	11	−24	16	−17	9	3	−9	8	−10	17	−11	−11	17	−21	−32	−19	−27	−18	−12	−26	5
Jap.	16	−5	23	−6	18	5	−2	23	−14	−14	−38	−38	−14	−5	−33	−38	−5	−28	−18	−25	−7
U.K.	−18	−13	27	−12	15	6	−10	1	3	13	−22	−22	13	−8	−17	−26	−5	−27	−10	−24	−16

TABLE 4-2C Correlation Matrix of the Errors

Consumption

		U.S. D	U.S. N	U.S. S	Can. D	Can. N	Can. S	Fra. D	Fra. N	Fra. S	Ger.	It.	Jap. D	Jap. N	Jap. S	U.K. D	U.K. N	U.K. S
U.S.	N	73																
	S	55	65															
Can.	D	51	40	32														
	N	17	15	16	46													
	S	11	18	24	33	8												
Fra.	D	20	33	28	24	7	−0											
	N	37	55	42	51	23	17	76										
	S	51	55	40	49	27	12	56	72									
Ger.		15	24	22	23	5	−11	24	33	12								
It.		12	12	−8	−0	−4	−7	16	−7	−6	17							
Jap.	D	19	34	12	12	−15	2	20	31	29	43	29						
	N	4	19	1	−5	−23	3	1	7	−4	27	6	37					
	S	−0	9	8	−9	−18	−14	−7	−2	−3	−5	−1	19	30				
U.K.	D	21	41	33	13	−2	12	33	29	28	43	33	28	1	12			
	N	36	45	30	22	2	−2	20	31	17	44	40	42	16	24	72		
	S	12	34	33	9	1	12	15	23	10	10	24	6	1	21	41	49	
		D	N	S	D	N	S	D	N	S	Ger.	It.	D	N	S	D	N	S
			U.S.			Can.			Fra.					Jap.			U.K.	

Consumption

Investment

	U.S. D	N	S	Can. D	N	S	Fra. D	N	S	Ger.	It.	Jap. D	N	S	U.K. D	N	S
U.S. NE	72	64	44	49	24	-0	12	36	43	12	27	27	-15	-1	21	50	25
NS	40	29	20	24	6	-11	3	9	21	17	39	20	-19	-4	16	30	20
R	77	87	64	55	23	16	41	67	64	30	8	29	4	-11	38	46	33
I	-1	1	-25	-3	-8	14	-5	7	-5	-3	22	8	8	-37	4	9	-9
Can. F	17	6	2	59	20	25	-0	16	17	29	-2	11	-16	-10	-7	5	16
N	-21	6	-10	-10	-8	-8	29	38	26	12	-0	29	-7	-5	21	6	-4
R	17	14	6	12	-5	-1	34	15	20	7	38	14	-4	8	6	1	2
I	-3	12	-0	38	26	7	58	54	46	19	14	16	-10	-9	24	26	27
Fra. N	-13	-3	-19	-5	1	-16	29	7	-11	-1	28	-5	1	-3	2	14	-10
R	17	21	12	33	7	10	48	34	35	23	37	34	-18	-14	48	41	37
I	-4	20	-6	19	8	16	21	25	18	-0	20	17	44	8	-3	2	10
Ger. F	34	39	14	38	11	4	44	35	45	15	48	14	-9	-18	25	30	14
N	-8	17	19	30	17	24	49	46	33	21	-4	-4	-8	-13	24	2	9
R	17	50	18	26	8	7	35	52	47	40	20	61	34	12	23	28	23
It. I	10	32	6	-10	-21	2	9	18	3	22	8	34	12	6	12	13	8
F	18	23	5	33	16	-8	30	38	20	33	15	23	-14	-24	3	18	22
N	32	40	8	13	13	-4	15	26	23	-8	33	21	-11	8	30	41	18
Jap. R	21	41	40	-3	-2	8	11	28	21	19	-0	-23	6	12	26	25	29
U.K. I	30	31	-1	12	3	-6	8	9	11	1	21	12	33	6	-13	10	-11
	U.S.			Can.			Fra.			Ger.	It.	Jap.			U.K.		

Consumption

TABLE 4-2D Correlation Matrix of the Errors

LEX

	U.S. D	U.S. N	U.S. S	Can. D	Can. N	Can. S	Fra. D	Fra. N	Fra. S	Ger. D	Ger. N	Ger. S	It. D	It. N	It. S	Jap. D	Jap. N	Jap. S	U.K. D	U.K. N	U.K. S
U.S.	13	14	-9	27	13	9	2	10	-1	5	38	30	4	-5	-5	27	14				
Can.	23	16	9	28	18	8	6	8	7	-5	19	-19	-8	-18	3	13	11				
Fra.	37	43	36	16	27	15	12	12	26	-11	9	20	2	7	2	10	8				
Ger.	14	4	-4	11	22	-13	30	24	20	15	10	9	-10	-37	3	13	-27				
It.	21	2	9	-1	10	-11	-9	-5	-2	-10	0	20	3	-11	-36	-12	-17				
Jap.	10	9	9	6	-5	22	1	10	10	-18	12	-21	-12	-25	14	4	11				
U.K.	-1	-7	1	-15	-3	-8	-19	-24	-13	12	3	15	15	4	11	4	-15				

LIM

	U.S. D	U.S. N	U.S. S	Can. D	Can. N	Can. S	Fra. D	Fra. N	Fra. S	Ger. D	Ger. N	Ger. S	It. D	It. N	It. S	Jap. D	Jap. N	Jap. S	U.K. D	U.K. N	U.K. S
U.S.	10	9	6	2	-16	17	-18	2	-5	-24	-9	-5	12	-4	-4	2	-3				
Can.	11	11	-4	42	20	19	-9	10	10	9	16	12	-6	0	3	9	-5				
Fra.	7	-8	-13	16	27	7	35	14	1	-10	30	-18	-8	-12	0	5	-7				
Ger.	-0	-14	1	-13	21	-12	-6	-16	-15	26	11	5	32	-1	2	-7	3				
It.	14	3	7	28	21	17	13	16	10	11	32	14	-7	-16	1	14	-3				
Jap.	-3	5	-20	-1	12	-8	16	16	2	-14	25	2	-7	-10	-15	-8	4				
U.K.	4	9	0	4	9	-0	16	15	18	-2	28	18	-1	3	29	24	-1				

LX

	U.S. D	U.S. N	U.S. S	Can. D	Can. N	Can. S	Fra. D	Fra. N	Fra. S	Ger. D	Ger. N	Ger. S	It. D	It. N	It. S	Jap. D	Jap. N	Jap. S	U.K. D	U.K. N	U.K. S
U.S.	23	27	20	23	19	5	20	35	20	27	-4	12	22	-12	-0	18	14				
Can.	5	17	-8	1	-11	-6	19	18	19	-7	1	-11	-17	-1	8	3	20				
Fra.	3	6	-2	19	19	-2	53	47	44	6	4	-8	-2	-13	18	11	-3				
Ger.	1	10	-0	19	6	-3	43	35	29	21	8	13	4	9	10	10	7				
It.	-4	-26	-19	-30	-25	-5	-23	-51	-29	-30	25	-22	-8	2	5	-5	1				
Jap.	-17	-34	-12	-17	-19	6	-33	-34	-24	-17	-23	-8	15	39	-25	-21	-24				
U.K.	-17	-20	3	-30	-30	-19	-10	-11	-7	18	-4	4	22	13	9	-0	-14				

Consumption

LP

	U.S.			Can.			Fra.			Ger.		It.		Jap.		U.K.	
	D	N	S	D	N	S	D	N	S	D	N	D	N	D	N	D	N
U.S.	5	−14	−22	19	2	−21	−9	15	9	14	−14	17	21	14	−22	−1	−36
Can.	−1	8	−1	39	27	−4	39	49	43	47	4	28	−8	−19	21	16	−2
Fra.	−24	−15	−16	−5	8	−17	20	5	0	22	9	10	22	2	5	9	−6
Ger.	−21	−12	−16	−3	−16	−4	9	12	−3	5	13	25	12	2	2	10	18
It.	8	36	16	39	31	16	50	68	57	30	−16	31	1	−10	16	14	3
Jap.	0	26	−2	14	19	13	35	45	19	20	22	21	−6	−31	9	10	17
U.K.	−31	−16	−21	−14	−25	7	−20	−23	−10	−14	−18	6	28	40	−12	−15	16

LPIM

	U.S.			Can.			Fra.			Ger.		It.		Jap.		U.K.	
	D	N	S	D	N	S	D	N	S	D	N	D	N	D	N	D	N
U.S.	−5	−14	−13	12	24	−7	9	4	−3	−8	16	5	−49	−24	−10	4	3
Can.	6	6	−1	17	−3	10	5	20	9	−19	−21	3	4	−9	−42	−15	0
Fra.	5	4	0	25	19	8	13	20	16	24	19	30	−5	−24	2	15	−8
Ger.	−1	3	−5	18	1	−1	8	4	4	5	16	37	−10	−21	−5	5	−3
It.	0	0	−27	20	27	−9	11	10	14	−5	32	15	−22	−4	6	5	−17
Jap.	3	−16	−25	29	16	18	3	−4	−7	3	39	16	−29	−18	−2	12	−5
U.K.	−11	−13	−17	18	23	5	11	7	−3	−1	22	11	−45	−27	−6	−0	−4

LPEX

	U.S.			Can.			Fra.			Ger.		It.		Jap.		U.K.	
	D	N	S	D	N	S	D	N	S	D	N	D	N	D	N	D	N
U.S.	−3	−3	−11	11	14	12	1	0	−4	5	19	15	7	12	7	31	−9
Can.	−18	−9	−4	16	−4	16	−3	4	−16	9	19	28	−12	−1	11	24	12
Fra.	−8	−22	−8	4	4	6	3	−12	−6	−17	18	−8	−21	−7	−11	−7	−14
Ger.	−2	−12	−14	8	10	−0	7	−4	−8	−10	32	10	−35	−20	−3	5	−16
It.	−20	−15	−22	−2	7	−5	−7	−12	3	−16	13	5	−5	4	−9	−11	−20
Jap.	9	−27	−25	16	25	12	6	−2	8	−2	27	−0	−13	−11	−6	4	−11
U.K.	−14	−16	−37	3	8	21	−10	−10	−5	−22	19	7	−13	−4	−3	3	2

Consumption

TABLE 4-2E Correlation Matrix of the Errors

Investment

Row	NE	NS	R	I	F	N	R	I	F	I	F	I	N	R	I	N	R	I
U.S. NS	65																	
U.S. R	72	45																
U.S. I	22	19	11															
Can. F	24	35	24	−11														
Can. N	−0	20	13	31	−9													
Fra. R	17	28	13	−18	6	−1												
Fra. I	23	17	34	13	38	35	12											
Ger. F	−1	−20	−7	1	−34	2	32	19										
Ger. I	29	27	33	2	35	18	32	52	10									
It. F	8	−1	10	28	9	22	11	32	10	7								
It. I	44	43	44	5	27	16	43	48	30	46	45							
Jap. N	−0	−18	23	−7	6	10	24	41	33	24	28	28						
Jap. R	32	34	47	15	28	31	27	41	0	35	43	28	26					
U.K. I	12	15	22	14	7	9	19	−8	−15	11	2	−1	−10	40				
U.K. N	29	17	33	0	20	26	20	35	22	41	13	35	27	29	9			
U.K. R	39	23	39	18	−7	1	5	11	10	23	5	15	3	14	18	−0		
U.K. I	7	3	33	−18	−3	4	−3	−3	−5	−2	5	12	4	13	31	1	14	
U.K. I	32	4	20	8	−13	7	7	6	29	−14	21	20	−5	7	7	22	17	−0

NE NS R I	F I N R I	F I N R I	F I N R I	F I N R I	N R I
U.S.	Can.	Fra.	Ger.	It.	Jap.	U.K.

TABLE 4-2F Correlation Matrix of the Errors

LEX

	U.S.				Can.			Fra.			Ger.		It.		Jap.		U.K.	
	NE	NS	R	I	F	I	N	R	I	N	F	I	F	I	R	I	R	I
U.S.	42	48	25	29	27	20	23	32	25	32	23	36	-5	40	41	10	-6	24
Can.	41	21	21	28	13	-31	22	17	3	15	26	26	13	-2	2	31	-20	8
Fra.	30	16	38	-2	14	-17	-9	10	-20	14	3	3	7	-5	-8	41	23	9
Ger.	28	3	13	20	-14	-1	9	20	36	4	-4	19	-15	-5	21	16	-12	16
It.	22	26	12	1	6	5	-9	-5	-9	-6	-19	-3	12	0	9	16	-8	16
Jap.	28	24	20	41	-14	25	-1	16	3	3	29	25	-48	2	4	-15	7	9
U.K.	-12	10	-8	-13	-15	-11	17	-30	2	6	-30	-14	-17	-15	-14	-0	-4	-7

LIM

	NE	NS	R	I	F	I	N	R	I	N	F	I	F	I	R	I	R	I
U.S.	20	18	13	41	-24	23	-20	-14	-7	-4	-2	-3	-8	-7	7	9	-13	17
Can.	36	40	16	30	49	21	20	22	-20	22	27	1	-5	22	4	22	-7	1
Fra.	10	10	3	4	-13	3	42	33	65	26	31	22	-19	-9	26	13	-12	25
Ger.	-18	-4	-13	-4	-10	-30	10	-17	-15	-4	-17	-10	8	-4	-1	-17	2	-9
It.	27	21	15	4	17	2	25	18	25	7	28	38	-14	16	35	7	-5	16
Jap.	22	33	8	43	5	34	2	31	7	19	37	-11	10	17	28	10	-2	20
U.K.	26	21	18	24	-27	21	2	33	27	26	14	7	-10	5	1	36	-12	14

LX

	NE	NS	R	I	F	I	N	R	I	N	F	I	F	I	R	I	R	I
U.S.	27	2	32	4	-3	-0	0	18	1	1	10	14	4	22	29	-1	-6	33
Can.	-4	2	14	0	7	27	0	29	17	25	25	10	1	3	20	8	16	-0
Fra.	5	-21	17	18	-15	21	-5	53	35	21	27	44	-21	11	17	9	-8	20
Ger.	3	-5	9	-14	12	28	27	35	22	35	24	38	-11	28	43	5	-12	30
It.	-19	-12	-33	-3	-21	-38	-11	-16	7	-7	2	-34	-22	-46	-44	-4	-8	-9
Jap.	-30	-34	-45	-17	-21	-14	-16	-32	-3	-51	-34	-30	-29	-41	-18	-38	-15	-3
U.K.	-16	-10	-25	5	-25	13	-13	-20	-17	-10	-19	-12	3	-4	-18	-13	-7	9

	NE	NS	R	I	F	I	N	R	I	N	F	I	F	I	N	R	I	N	R	I
	U.S.				Can.			Fra.			Ger.		It.			Jap.			U.K.	

Investment

(Continued)

Table 4-2F (Continued)

LP

	NE	NS	R	F	I	N	R	F	I	N	R	F	I	N	R	F	I	N	R	F	I	N	R	I
U.S.	12	4	−4	18	16	6	−20	−0	−13	24	−3	−9	17	9	−8	9	−23	11						
Can.	9	16	25	11	28	44	2	47	−2	13	31	38	37	−5	50	−5	0	−1						
Fra.	−13	−5	−13	−3	14	9	−6	36	27	10	17	10	13	19	−21	−16	−0	1	11					
Ger.	5	−0	−5	13	1	7	13	20	5	10	17	−8	17	16	9	3	24	−5	15					
It.	19	10	41	2	21	54	14	48	12	28	6	31	52	53	6	51	6	11						
Jap.	23	14	35	45	10	38	11	41	23	19	28	21	37	50	26	34	22	17	21					
U.K.	−30	−13	−25	−23	6	−4	7	−2	2	−0	13	−22	−2	13	4	−27	−14	10	−11					

LPIM

	NE	NS	R	F	I	N	R	F	I	N	R	F	I	N	R	F	I	N	R	F	I	N	R	I
U.S.	15	13	3	−7	25	3	17	21	23	29	−7	25	5	−14	−9	29	9	−0	−24					
Can.	27	0	15	22	8	13	8	32	13	−2	33	13	12	10	−6	32	−9	−9	22					
Fra.	21	18	11	12	21	17	16	16	10	10	27	32	13	12	−13	30	−2	3	−5					
Ger.	16	20	6	3	17	14	17	13	4	17	5	13	−2	20	−6	13	9	−10	1					
It.	11	23	3	10	15	34	15	18	−0	18	30	40	−0	10	−4	18	20	−16	−2					
Jap.	16	21	−7	10	39	−6	20	18	1	23	5	26	−6	−11	−5	20	10	−26	−6					
U.K.	8	16	−4	17	29	21	14	20	11	34	7	24	2	2	−13	33	14	−16	−23					

LPEX

	NE	NS	R	F	I	N	R	F	I	N	R	F	I	N	R	F	I	N	R	F	I	N	R	I
U.S.	14	2	−4	11	16	−2	−0	10	16	13	23	15	12	2	−15	−13	16	−19	5					
Can.	14	6	−0	22	13	14	−1	22	16	15	8	7	18	8	−14	22	−10	3	−21					
Fra.	7	8	−23	6	−4	−4	8	−7	5	−11	11	13	−4	−30	−24	−11	−13	−32	−6					
Ger.	13	21	−5	11	4	26	23	9	22	17	4	29	−14	−10	−15	24	7	−14	1					
It.	−7	4	−17	6	4	15	−5	13	5	−6	31	15	9	−3	−22	−5	19	−20	3					
Jap.	16	19	−10	26	22	3	6	25	−1	17	16	25	−8	−17	−17	11	−8	−12	12					
U.K.	−8	−5	−17	17	4	8	−6	7	14	11	5	9	−9	−13	−29	5	6	−13	−2					

NE	NS	R		F	I	N	R		F	I	N	R		F	I	N	R		F	I	N	R		F	I	N	R		I
	U.S.			Can.					Fra.					Ger.					It.					Jap.					U.K.

Investment

TABLE 4-2G Correlation Matrix of the Errors

LEX

	U.S.	Can.	Fra.	Ger.	It.	Jap.
Can.	1					
Fra.	−5	20				
Ger.	−4	28	21			
It.	34	−10	18	9		
Jap.	10	25	3	25	−15	
U.K.	0	−9	6	3	−3	−19

LIM

	U.S.	Can.	Fra.	Ger.	It.	Jap.	U.K.		U.S.	Can.	Fra.	Ger.	It.	Jap.
	\textit{LEX}								\textit{LIM}					
U.S.	20	15	−4	−8	11	51	18							
Can.	35	54	15	1	6	19	−11		14					
Fra.	30	21	5	42	−1	31	7		11	3				
Ger.	−14	20	9	8	6	−5	28		−9	−6	3			
It.	39	−13	17	30	17	−29	4		20	28	−0			
Jap.	48	14	12	5	26	36	−31		18	29	24	16		
U.K.	20	7	17	31	−0	43	30		36	−5	34	7	13	

LX

	U.S.	Can.	Fra.	Ger.	It.	Jap.	U.K.		U.S.	Can.	Fra.	Ger.	It.	Jap.	U.K.		U.S.	Can.	Fra.	Ger.	It.	Jap.
	\textit{LEX}								\textit{LIM}								\textit{LX}					
U.S.	20	−6	18	8	17	−16	13		−0	15	15	11	7	−3	6							
Can.	13	−22	−19	8	17	−37	7		−7	24	−23	12	26	−14	24		6					
Fra.	−2	24	−7	−16	12	−21	2		−4	25	3	10	8	32	6		18	29				
Ger.	1	−3	−8	−28	−15	−8	−20		8	26	−17	7	3	−2	6		24	14	−34			
It.	−19	14	6	−15	−5	4	−8		−19	1	14	−23	−0	2	−28		6	12	−19	−25	18	
Jap.	−19	−19	−7	−1	12	−1	8		−12	−5	6	−13	−16	−10	−7		−28	−15	7	2	18	
U.K.	−26	−5	−27	−1	14	11	27		−2	−23	19	−6	−13	12	13		−7	−8	11	−4	−4	9

(Continued)

TABLE 4-2G (Continued)

LP

	LEX							LIM							LX						
	U.S.	Can.	Fra.	Ger.	It.	Jap.	U.K.	U.S.	Can.	Fra.	Ger.	It.	Jap.	U.K.	U.S.	Can.	Fra.	Ger.	It.	Jap.	U.K.
U.S.	4	-1	-17	2	10	-8	-14	23	26	-17	-8	9	12	-0	3	1	4	-6	-17	5	33
Can.	21	-22	-12	21	-11	-1	2	-7	11	1	-18	24	15	16	4	-6	22	37	-54	-20	-2
Fra.	15	-8	-3	-2	6	-24	-10	-25	13	8	-4	8	12	14	-26	15	24	25	0	-9	14
Ger.	20	24	-10	6	-13	7	8	18	12	8	1	-1	2	29	26	-8	13	15	-7	-29	21
It.	16	-9	5	15	-17	1	3	11	16	17	-24	11	6	16	21	4	31	59	-69	-32	-6
Jap.	47	-6	-6	7	-7	10	-24	-1	4	18	-25	23	36	16	23	18	20	23	-42	-56	-23
U.K.	-2	-12	-1	-35	-23	-9	16	-10	0	-3	9	-32	-21	-2	-6	-0	-4	1	9	14	-8

LPIM

	LEX							LIM							LX						
	U.S.	Can.	Fra.	Ger.	It.	Jap.	U.K.	U.S.	Can.	Fra.	Ger.	It.	Jap.	U.K.	U.S.	Can.	Fra.	Ger.	It.	Jap.	U.K.
U.S.	32	7	16	32	14	10	4	-7	13	32	-12	18	16	7	-0	7	-12	-18	-5	6	-47
Can.	30	18	3	17	13	34	-14	32	13	18	-14	4	20	17	28	5	13	8	-24	17	-22
Fra.	19	11	13	49	3	8	10	-8	31	7	-1	24	-1	5	-1	-39	1	1	-28	14	-21
Ger.	26	-4	4	11	5	-5	-2	-14	11	5	-30	7	-4	4	13	-26	-19	9	-14	-9	-27
It.	18	-5	8	9	-11	14	-5	-4	30	14	-17	14	28	18	-6	-10	-1	13	-20	-6	-20
Jap.	22	22	12	29	6	5	-5	-19	33	18	-3	30	7	7	-2	-24	-9	-4	1	16	-40
U.K.	38	4	6	12	12	-5	-1	-7	37	13	-27	25	26	-5	-15	-2	-15	-1	-18	-1	-34

LPEX

	LEX							LIM							LX						
	U.S.	Can.	Fra.	Ger.	It.	Jap.	U.K.	U.S.	Can.	Fra.	Ger.	It.	Jap.	U.K.	U.S.	Can.	Fra.	Ger.	It.	Jap.	U.K.
U.S.	22	7	2	1	-6	-7	10	9	28	6	-18	24	-4	7	0	-23	-4	-3	-10	9	-4
Can.	50	-12	-14	1	-4	14	-11	1	8	1	-15	23	10	19	-0	-8	-7	-12	-13	17	-33
Fra.	-18	20	3	32	21	24	-0	-0	8	11	-6	8	-5	16	-12	-51	-2	-4	7	36	-5
Ger.	37	-5	-2	25	18	37	-4	-4	22	32	-27	27	28	16	-5	-4	-12	3	-10	12	-28
It.	2	-5	15	18	37	8	8	5	15	12	-9	9	16	29	-2	-12	-1	6	-15	17	3
Jap.	24	20	12	27	23	-5	-5	-0	25	37	17	26	30	19	4	-10	18	-1	9	20	-11
U.K.	31	-6	6	-5	-7	-1	-1	11	15	16	-28	8	12	2	-10	2	-4	-15	17	26	-33

TABLE 4-2H Correlation Matrix of the Errors

		LP							LPIM							LPEX					
		U.S.	Can.	Fra.	Ger.	It.	Jap.	U.K.	U.S.	Can.	Fra.	Ger.	It.	Jap.	U.K.	U.S.	Can.	Fra.	Ger.	It.	Jap.
LP	U.S.																				
	Can.	19																			
	Fra.	21	13																		
	Ger.	6	2	11																	
	It.	9	62	14	8																
	Jap.	−8	39	17	36	43															
	U.K.	−16	−27	7	21	−8	−14														
LPIM	U.S.	−12	18	−18	8	5	11	−10													
	Can.	5	2	−16	−13	21	16	13	22												
	Fra.	4	48	−14	−15	29	2	−16	50	23											
	Ger.	−8	27	−24	26	12	27	14	38	16	42										
	It.	15	44	−17	−15	26	11	−14	41	−4	49	43									
	Jap.	−6	23	−24	−6	−4	−2	−15	61	15	66	47	61								
	U.K.	3	41	−9	−12	19	21	−29	70	11	61	41	56	66							
LPEX	U.S.	33	16	18	−5	16	−4	−13	27	7	35	8	30	39	41						
	Can.	−13	23	2	10	2	28	0	44	35	37	32	15	42	39	26					
	Fra.	−4	10	−23	−9	−6	−25	−11	32	9	56	40	49	64	32	31	16				
	Ger.	−15	28	−23	−10	0	12	−16	61	16	50	55	67	66	68	19	35	50			
	It.	−0	22	−7	−2	8	−6	14	27	17	35	33	59	39	29	27	16	41	50		
	Jap.	5	23	5	3	−1	7	−13	37	13	40	6	39	58	33	25	19	44	38	25	
	U.K.	3	17	−3	−6	3	6	2	46	−2	42	28	38	47	62	39	29	25	34	12	39

term structure. Because the estimated structural residuals turned out to be highly serially correlated, I assumed that they behave according to a first-order autoregressive process.[2]

Consider now the correlation between the shocks to the equations of the financial sector. A higher correlation is found among risk-premia shocks (for both exchange rates and long-term interest rates) in different countries than among shocks to money demand (short-term interest-rate shocks).[3] The highest correlation coefficient between short-term interest-rate shocks is only .3, and seventeen of twenty-one are less than .2 in absolute value. Although changes in regulations that affect money demand might be expected to be uncorrelated, it is surprising that technological changes affecting money demand worldwide do not create more correlation across countries.[4]

In comparison, shocks to the exchange-rate equations in the different countries are highly correlated. The correlation is positive between all pairs of exchange rates, except between the Canadian dollar and the other currencies. Recall that all the interest-rate parity equations are written relative to the U.S. dollar. Hence, with the exception of the Canadian dollar, there is a positive relationship between risk premia against the dollar. To the extent that this simply represents factors relating to the United States, this is not surprising—political developments in the United States or changes in the perception of the United States as a safe haven would explain these correlations quite well. The negative correlations with the U.S. dollar/Canadian dollar exchange rate raises the possibility that some of these same factors may have been applying to Canada and the United States at the same time.

Another set of high correlations is between term-premium shocks in the different countries, and more than twice as many correlations are positive as are negative. Perhaps this reflects worldwide shifts in uncertainty about future inflation that would tilt the yield curve simultaneously in different countries. However, note the two large negative correlations between term-premia shocks in the United Kingdom and France and between the United Kingdom and Italy. Examining the time series of these shocks indicates that the correlations are due to low-frequency movements with term premia being generally negative in France and Italy in the 1970s and generally positive in the United Kingdom in the same period with a reversal taking

---

[2]The autoregressive coefficient is not estimated separately for each equation. The coefficient is simply calibrated to .5 for all countries; this appeared to be a rough average. Although admittedly not as good as an econometric estimate for each country, the assumed .5 value is certainly better than 0. As the standard deviation reported in Table 4-1 refers to the serially uncorrelated shock to this autoregressive process, the standard deviation of the correlated risk-premium shock is slightly larger ($(1 - .5^2)^{-1} = 1.33$ times the standard deviation reported in Table 4-1).

[3]As we show below there is also a relatively high correlation among price shocks in the different countries and a relatively low correlation among goods-market shocks in different countries.

[4]Note, however, that some of the money-demand equations contain dummy shifts that may account for technological change.

place in the late 1970s and 1980s. A reduction in future inflation uncertainty in the United Kingdom in the late 1970s may have accompanied the change in governments, and perhaps similar factors were occurring in reverse in France and Italy. The term premium in the United States turned negative in the late 1970s and early 1980s, but this reversed in late 1982 and may have been due to business-cycle developments. In any case there is almost no correlation between the term premium in the United States and in the United Kingdom.

Goods-Market Shocks

Several important features of the variance-covariance matrix relate to the goods markets. Consider first the size of the shocks as measured by the standard deviations (see Table 4-1). The shocks to the more volatile components of spending are relatively large: shocks to durable-goods consumption are larger than shocks to nondurable consumption, which are in turn larger than shocks to services consumption (in percentage terms); shocks to inventory investment are larger than shocks to residential investment, which in turn are larger than shocks to business fixed investment. Shocks to exports and imports are of a magnitude between that of durables and nondurables consumption and of about the same size as that of business fixed investment.

Usually, the larger volatility of durable consumer goods compared to service and nondurables is attributed to their larger interest-rate sensitivity, but according to these results there are other factors at work, as the model explicitly accounts for the interest rate. For example, shifts in consumer confidence might affect big-ticket consumer durables items more than nondurables or services.

The size of the spending shocks in the different countries are surprisingly similar. The standard deviation of export shocks and import shocks hovers close to 3 percent in most countries. The standard deviation of consumer-services shocks rounds to exactly 1 percent in all countries for which we have measures of such shocks. In general, the difference between the size of the shocks to different categories of spending in a given country is larger than the difference between the size of spending shocks for a given category of spending in different countries.

Next, consider the correlation between spending shocks. Typically the correlation between components of spending in a given country is larger than the correlation found between components of spending in different countries. This is not surprising, and it offers us some measure of reassurance to see that the computational approach is generally on the right track. The correlation between the shocks to demand in different countries is by no means negligible, however, and cannot be ignored. Moreover, the vast majority of investment, consumption, export, and import shocks tend to be positively correlated between countries. Hence, there is little tendency for "*IS* curve" shocks to cancel out across countries.

Price Shocks

The data in Table 4-1 show that the shocks to wages tend to be larger than the shocks to aggregate prices (which are markup shocks). In fact, the size of the shocks to markups are surprisingly small in all countries. Note, however, that the aggregate-price shocks follow a first-order autoregressive process and that we are looking at the standard deviation of the shocks to the autoregressive process. Hence, the variability of the measured markup will show larger variation. Shocks to export prices and import prices are generally larger than the markup shocks; these are likely to be influenced by oil and other commodity price shocks.

The correlations between the export price and import price shocks are all positive (with one minor exception) and are frequently large. These positive correlations are most likely due to oil prices as suggested by Figure 4-1. The omission of oil-price equations is probably appropriate given that the stochastic simulations of the model are designed to capture oil shocks that are unpredictable. A regression equation for oil prices might include as explanatory functions items, such as war in the Middle East, that are similarly unpredictable.

On the other hand, there is very little correlation between wage shocks in the different countries, and correlation coefficients are almost as likely to be negative as positive. To the extent that price shocks originate in wages, they are unlikely to be a source of business-cycle correlation across countries. Also, little correlation appears in markup shocks across countries. I find it surprising that the correlation between wage shocks and both markup shocks and import-price shocks is frequently negative. Note the very large negative correlations between wage shocks and markup shocks in both Japan and Italy.

Correlation between Shocks in Different Groups

The most notable general correlations between shocks in the different groups appear to be between the financial-sector shocks and the price shocks. For example, the correlation matrix shows significant correlation coefficients between exchange-rate shocks and both price and wage shocks. One particular example is the large negative correlation $(-.54)$ between shocks to the French exchange rate and the shock to French wages. Also relatively systematic negative correlations between term-structure premium shocks and almost all of the price shocks are evident. Finally, we find a relatively large negative correlation between all three financial-sector shocks and the three types of consumption in France.

4.4   Conclusion

This chapter focused on the structural residuals to the equations of the multicountry model and looked, in particular, at the variance-covariance matrix of the shocks. The variance-covariance matrix shows considerable differences in the size of shocks in the different sectors and different countries. Importantly, it also shows a high degree of correlation between shocks in different countries, especially financial shocks and price shocks. The variance-covariance matrix is far from being a diagonal matrix and even farther from being a scalar matrix. This suggests that theoretical shortcuts that assume that shocks are independent either across countries or across sectors are unlikely to yield satisfactory answers. An empirical policy analysis using the estimated variance-covariance matrix provided here appears necessary. This is the objective of Chapter 6. However, it is necessary to first look at the impact of changes in the instruments of fiscal and monetary policy in Chapter 5.

Reference Notes

That the average of the sum of squared estimated residuals and their cross-products gives consistent estimates of the covariance matrix of the shocks follows directly from the consistency proofs in Anderson (1971, Chapter 8). This requires that the estimators of the parameters of each equation of the multicountry model be consistent so that the estimates of the residuals are consistent. The consistency of the parameter estimates follows from Hansen (1982).

I am not aware of other research that has presented estimates of the covariance matrix for a multicountry model with rational expectations. Fair (1984) emphasizes the use of stochastic simulation for forecasting with nonlinear models and for model evaluation. Fair and Taylor (1983) describe how to compute the residuals by replacing the conditional expectations in each equation using the extended path method, although the aim there was primarily maximum-likelihood estimation, a task which has not yet been attempted in this large model.

The singularity of the covariance matrix prevents the use of the Cholesky decomposition algorithm (see Faddeeva, 1959, pp. 81–84) used by some random-number generators, but, as described in Appendix 2, it is still possible to draw random numbers from a singular normal distribution.

5

The Impact of Monetary and Fiscal Instruments

Changes in the instruments of monetary and fiscal policy have powerful effects on real economic activity according to the estimated multicountry model presented in Chapter 3. Despite the presence of rational expectations, short-term nominal price and wage rigidities translate changes in the money supply into changes in real interest rates and exchange rates and hence into changes in real output and employment. The effects are temporary, however; eventually real output returns to the path it was previously following, as it did in the stylized model presented in Chapter 1.

For most practical policy applications we need to estimate the size of these effects. By how much can we expect output, inflation, long-term interest rates, and exchange rates to change if the Federal Reserve lowers the federal funds rate by 1 percent? Does it matter if the Bundesbank or the Bank of Japan lower their interest rate target at the same time? Presumably the dollar depreciates if the Fed eases monetary policy. But does it overshoot? Does the depreciation cause more inflation in the United States and less inflation abroad? How long does it take before the depreciation improves the trade balance? Or is the improvement in the trade balance offset by the increased demand for imports due do the expansion in the U.S. economy? Do the answers to these questions change if easing of monetary policy is anticipated to occur several quarters in the future?

Knowing the magnitude of the impact of the instruments of fiscal policy is also important. What is the size of the effect of a 1-percent decrease in government purchases in the United States? Do real interest rates fall by enough to have a net stimulative effect on economic activity? Does the exchange rate depreciate by enough to stimulate exports and add to this effect? How large is the impact on other countries? And as with the questions pertaining to monetary policy, does it matter if the spending cut is anticipated?

This chapter provides quantitative estimates of the dynamic—short-run and long-run—impact of changes in the *instruments* of monetary and fiscal policy by using the empirical mulitcountry model described in Chapter 3. When combined with the information about the stochastic structure of the model presented in Chapter 4, the estimates provide the raw material for the analysis of how monetary and fiscal policy *rules* should be designed, implemented, and operated in an uncertain and dynamic world environment.

I focus the analysis on two canonical policy shocks: a monetary policy shock and a fiscal policy shock. The monetary policy shock is a permanent increase in the money supply. The fiscal policy shock is a permanent increase in real government spending. Recall that these are the two policy shocks considered in the stylized two-country model of Chapter 1. The effects of the shocks on the behavior of output, investment, consumption, the trade balance, inflation, exchange rates, and other key variables in the United States and other countries are examined by deterministically simulating the estimated multicountry model, using the extended path method described in Chapter 1. Both anticipated and unanticipated policy changes are studied. From this information one can easily determine the effects of combinations of the two canonical shocks, such as the effect of a combined tightening of fiscal policy and loosening of monetary policy.

It should already be clear that the rational expectations assumption plays a role in evaluating the impact of anticipated changes in policy. However, the quantitative significance of this role is an empirical question that is answered here by using the parameters estimated in Chapter 3. Of course, the rational expectations assumption plays a role even in the case of unanticipated shocks, especially in an international model, when the behavior of exchange rates is heavily influenced by expectations. For example, when the money supply increases, the exchange rate usually changes by a larger amount in a forward-looking model than in a traditional model.

In addition to providing quantitative input to policy analysis, these deterministic simulations provide useful insights into the dynamic properties of the model. These insights are of help in interpreting more complex stochastic simulations used to evaluate the effect of different monetary rules such as fixed exchange-rate rules versus floating exchange-rates rules. The insights from these deterministic simulations remain even if these particular canonical changes in the paths of the monetary and fiscal instruments never occur.

The next section describes how the simulations were performed. Subsequent sections then present the impacts of unanticipated monetary and fiscal shocks under flexible and fixed exchange rates. Finally the impacts of anticipated monetary and fiscal policy shocks are considered. A summary is provided in the final section.

5.1   The Nature of the Simulations

We are generally interested in obtaining "elasticity type" information: the percentage changes in output, employment, or other variables that occur in response to a given percentage change in a policy instrument. Because the multicountry model is neither log-linear nor linear, the initial starting values for the variables and for the period over which one conducts policy experiments can in principle make a difference for these percentage changes. In practice, however, the time period and the level of the variables appear to make only small differences for this model. To a close approximation, the percentage changes do not depend on the level of the variables or the time period. Hence, although these simulations focus on a particular ten-year period—1975:1 through 1984:4—they can be interpreted as applying to any other ten-year period, for example, from 1993:1 through 2002:4.

The simulation procedure differs according to whether the policy change is anticipated or unanticipated. In the case of *unanticipated* changes, the first period in which the policy instruments differ from the baseline values is the first quarter of the simulation; the results are reported through the full ten years of the simulation. In the case of *anticipated* changes, the first period in which people learn about the policy change is the first quarter of the simulation, even though the actual change does not occur until two years later. The results are again reported through the full ten-year period. (In order to solve the model for ten years, it is of course necessary to solve beyond ten years when using the extended path method, but the results are only reported for ten years.)

For the *baseline* simulation—that is, the simulation with no change in policy instruments—the endogenous variables are set so as to track the actual historical values perfectly. This is done by adding residuals to each equation. The residuals are computed as if the future expectations of the endogenous variables that appear in the model are equal to the actual values. These residuals therefore include not only the shocks to the equations, but also the forecasting errors. They are not the structural errors computed in Chapter 4. The historical path is a natural baseline for such comparisons. A less attractive alternative from this perspective would be to set the residuals to zero—their unconditional mean. As already mentioned, however, the results of the experiments on this model—stated as percentage deviations of the variables from the baseline path—do not seem to be much affected by the choice of baseline path or historical period.

The experiments reported in this chapter begin with changes in United States policy variables and then go on to consider policy in other countries. For most of the experiments, flexible exchange rates are assumed with the levels of money supplies in each country held to the baseline path with the exception of the country whose monetary policy is being investigated. For fixed exchange-rate simulations, one country keeps its money supply on a set exogenous path and all other countries must manipulate their money supplies to keep their exchange rates fixed with respect to the dollar. Although this characterization of fixed exchange rates is probably a historically accurate description of the dollar standard that existed under the Bretton Woods agreement, it is not the only fixed exchange-rate system. For example, another type of a fixed exchange-rate system would hold *world* money growth—a weighted average of money in the different countries—constant. This and other variants of a fixed exchange-rate regime are not considered in the results reported in this chapter.

The results of the experiments are summarized in graphical form in Figures 5-1 through 5-17. These charts are easier to digest than numerical tables. Although there are many charts, only a selection of the variables is reported. The charts all show the percentage deviation of a particular variable—real output, price level, and so on—from the baseline path. Note that in the case of interest rates, the charts show percentage *point* deviations from the baseline. Note also that when the change is large relative to the baseline values—as is sometimes the case with inventory investment—the fluctuations in the percentage change can be influenced by fluctuations in the baseline path. This is one explanation for the occasional finding that the impacts display a nonsmooth path over time.

5.2   Unanticipated Increase in Money Supply

Consider the case of an unanticipated permanent 3-percent increase in the level of the money supply relative to the historical baseline in one country. The money supplies in all other countries are held to the baseline path, and exchange rates are flexible. The 3-percent increase is completed in one year but is phased in gradually during the year at an average increase of 3/4 percentage points per quarter.[1] Thereafter, the money supply is 3 percent greater than the baseline path. Although unanticipated at the time of the initial increase, the entire path of the money supply is assumed to be incorporated into people's forecasts as of the first quarter of the simulation. In particular, people know that the increase in money is permanent.

Theoretical Insights

Money is neutral in the long run in the multicountry model. Hence, in the long run, the price level should increase by 3 percent above its baseline along with nominal wages and other prices, and the exchange rate should depreciate by 3 percent. Real output, the components of real spending, real interest rates, and real exchange rate should return to the baseline. In the other countries, all variables—real and nominal—should return to the baseline. *(continued on p. 206)*

---

[1]The exact pattern of the percentage increase in the money supply from the baseline in the first four quarters was .14, .73, 1.88, and 2.80. This pattern was chosen to conform with a model comparison project organized by Lawrence Klein in the late 1980s and described in Klein (1991).

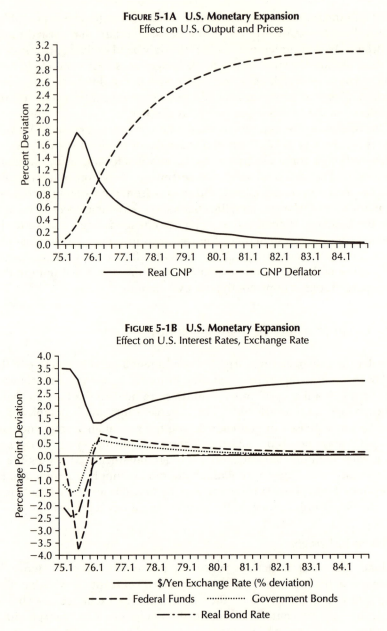

FIGURE 5-1A   U.S. Monetary Expansion
Effect on U.S. Output and Prices

FIGURE 5-1B   U.S. Monetary Expansion
Effect on U.S. Interest Rates, Exchange Rate

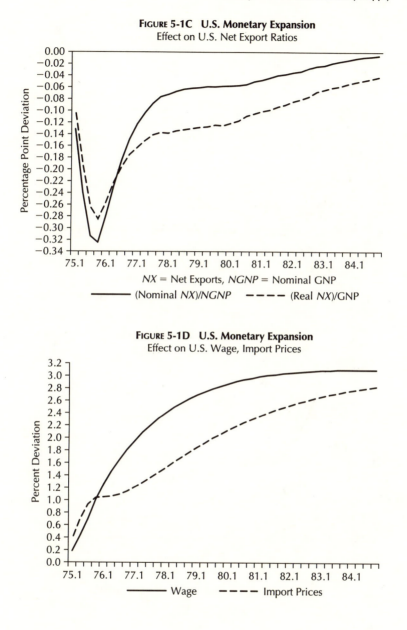

FIGURE 5-1C   U.S. Monetary Expansion
Effect on U.S. Net Export Ratios

NX = Net Exports, *NGNP* = Nominal GNP
———— (Nominal *NX*)/NGNP   – – – – (Real *NX*)/GNP

FIGURE 5-1D   U.S. Monetary Expansion
Effect on U.S. Wage, Import Prices

———— Wage   – – – – Import Prices

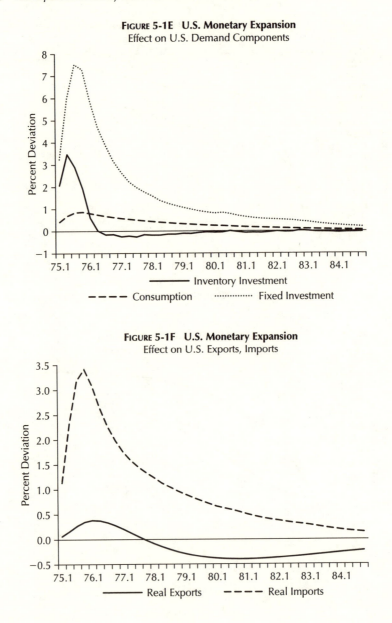

FIGURE 5-1E   U.S. Monetary Expansion
Effect on U.S. Demand Components

—— Inventory Investment
– – – Consumption   ·········· Fixed Investment

FIGURE 5-1F   U.S. Monetary Expansion
Effect on U.S. Exports, Imports

—— Real Exports   – – – Real Imports

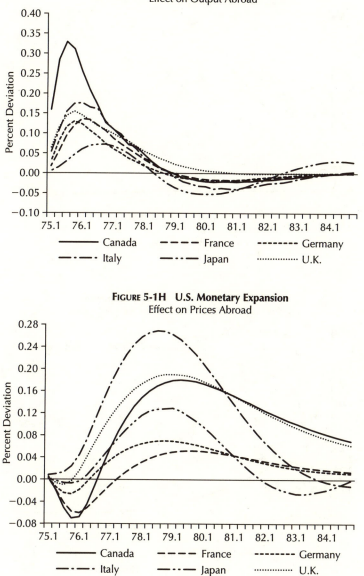

FIGURE 5-1G   U.S. Monetary Expansion
Effect on Output Abroad

FIGURE 5-1H   U.S. Monetary Expansion
Effect on Prices Abroad

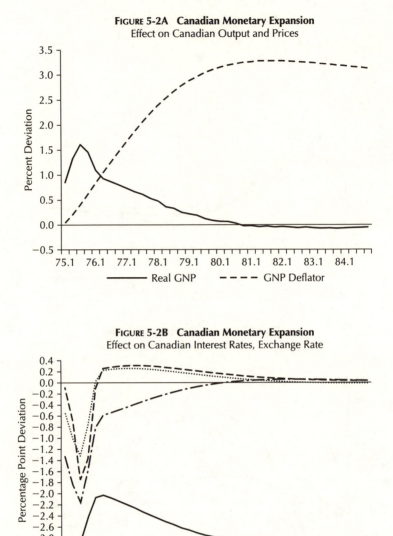

FIGURE 5-2A   Canadian Monetary Expansion
Effect on Canadian Output and Prices

FIGURE 5-2B   Canadian Monetary Expansion
Effect on Canadian Interest Rates, Exchange Rate

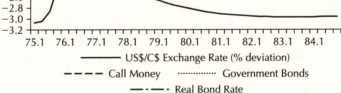

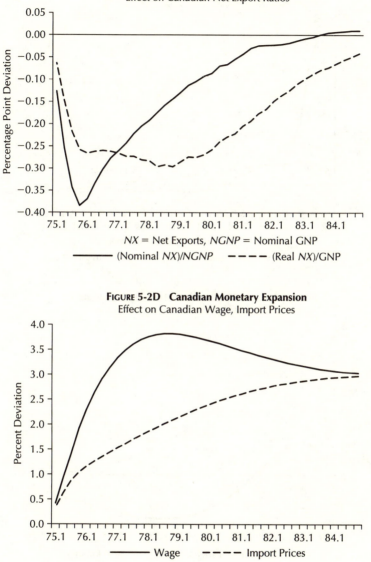

FIGURE 5-2C   Canadian Monetary Expansion
Effect on Canadian Net Export Ratios

NX = Net Exports, *NGNP* = Nominal GNP

——— (Nominal *NX*)/*NGNP*   – – – – (Real *NX*)/GNP

FIGURE 5-2D   Canadian Monetary Expansion
Effect on Canadian Wage, Import Prices

——— Wage   – – – – Import Prices

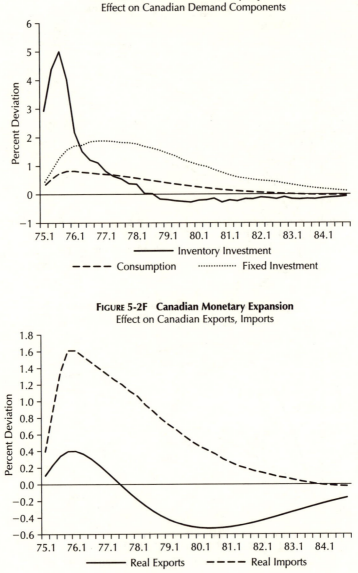

FIGURE 5-2E   Canadian Monetary Expansion
Effect on Canadian Demand Components

——— Inventory Investment

– – – Consumption   ·········· Fixed Investment

FIGURE 5-2F   Canadian Monetary Expansion
Effect on Canadian Exports, Imports

——— Real Exports   – – – – Real Imports

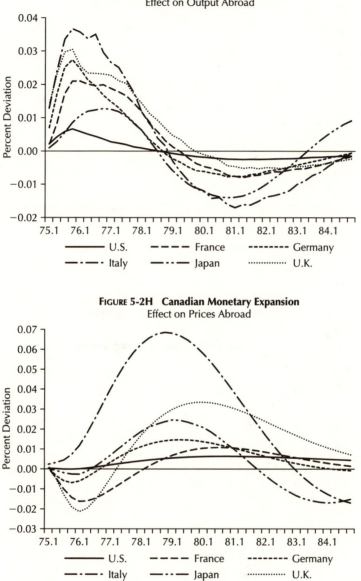

Figure 5-2G   Canadian Monetary Expansion
Effect on Output Abroad

Figure 5-2H   Canadian Monetary Expansion
Effect on Prices Abroad

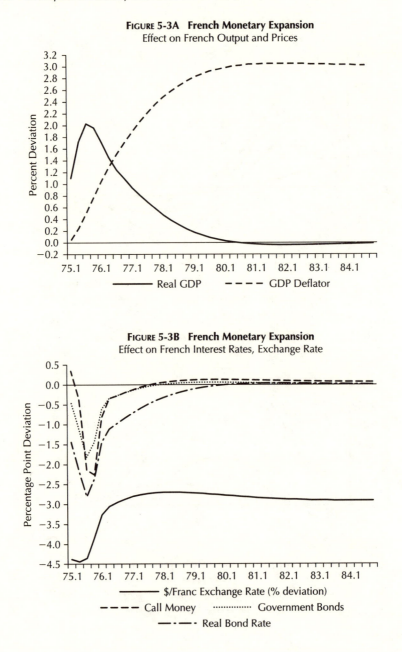

FIGURE 5-3A   French Monetary Expansion
Effect on French Output and Prices

FIGURE 5-3B   French Monetary Expansion
Effect on French Interest Rates, Exchange Rate

FIGURE 5-3C French Monetary Expansion
Effect on French Net Export Ratios

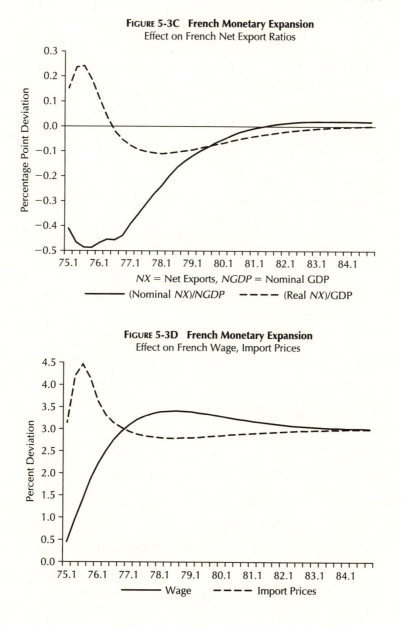

NX = Net Exports, *NGDP* = Nominal GDP
——— (Nominal *NX*)/*NGDP*   – – – – (Real *NX*)/GDP

FIGURE 5-3D French Monetary Expansion
Effect on French Wage, Import Prices

——— Wage   – – – – Import Prices

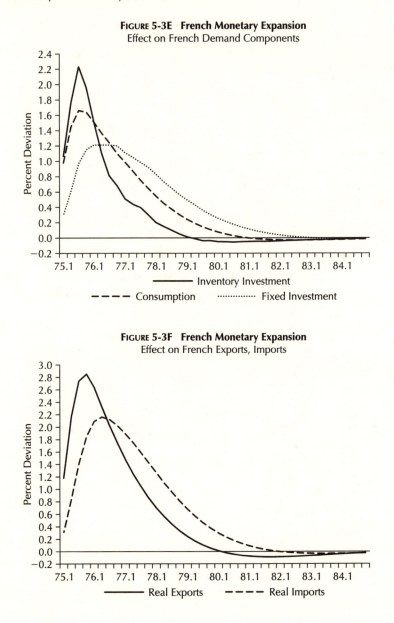

FIGURE 5-3E   French Monetary Expansion
Effect on French Demand Components

FIGURE 5-3F   French Monetary Expansion
Effect on French Exports, Imports

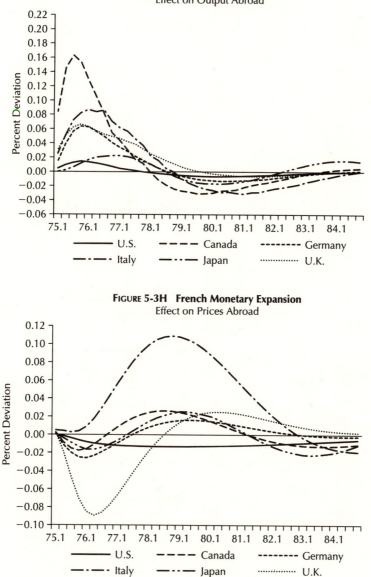

FIGURE 5-3G   French Monetary Expansion
Effect on Output Abroad

FIGURE 5-3H   French Monetary Expansion
Effect on Prices Abroad

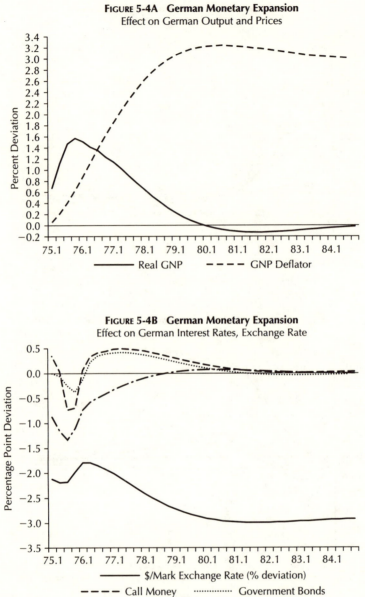

FIGURE 5-4A   German Monetary Expansion
Effect on German Output and Prices

—— Real GNP   - - - - GNP Deflator

FIGURE 5-4B   German Monetary Expansion
Effect on German Interest Rates, Exchange Rate

—— $/Mark Exchange Rate (% deviation)
- - - - Call Money   ·········· Government Bonds
—·—· Real Bond Rate

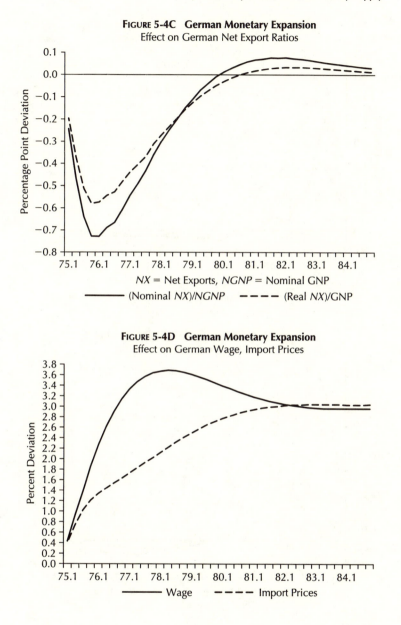

FIGURE 5-4C   **German Monetary Expansion**
Effect on German Net Export Ratios

NX = Net Exports, *NGNP* = Nominal GNP
———— (Nominal *NX*)/*NGNP*   – – – – (Real *NX*)/GNP

FIGURE 5-4D   **German Monetary Expansion**
Effect on German Wage, Import Prices

———— Wage   – – – – Import Prices

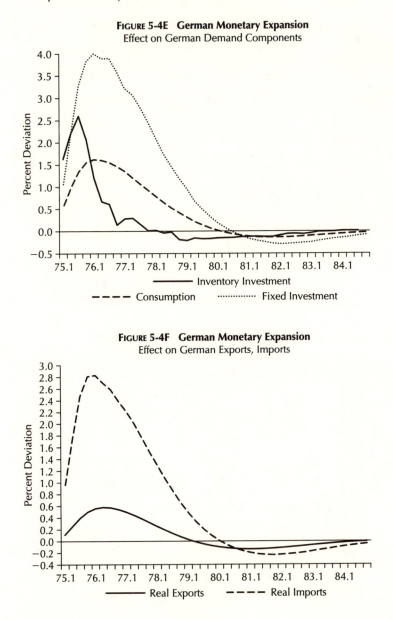

FIGURE 5-4E   German Monetary Expansion
Effect on German Demand Components

——— Inventory Investment

– – – Consumption   ·············· Fixed Investment

FIGURE 5-4F   German Monetary Expansion
Effect on German Exports, Imports

——— Real Exports   – – – Real Imports

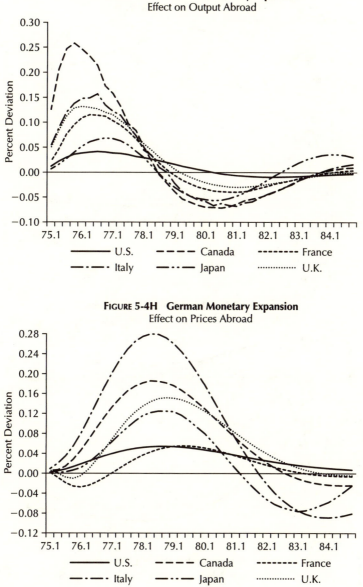

FIGURE 5-4G   German Monetary Expansion
Effect on Output Abroad

Legend: U.S. ——— Canada —————— France ----------
Italy —·—·— Japan —··—··— U.K. ··············

FIGURE 5-4H   German Monetary Expansion
Effect on Prices Abroad

Legend: U.S. ——— Canada —————— France ----------
Italy —·—·— Japan —··—··— U.K. ··············

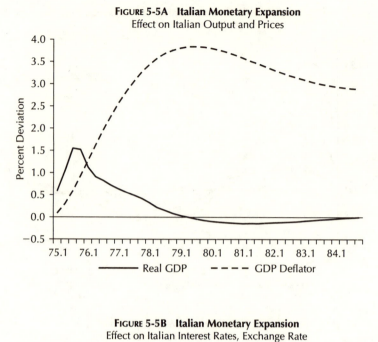

FIGURE 5-5A   Italian Monetary Expansion
Effect on Italian Output and Prices

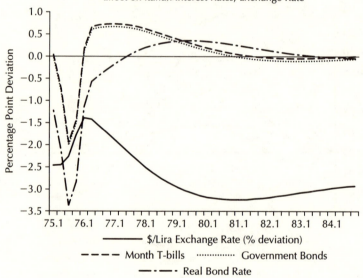

FIGURE 5-5B   Italian Monetary Expansion
Effect on Italian Interest Rates, Exchange Rate

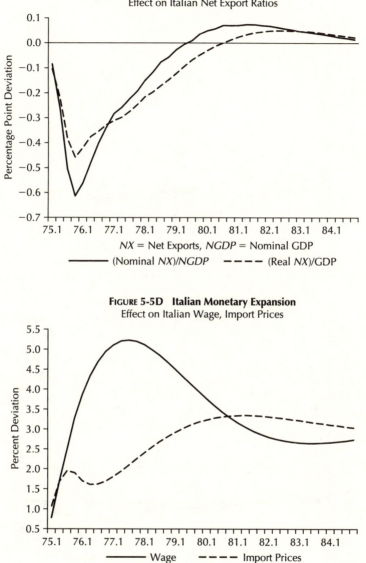

FIGURE 5-5C   Italian Monetary Expansion
Effect on Italian Net Export Ratios

NX = Net Exports, *NGDP* = Nominal GDP
——— (Nominal *NX*)/*NGDP*   – – – – (Real *NX*)/GDP

FIGURE 5-5D   Italian Monetary Expansion
Effect on Italian Wage, Import Prices

——— Wage   – – – – Import Prices

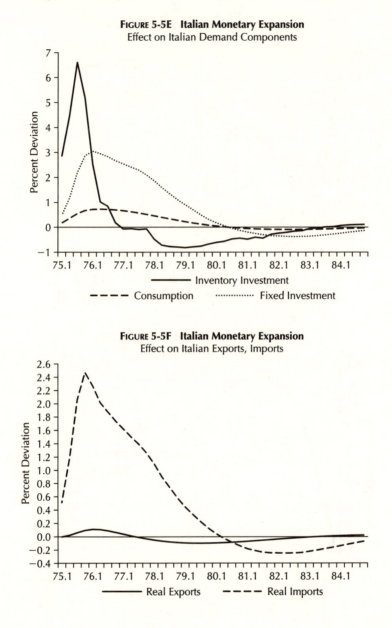

FIGURE 5-5E   Italian Monetary Expansion
Effect on Italian Demand Components

Inventory Investment

---- Consumption   ············· Fixed Investment

FIGURE 5-5F   Italian Monetary Expansion
Effect on Italian Exports, Imports

——— Real Exports   ———— Real Imports

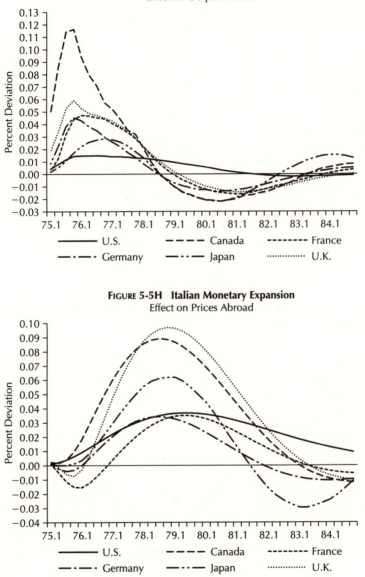

FIGURE 5-5G   Italian Monetary Expansion
Effect on Output Abroad

FIGURE 5-5H   Italian Monetary Expansion
Effect on Prices Abroad

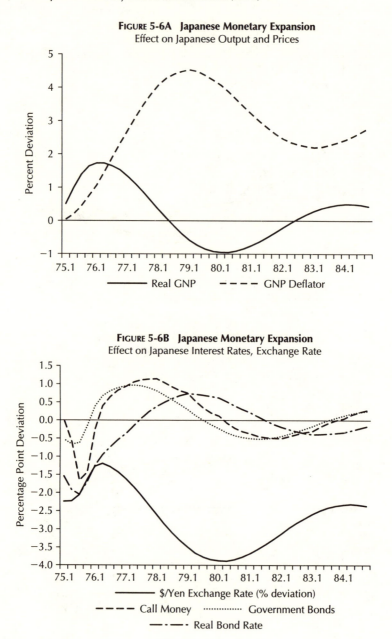

FIGURE 5-6A   Japanese Monetary Expansion
Effect on Japanese Output and Prices

—— Real GNP   – – – GNP Deflator

FIGURE 5-6B   Japanese Monetary Expansion
Effect on Japanese Interest Rates, Exchange Rate

—— $/Yen Exchange Rate (% deviation)
– – – Call Money   ·········· Government Bonds
–·–·– Real Bond Rate

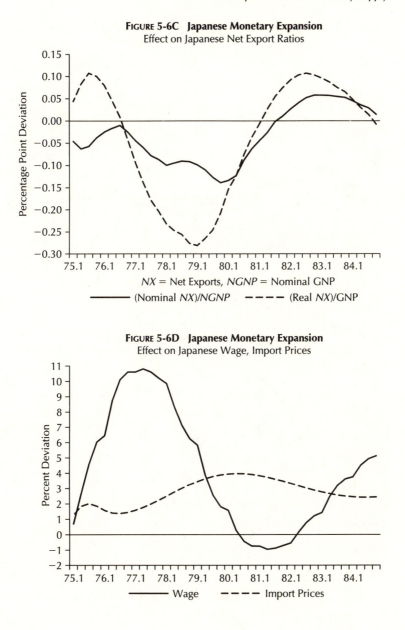

FIGURE 5-6C   Japanese Monetary Expansion
Effect on Japanese Net Export Ratios

NX = Net Exports, *NGNP* = Nominal GNP
——— (Nominal *NX*)/*NGNP*   – – – – (Real *NX*)/GNP

FIGURE 5-6D   Japanese Monetary Expansion
Effect on Japanese Wage, Import Prices

——— Wage   – – – – Import Prices

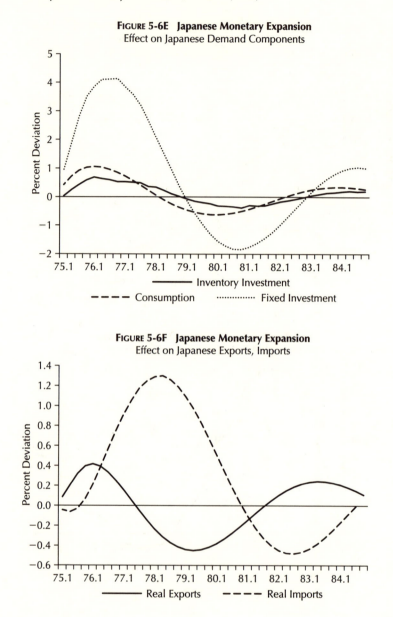

FIGURE 5-6E   Japanese Monetary Expansion
Effect on Japanese Demand Components

——— Inventory Investment
– – – Consumption   ·········· Fixed Investment

FIGURE 5-6F   Japanese Monetary Expansion
Effect on Japanese Exports, Imports

——— Real Exports   – – – Real Imports

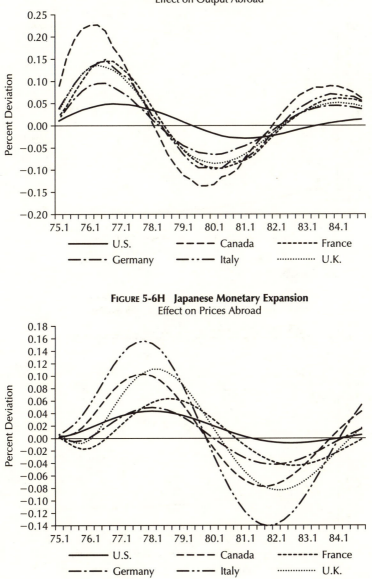

FIGURE 5-6G Japanese Monetary Expansion
Effect on Output Abroad

FIGURE 5-6H Japanese Monetary Expansion
Effect on Prices Abroad

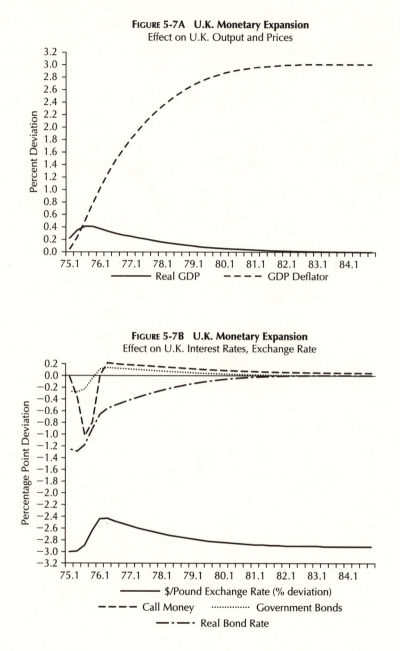

FIGURE 5-7A   U.K. Monetary Expansion
Effect on U.K. Output and Prices

Real GDP ———   GDP Deflator – – – –

FIGURE 5-7B   U.K. Monetary Expansion
Effect on U.K. Interest Rates, Exchange Rate

——— $/Pound Exchange Rate (% deviation)
– – – Call Money   ·············· Government Bonds
—·—·— Real Bond Rate

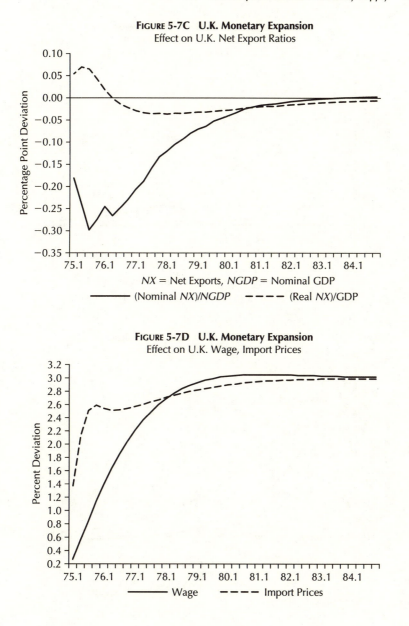

FIGURE 5-7C   U.K. Monetary Expansion
Effect on U.K. Net Export Ratios

NX = Net Exports, *NGDP* = Nominal GDP
——— (Nominal *NX*)/*NGDP*   − − − − (Real *NX*)/GDP

FIGURE 5-7D   U.K. Monetary Expansion
Effect on U.K. Wage, Import Prices

——— Wage   − − − − Import Prices

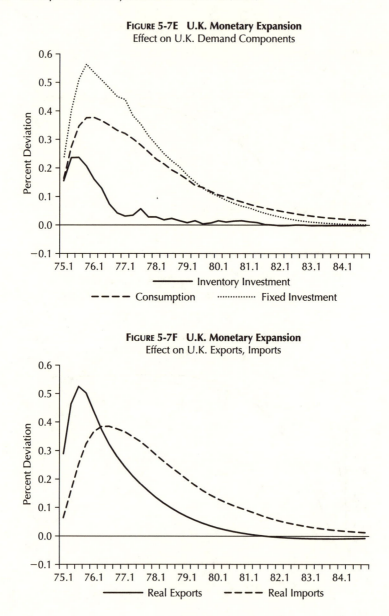

FIGURE 5-7E   U.K. Monetary Expansion
Effect on U.K. Demand Components

FIGURE 5-7F   U.K. Monetary Expansion
Effect on U.K. Exports, Imports

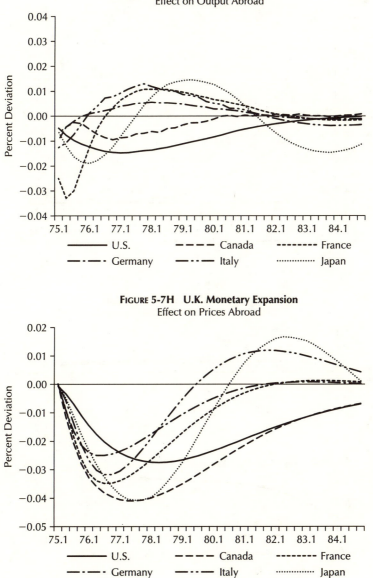

FIGURE 5-7G   U.K. Monetary Expansion
Effect on Output Abroad

FIGURE 5-7H   U.K. Monetary Expansion
Effect on Prices Abroad

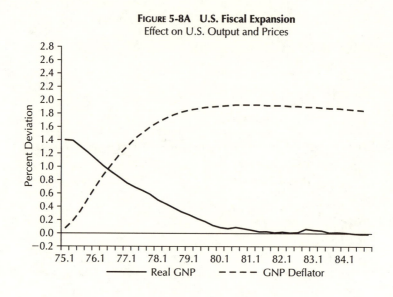

FIGURE 5-8A   U.S. Fiscal Expansion
Effect on U.S. Output and Prices

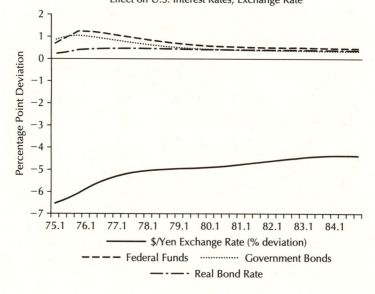

FIGURE 5-8B   U.S. Fiscal Expansion
Effect on U.S. Interest Rates, Exchange Rate

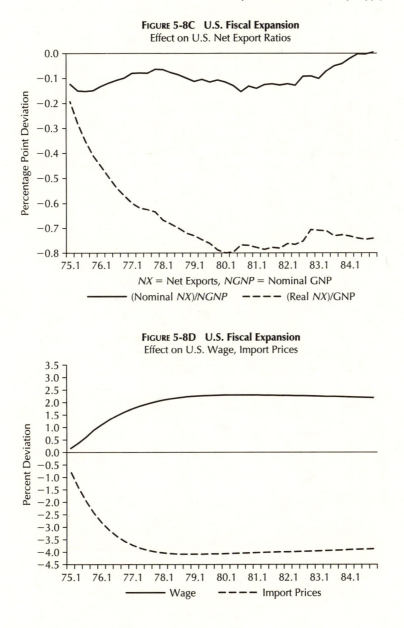

FIGURE 5-8C   U.S. Fiscal Expansion
Effect on U.S. Net Export Ratios

NX = Net Exports, *NGNP* = Nominal GNP
———— (Nominal *NX*)/*NGNP*   – – – – (Real *NX*)/GNP

FIGURE 5-8D   U.S. Fiscal Expansion
Effect on U.S. Wage, Import Prices

———— Wage   – – – – Import Prices

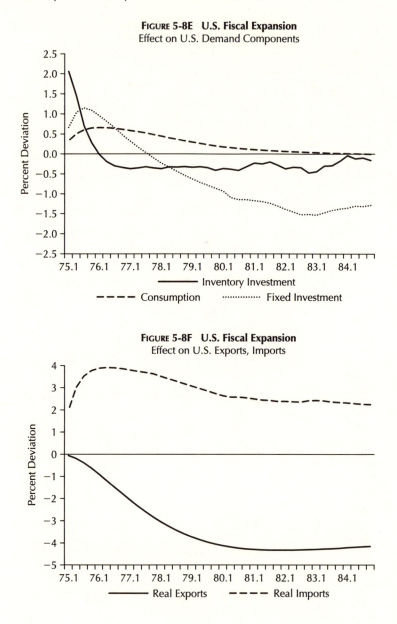

FIGURE 5-8E   U.S. Fiscal Expansion
Effect on U.S. Demand Components

FIGURE 5-8F   U.S. Fiscal Expansion
Effect on U.S. Exports, Imports

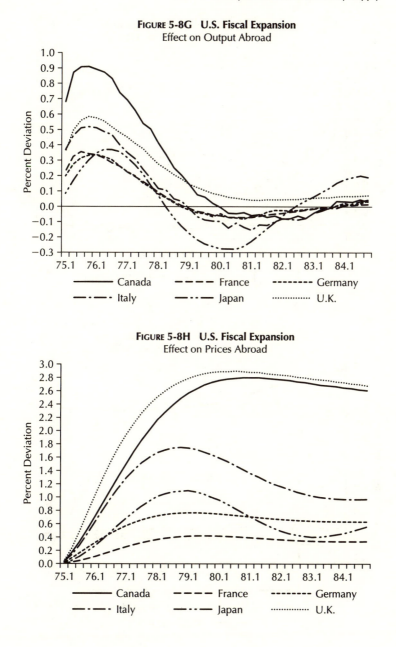

FIGURE 5-8G   U.S. Fiscal Expansion
Effect on Output Abroad

FIGURE 5-8H   U.S. Fiscal Expansion
Effect on Prices Abroad

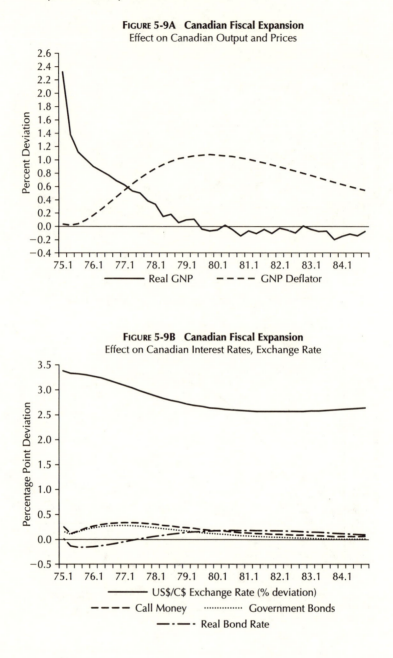

FIGURE 5-9A   Canadian Fiscal Expansion
Effect on Canadian Output and Prices

Real GNP   GNP Deflator

FIGURE 5-9B   Canadian Fiscal Expansion
Effect on Canadian Interest Rates, Exchange Rate

US$/C$ Exchange Rate (% deviation)

Call Money   Government Bonds

Real Bond Rate

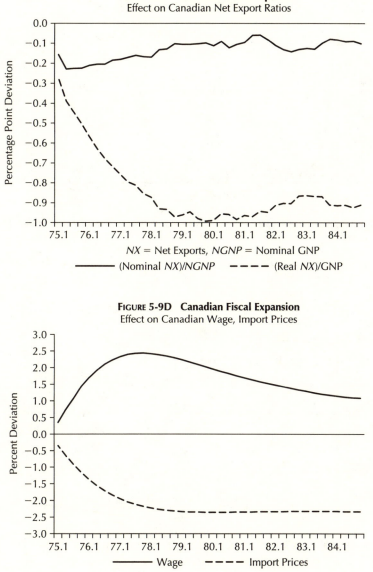

FIGURE 5-9C   Canadian Fiscal Expansion
Effect on Canadian Net Export Ratios

NX = Net Exports, *NGNP* = Nominal GNP

——— (Nominal *NX*)/*NGNP*   – – – – (Real *NX*)/GNP

FIGURE 5-9D   Canadian Fiscal Expansion
Effect on Canadian Wage, Import Prices

——— Wage   – – – – Import Prices

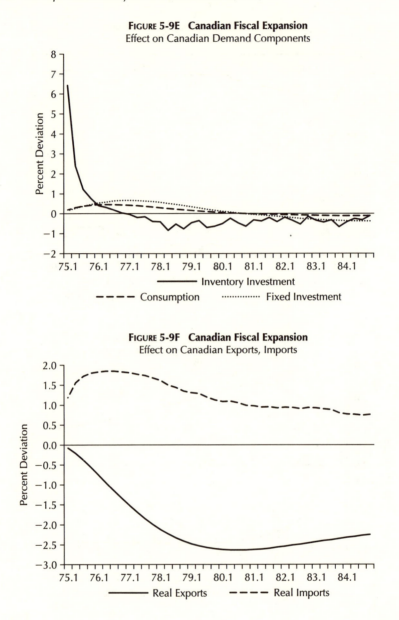

FIGURE 5-9E Canadian Fiscal Expansion
Effect on Canadian Demand Components

Inventory Investment

- - - - Consumption   ·············· Fixed Investment

FIGURE 5-9F Canadian Fiscal Expansion
Effect on Canadian Exports, Imports

——— Real Exports   - - - - Real Imports

FIGURE 5-9G   Canadian Fiscal Expansion
Effect on Output Abroad

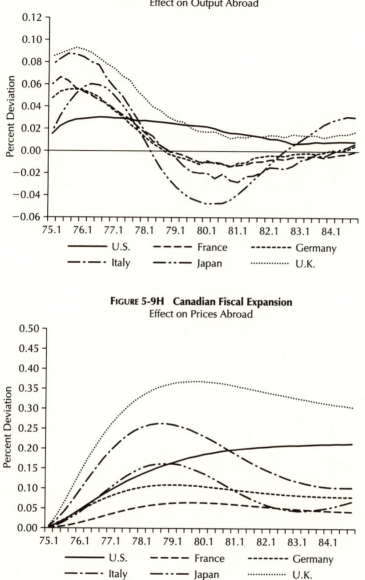

FIGURE 5-9H   Canadian Fiscal Expansion
Effect on Prices Abroad

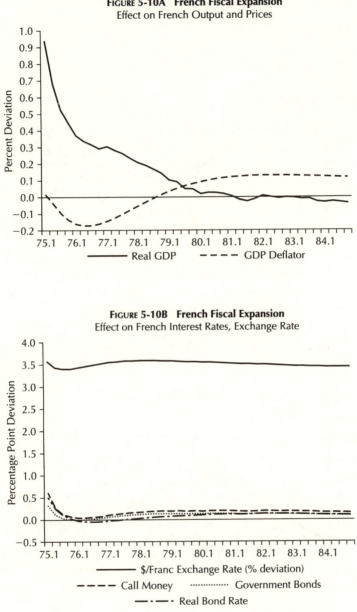

FIGURE 5-10A   French Fiscal Expansion
Effect on French Output and Prices

FIGURE 5-10B   French Fiscal Expansion
Effect on French Interest Rates, Exchange Rate

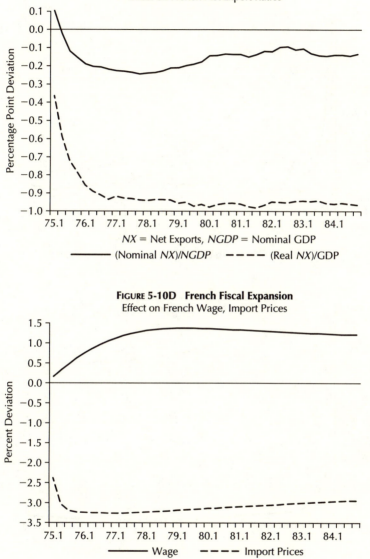

FIGURE 5-10C   French Fiscal Expansion
Effect on French Net Export Ratios

NX = Net Exports, *NGDP* = Nominal GDP
———— (Nominal *NX*)/*NGDP*   – – – – (Real *NX*)/GDP

FIGURE 5-10D   French Fiscal Expansion
Effect on French Wage, Import Prices

———— Wage   – – – – Import Prices

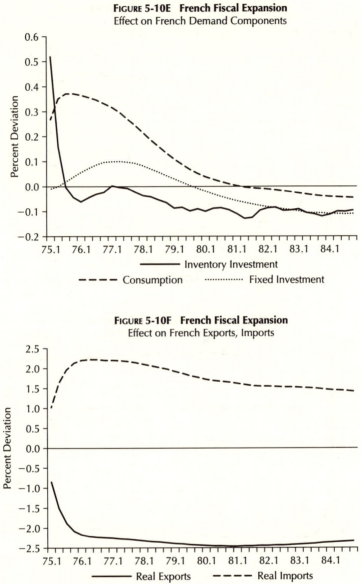

FIGURE 5-10E   French Fiscal Expansion
Effect on French Demand Components

Inventory Investment
Consumption   Fixed Investment

FIGURE 5-10F   French Fiscal Expansion
Effect on French Exports, Imports

Real Exports   Real Imports

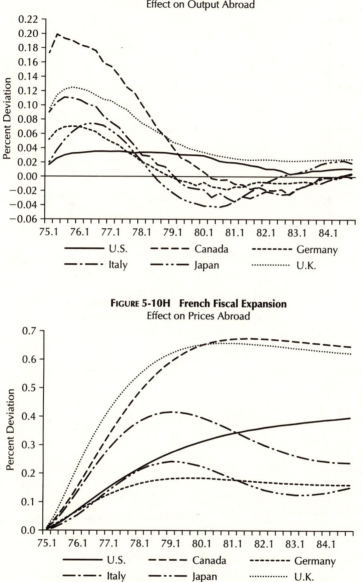

FIGURE 5-10G   French Fiscal Expansion
Effect on Output Abroad

FIGURE 5-10H   French Fiscal Expansion
Effect on Prices Abroad

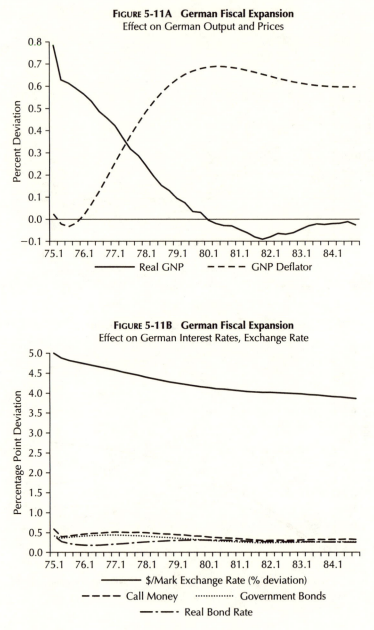

FIGURE 5-11A   German Fiscal Expansion
Effect on German Output and Prices

Real GNP   - - - - GNP Deflator

FIGURE 5-11B   German Fiscal Expansion
Effect on German Interest Rates, Exchange Rate

$/Mark Exchange Rate (% deviation)

- - - Call Money   ·············· Government Bonds

—·—· Real Bond Rate

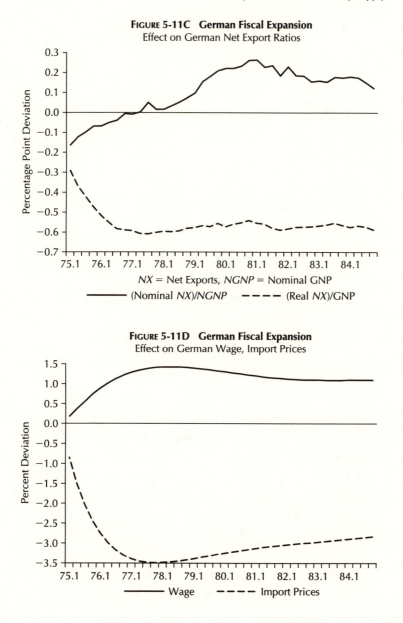

FIGURE 5-11C   German Fiscal Expansion
Effect on German Net Export Ratios

NX = Net Exports, *NGNP* = Nominal GNP
———— (Nominal *NX*)/*NGNP*   — — — — (Real *NX*)/GNP

FIGURE 5-11D   German Fiscal Expansion
Effect on German Wage, Import Prices

———— Wage   — — — — Import Prices

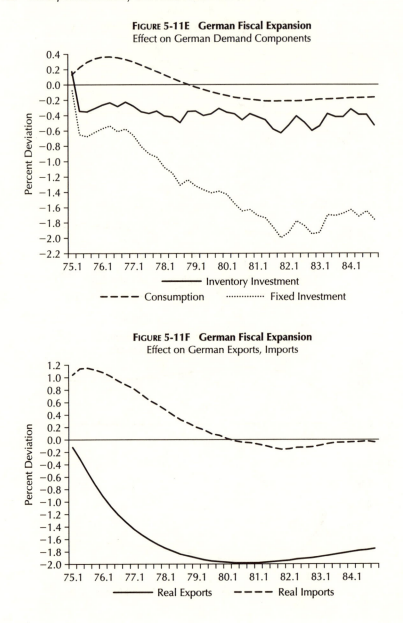

FIGURE 5-11E   German Fiscal Expansion
Effect on German Demand Components

——— Inventory Investment

– – – Consumption   ·············· Fixed Investment

FIGURE 5-11F   German Fiscal Expansion
Effect on German Exports, Imports

——— Real Exports   – – – Real Imports

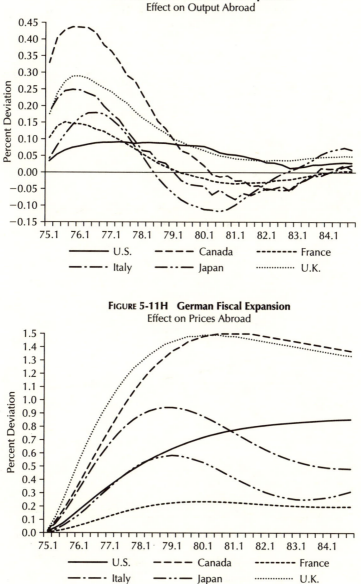

FIGURE 5-11G German Fiscal Expansion
Effect on Output Abroad

FIGURE 5-11H German Fiscal Expansion
Effect on Prices Abroad

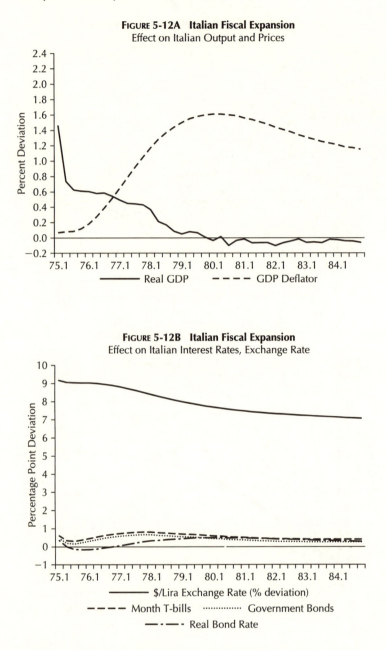

FIGURE 5-12A   Italian Fiscal Expansion
Effect on Italian Output and Prices

FIGURE 5-12B   Italian Fiscal Expansion
Effect on Italian Interest Rates, Exchange Rate

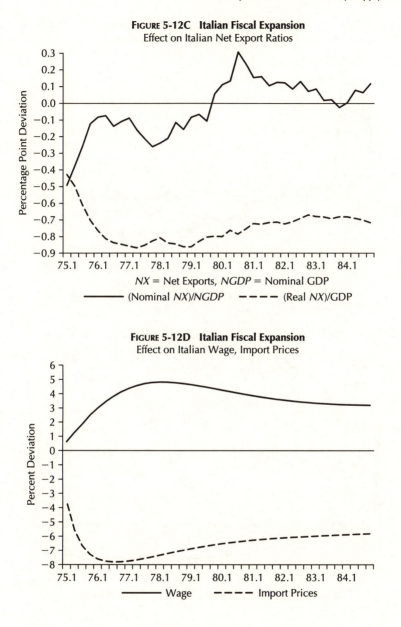

FIGURE 5-12C   Italian Fiscal Expansion
Effect on Italian Net Export Ratios

NX = Net Exports, *NGDP* = Nominal GDP

———— (Nominal *NX*)/*NGDP*   – – – – (Real *NX*)/GDP

FIGURE 5-12D   Italian Fiscal Expansion
Effect on Italian Wage, Import Prices

———— Wage   – – – – Import Prices

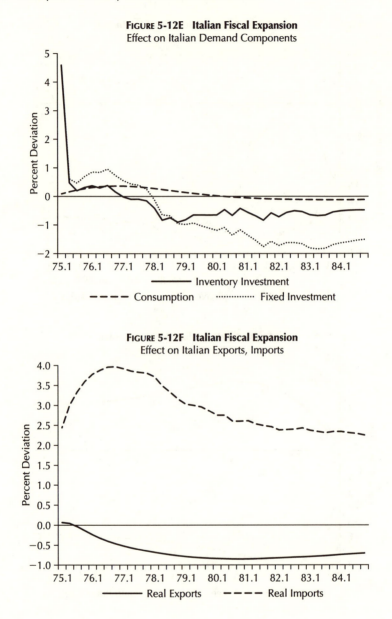

FIGURE 5-12E **Italian Fiscal Expansion**
Effect on Italian Demand Components

Inventory Investment
Consumption   Fixed Investment

FIGURE 5-12F **Italian Fiscal Expansion**
Effect on Italian Exports, Imports

Real Exports   Real Imports

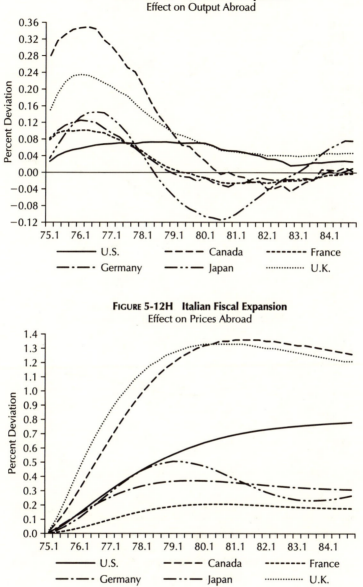

FIGURE 5-12G   **Italian Fiscal Expansion**
Effect on Output Abroad

| ——— U.S. | – – – Canada | ------- France |
| —·—· Germany | —··— Japan | ············· U.K. |

FIGURE 5-12H   **Italian Fiscal Expansion**
Effect on Prices Abroad

| ——— U.S. | – – – Canada | ------- France |
| —·—· Germany | —··— Japan | ············· U.K. |

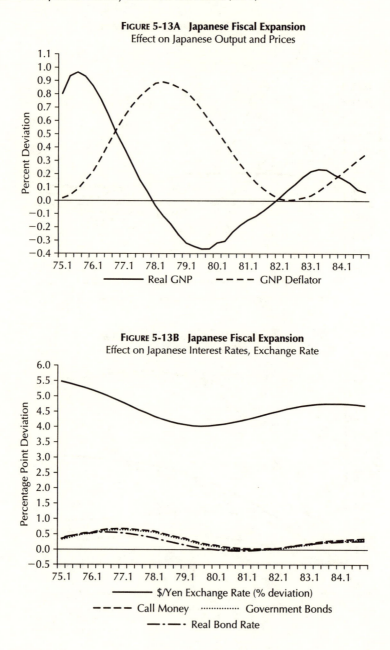

FIGURE 5-13A   Japanese Fiscal Expansion
Effect on Japanese Output and Prices

——— Real GNP   – – – – GNP Deflator

FIGURE 5-13B   Japanese Fiscal Expansion
Effect on Japanese Interest Rates, Exchange Rate

——— $/Yen Exchange Rate (% deviation)
– – – – Call Money   ·············· Government Bonds
–·—·– Real Bond Rate

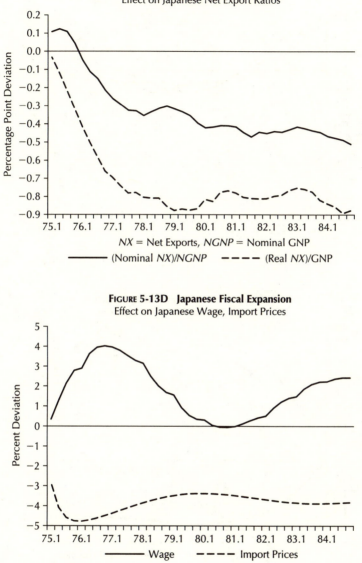

FIGURE 5-13C   Japanese Fiscal Expansion
Effect on Japanese Net Export Ratios

NX = Net Exports, *NGNP* = Nominal GNP
——— (Nominal *NX*)/*NGNP*   — — — (Real *NX*)/GNP

FIGURE 5-13D   Japanese Fiscal Expansion
Effect on Japanese Wage, Import Prices

——— Wage   — — — Import Prices

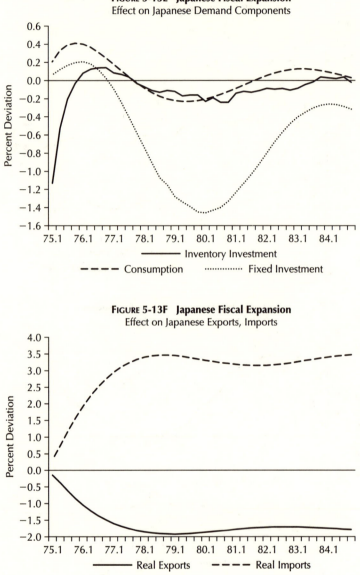

FIGURE 5-13E   Japanese Fiscal Expansion
Effect on Japanese Demand Components

FIGURE 5-13F   Japanese Fiscal Expansion
Effect on Japanese Exports, Imports

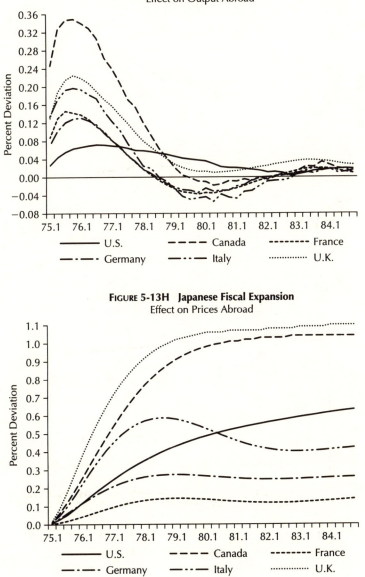

FIGURE 5-13G   Japanese Fiscal Expansion
Effect on Output Abroad

FIGURE 5-13H   Japanese Fiscal Expansion
Effect on Prices Abroad

FIGURE 5-14A U.K. Fiscal Expansion
Effect on U.K. Output and Prices

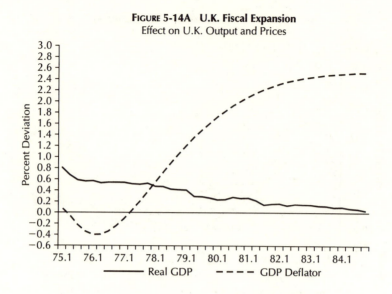

FIGURE 5-14B U.K. Fiscal Expansion
Effect on U.K. Interest Rates, Exchange Rate

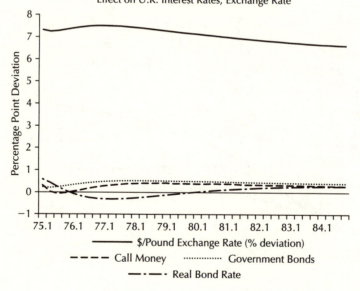

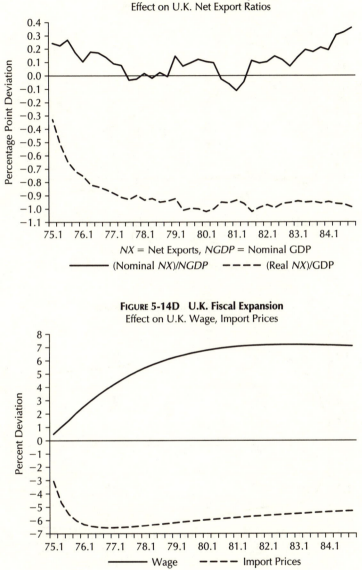

FIGURE 5-14C   U.K. Fiscal Expansion
Effect on U.K. Net Export Ratios

NX = Net Exports, $NGDP$ = Nominal GDP
———— (Nominal NX)/$NGDP$ – – – – (Real NX)/GDP

FIGURE 5-14D   U.K. Fiscal Expansion
Effect on U.K. Wage, Import Prices

———— Wage   – – – – Import Prices

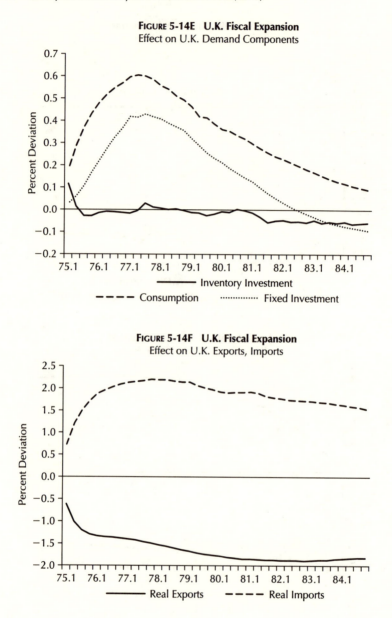

FIGURE 5-14E   U.K. Fiscal Expansion
Effect on U.K. Demand Components

FIGURE 5-14F   U.K. Fiscal Expansion
Effect on U.K. Exports, Imports

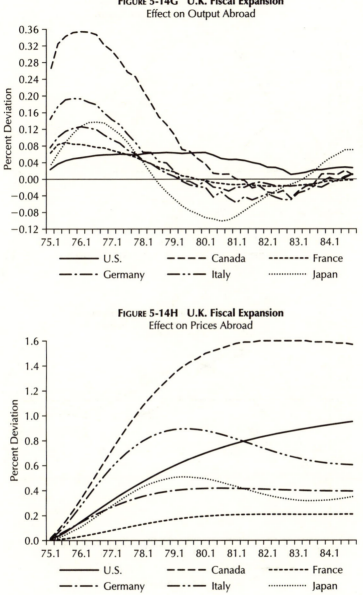

FIGURE 5-14G U.K. Fiscal Expansion
Effect on Output Abroad

FIGURE 5-14H U.K. Fiscal Expansion
Effect on Prices Abroad

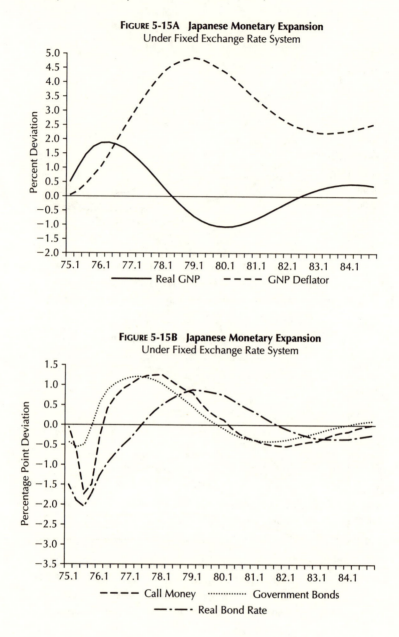

FIGURE 5-15A   Japanese Monetary Expansion
Under Fixed Exchange Rate System

Real GNP   GNP Deflator

FIGURE 5-15B   Japanese Monetary Expansion
Under Fixed Exchange Rate System

Call Money   Government Bonds
Real Bond Rate

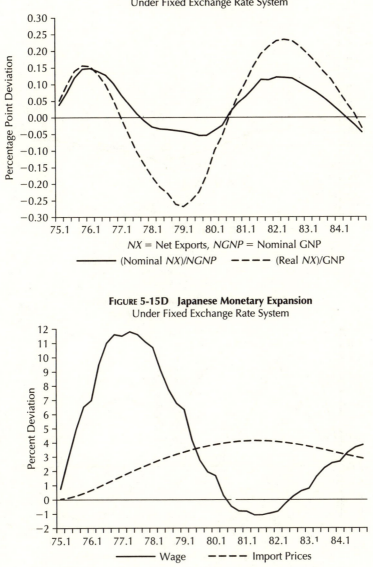

FIGURE 5-15C   Japanese Monetary Expansion
Under Fixed Exchange Rate System

NX = Net Exports, *NGNP* = Nominal GNP

——— (Nominal *NX*)/*NGNP*   – – – – (Real *NX*)/GNP

FIGURE 5-15D   Japanese Monetary Expansion
Under Fixed Exchange Rate System

——— Wage   – – – – Import Prices

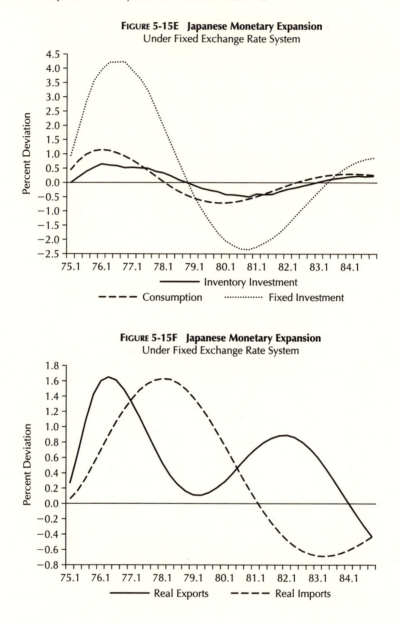

FIGURE 5-15E   Japanese Monetary Expansion
Under Fixed Exchange Rate System

FIGURE 5-15F   Japanese Monetary Expansion
Under Fixed Exchange Rate System

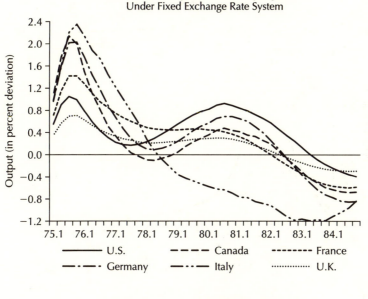

FIGURE 5-15G   Japanese Monetary Expansion
Under Fixed Exchange Rate System

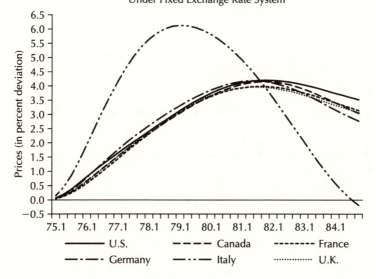

FIGURE 5-15H   Japanese Monetary Expansion
Under Fixed Exchange Rate System

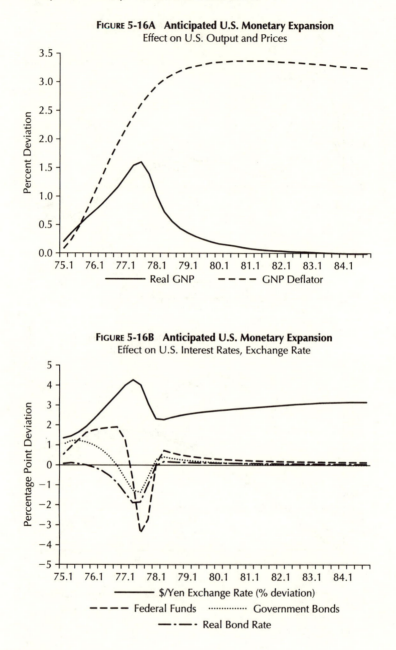

FIGURE 5-16A   Anticipated U.S. Monetary Expansion
Effect on U.S. Output and Prices

Real GNP   GNP Deflator

FIGURE 5-16B   Anticipated U.S. Monetary Expansion
Effect on U.S. Interest Rates, Exchange Rate

$/Yen Exchange Rate (% deviation)

Federal Funds   Government Bonds

Real Bond Rate

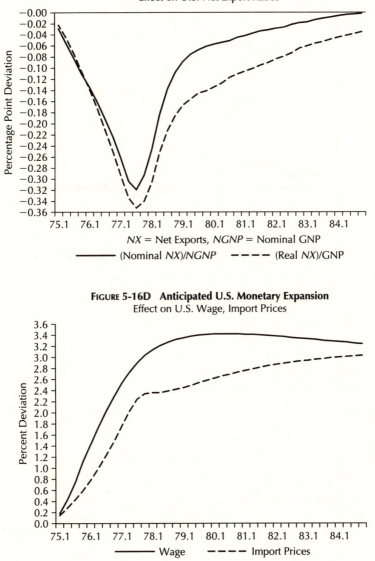

FIGURE 5-16C   Anticipated U.S. Monetary Expansion
Effect on U.S. Net Export Ratios

NX = Net Exports, *NGNP* = Nominal GNP

———— (Nominal *NX*)/*NGNP*   – – – – (Real *NX*)/GNP

FIGURE 5-16D   Anticipated U.S. Monetary Expansion
Effect on U.S. Wage, Import Prices

———— Wage   – – – – Import Prices

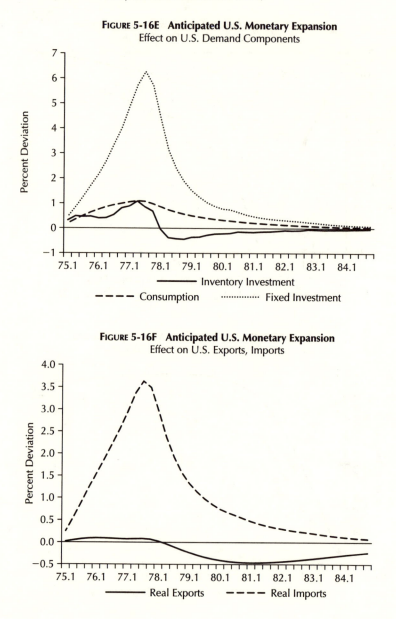

FIGURE 5-16E   **Anticipated U.S. Monetary Expansion**
Effect on U.S. Demand Components

——— Inventory Investment
– – – – Consumption   ············· Fixed Investment

FIGURE 5-16F   **Anticipated U.S. Monetary Expansion**
Effect on U.S. Exports, Imports

——— Real Exports   – – – – Real Imports

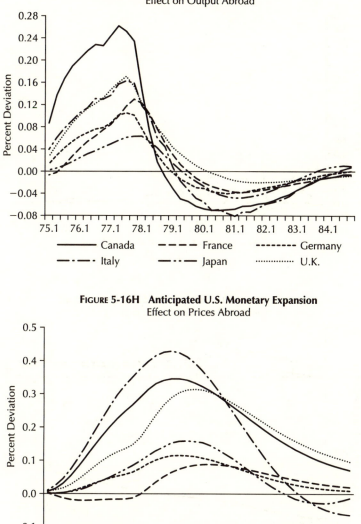

FIGURE 5-16G Anticipated U.S. Monetary Expansion
Effect on Output Abroad

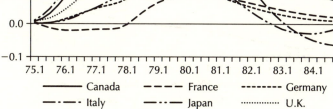

FIGURE 5-16H Anticipated U.S. Monetary Expansion
Effect on Prices Abroad

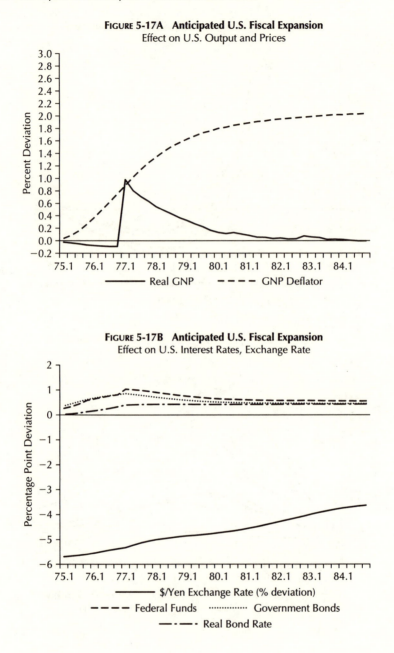

FIGURE 5-17A   Anticipated U.S. Fiscal Expansion
Effect on U.S. Output and Prices

Real GNP ——— GNP Deflator – – – –

FIGURE 5-17B   Anticipated U.S. Fiscal Expansion
Effect on U.S. Interest Rates, Exchange Rate

——— $/Yen Exchange Rate (% deviation)
– – – Federal Funds   ·········· Government Bonds
—·—· Real Bond Rate

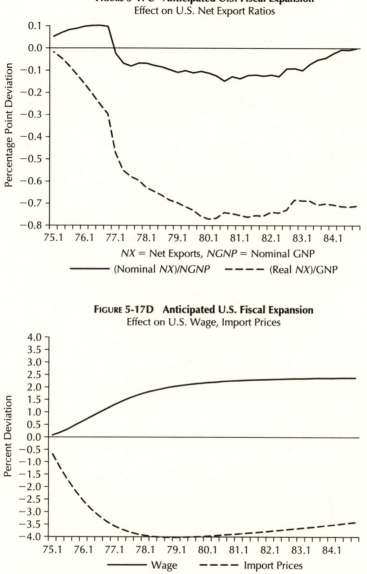

FIGURE 5-17C Anticipated U.S. Fiscal Expansion
Effect on U.S. Net Export Ratios

NX = Net Exports, *NGNP* = Nominal GNP
——— (Nominal *NX*)/*NGNP* − − − − (Real *NX*)/GNP

FIGURE 5-17D Anticipated U.S. Fiscal Expansion
Effect on U.S. Wage, Import Prices

——— Wage − − − − Import Prices

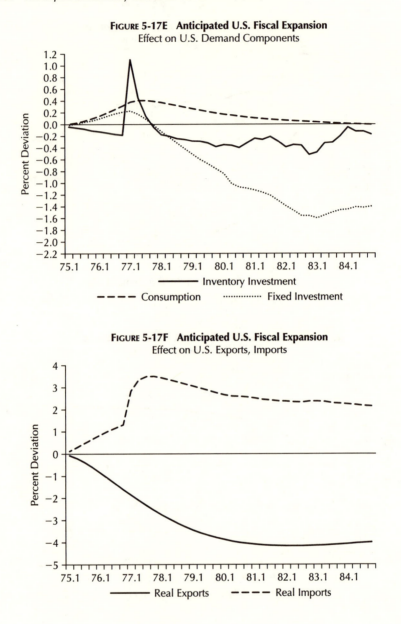

FIGURE 5-17E   **Anticipated U.S. Fiscal Expansion**
Effect on U.S. Demand Components

FIGURE 5-17F   **Anticipated U.S. Fiscal Expansion**
Effect on U.S. Exports, Imports

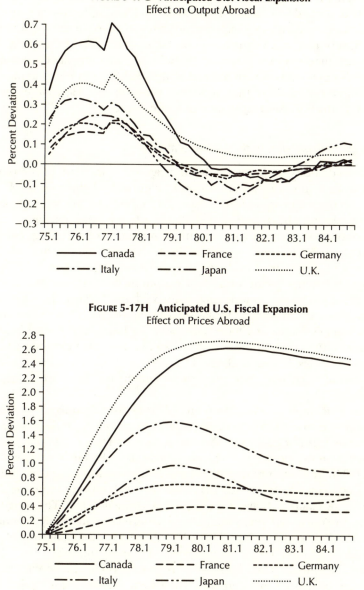

FIGURE 5-17G   Anticipated U.S. Fiscal Expansion
Effect on Output Abroad

| Canada | France | Germany |
| Italy | Japan | U.K. |

FIGURE 5-17H   Anticipated U.S. Fiscal Expansion
Effect on Prices Abroad

| Canada | France | Germany |
| Italy | Japan | U.K. |

The difficult questions concern what happens in the short and medium runs. As described in Chapter 1, the Mundell-Fleming fixed-price models, which ignore exchange-rate expectations, predict an expansion of output in the home country and a contraction of output in the rest of the world. The Dornbusch model, which incorporates rational exchange-rate expectations in a small open economy, predicts that the exchange rate will depreciate in the short run by more than it does in the long run. How large are the short-run effects in this empirical multicountry model?

Monetary Expansion in the United States

The predictions of the model for the case of an increase in the money supply in the United States are shown in Figures 5-1A through 5-1H. The impact on the major variables are reported in the following order for every country: real output, the output deflator, interest rates, exchange rates, net exports, wages, import prices, the components of spending, exports, imports, and finally, real output and prices in the other countries. This same order is maintained in the other experiments.

There is a sharp expansion in U.S. output in the first year as real long-term interest rates fall, stimulating residential and business investment as well as consumer durables. Displaying a hump-shaped pattern over time, output reaches a peak of 1.8 percent above the baseline after two quarters and then returns monotonically to the baseline over the next several years. With the increase in demand, the U.S. price level rises gradually as does the nominal wage level; the gradual movement is due to the staggered wage-setting assumptions.

Short-term interest rates drop sharply and then bounce back before gradually returning to normal. Because of the *ex ante* interest-rate parity conditions, this fluctuation in short-term interest rates requires a parallel fluctuation in the expected exchange rate, as described below. (This sharp initial fall in interest rates is probably due to the very low short-run elasticity of money demand. As already discussed, the interest-rate targeting rules I explore in Chapter 6 are not affected by this elasticity.) The long-term interest rate fluctuates with a similar time pattern but is naturally attenuated relative to the short-term rate. The real interest rate falls below the nominal rate because of the increase in the expected rate of inflation.

Fixed investment rises more than consumption in percentage terms (7 percent compared to 1 percent). The rise of durable consumption (not shown in the figures) is larger than that of nondurable consumption because of the larger interest-rate elasticity for durables. Of the components of investment, producers equipment rises by most in percentage terms, and structures (with a relatively low interest-rate elasticity) have the smallest response.

The pattern of the exchange rate is consistent with the fluctuations in short-term interest rates (only the dollar/yen exchange rate is shown, but the other exchange rates display a similar pattern). Because foreign interest rates do not change by much, U.S. interest rates fall below foreign interest rates for several quarters but then rise above foreign interest rates. The dollar quickly depreciates by about 3 ½ percent and then is expected to appreciate for about three quarters while the U.S. interest rate is below interest rates in the rest of the world. The appreciation takes the dollar above the long-run equilibrium, however, and the dollar then begins to gradually depreciate, eventually converging at 3 percent below normal. During this depreciation, the U.S. short-term interest rate is above foreign interest rates.

The monetary expansion causes a large decrease in net exports that is due almost entirely to a large increase in imports as the economy expands. Exports fluctuate by a relatively small amount. Both price and income elasticities are smaller in the export equation than in the import equation for the United States. Moreover, demand in the other economies does not fluctuate by much. Hence, the favorable effects on net exports of the dollar depreciation are overwhelmed by the increase in import demand brought about by the expansion in the U.S. economy.

The effects of the U.S. monetary expansion on output and prices in the other countries are small. The largest impact on output is in Canada, but it is still only about 20 percent of the expansion in the United States. The impact on output in the other countries is less than 10 percent of the United States. (Note that the scale is much larger for these figures.) In all cases, however, the short-term effects on output are positive, unlike with the simple Mundell-Fleming model but like with the model of Chapter 1. It appears that most of the positive effect on output in the other countries is due to the increased demand for their products brought on by the expansion of income in the U.S. economy.

For all countries except Italy, the price level initially declines relative to the baseline path. The appreciation of the currencies has a short-term negative effect on inflation. Eventually, this is offset by the expansion in demand for domestically produced goods, which drives up wages and prices. However, prices rise by less than 10 percent of the increase in the United States and eventually return to the baseline.

Monetary Expansion in Other Countries

Figures 5-2A through 5-7H show the effects of the same type of monetary expansion in each of the other G-7 countries, again holding money growth to the baseline path in the countries not experiencing a monetary expansion. The order of the figures is the same as in the U.S. presentation, and the countries are in alphabetical order. As with the United States, for each of the other countries, there is an initial increase in real output, which builds up for several quarters before gradually returning to the baseline. In other words, there is the same "hump-shape" pattern as that observed for the United States. The impact on output is largest for France and smallest for the United Kingdom. As in the United States, a monetary expansion causes a decline in the real long-term interest rate and this temporarily stimulates the demand for investment and consumer durables.

Unlike in the United States, there is overshooting of the price level in some of the countries, especially Japan. The overshooting of the price level is associated with damped cycles in real output that are most prominent in Japan. After eventually rising, real output drops below the baseline by about 1 percent in Japan before rising again. It appears that the different wage dynamics in Japan are the source of these swings. To test this, the model was simulated with the wage coefficients in Japan set equal to those of the United States. This change resulted in wage-price dynamics as well as output dynamics that are much closer to those in the United States and that did not show the large cyclical swings.[2]

The general time pattern of short-term interest rates is similar to that of the United States, but the magnitudes are different. Short-term interest rates fall less in the other countries than in the United States, reflecting the larger short-run interest-rate elasticity of money demand in these countries. In every country the real long-term interest rate falls more than the nominal long-term interest rate because of the increase in the expected rate of inflation that results from the monetary expansion.

Exchange rates sharply depreciate in every country when there is a domestic monetary expansion. The initial depreciation is smaller in Germany and Japan than was observed for the United States. Surprisingly, the initial impact in these two countries is less than the long-run impact, so that there is no overshooting of the type observed in the other countries.

It was noted above that net exports decline in the United States when there is monetary expansion, despite the depreciation of the dollar. The same is generally true for each of the other countries; an easier monetary policy tends to make the trade deficit larger (or the surplus smaller) because of the short-run stimulus to domestic demand. Imports eventually rise more than exports in each of the countries. However, in the short run, exports rise more than imports in France, Japan, and the United Kingdom, so there is some transitory improvement of the trade account before deterioration takes place.

There are positive effects of monetary expansion on all the components of domestic aggregate demand, but the size of these effects vary widely from country to country. In percentage terms, fixed investment increases more than consumption in all countries except France. Although inventory investment moves by a relatively large amount in the United States, only a relatively small movement occurs in Japan.

Finally, consider the transmission of the monetary shocks abroad. Recall that the U.S. monetary expansion led to positive impacts on real output in the other countries, contrary to the predictions of a simple Mundell-

---

[2]More sensitive wages will tend to be stabilizing if the shocks to the economy come from the supply side. These demand-side disturbances are magnified by the very sensitive wage equations.

Fleming model. For the U.S. expansion, the transmission effect was very small in all countries except Canada where it was about 20 percent of the impact in the United States. Although the size of the transmission effects vary for the other countries, they are positive in the first few years for all countries except the United Kingdom. Perhaps this is due to the fact that the expansion of demand in the United Kingdom itself is small. But in any case, the most important feature of these transmissions is that they are very small. Not surprisingly, a monetary expansion in Canada has the smallest effects on the other countries. The impacts on prices abroad are also small. Monetary expansion in any of these countries—under a flexible exchange rate—has very small effects on inflation in the other countries, compared with the effects on domestic inflation.

5.3   Unanticipated Increase in Government Purchases

Consider next an unanticipated increase in government spending above the baseline by 1 percent of real output. The increase occurs in the first year and government spending remains at 1 percent of real output above baseline in all following years. This represents a permanent fiscal shock with a magnitude fixed in terms of the growing trend in real output.

Theoretical Insights

Some of the long-run effects of the fiscal shock can be assessed theoretically. Such a fiscal shock is assumed to have no long-run demand effects on real output. Of course, if the share of investment declines, then a slower growth of the capital stock will reduce potential output. But the economy will still return to potential output. The model is designed this way. Hence, in the country where the fiscal shock takes place, the share of the non-government components of real spending (consumption, investment, and net exports) should decline in the long run by the amount of the increase in the government share. Prices rise by enough to reduce real-money balances to the point where higher interest rates crowd out investment and a stronger home currency reduces net exports. Because the real wage does not change, wages rise by as much as prices. Hence, prices, wages, interest rates, and the real exchange rate all permanently rise. In the other countries, prices and interest rates also permanently rise in the long run in order to offset the positive net export effects of the depreciated currencies in those countries. The magnitudes of all these long-run effects must be estimated empirically since they depend on the elasticities of the model.

Fiscal Expansion in the United States

Figures 5-8A through 5-8H describe what would happen during the ten years following such a fiscal shock in the United States. Real output in the

United States increases quite sharply during the first year, and then gradually returns to the baseline path. The large real output increase during the first year is due to increases in consumption, fixed investment, and inventory investment as well as government purchases. Consumption and investment rise because the increase in expected income and sales outweighs the negative effect from the real interest-rate increase.

The real interest-rate increase is small, however, because of changes in inflation expectations. The fiscal expansion implies that prices must rise in the future. People realize this and raise their inflationary expectations. By definition, this reduces the real interest rate relative to what it otherwise would be. In fact, prices do increase in the simulations and this reduces crowding out of durable consumption and investment. Eventually, however, the expected rate of inflation returns to the baseline value, the real interest rate increases further, and the investment components of demand are entirely crowded out.

In the long run, the simulations indicate that prices rise by about 3 percent. This reduces real-money balances by a sufficient amount to increase interest rates, so that investment and durable consumption fall as a share of output to make room for more government purchases. The interest-rate rise is less than 1 percent in the long run.

The fiscal expansion causes the trade deficit to increase as imports rise and exports fall. The transmission channel is through the appreciation of the dollar that raises the price of exports and lowers the price of imports. The decline in net exports is a type of crowding out and occurs both in the short run and in the long run.

Fiscal expansion in the United States induces a positive effect on output in all the other countries, with Japan and Germany experiencing the smallest impact and Canada the largest. The effects are smaller than in the United States but are slightly larger than those abroad in the case of a monetary expansion. Prices rise in all other countries, but by less than in the United States.

Net exports increase in all the other countries (not shown in the figures) because of the depreciation of their currencies. This increase in net exports must eventually be offset by a decline in investment and durable consumption since real GNP is to remain unaffected. Hence, interest rates rise in the rest of the world. As exchange rates settle down to the baseline, this increase in world interest rates matches that in the United States.

Fiscal Expansion in Other Countries

Now consider a fiscal expansion in each of the other six countries. The results are shown in Figures 5-9A through 5-14G. A permanent increase in real government purchases causes output to expand in each of the other countries. With the exception of Japan, the largest effect occurs in the first quarter. In Japan, there is a cyclical swing much like the one observed for the money shock. Eventually, prices rise in all countries, and real output returns to the baseline.

The fiscal expansion causes a large exchange-rate appreciation and a rise in interest rates in each country that experiences a fiscal expansion. The real net exports decline in each country as imports rise and exports fall due to the appreciation of the exchange rate. Hence, the fiscal deficit leads to a worsened trade account.

The transmission effects of the fiscal expansion in the other countries are of the same qualitative form as for the United States. A domestic fiscal expansion causes output to expand in the other countries; the lower exchange rate in those countries, as well as the expansion of output abroad, cause net exports to rise. This in turn stimulates production abroad. The transmission effects are, however, smaller for the other countries than what was observed for the United States.

5.4 Fixed Exchange Rates

Thus far all of the experiments have assumed flexible exchange rates with the money supplies in all countries being exogenous. Now consider the polar opposite case; money supplies are manipulated to keep the exchange rate pegged. Although one could consider changes in the policy instrument in every country, only Japan is considered here. In particular, consider a 3-percent increase in the Japanese money supply with a fixed exchange-rate system. The other six countries adjust their money supplies endogenously to keep exchange rates pegged.

Technically, the model is changed in two ways. First, the short-term interest-rate equations in all countries except Japan are rearranged with money on the left-hand side. This makes money in each of the countries an endogenous variable. Second, the interest rates in all countries are made endogenous by placing them on the left-hand side of the interest-rate parity equations. Interest-rate changes in the other countries then match movements in the U.S. interest rate because the expected change in the exchange rate relative to the U.S. dollar is assumed to be zero in the interest-rate parity equations.

Theoretical Considerations

Since money is neutral in the long run, prices and wages in Japan will eventually increase by 3 percent, and output and the components of demand will return to their baseline values. With exchange rates fixed, prices and wages in all the other countries must also eventually increase by 3 percent. The money supplies in all the other countries will eventually increase by 3 percent to bring about the required inflation. In this sense it doesn't matter which country started the money expansion, as all will follow suit in any case. In the long run, output and the components of demand in the other countries also return to the baseline path.

Simulation Results

In the short run, there will be effects on output, the components of demand, and the trade balance from an increase in the money supply in Japan. Figures 5-15A through 5-15H show the results. They are strikingly different from those obtained in the flexible exchange-rate case. In that case, Japanese output expanded by a significant amount, and there was almost no effect on output in the United States, Germany, and the other countries. With fixed exchange rates, there is a big effect of the Japanese monetary expansion on both the United States and Germany. The impact on Japanese output is still about the same, but Germany's output expands by almost the same amount, and U.S. output expands by almost half as much as in Japan.

The reason for these changes is clear. In order to keep the exchange rates on target, the other central banks must expand their money supplies and reduce their interest rates when the Bank of Japan's monetary expansion puts downward pressure on short-term interest rates. The monetary expansion in the other countries in turn stimulates demand in these countries because wages and prices adjust slowly. Real-money balances rise, and this causes nominal interest rates to fall along with Japan's interest rates. Real interest rates in the other countries drop by a different amount from that in Japan because wages and prices rise (and are expected to rise) at different rates from those in Japan. The drop in real interest rates affects investment and durable consumption by amounts that depend on the size of real interest-rate elasticities. As the simulations show, the effect in some of the other countries of the Japanese monetary expansion is even larger than in Japan.[3]

5.5   An Anticipated Increase in the Money Supply

To examine the effects of anticipated changes in the instruments, we return to the world of flexible exchange rates. We focus our discussion on the United States. The qualitative differences between anticipated and unanticipated shocks are similar in the other countries.

Consider an increase in the money supply of 3 percent, just as in Section 5.2, except that the increase is anticipated eight quarters in advance.

---

[3]Note that this particular fixed exchange-rate system imposed on the model is not the only possibility. This system leads to a situation where all countries must match the increase in money growth undertaken by Japan. An alternative fixed exchange-rate arrangement would be to make world money exogenous. However, if the simulation was for the world money supply to increase by 3 percent, then the results would be similar since the money supply would increase by 3 percent in every country.

Because of the expectations effects, the anticipation of this change in policy will lead to immediate impacts. Additional impacts will occur at the time of the actual policy change. In the long run, however, the money increase will be neutral with the same effects studied as those in Section 5.2.

The effects on U.S. variables are shown in Figures 5-16A through 5-16H. There is a small expansionary effect on real output at the time of announcement. The stimulative effect occurs largely because investment and consumption depend on expectations of future sales and income, both of which rise as soon as the monetary expansion is expected to occur. In addition, there is a small decline in the real long-term interest rate in the first few quarters following the announcement. The effect on real output gradually builds up and reaches a maximum during the year in which the money supply is increased. The maximum increase at the time of impact is smaller than the initial impact in the unanticipated case (compare Figure 5-1A with Figure 5-16A). However, the speed of decline in output after the maximum effect is very similar to the unanticipated case.

Prices and wages rise gradually from the date of announcement. Because the money supply has not yet risen, this inflation reduces real-money balances and causes interest rates to rise in the first few quarters before they decline at the time of impact. This rise in nominal interest rates is more than offset by the increase in the expected rate of inflation, so that real interest rates fall slightly and stimulate investment and the purchase of durables.

Very little stimulus to demand is coming from exports in the initial quarters. The dollar depreciates starting in the period of the announcement, but this is not large enough to stimulate exports by more than a small amount. The depreciation starts with a 1-percent downward jump. This is followed by a more gradual fall to about 4.5 percent below the baseline—an overshoot of the final 3 percent. Then there is an appreciation back to a level 3 percent below the baseline in the first few quarters after the money supply increase.

The output effects in the other countries are even smaller than in the unanticipated case. The overall effect of the anticipated monetary change compared to the unanticipated change is to smooth out the effects on output and the components of demand in the United States and other countries. The impacts are smaller, but they last longer.

5.6 Anticipated Increase in Government Spending

Suppose now that the unanticipated expansion in government spending described in Section 5.3 is anticipated two years in advance. In the long run the effects will be identical to those in the unanticipated case, but in the short run the effects are much different. Again we focus on the United States. The effects are shown in Figures 5-17A through 5-17H.

At the time of the announcement there is a small decline in output relative to the baseline. By the seventh quarter after the announcement—but still before the fiscal shock occurs—output is still slightly below baseline. In a growing economy this decline would not be large enough to be registered as a recession, but a slowdown in economic growth might be observed. When the increase in government spending actually takes place, the economy goes into a boom as output rises about 1 percent above normal. Hence, the size of the expansion, once it occurs, is about 70 percent as large as in the unanticipated case.

The cause of the decline in output at the time of the fiscal announcement is primarily the increase in interest rates and an appreciation of the dollar. Long-term interest rates rise because people expect short-term interest rates to rise in the future when the fiscal expansion actually occurs. The rise in long-term interest rates chokes off investment well before the increase in government spending occurs.

The sharp appreciation of the dollar occurs for similar reasons. People realize at the time of announcement that the dollar will appreciate in the future. If interest rates did not change, then the dollar would have to jump up immediately in order to keep interest-rate parity. In this case, U.S. interest rates rise above foreign interest rates at the time of announcement. Hence, the dollar must appreciate even further so that it can be expected to depreciate while the spread between U.S. interest rates and world interest rates is greater than normal.

The appreciation of the dollar has a positive impact on imports and has a negative impact on exports. The trade deficit gradually grows until the time of the fiscal shock when it increases sharply. The sharp increase in the trade deficit is due to the large increase in domestic demand at the time government spending increases. The decline in net exports is more than offset by an increase in consumption and investment, and the economy goes into a boom as described before.

5.7   Empirical Overview

This chapter began by emphasizing the importance of obtaining empirical information about the impact of the policy instruments. The many charts presented here provide that information and form the basis of the policy analysis that follows in the last three chapters of the book. In this section, I attempt to glean several key empirical rules of thumb about the overall effects on real output and prices from the simulations.

Monetary Policy Effects on Real Output and Prices

Short Run.   An unanticipated increase in the money supply has significant short-run impact on real output in all seven countries. A *3-percent increase in the money supply* temporarily reduces the short-term interest rate by about 2 percentage points on the average and *raises real output* by an average maximum of *about 1½ percent* above the baseline. The maximum effect usually occurs about two quarters after the monetary shock. At this point prices are about ½ percent above baseline. Anticipated increases in the money supply also have a significant effect on real output. The impact starts before the increase, and the maximum is slightly less than the unanticipated increase.

Medium to Long Run. The impact on real output dies out slowly. After three years, real output is still above baseline in all the countries, having returned about 75 percent of the distance back to the baseline. At this three-year point, prices, on average, are still less than 3 percent above baseline. In the long run, of course, effects on real output disappear, and prices rise by 3 percent.

Monetary Policy Effects on the Trade Balance and on Other Countries

In every country net exports decline in response to a monetary expansion. The maximum short-run decline is slightly less than ½ percentage points of GNP on average for the 3-percent money expansion. Of course, this effect is short-lived; eventually net exports return to the baseline.

With flexible exchange rates, monetary policy has a small but positive short-run effect on real output in other countries. The average impact is about one-tenth of a percent increase.

With fixed exchange rates, however, a monetary expansion has huge effects abroad. The impact in foreign countries averages to about the same as in the country expanding the money supply.

Fiscal Policy Effects on Real Output and Prices

Short Run. An unanticipated change in government purchases also has a significant effect on real output in the short run. An increase in real government purchases by 1 percent above the baseline raises real output by an average maximum of 1¼ percent. Hence, the multiplier is about 1¼ on average. The maximum effect occurs in the first quarter during which government spending increases. Prices rise by only a small amount in this first quarter.

Medium to Long Run. The impact on real output dissipates slowly as other components of spending decline. After three years, real output is still about one-third of a percentage point above the baseline. In the long run, of course, there is complete crowding out, and real output returns to the baseline.

Fiscal Policy Effects on the Trade Balance and on Other Countries

The expansionary fiscal policy reduces real net exports in every country. The long-run impact is larger than the short-run impact. In the long run the increase in government spending by 1 percent of real output reduces net exports by an average of about .8 percent of real output. Thus, most of the long-run crowding out caused by the fiscal expansion occurs in net exports. However, even the short-run crowding out is significant. Real net exports decline by about .3 percent of real output on average in the quarter in which government spending increases. This is caused by a large appreciation of the currency that occurs just as the fiscal expansion occurs.

Assessing the Magnitude of the Impact in the 1980s

Finally, to give some sense of the magnitude of these effects, consider some well-publicized events of the 1980s. An important public policy issue in the 1980s was whether the U.S. budget deficit and expected future budget deficits were the cause of the large dollar appreciation—about 60 percent from 1980 to 1985 on a trade-weighted basis. As the simulations in this chapter make clear, both current and expected future budget deficits—caused, for example, by an increase in government spending—make the dollar appreciate.

Is the size of the effect large enough to explain the appreciation of the dollar observed in the early 1980s? The simulation results suggest that an unanticipated permanent increase in the budget deficit by 1 percent of GNP causes the dollar to appreciate by about 6 percent (the impact effect). The budget deficit in the United States during the 1980s reached a peak of about 5 percent of GNP, indicating that a 30-percent dollar appreciation in the early 1980s could be attributed to the budget deficits. This is only the impact effect. Over time, the size of effect on the exchange rate diminishes.

Anticipated budget deficits also affect the exchange rate. An increase in the budget deficit of 1 percent of GNP (anticipated two years in advance) causes the dollar to appreciate by about another 6 percent. Hence, it is possible that projections of large future deficits that had not yet occurred would have raised the exchange rate even further. But projections of deficits of over 10 percent of GNP would have been necessary to explain the dollar appreciation observed at that time. It appears that other factors, perhaps monetary policy, also had a role to play in the dollar's high value. The simulations in this chapter imply that a tighter monetary policy would temporarily appreciate the dollar.

Reference Notes

Starting in the mid-1980s, several research efforts have been devoted to comparing deterministic simulations, like those in this chapter, from different econometric models. This multicountry model was a participant in most of these comparison projects, so it is possible to compare the policy impacts with conventional models or with other rational expectations models. My assessment is that there are large differences between the simulations with rational expectations models and those with conventional models. However, since most of the comparisons are for simulations of unanticipated changes in the policy instruments—where expectations effects play a smaller role—there is less difference between conventional and rational expectations models than a casual observer might expect.

The first set of comparisons—in which an early version of this multicountry model participated—is reported in the two-volume work by Bryant et al. (1988a). The paper by Hickman (1988) in the first of these volumes summarizes the different simulations by using stanadard textbook graphs and is a very useful way for the uninitiated to assess the results. The results of a second comparison, focusing on the trade deficit effects, were published by Bryant, Holtham, and Hooper (1988b). In addition, a model comparison project focusing mostly on quarterly econometric models of the U.S. economy was organized by Lawrence Klein and has met regularly since 1986. The results of a comparison of the deterministic simulations for this group of models is reported in Klein (1991). The comment by Shiller (1991) in the later volume points to some of the fundamental differences between simulations of conventional models and rational expectations models.

III

Econometric Policy Evaluation

6

Design of Policy Systems

This chapter considers the design of macroeconomic policy systems. Three questions are addressed. First, is a worldwide system of fixed exchange rates between the major currencies desirable? Second, are there gains from designing monetary policy rules in coordination with other countries? Third, does a price rule, a nominal-income rule, or some other rule for monetary policy give the best domestic economic performance? The first two questions relate to international monetary policy, the third to domestic monetary policy. If one could reliably answer all three questions, and if there *was* a consensus about the answers, then policymakers would have a pretty good fix on what a macroeconomic policy system should look like in today's economy. Hence, these questions seem like a good place to begin an investigation of policy design.

In principle, the three questions are not separable. For example, the choice of a domestic policy rule (Question 3) affects the choice of an exchange-rate system (Question 1). One could imagine a poorly designed rule for domestic monetary policy that would make either a fixed or a flexible exchange-rate system look bad. However, it is a monumental task to consider all three questions simultaneously within one grand policy-optimization problem, and the complexity of the task would make for a nearly impossible interpretation of the results. Hence, the analysis does not attempt to address all three questions at once. Rather, it is a sequential analysis: first, the exchange-rate system, second, international coordination, and finally, the optimal domestic monetary policy rule. As will become clear, the order has some logic to it and makes the analysis easier.

The multicountry model with the stochastic shocks and the dynamic policy effects described in the previous three chapters is used for each of the design problems. The method of analysis—stochastic simulation of the multicountry model—is directly analogous to both the simple theoretical evaluation of policy using the stylized model in Chapter 1 and the empirical evaluation using the model of the United States in Chapter 2. However, because of the size and the nonlinearity of the model, the method may appear more opaque.

The stochastic simulations are conducted over a representative future ten-year period—the particular period makes little difference for the analysis. The shocks for the stochastic simulation are drawn from the estimated distribution of shocks described in detail in Chapter 4. The performance of the seven countries is examined under the different macroeconomic policy systems. The alternative policy systems are ranked according to how successful they are in reducing the fluctuations in inflation, real output, the components of spending, exports, and imports. Of course, other factors may be relevant for policy decisions, such as the impact on long-term growth, income distribution, and even national security.

This approach deals explicitly with several issues raised by the Lucas critique of traditional econometric policy-evaluation methods. In fact, the three examples used in the original critique paper of Lucas—consumption demand, price determination, and investment demand—are part of the multicountry model. Endogenizing expectations by using the rational expectations assumption, as Lucas did in his original paper, is precisely what automatically happens in the multicountry model. To be sure, the equations of the model could benefit from more theoretical research, and the rational expectations assumption may not be appropriate in periods immediately following a policy reform (when market participants are learning about the policy). The transition to new policy systems is the focus of Chapter 7. Nevertheless, the approach does seem appropriate for estimating the long-term effects of policy regimes.

Another advantage with the approach—and an important methodological innovation for international monetary policy research—is the use of a statistically estimated distribution of shocks. In contrast, the stylized analysis of international monetary systems presented in Chapter 1 was based on *assumed parameter values* for the equations and *assumed distributions* for the shocks to the equations. However, this is also true of many previous attempts to evaluate international policy rules from a stochastic viewpoint.[1] These previous theoretical studies are useful for highlighting key parameters that affect the answers. For example, in a static non-rational expectations model that can be put into an ISLM framework, a fixed exchange-rate system will work better if country-specific shocks to the *LM* equations have a relatively large variance. In that case, a fixed exchange-rate system offers the same advantages as interest-rate targeting. On the other hand, a flexible exchange-rate system will work better if country-specific shocks to the *IS* equations have a relatively large variance. To get any further than this

---

[1]See Carlozzi and Taylor (1985), McKibbin and Sachs (1989), or Fukuda and Hamada (1987). Poole (1970) was one of the first to study the effect of different types of shocks in a single-country, theoretical ISLM framework without rational expectations.

requires estimates of the size of the shocks. Moreover, the proofs of these theoretical results depend on a number of simplifying assumptions that are most likely unrealistic. For example, it is typically assumed that the *IS* and *LM* shocks are either uncorrelated or perfectly correlated between countries and that there are no other shocks—such as labor-market shocks, exchange-rate shocks, or commodity-price shocks. The proofs also require that the demand and supply elasticities be in a certain range (usually the same in all countries). An empirical framework provides guidance about such assumptions. The estimated parameters and estimated distributions of the shocks used in this chapter are based on real-world data. As will be discussed below, applying this technique raises several new and interesting issues—such as how the probability distribution of the shocks may change when policy changes—and it is not without its own shortcomings.

The policy-design issues considered in this chapter focus entirely on monetary policy. The study of fiscal policy rules—automatic stabilizers or budget-balancing strategies—could be considered by using the same approach. For this analysis, however, we take government purchases as exogenous and assume that other components of the government budget—tax revenues and transfers—affect income and thereby private spending as they did during the sample period of the multicountry model. For example, automatic stabilizers affect the response of disposable income to changes in national income and, thereby, affect the response of consumption to national income incorporated in the consumption equations discussed in Chapter 3.

The design of fiscal policy rules is an important element of macro-economic policy analysis, despite the well-known problems with discretionary fiscal policy. Automatic stabilizers remain an important part of macroeconomic policy and help mitigate recessions. However, automatic stabilizers in most countries are affected by goals that go well beyond those of macroeconomic policy. For example, changes in the progressivity of the tax system affect the responsiveness of the automatic stabilizers but are not made with stabilization policy in mind.

6.1   The International Monetary System: Fixed or Flexible Rates?

One of the most important questions about the design of international monetary policy concerns the role of the monetary authorities in stabilizing exchange rates. The classic question is simply, "Should exchange rates be fixed or flexible?" In reality, the question is less black and white. Target zones—in which the monetary authorities permit exchange rates to fluctuate within rather wide margins around a fixed parity—are frequently proposed as a more practical alternative to fixed rates. Fixing exchange rates among a group of countries (such as the countries in the European Monetary System) while allowing the exchange rate for members of the group to fluctuate freely against other countries is another alternative. Despite the continuing importance of the exchange-rate questions, surprisingly few empirical studies have attempted to evaluate the effects of fixed-versus-flexible exchange rates. In particular, there have been no econometric policy evaluations that have addressed these questions while dealing with expectational issues and capital mobility, both of which are widely viewed as crucial to exchange-rate behavior. Policy advisors, therefore, have had to rely on the ambiguous theoretical studies or on intuitive judgments.

Assumptions about Monetary Policy Rules

In comparing the fixed-versus-flexible exchange-rate system, I assume that monetary policy is conducted according to a particular policy rule in which the short-term interest rate is assumed to be the primary instrument of monetary policy. In recent years, the short-term interest rate—the federal funds rate in the United States, for example—has been used in practice by central bankers much more frequently than money supply as the operating instrument for monetary policy decisions. Although the money supply has been used as a guide to monetary policy in varying degrees from time to time, deciding on a setting for interest rates is a better characterization of how policy is operated today in most countries. At an early stage of my research, I investigated fixed-versus-flexible exchange rates within the context of money-supply rules. The results on the choice of an exchange-rate system are similar, but interest-rate rules provide a cleaner comparison because they automatically eliminate velocity shocks, which are quite large in some of the equations.

For all the policy rules considered in this section, the interest rate is assumed to react to deviations of a price index from a target level. Alternatives in which the interest rate reacts to other indicators—such as real output—are considered later in the chapter when discussing the design of an optimal domestic monetary policy rule. The comparisons of fixed-versus-flexible rates described in this chapter could also be made for these alternative assumptions about the monetary policy rule. The results do not appear to be sensitive to this assumption, although an extensive analysis has not yet been performed.

According to the multicountry model, sterilized intervention in the foreign-exchange markets—that is, for which the monetary base does not change—has no effect on exchange rates. International financial markets are characterized by perfect capital mobility and perfect substitution between domestic and international assets. Fundamental changes in monetary or fiscal policy are required to move exchange rates. This property is realistic for the quarterly time interval for which the model is estimated and simulated. Under flexible exchange rates, the nominal interest-rate spread between each pair of countries is equal to the expected depreciation of the exchange rate between the same two countries. In this model, expectations of exchange-rate changes are forward-looking, computed by using the entire model. Although capital flows among countries may be quite large with perfect capital mobility, the accumulated stocks of foreign assets do not affect the analysis.

Interest-Rate Rules under Flexible Rates

For the flexible exchange-rate regime, I assume that each central bank adjusts its short-term interest-rate target in response to changes in the price level. This type of response for monetary policy is sometimes called a price rule. To be specific, I assume that a 1-percent rise in the domestic price level—measured by the output (GNP or GDP) deflator—brings about a monetary response of about a 1½ percentage point rise in the short-term interest rate.[2] For example, suppose that the inflation rate in the United States rises to 5 percent and that this is above the U.S. target of, say, 3 percent. Hence, the price level rises by 2 percent above its target level. According to the policy rule, the Federal Reserve Bank responds by taking actions to raise the federal funds rate by 3 percentage points. The same is true for the other countries. To give another example, if the price level in Japan falls by 1 percent below its target, then the Bank of Japan lowers the call-money rate by about 1½ percentage points. Such interest-rate adjustments should be made in real terms; that is, the central bank's target interest rate should be higher if there is a higher expected inflation rate than if there is a lower expected inflation rate. In general, therefore, the interest-rate rule for each country (i) can be written algebraically as

$$RS_i - RS_i^* = LP_i(+4) - LP_i + g(LP_i - LP_i^*) \tag{6.1}$$

if $RS_i > .01$ and $RS_i = .01$ otherwise. The notation of Equation (6.1) is essentially the same as that of Chapter 3; RS is the short-term interest rate and LP is the log of the price level. The target for the (log of the) price level is LP^* and g is the reaction coefficient. RS^* is the (real) interest rate consistent with the price level being on target. Note that $LP(+4)$ is the rational forecast of the (log of the) price level four quarters ahead. Hence, $LP(+4) - LP$ is the expected inflation rate, and Equation (6.1) is effectively a real interest-rate rule. Of course, this does not mean that the central bank is attempting to peg the real interest rate. The interest rate adjusts depending on what happens to the price level. The real interest rate is the *ex ante* real interest rate based on the rational forecast of inflation from the multicountry model. Without truncation from below, the semi-log functional form in Equation (6.1) does not rule out the possibility that the nominal interest rate RS becomes negative. If the price level falls 10 percent below the target, for example, then the functional form could call for a negative nominal interest rate. Since negative nominal interest rates are not

---

[2]The exact interest-rate response in the simulations is 1.6 percentage points. The precise value for this response coefficient does not matter for the choice between fixed and flexible exchange rates. Alternative values are considered below.

feasible, Equation (6.1) must be truncated below some nonnegative value, which is taken to be 1 percent in this analysis ($RS_i = .01$). In other words, whenever the function in Equation (6.1) calls for a nominal interest rate below 1 percent, the nominal interest rate is set to 1 percent. This truncated form of Equation (6.1) is the policy rule that the monetary authorities are assumed to follow.

When the model is simulated under the flexible exchange-rate regime, the interest-rate rules in Equation (6.1) replace the inverted money-demand equations that would be in operation if money-supply rules were used as the policy variable. Money is now endogenous and the behavior of the money supply can be computed directly from the money-demand equations. Recall that the money supply only enters the model through the interest-rate effects captured in Equation (6.1).

Interest-Rate Rules in the Fixed Exchange-Rate System

For the fixed exchange-rate system, the interest rates in the individual countries cannot be set independently of one another. For example, if the Federal Reserve raised the federal funds rate above the Japanese call-money rate, funds would flow quickly into the United States, putting upward pressure on the dollar and threatening the fixed rate unless the Bank of Japan likewise raised the call-money rate. In order to keep exchange rates from fluctuating, therefore, a common target for the "world" short-term interest rate must be chosen. Short-term interest rates with similar maturities and risk characteristics cannot diverge from one another. Hence, short-term interest rates are equated throughout the world, and a policy rule for the "world" short-term interest rate is needed. Analogously with the flexible exchange-rate case, it is assumed that world short-term interest rates rise if the world price level rises above the target. That is,

$$RS_i - RS_i^* = LP_w(+4) - LP_w + g(LP_w - LP_w^*) \tag{6.2}$$

if $RS_i > .01$ and $RS_i = .01$ otherwise. The log of the world price level LP_w is defined as a weighted average of the price levels in the G-7 countries, and LP_w^* is the target value.[3] Note that according to Equation (6.2), the interest rates are the same in all the countries. Several alternative sets of weights for computing world average price LP_w are possible. For the results reported here, I focus on the following set of weights: United States = .3, Canada = .05, France = .05, Germany = .2, Italy = .05, Japan = .3, United Kindgom = .05. The weights were chosen after some preliminary simulations. As explained below, the relatively high weight on Japan was chosen in order to reduce the size of the output fluctuations in Japan. Lower weights on Japan will increase fluctuations in Japan and tend to worsen the performance of the fixed exchange-rate system. The values for the short-term

---

[3]As in the flexible exchange-rate case, the exact value of g used in the simulations is 1.6.

interest rates are truncated in Equation (6.2) as in Equation (6.1) to rule out negative nominal interest rates.

As in the case of flexible exchange rates, the interest-rate rules in Equation (6.2) replace the inverted money-demand equations. However, because the interest rates in different countries are equated in Equation (6.2), the interest-rate differentials in the interest-rate parity equations are set to zero. Therefore, the expected change in the exchange rate is zero, which is implied by a credible fixed exchange-rate system.

Baseline and Targets for Price Levels and Real Output

The baseline for these experiments (that is, for the path for the world economy with no shocks to any equations) was chosen so that real output growth in all countries is the same rate as potential output growth. The measure of performance is based on the mean square distance of the economy from this baseline. However, the actual baseline position of the economy for these experiments does not appear to matter much. On the baseline, the actual price level P equals the target price level P^*, so that the interest rate RS equals RS^*. If there were no shocks, there would be no movements in the interest rate away from this baseline value.[4]

For the purposes of stochastic simulation, the model is solved using the extended path algorithm discussed in Chapter 1. For every period and for each stochastic shock, the model is solved dynamically with future disturbances set to their mean values.

The Stochastic Structure under Alternative Regimes

The preceding section described how the interest-rate equations of the model are changed for the stochastic simulation. Here we consider the covariance matrix and how it is modified. Recall that for stochastic simulation, it is necessary to estimate the variance-covariance matrix of the shocks to the structural equations. The exchange-rate equations are part of the structural equation system, along with interest rates, consumption, investment, wages, and so on. As described in Chapter 4, the covariance matrix was estimated from the residuals of the ninety-eight stochastic structural equations over the period from 1972:1 through 1986:4. The variance-covariance matrix was summarized in Tables 4-1 and 4-2. It is useful to look through those tables again with the following policy analysis in mind.

One of the most difficult questions concerning a possible change in regime from flexible exchange rates to fixed exchange rates concerns the behavior of the shocks to the interest-rate parity equations that link interest-

---

[4]The target price levels need not be fixed, and in the simulations they were assumed to rise at a constant inflation rate. If the target price levels grow at different rates in the different countries, then the target exchange rates in the "fixed" exchange-rate case should change at a preannounced deterministic rate of crawl. In this case, there would be an average differential between the short-term interest rate that would depend on the inflation-rate differentials.

rate differentials to expected changes in the exchange rate in different countries. Would the behavior of these shocks remain stable across exchange-rate regimes? The question is made more difficult by the fact that the reason for the shocks is not clear and by the fact that we have never had a full fixed-rate system in operation along with the high degree of capital mobility that we now find in the G-7 countries. If the shocks are due to time-varying risk premia, then a fully credible fixed-exchange rate regime should eliminate the shocks. If the exchange-rate system was not fully credible, then the risk premia would persist. Similarly, if the shocks are due to speculative bubbles, a credible fixed exchange-rate system should eliminate the shocks. Indeed, a frequently stated advantage of a fixed exchange-rate system is that speculative swings would be mitigated. However, it is not clear that the shocks are due to speculative bubbles.

In any case, the assumption made here is that the shocks disappear under fixed exchange rates. In other words, when I simulate the flexible exchange-rate case, I assume that the exchange-rate shocks have the standard deviations shown in Table 4-1, but when I simulate the fixed exchange-rate case, I assume that the exchange-rate shocks have zero variances. It is not clear what the relationship among interest rates would be if exchange rates were fixed permanently and if capital markets were unrestricted, but the best guess is that short-term interest rates would be equal in different countries. In any case, this is the assumption made here.

This assumption tends to disadvantage a flexible exchange-rate system in comparison with a fixed exchange-rate system. If one did not make this assumption and instead left the shocks in the interest-rate parity equations for the fixed exchange-rate simulations, the performance of the fixed exchange-rate system would deteriorate. Fluctuations in interest rates would be required to stabilize the exchange rates in the face of risk-premium shocks. The fluctuations in interest rates would lead to fluctuations in output and prices.

Drawing the Shocks

Shocks were drawn from the covariance matrix by using a normal random-number generator. In other words, the shocks are assumed to have a normal distribution with zero mean and the sample covariance matrix of the structural residuals. For the stochastic simulations, ten draws were made over the forty quarter periods, and the model was dynamically simulated with these draws. Each of the draws represented one realization of the stochastic process, and the performance of the macroeconomic variables were averaged across the draws. For each of the ten draws of forty quarters, both the fixed and the flexible exchange-rate systems were examined. In other words, the specific question being addressed is whether a flexible exchange-rate system or a fixed exchange-rate system would work better over a representative ten years, assuming that the shocks to the economy will be drawn from the same universe that shocked the world during the 1970s and early 1980s.

As described in Chapter 4, an alternative simulation procedure, also reported here, is to use the actual structural residuals directly in the simulations, rather than to first use these residuals to estimate the covariance matrix and then take draws from the covariance matrix. The direct approach has the advantage of not relying on normality—during the sample period, the shocks are not normal, and there were some large "outliers." Simulating with the actual shocks may therefore bring in important nonnormalities.

Macroeconomic Performance

The results for the comparison of the flexible exchange-rate system with the fixed exchange-rate system are shown in Table 6-1. As stated above, averages are taken over ten stochastic simulations for the forty-quarter period. There are three columns in the table. The first two columns list the standard deviation of the percentage deviation from the baseline of real output, the output deflator, the price level, the exchange rate, and so on. Also shown is the standard deviation of the percentage-point deviation of the short-term interest rate from the baseline. The third column shows the number of times out of the ten simulations in which the variance under the fixed-rate system is greater than the variance with the flexible-rate system.

The main results can be summarized as follows. The fluctuations in real output are much larger in the United States, France, Germany, Italy, and especially Japan when exchange rates are fixed, compared with when they are flexible. The fluctuations are also larger in the United Kingdom under fixed rates, though the differences are not so large as in the other countries. The standard deviation of output nearly doubles in Germany and Japan under fixed exchange rates in comparison with flexible exchange rates. The fluctuations in real output in Canada are slightly less under fixed rates than under flexible rates. But, as discussed below, there is a deterioration of price stability in Canada under fixed exchange rates. A change in the Canadian domestic policy rule under flexible exchange rates (for example, lowering the response coefficient g in the policy rule) could easily match the output stability of the fixed exchange rate case with more price stability. In this sense, the flexible exchange-rate system dominates.

The deterioration of performance under the fixed exchange-rate regime for Germany and Japan comes from all components of demand as shown in Table 6-1. In Germany, the standard deviation of investment around the baseline sharply rises under fixed exchange rates. The variance of imports also increases. The variance of exports decreases, although by a very small amount. Exports vary slightly less in Germany under fixed exchange rates, despite the general deterioration of economic performance. In Japan, the variance of consumption and investment also increases with fixed exchange rates, but the variance of imports is not affected much by the regime change.

Table 6-2 shows a variance decomposition of the components of real output that takes account of the relative size of each component. In the United States, Germany, and Italy, consumption, investment, and net exports all contribute to the lower output stability under the fixed exchange-rate

TABLE 6-1   Comparison of Fixed and Flexible Exchange Rates

The monetary policy rules are given in Equations (6.1) and (6.2). The world price level for fixed exchange rates has weights of .3 for the United States, .2 for Germany, .3 for Japan, and .05 for each of the other countries. (Results are averages over ten stochastic simulations. Each entry in the table shows the root mean squared percentage deviation of the variable from its baseline path.)

	Fixed	Flexible	Number of Simulations (with fixed greater than flexible)
Output			
U.S.	3.52	2.13	9
Canada	8.20	10.16	1
France	5.61	3.85	8
Germany	5.96	2.78	9
Italy	5.21	3.48	9
Japan	8.03	4.56	9
U.K.	2.71	2.23	7
Prices			
U.S.	2.82	1.33	10
Canada	9.09	4.93	10
France	8.33	3.79	10
Germany	4.24	1.80	9
Italy	9.43	3.57	9
Japan	9.09	3.99	9
U.K.	4.88	3.45	8
Interest Rates			
U.S.	0.021	0.019	5
Canada	0.021	0.063	0
France	0.021	0.058	0
Germany	0.021	0.022	4
Italy	0.021	0.042	1
Japan	0.021	0.044	0
U.K.	0.021	0.047	0
Exchange Rates			
Canada	0.00	11.09	0
France	0.00	19.61	0
Germany	0.00	23.27	0
Italy	0.00	14.78	0
Japan	0.00	19.72	0
U.K.	0.00	14.93	0
Real Net Exports (% of real output)			
U.S.	1.24	1.01	8
Canada	2.25	2.44	4
France	1.51	2.74	1
Germany	3.48	2.70	9
Italy	2.34	1.74	7
Japan	2.62	2.70	5
U.K.	1.59	1.77	2

TABLE 6-1   (Continued)

	Fixed	Flexible	Number of Simulations (with fixed greater than flexible)
Investment			
U.S.	15.62	9.99	10
Canada	23.14	32.14	1
France	7.07	8.69	3
Germany	22.83	13.05	9
Italy	24.10	16.76	9
Japan	21.96	13.29	9
U.K.	7.25	7.66	4
Exports			
U.S.	6.50	6.30	5
Canada	12.05	12.38	6
France	11.02	10.61	6
Germany	9.27	9.65	7
Italy	6.39	6.17	6
Japan	10.45	11.25	5
U.K.	5.74	5.47	5
Imports			
U.S.	8.37	5.52	9
Canada	10.23	13.52	1
France	7.51	4.98	8
Germany	10.76	5.18	9
Italy	10.15	6.69	9
Japan	7.87	7.77	5
U.K.	4.94	4.59	8
United States			
CD	5.39	3.73	10
CN	2.89	1.61	9
CS	2.24	1.36	8
Canada			
CD	12.03	16.02	1
CN	4.08	5.35	1
CS	4.99	6.05	4
France			
CD	10.55	8.50	8
CN	4.47	2.82	9
CS	5.60	2.85	8
Germany-C	6.53	2.48	9
Italy-C	3.80	2.05	9

TABLE 6-1   (Continued)

	Fixed	Flexible	Number of Simulations (with fixed greater than flexible)
Japan			
CD	16.73	9.28	9
CN	3.21	2.05	9
CS	6.43	3.61	9
United Kingdom			
CD	6.01	5.43	8
CN	2.21	1.95	6
CS	2.26	2.17	3
Wages			
U.S.	2.97	1.12	10
Canada	19.93	14.49	10
France	9.85	3.72	10
Germany	7.10	2.32	10
Italy	18.41	10.59	9
Japan	58.54	29.65	9
U.K.	6.74	5.96	8
Import Prices			
U.S.	9.76	10.11	3
Canada	12.56	13.08	5
France	19.61	18.10	6
Germany	13.12	14.48	4
Italy	9.32	12.09	1
Japan	12.19	14.64	2
U.K.	10.43	13.04	2
Real Interest Rates			
U.S.	0.025	0.023	6
Canada	0.058	0.076	1
France	0.028	0.060	1
Germany	0.038	0.032	8
Italy	0.079	0.066	6
Japan	0.076	0.058	7
U.K.	0.044	0.062	1

system. In France and Japan, net exports tend to add to the variance, but this is offset by declines in the variability of the other components or in changes in the covariances. Changes in the covariance terms have a big impact on the differences between output volatility across the two regimes.

The source of the large deterioration in the performance of the Japanese and the German economies is obviously related to monetary policy. But how? The intuitive explanation is that the fixed rate system does not permit the Bank of Japan and the Bundesbank to react enough to internal price developments. For example, if there is a rise in inflation in Japan, the

TABLE 6-1 *(Continued)*

	Fixed	Flexible
Nominal GNP		
U.S.	5.6	2.5
Canada	10.0	6.8
France	11.9	5.3
Germany	8.7	3.1
Italy	12.2	3.5
Japan	11.5	3.9
U.K.	5.3	3.5
Money		
U.S.	9.6	9.2
Canada	17.1	23.8
France	15.2	13.1
Germany	11.2	5.1
Italy	16.2	10.4
Japan	10.9	6.5
U.K.	11.7	24.5
Velocity		
U.S.	10.0	9.1
Canada	16.6	20.9
France	14.2	15.4
Germany	6.6	5.4
Italy	9.4	10.3
Japan	6.6	7.4
U.K.	12.2	26.4
Velocity/Money Correlation		
U.S.	−0.76	−0.95
Canada	−0.68	−0.97
France	−0.84	−0.96
Germany	−0.59	−0.79
Italy	−0.60	−0.93
Japan	−0.22	−0.82
U.K.	−0.83	−0.98

Bank of Japan cannot immediately tighten by raising interest rates as much as it could under a flexible exchange-rate system. According to the rules of the fixed exchange-rate system, the run-up in prices must first have an impact abroad and thereby raise world prices and foreign interest rates. This intuitive explanation is supported by the finding that the variance of short-term nominal interest rates is generally lower under the fixed exchange-rate regime (see Table 6-1).

Inflation performance is also better with the flexible exchange-rate system than with the fixed-rate system. Price volatility—as measured by the standard deviation of the output deflator around its target—is greater in all

TABLE 6-2 Variance Decompositions for Output in Fixed and Flexible Exchange-Rate Simulations

The simulations are the same as those in Table 6-1.

	Variances and Covariances of Components (weighted)						
Fixed	Y	C	I	NX	C, I	C, NX	I, NX
U.S.	12.4	3.3	7.3	1.7	13.5	−21.6	−5.1
Canada	67.3	9.7	25.0	5.7	8.6	1.5	1.2
France	31.5	13.0	2.5	2.2	−56.9	1.6	0.7
Germany	35.6	12.9	22.0	10.1	2.7	−73.0	−27.2
Italy	27.1	5.9	20.5	4.6	−60.7	−52.0	−16.1
Japan	64.5	10.0	29.5	6.8	28.4	−31.6	−16.0
U.K.	7.3	2.0	1.7	2.4	−26.6	−4.3	−1.1
Flexible	Y	C	I	NX	C, I	C, NX	I, NX
U.S.	4.5	1.1	3.0	1.1	2.9	−8.9	−2.4
Canada	103.3	15.9	48.1	5.8	−27.3	−28.0	−9.7
France	14.8	4.2	3.8	7.8	−14.5	−24.3	−9.0
Germany	7.7	1.9	7.2	7.5	5.4	−32.2	−11.1
Italy	12.1	1.7	9.9	2.8	−12.4	−22.7	−6.2
Japan	20.8	3.0	10.8	7.3	−6.9	−25.0	−11.4
U.K.	5.0	1.6	1.9	3.1	33.8	−8.7	−2.5

countries under fixed exchange rates (see Table 6-1). Japan and Germany have more than twice as much price volatility under the system that fixes their exchange rate with the dollar.

A reduction in wage variability under flexible rates apparently explains the reduction in price variability (see Table 6-1). Not surprisingly, import prices are usually more volatile when exchange rates are flexible. For all countries except France, import prices were on average more volatile under flexible rates. Hence, greater wage stability outweighs greater import price volatility and yields more stable prices under flexible exchange rates. Why are wages more stable under flexible rates? According to the contract-wage equations, smaller wage variability could be due to the smaller variability of demand.

Note in Table 6-1 that the variance of nominal income is reduced for all countries including Canada. The breakdown of nominal GNP variability between money variability and velocity variability and the correlation between money and velocity indicate that money is used to offset velocity shocks more freely under the flexible rate system. The negative correlation between velocity and money is larger in the flexible exchange-rate system than in the fixed exchange-rate system for all countries.

Not all aspects of the fixed exchange-rate system are inferior to the flexible exchange-rate system. Nominal interest rates are more volatile under the flexible exchange-rate system, presumably because the monetary authorities are able to react more to internal developments. Real interest rates are also more variable. And, of course, there is much more nominal exchange-rate volatility under the flexible exchange-rate system.

The difference in exchange-rate stability is clear in Table 6-1. It is very important to observe, however, that most of the increase in exchange-rate volatility under flexible rates is due to the fact that I am shocking the exchange rates more heavily; recall that the shock to interest-rate parity is assumed to have zero variance in the fixed exchange-rate regime. It is possible that a credible monetary policy rule would eliminate much of this exchange-rate volatility even under the flexible exchange-rate system. It should also be emphasized that at least part of the estimated variance of shocks to interest-rate parity was due to restrictions on capital mobility during the sample period. Most of these restrictions are now lifted. Taking all these factors into account indicates that a flexible exchange-rate system may generate considerably more exchange-rate stability than indicated in the tables.

Comparative Performance for One Draw of Shocks

A visual picture of the macroeconomic performance in four of the countries—the United States, Japan, Germany, and the United Kingdom— is given in Figure 6-1 for one of the ten stochastic draws. Real output and the price level are shown in the diagrams. The picture clearly shows that output and the price level are more stable in the flexible exchange-rate regime. With this set of shocks, output and prices hover close to target for a number of quarters in the simulations before they are sent off-course. A comparison of Japan with the other three countries during the latter half of the simulation gives some indication of why the flexible exchange-rate system works better. Look first at the United States and Japan. Real output deviates from potential in opposite directions in Japan and in the United States. The deviations of the price level from the target are also in opposite directions. There is an inflationary boom in Japan and a disinflationary slump in the United States. However, the fixed exchange-rate regime does not permit U.S. and Japanese monetary policy to deviate from each other— short-term interest rates must move in tandem. The Bank of Japan would have been better off with a tighter monetary policy than with fixed exchange rates, and the Federal Reserve would have been better off with an easier monetary policy. When the two central banks are able to run independent monetary policies—the case of flexible exchange rates, the boom in Japan is moderated as is the slump in the United States. The fixed-exchange-rate policy also leads to a larger slump in Germany and in the United Kingdom than could have been achieved with a flexible exchange-rate system.

Sensitivity Analysis—1: Simulation with Actual Residuals

Figure 6-2 shows a comparison of the same two regimes with the shocks drawn directly from the structural residuals estimated during the sample period of the multicountry model. The ten-year period for the estimated

(continued on p. 244)

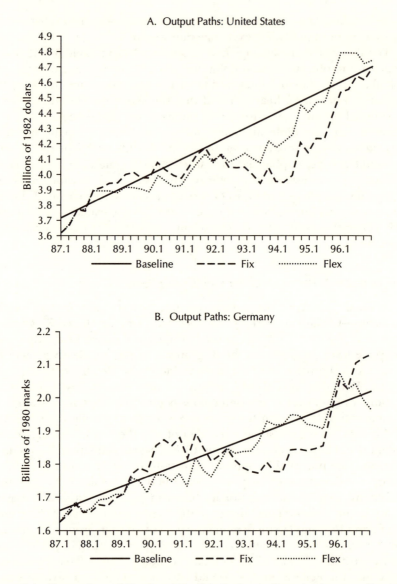

FIGURE 6-1   Comparison of Fixed and Flexible Exchange Rates (with one realization of the shocks)

C. Output Paths: Japan

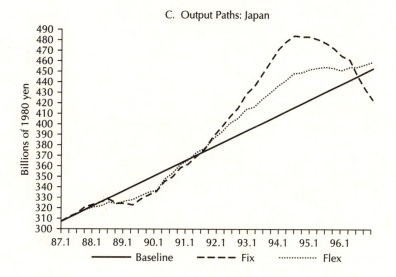

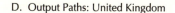

D. Output Paths: United Kingdom

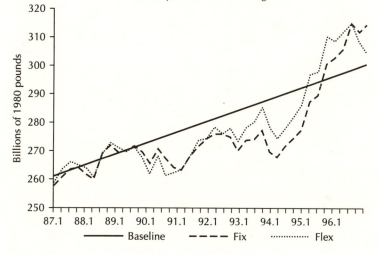

FIGURE 6-1   (Continued)

E. Price Paths: United States

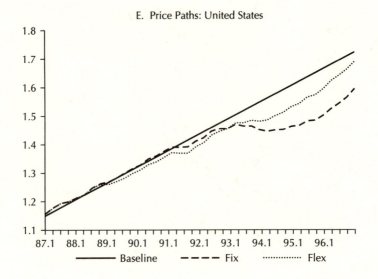

F. Price Paths: Germany

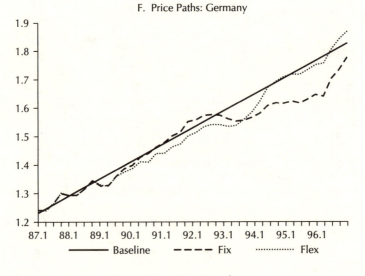

FIGURE 6-1 *(Continued)*

G. Price Paths: Japan

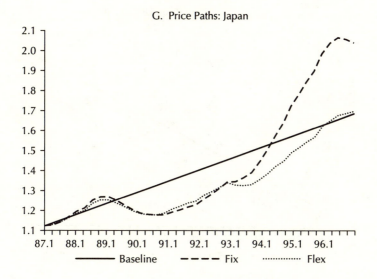

H. Price Paths: United Kingdom

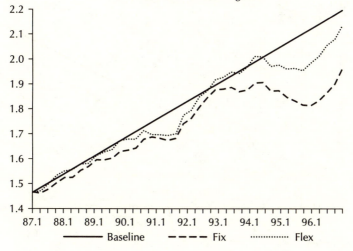

FIGURE 6-1   *(Continued)*

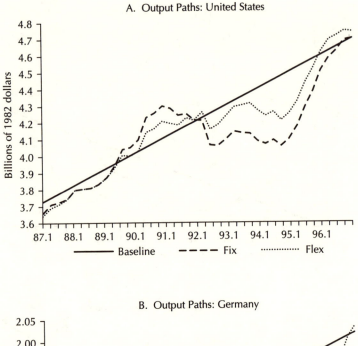

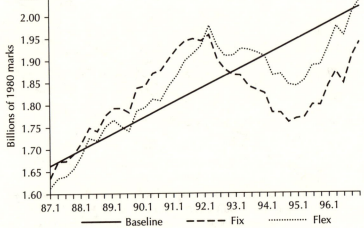

Figure 6-2   Comparison of Fixed and Flexible Exchange Rates (with actual shocks)

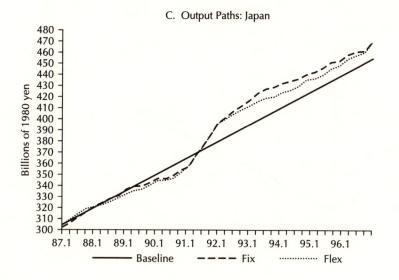

C. Output Paths: Japan

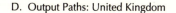

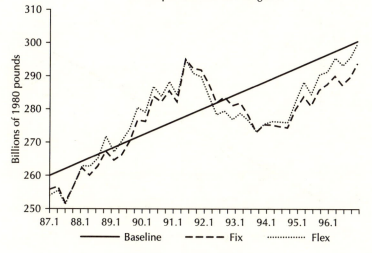

D. Output Paths: United Kingdom

FIGURE 6-2   *(Continued)*

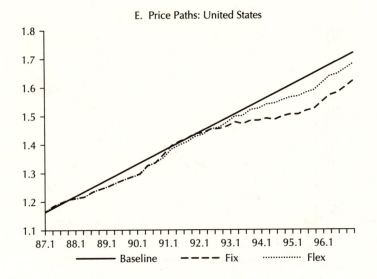

E. Price Paths: United States

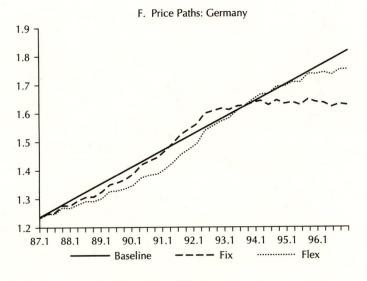

F. Price Paths: Germany

Figure 6-2   *(Continued)*

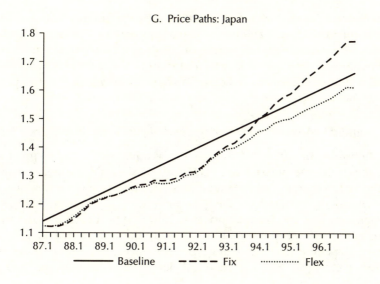

G. Price Paths: Japan

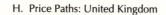

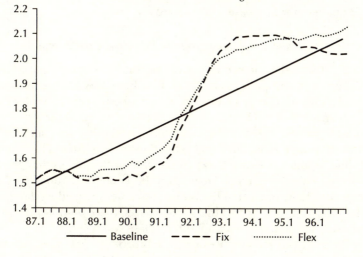

H. Price Paths: United Kingdom

FIGURE 6-2 *(Continued)*

shocks is 1975:1 to 1984:4. The results confirm the findings from the stochastic simulation. Output and price fluctuations are larger with fixed exchange rates. The intuitive explanation again appears to be related to monetary independence. Asymmetric booms and slumps in the different countries require different monetary policies. The fixed exchange-rate system prevents this from happening.

Sensitivity Analysis—2: Altering the Weights on the World Price Index

Consider the effects of shifting the weights on the world price index in the price rule under fixed exchange rates. Could the performance of the fixed exchange-rate system be improved by altering the weights? Table 6-3 shows the results for raising the weight on Japan from .3 to .5. The weights on U.S. and German prices are lowered by .1 each in order to keep the sum of the weights equal to 1. Raising the weight on Japanese prices makes Japanese macroeconomic performance significantly better under fixed exchange rates. The standard deviation of both output and price fluctuations is reduced.

However, raising the weight on Japan leads to less price stability in some of the other countries, and the flexible exchange rate continues to dominate by a large margin. The basic conclusions are not changed.

Sensitivity Analysis—3: Changing the Response Coefficients

Finally, I consider the robustness of the results to changing the response coefficient g in the policy rule. Table 6-4 shows the macroeconomic performance with simulations based on the actual estimated residuals but with $g = 1.0$ and $g = 2.5$. (Recall that the results thus far show $g = 1.6$.) For both these values of g, there appears to be generally more stability under flexible exchange rates than under fixed exchange rates. The variance of both output and prices are lower in the case of flexible exchange rates in the United States, Germany, Japan, and the United Kingdom. In Canada, France, and Italy, price stability is also lower under fixed exchange rates, but for these values of g and this set of shocks, there is an improvement in output stability, so there is a trade-off in these countries.

In the next two sections I examine a broader policy question: can the central banks improve economic performance by (1) coordinating policy with other countries or (2) choosing a policy rule other than the price rule considered thus far? In light of the previous results, in answering this question I will maintain the flexible exchange-rate regime.

6.2   Coordination in the Design of Policy Rules?

When one thinks of macroeconomic policy coordination, one usually thinks of the annual Economic Summit involving the heads of government of the G-7 countries or the more frequent meetings of the G-7 finance ministers and central bank governors. The coordination, or negotiation, in these

TABLE 6-3   Sensitivity Analysis: Changing the Weights for the World Price Level in the Fixed-versus-Flexible Exchange-Rates Comparison

The first and third columns correspond to Table 6-1. The second column lowers the weight for the United States and Germany by .1 and raises the weight for Japan by .2. (Results are averages over ten stochastic simulations. Each entry in the table shows the root mean squared percentage deviation of the variable from its baseline path.)

	Fixed (1)	Fixed (2)	Flexible
Output			
U.S.	3.52	3.33	2.13
Canada	8.20	8.08	10.16
France	5.61	5.34	3.85
Germany	5.96	5.73	2.78
Italy	5.21	5.73	3.48
Japan	8.03	5.20	4.56
U.K.	2.71	2.71	2.23
Prices			
U.S.	2.82	2.80	1.33
Canada	9.09	8.82	4.93
France	8.33	8.74	3.79
Germany	4.24	4.55	1.80
Italy	9.43	12.02	3.57
Japan	9.09	5.42	3.99
U.K.	4.88	5.14	3.45
Interest Rates			
U.S.	0.021	0.026	0.019
Canada	0.021	0.026	0.063
France	0.021	0.026	0.058
Germany	0.021	0.026	0.022
Italy	0.021	0.026	0.042
Japan	0.021	0.026	0.044
U.K.	0.021	0.026	0.047
Exchange Rates			
Canada	0.00	0.00	11.09
France	0.00	0.00	19.61
Germany	0.00	0.00	23.27
Italy	0.00	0.00	14.78
Japan	0.00	0.00	19.72
U.K.	0.00	0.00	14.93
Real Net Exports (% of real GNP)			
U.S.	1.24	1.15	1.01
Canada	2.25	2.20	2.44
France	1.51	1.46	2.74
Germany	3.48	3.21	2.70
Italy	2.34	2.52	1.74
Japan	2.62	2.16	2.70
U.K.	1.59	1.52	1.77

TABLE 6-4 Sensitivity Analysis: Changing the Response Coefficients in the Fixed-versus-Flexible Exchange-Rates Comparison

The response coefficient g in the policy rules is shown at the top of each column. Results are from single stochastic simulations using the actual residuals from 1975:1 to 1984:4. (Each entry in the table shows the root mean squared percentage deviation of the variable from its baseline path.)

	g = 1.0		g = 2.5	
	Fixed	*Flexible*	*Fixed*	*Flexible*
Output				
U.S.	4.41	2.37	3.89	2.01
Canada	4.95	7.49	5.62	8.57
France	4.43	4.94	4.42	5.00
Germany	5.34	3.32	5.32	3.26
Italy	5.89	7.04	6.59	7.65
Japan	4.78	3.41	4.71	3.81
U.K.	3.14	2.75	3.07	3.23
Prices				
U.S.	3.37	1.43	3.20	1.09
Canada	6.28	3.67	5.53	2.80
France	8.10	5.75	7.73	4.32
Germany	3.74	2.16	3.90	1.58
Italy	15.07	8.04	15.42	5.19
Japan	5.08	3.40	2.97	2.24
U.K.	6.26	4.98	6.31	3.96
Interest Rates				
U.S.	0.018	0.014	0.023	0.024
Canada	0.018	0.029	0.023	0.046
France	0.018	0.044	0.023	0.052
Germany	0.018	0.020	0.023	0.029
Italy	0.018	0.081	0.023	0.088
Japan	0.018	0.020	0.023	0.028
U.K.	0.018	0.040	0.023	0.079
Exchange Rates				
Canada	0.00	6.61	0.00	6.96
France	0.00	11.21	0.00	10.51
Germany	0.00	12.98	0.00	12.46
Italy	0.00	9.44	0.00	8.91
Japan	0.00	11.84	0.00	11.42
U.K.	0.00	13.40	0.00	14.17
Real Net Exports (of real GNP)				
U.S.	1.68	1.33	1.54	1.51
Canada	1.95	1.83	2.04	2.07
France	1.76	1.91	1.78	1.99
Germany	2.20	1.46	2.08	1.71
Italy	3.73	1.98	3.92	2.62
Japan	1.73	1.46	1.52	1.42
U.K.	1.60	1.62	1.63	1.67

meetings is most frequently about the settings of the instruments of policy—for example, whether the United States should reduce its budget deficit, whether the Bank of Japan should ease, whether the Bundesbank should tighten, and so on. Hence, the coordination is more about the implementation or operation of policies rather than about the design of policies as I have defined the terms in this book. Proposals to change the exchange rate system arise in international discussion from time to time and could be thought of as international policy coordination. That was the subject of the previous section.

In this section I consider a broader set of international coordination issues that are essentially questions of policy design. The questions take as given the result of the preceding section that the exchange-rate system among the major industrial countries must retain some degree of flexibility. Given a flexible exchange-rate system, they ask whether there should be coordination or negotiation in designing domestic monetary policy rules. For example, is it necessary or helpful for the United States and Japan to come to some agreement about the choice of the response coefficient g in their respective Equation (6.1), their policy rule? If so, how should they come to agreement? Should there be a grand multilateral negotiation—like a trade negotiation—where the United States asks Japan and Europe to use, for example, a lower g, by offering to use a lower g itself? Asking whether coordination or negotiation is needed or helpful here is equivalent to asking the following type of specific question: "Are there economic gains to jointly setting the response coefficients of monetary policy rules—whether price rules such as those of Equation (6.1), or nominal income rules, or something else?" This is the specific design question I take up in this section.[5]

Table 6-5 shows the results of stochastic simulations of the multicountry model that are aimed at the question. It shows the effect on price and output stability in each country when the policy rule in another country is changed. I focus on policy rules in Table 6-5 that are nominal-income rules, rather than price rules. The interest rate is increased or decreased according to whether nominal income is above or below a target. The algebra of a nominal-income rule is as follows:

$$RS_i - RS_i^* = LP_i(+4) - LP_i + g(LP_i - LP_i^*) + g(LY_i - LY_i^*) \qquad (6.3)$$

if $RS_i > .01$ and $RS_i = .01$ otherwise. The last term in Equation (6.1) is the log of real income less the log of target real income. The sum of the last two terms is equal to the deviations of nominal income from a target, and this is why Equation (6.3) is called a nominal-income rule. Equation (6.3) makes it clear that a nominal-income rule differs from a price rule in that

[5]The closest that practical discussions have come to this type of design issue of which I am aware is the proposal in the late 1980s to use "conjunctural" indicators to guide policy. Conjunctural indicators are simply economic data from each country around which policymakers at the OECD or the G-7 agree to center their discussions. They are usually tabulated and presented by the staff of the OECD or of the IMF.

TABLE 6-5 Effect on Economic Performance Abroad of Alternative Response Coefficients under Flexible Exchange Rates

The monetary policy rule is shown in Equation (6.3). The value of g is .05 in France and in the United Kingdom and 1.5 in the other countries, unless otherwise indicated. (Results are averages over ten stochastic simulations. Each entry in the table shows the root mean squared percentage deviation of the variable from its baseline path.)

	U.S. Value of g	
	1.5	2.5
Output		
U.S.	1.65	1.52
Canada	5.80	5.79
France	3.85	3.83
Germany	1.58	1.57
Italy	2.72	2.71
Japan	3.30	3.33
U.K.	2.15	2.14
Prices		
U.S.	1.38	1.25
Canada	7.02	7.01
France	6.56	6.54
Germany	1.73	1.73
Italy	5.11	5.11
Japan	5.36	5.40
U.K.	4.41	4.39

	Japan Value of g	
	1.5	1.8
Output		
U.S.	1.65	1.65
Canada	5.80	5.80
France	3.85	3.90
Germany	1.58	1.58
Italy	2.72	2.72
Japan	3.30	3.12
U.K.	2.15	2.16
Prices		
U.S.	1.38	1.38
Canada	7.02	7.03
France	6.56	6.58
Germany	1.73	1.74
Italy	5.11	5.12
Japan	5.36	4.89
U.K.	4.41	4.41

TABLE 6-5   *(Continued)*

	German Value of g	
	0.5	*1.5*
Output		
U.S.	1.65	1.65
Canada	5.82	5.80
France	3.92	3.85
Germany	2.11	1.58
Italy	2.73	2.72
Japan	3.25	3.30
U.K.	2.18	2.15
Prices		
U.S.	1.39	1.38
Canada	7.03	7.02
France	6.62	6.56
Germany	2.34	1.73
Italy	5.10	5.11
Japan	5.29	5.36
U.K.	4.42	4.41

real output appears in the reaction function along with the price level and with the same coefficient *g* as the price level.

The nominal-income rules for the United States, Germany, and Japan in Table 6-5 are each changed, while the reaction coefficients in the other countries remain the same. For example, in the top panel of Table 6-5, the United States changes its reaction coefficient from 1.5 to 2.5, while there is no change in the other countries. In the middle panel of Table 6-5, Japan changes its reaction coefficient from 1.5 to 1.8, while the other countries remain the same. In the bottom panel, Germany changes its reaction coefficient from .5 to 1.5, and the other countries remain the same. The table, therefore, shows what happens to the other countries when either the United States, Japan, or Germany change their policy rules. What is most striking about Table 6-5 is that a change in the policy rule within these ranges has a very small impact abroad.[6] For example, changing the U.S. policy rule changes the standard deviation of real output and the price level in the United States by many multiples of the change in all the other countries. Raising the Japanese reaction coefficient from 1.5 to 1.8 reduces both output and price variability in Japan but has virtually no effect on either the United States, Germany, or the other countries. The same is true for a change in the German policy rule.

---

[6]Recall that this same type of result was found in the stylized two-country model of Chapter 1. Using a less structural modeling approach I found stronger cross-country effects in earlier work (see Taylor [1985]).

The simulation results suggest that there is not much need to coordinate or negotiate on the design of monetary policy rules among countries. Of course, to reduce uncertainty, it is important for each central bank to communicate with other central banks about what type of policy system is guiding the setting of the policy instruments.

This is a surprising result. Recalling the deterministic simulations of the instruments of monetary policy in Chapter 5 might help understand it. Those simulations showed that an increase in the money supply in one country has a much larger effect on real output and prices at home than abroad. The effects abroad are positive, rather than negative as in the Mundell-Fleming models, but in almost all cases they are very small.

The evidence presented here pertains to nominal GNP rules only. Similar simulations (not reported here) show similar results when the reaction coefficients of price rules are varied, but the effect of more drastic changes in the rule has yet to be examined. And it should be emphasized that the result applies to monetary rules only. The deterministic simulations of Chapter 5 indicate that changes in fiscal policy rules—for example, changing the automatic stabilizers—would be likely to have larger effects abroad.

6.3   Looking for a Better Monetary Policy Rule

Aside from the surprising result on coordination, the simulation results discussed above indicate that, for flexible exchange-rate systems, nominal-income rules that weigh output deviations as well as price deviations in the central banks' reaction function frequently perform better than price rules. Compare the output and price variances in Table 6-1 on price rules with Table 6-5 on nominal-income rules. For Germany and the United States, for example, output and price variability are lower when these countries use nominal-income rules rather than price rules. The improvement in real output stability is especially large. Although an improvement for both output and prices is not observed for Japan, this finding suggests that by examining a wider array of policy reaction functions we could find improvements in macroeconomic stability.

In principle, the objective is to search for a monetary policy rule, among a very large class, that maximizes macroeconomic performance along a number of dimensions by using an appropriate social utility function, perhaps by solving a dynamic stochastic optimal control problem.[7] Computationally, such a general optimization approach is not yet possible with a nonlinear rational expectations model of the size used in this research. It is still too expensive to do extensive stochastic simulations. For this reason, I take a simpler approach. The simpler approach also offers the advantage of being somewhat easier to interpret. Future research might take these results as a starting point in a more formal search for optimal policy rules.

---

[7]This is the approach used in Taylor (1979), where formal dynamic optimization methods were employed to find optimal rules for monetary policy in very simple linear models.

The search for better policy rules in the G-7 countries is made much simpler if we take the findings of the preceding two sections as given: (1) a flexible exchange-rate system works better than a fixed exchange-rate system, and (2) within a flexible exchange-rate regime, the choice of the coefficients of a monetary policy rule in one country has little effect on economic performance in other countries. Thus, one can simply search across policy rules in each country individually and not simultaneously consider reaction functions in other countries.

As a further simplification, rather than optimize across a very general class of policies, I examine a limited, but widely discussed, class of policy rules in which only price and real output appear in the interest-rate reaction function for each central bank. However, the weights on output and the price level need not be the same. These policy rules take the form

$$RS_i - RS_i^* = LP_i(+4) - LP_i + g_1(LP_i - LP_i^*) + g_2(LY_i - LY_i^*) \quad (6.4)$$

if $RS_i > .01$ and $RS_i = .01$ otherwise. This is a more general class of rules than either price rules, where all the weight is on the price level ($g_2 = 0$), or nominal GNP rules where the weight is the same for both price and output ($g_1 = g_2$).

A summary of results are presented in Table 6-6 and Table 6-7. I focus on the stability of real output and the price level. The results show that it is possible to improve on either the price rule or the nominal-income rule in most of the countries. The more general rule places relatively less weight on real output than the nominal-income rule but more weight than a pure-price rule. Compared to the nominal-income rule, a more general rule seems to work better in most countries. For these calculations, simulations were run using ten sets of shocks from a random-number generator.

A general conclusion from these results is that placing some weight on real output in the interest rate reaction function is likely to be better than a pure price rule. A more general rule that places less weight on real output than a nominal-output rule stabilizes the price level better than a nominal-income rule. Finally, all of these rules seem to result in exchange-rate fluctuations that are not excessive, even though the exchange-rate equations are being shocked by time-varying risk premia. Although these policies focus the reaction functions on domestic indicators, they have the potential of achieving a surprising amount of exchange-rate stability.

6.4 Conclusions

The main objective of this chapter has been to apply the new rational expectations empirical approach to the policy problem of designing monetary policy rules or systems. The approach is novel in its use of empirical measures of the shocks and thereby, the probability distribution of shocks to the economic relations. In addition, the quarterly empirical model incorporates a highly mobile world capital market, rational expectations of the

TABLE 6-6 Effect on Economic Performance of Alternative Rules

The response coefficients on prices and output under each of the rules are as follows: for the price rule, (1.5, 0.0) for all countries except France and the United Kingdom, where they are (0.5, 0.0); for the nominal-income rule, (1.5, 1.5) for all countries except France and the United Kingdom, where they are (0.5, 0.5); for the general rule, (2.0, 0.8) for all countries except the United States, where they are (2.5, 0.8). Results are averages over ten stochastic simulations. (Each entry in the table shows the root mean squared percentage deviation of the variable from its baseline path.)

	Price Rule	Nominal-Income Rule	General Rule
Output			
U.S.	2.23	1.65	1.90
Canada	9.21	5.80	7.67
France	4.76	3.85	3.22
Germany	2.74	1.58	1.98
Italy	3.96	2.72	3.56
Japan	4.06	3.30	3.60
U.K.	2.45	2.15	2.19
Prices			
U.S.	1.39	1.38	1.16
Canada	5.10	7.02	5.66
France	7.54	6.56	3.20
Germany	1.74	1.73	1.59
Italy	4.30	5.11	4.39
Japan	3.76	5.36	3.87
U.K.	4.57	4.41	3.08
Interest Rates			
U.S.	0.019	0.029	0.026
Canada	0.060	0.052	0.055
France	0.045	0.053	0.063
Germany	0.020	0.029	0.026
Italy	0.043	0.041	0.048
Japan	0.041	0.043	0.043
U.K.	0.029	0.033	0.047
Exchange Rates			
Canada	11.27	9.42	10.19
France	21.00	20.60	20.07
Germany	22.94	22.99	22.78
Italy	14.33	14.40	14.10
Japan	19.89	19.64	19.64
U.K.	15.56	15.41	14.62
Real Net Exports (% of real GNP)			
U.S.	1.04	1.02	1.07
Canada	2.41	2.53	2.38
France	2.00	2.15	2.71
Germany	2.49	2.47	2.45
Italy	1.75	1.45	1.67
Japan	2.36	2.26	2.24
U.K.	1.61	1.54	1.61

TABLE 6-6 *(Continued)*

	Price Rule	Nominal-Income Rule	General Rule
Investment			
U.S.	10.25	8.05	9.61
Canada	29.61	15.58	23.54
France	6.50	5.99	8.24
Germany	12.81	10.74	11.69
Italy	18.77	12.67	17.25
Japan	13.07	11.19	12.10
U.K.	6.57	6.47	6.85
Exports			
U.S.	6.26	5.99	5.90
Canada	11.35	10.97	10.76
France	10.99	9.96	9.56
Germany	8.50	7.94	7.74
Italy	6.01	5.30	5.40
Japan	10.06	9.40	9.15
U.K.	5.52	4.73	4.72
Imports			
U.S.	5.57	5.01	5.51
Canada	12.13	7.90	10.21
France	5.14	3.88	4.56
Germany	5.06	3.25	3.88
Italy	7.81	5.89	7.19
Japan	7.21	7.32	7.37
U.K.	4.39	4.31	4.54
United States			
CD	3.91	3.49	3.65
CN	1.71	1.42	1.57
CS	1.40	1.18	1.24
Canada			
CD	14.58	8.40	11.95
CN	4.86	2.79	4.00
CS	5.19	3.77	4.55
France			
CD	7.80	5.90	7.41
CN	3.76	3.07	2.44
CS	4.42	3.51	2.64
Germany-C	2.58	1.79	2.14
Italy-C	2.53	1.87	2.31
Japan			
CD	8.39	7.11	7.62
CN	1.93	1.86	1.85
CS	3.26	2.99	3.03
United Kingdom			
CD	5.80	5.59	5.64
CN	1.65	1.44	1.90
CS	2.21	2.09	2.15

TABLE 6-6   (Continued)

	Price Rule	Nominal-Income Rule	General Rule
Prices			
U.S.	1.39	1.38	1.16
Canada	5.10	7.02	5.66
France	7.54	6.56	3.20
Germany	1.74	1.73	1.59
Italy	4.30	5.11	4.39
Japan	3.76	5.36	3.87
U.K.	4.57	4.41	3.08
Wages			
U.S.	1.19	1.23	1.01
Canada	14.29	15.46	14.51
France	7.80	6.87	3.55
Germany	2.32	2.09	2.00
Italy	11.65	12.64	12.10
Japan	26.21	26.07	25.46
U.K.	6.58	6.61	6.06
Import Prices			
U.S.	9.81	9.70	9.54
Canada	12.57	11.87	12.12
France	20.99	19.75	16.23
Germany	12.45	12.43	12.48
Italy	9.88	9.91	10.15
Japan	13.23	13.17	13.21
U.K.	13.00	12.69	11.41
Real Interest Rates			
U.S.	0.023	0.028	0.028
Canada	0.075	0.055	0.066
France	0.039	0.045	0.063
Germany	0.031	0.033	0.033
Italy	0.068	0.057	0.070
Japan	0.054	0.048	0.053
U.K.	0.037	0.037	0.062

future, and institutional differences between wage determination in different countries.

Of the several design issues considered, one is particularly striking: the question of fixed-versus-flexible exchange-rate systems. The results indicate that a flexible exchange-rate system works better than a fixed exchange-rate system. Not all countries and not all economic time series perform worse under the fixed exchange-rate system, but, in the vast majority of cases, all the G-7 countries except Canada have significantly worse macroeconomic performance under a fixed exchange-rate system. A policy-evaluation result

Table 6-6 (Continued)

	Price Rule	Nominal-Income Rule	General Rule
Nominal Income			
U.S.	2.4	2.1	1.9
Canada	6.1	3.1	3.6
France	9.8	8.1	4.1
Germany	3.0	1.9	2.0
Italy	3.6	3.3	2.6
Japan	3.1	4.1	2.5
U.K.	4.9	4.5	2.8
Money			
U.S.	9.4	9.6	9.8
Canada	19.3	14.6	17.2
France	14.0	13.5	13.8
Germany	4.8	4.8	5.0
Italy	10.5	9.2	10.6
Japan	6.1	5.9	6.3
U.K.	10.9	11.4	20.5
Velocity			
U.S.	9.3	10.2	10.0
Canada	16.9	16.3	17.0
France	14.8	15.7	15.7
Germany	4.9	5.9	5.7
Italy	10.1	9.8	10.5
Japan	6.9	7.6	7.2
U.K.	14.4	14.8	22.2
Velocity/Money Correlation			
U.S.	−0.95	−0.97	−0.97
Canada	−0.95	−0.97	−0.97
France	−0.91	−0.92	−0.98
Germany	−0.77	−0.94	−0.92
Italy	−0.94	−0.92	−0.96
Japan	−0.86	−0.80	−0.91
U.K.	−0.92	−0.95	−0.99

of this kind could not be obtained from purely theoretical considerations. It depends on the empirical nature of the economic relations and on the size and correlation of the shocks to these relations.

Of course, neither these three problems nor the model used to address them exhaust the possible applications of the approach. I do not view the analysis presented here as the last word. Improvements in the models, new and better data, or refinement of the questions may indeed lead to different results in future research. At the least the above analysis provides a useful benchmark to assess the impact of the different monetary policy systems.

TABLE 6-7   Variance Decompositions for Output for Different Rules

Same simulations as Table 6-6. Results are averages over ten stochastic simulations.

				Variances and Covariances of Components (weighted)			
Price Rule	Y	C	I	NX	C, I	C, NX	I, NX
U.S.	5.0	1.2	3.1	1.1	3.3	−9.6	−2.5
Canada	84.9	12.6	40.9	5.8	−24.8	−25.5	−9.8
France	22.6	7.7	2.1	4.0	−73.3	−4.8	−1.6
Germany	7.5	2.0	6.9	6.3	−13.2	−29.8	−11.1
Italy	15.7	2.6	12.4	2.6	−24.8	−27.7	−8.2
Japan	16.5	2.5	10.4	5.7	−13.1	−24.9	−11.0
U.K.	6.0	1.5	1.4	2.5	−26.7	−3.1	−0.9
Nominal-Income Rule	Y	C	I	NX	C, I	C, NX	I, NX
U.S.	2.7	0.9	1.9	1.0	2.0	−7.6	−2.0
Canada	33.6	4.7	11.3	7.2	17.8	−6.2	−2.4
France	14.9	4.6	1.8	4.7	−61.4	−9.5	−3.2
Germany	2.5	1.0	4.9	6.3	−12.1	−29.9	−11.1
Italy	7.4	1.4	5.7	1.9	−10.7	−14.3	−4.3
Japan	10.9	2.0	7.7	5.2	−11.8	−24.5	−10.8
U.K.	4.6	1.3	1.3	2.3	−3.9	−3.8	−1.1
General Rule	Y	C	I	NX	C, I	C, NX	I, NX
U.S.	1.9	1.0	2.8	1.2	3.6	−10.2	−2.7
Canada	7.7	8.8	25.8	6.0	−6.7	−15.7	−6.0
France	3.2	3.2	3.4	7.5	−1.9	−25.0	−8.3
Germany	2.0	1.4	5.8	6.1	−15.1	−30.6	−11.4
Italy	3.6	2.1	10.5	2.4	−22.0	−25.1	−7.4
Japan	3.6	2.1	9.0	5.1	−15.4	−24.2	−10.7
U.K.	2.2	1.6	1.5	2.3	33.8	−5.3	−1.5

Reference Notes

The use of simulation to evaluate policy rules has a long history in macro-economics, going back at least to simulations by A. W. Phillips (1954) of proportional, integral, and derivative policy rules adopted from the engineering literature. The work focused on dynamic Keynesian models as did the later work by Cooper and Fischer (1974), which performed stochastic simulations on estimated econometric models without rational expectations. Poole (1970) also considered stochastic Keynesian models, though his work focused more on how to cushion the static impact of shocks rather than on the dynamics or propagation effects. Phelps and Taylor (1977) and Fischer (1977) were the first to consider the evaluation of policy rules in theoretical stochastic rational expectations models, where policy is effective; Taylor (1979) considered the optimal policy rule in an estimated econometric model. This model was simple enough that the stochastic behavior of the endogenous variables could be derived analytically.

In the early 1990s there has been an increased interest in the use of stochastic simulations to evaluate policy rules. Bryant et al. (1989) edited a conference volume in which three papers reported results on the evaluation of policy using estimated multicountry models with rational expectations: Taylor (1989b), McKibbin and Sachs (1989), and Frenkel, Goldstein, and Masson (1989). These papers differ in their assessments of different exchange rate regimes. A follow-up Brookings conference focused entirely on the evaluation of policy rules using stochastic simulations of econometric models, although not all were rational expectations models. The results of this conference are reported in Bryant et al. (1992). The debate over fixed-versus-flexible exchange rates is an old one going back at least to Milton Friedman's (1948) proposals. McKinnon (1988) has recently argued in favor of fixed exchange rates, presenting very specific policy rules under which a fixed exchange-rate system would operate.

Although the reduced form of the multicountry model cannot be solved analytically to illustrate the way the coefficients change with change in the policy rules á la the Lucas critique, some reduced-form relationships can be estimated from the data generated by the stochastic simulations. A comparison of such reduced form equations under two regimes—fixed exchange rate and flexible exchange rates as in Section 6.1—was reported in Taylor (1989a). The coefficients of reduced-form consumption functions, Phillips curves, investment functions, and several vector autoregressions changed, as predicted by the Lucas critique, but perhaps less than one might have expected. Similar comparisons with different regime changes would be a good subject for future research.

7

Transitions to New Policy Systems

Most modern macroeconomic research on policy rules has focused on their optimal design. The preceding chapter is an example of this research and illustrates the tremendous progress and potential of empirical macroeconomics in policy analysis. However, questions about making a transition from one policy rule to a new one have been given relatively little attention. It is as if policy systems, after being proposed and analyzed by researchers, are put on the shelf waiting for policymakers to come and help themselves when the time is ripe, with few guidelines on how to handle the transition from one system to the next. Since the ripe time usually turns out to be an unanticipated crisis, such guidelines can rarely be developed on the spot.

This situation is not unique to macroeconomics. In general, economists have been better at determining what type of system works best than at determining how to make a transition to that system. In public finance, for example, there are many good arguments in support of a consumption tax, but there is little research on the important problem of how one makes the transition from an income tax to a consumption tax. In international-trade theory, not much is known about the appropriate speed at which one should move to free trade. And, perhaps most important of all, economists have shown the benefits of a market economy over a centrally planned economy but have little to go on when giving advice about the transition from one system to another.

In this chapter, I look at the problems of transition to new policy rules. Because there has been relatively little research in this area and because the problems are more difficult, the framework is less formal than for the design of policy rules. Nevertheless, I believe that quantitative economic analysis has something to say.

7.1   Analysis of Policy Transitions

Perhaps the most dramatic change in macroeconomic policy systems involves changes in exchange-rate regimes, such as the creation of the Bretton Woods system, its demise, or its partial re-creation in the European Monetary System. But there are many other more elementary examples, and the nature of transitions to new policies can be best illustrated with these examples. Most are related to the policy rules in Chapter 6.

Examples of Transitions

Suppose that it becomes clear that a policy in operation is not performing well and that a new policy system would work better. The most elementary example—though not the easiest—is when it is recognized that the target in the policy rule in Equation (6.1), (6.2), or (6.3) is wrong (see Chapter 6). Rather than aim for a target price level P^* that grows at 10 percent per year, it is recognized that a target price level growing close to 0 percent per year would be better for long-run economic performance. In this example, only the "intercept" term in the policy rule must be changed. This transition problem is, of course, none other than the problem of disinflation, and there are many examples of more sizeable changes in the targets. This macroeconomic transition from high inflation to low inflation has been part of the problem of overall transition to market economies in the formerly centrally planned economies in Eastern Europe and in the former Soviet Union.

Another example involves changes in the response coefficients of the policy rule. The optimal size of these response coefficients was the subject of the last part of Chapter 6. Suppose, for example, that a nominal-income target had been in operation, but a number of new studies show that a monetary rule with a smaller response coefficient on real output than on the price level would be better than a nominal-income rule. That is, it is recognized that g_2, the coefficient on real output in Equation (6.3), should be less than g_1, the coefficient on the price level, whereas previously they had been equal.

Similar examples can be given for fiscal policy rules. Analogous to a change in the intercept in the monetary policy rule would be a recognition that the budget deficit should be balanced at full employment. Analogous to a change in the response coefficient would be a recognition that an increase in the response of the automatic stabilizers to economic conditions would be desirable. The latter might entail a change in the unemployment compensation system that determines at what unemployment rate long-term unemployment benefits are automatically paid.

Why do we need any special treatment of these transitions? If a thorough design analysis—based on the work of a number of different analysts using different approaches—suggests that particular targets and response coefficients in a policy rule are appropriate, would it not be best to simply start doing what the rule says, immediately? Probably not, and this, for two reasons.

Learning

First, the research that underlies the design of policy rules assumes that expectations are rational. As I have argued, this makes sense when a policy is in operation for a long time. People will have adjusted their behavior to the policy in place, and expectations of policy and other variables are most likely to be unbiased. However, in the period immediately after a new policy rule has been put in place, people are unlikely to either know about or understand the new policy or to believe that policymakers are serious about maintaining it for long. Simply assuming that, during this transition period, people have rational expectations and know the policy rule is probably stretching things. Instead, people may base their expectations partly on past policy in a Bayesian way, or they may try to anticipate the credibility of the new policy by carefully studying the personalities of the policymakers (or of their economic advisers) and their past records, or by trying to assess whether the policy will work as advertised.

Because expectations only gradually converge during this transition period, the impact of the policy rule on the economy may be quite different from what is projected by an analysis that assumes rational expectations.[1] In most cases, uncertainty and bias in expectation formation will make the new policy work less well during a transition. In these cases, efforts to make the new policy credible will reduce the costs associated with a transition, and this is the great value of credibility to policymakers.

This problem of learning about a new policy during a transition was worked out in the case of a change in the price level, or inflation, target in a very simple model in Taylor (1975). It is optimal to make the new policy as credible as possible if the initial inflation rate is above the long-run inflation rate, as in the disinflation examples given above. However, in the case where the inflation rate is initially lower than is optimal, a welfare function that includes both inflation and unemployment can be increased by only gradually informing the public about the plans to move to a new policy. In this unusual case, the precise amount of information to release each period can be computed by using optimal control theory.

Rigidities

A second reason for worrying about transitions is that there are natural rigidities in the economy that prevent people from changing their behavior instantly. People may have committed themselves to projects, plans, or contracts under the assumption that the old policy was in place. Moreover,

---

[1] That was the main point of Taylor (1975).

they may have assumed that other people they deal with have similar commitments. The long-term wage-setting commitments used throughout this
book are primary examples, but there are many others, including long-term
investment projects and loan contracts. Such rigidities usually suggest that
the transition to a new policy rule should be gradual and announced pub-
licly. This gives people a chance to unravel previous commitments without
significant losses.

In the remainder of this chapter I look at these transition problems more
explicitly for two important macroeconomic cases: (1) the transition to a
monetary policy rule with a zero-inflation target, and (2) the transition
toward a fiscal policy rule with a balanced full-employment government
budget.

7.2   Transition to a Monetary Policy Rule with "Zero" Inflation

This section considers the problem of transition toward a zero-inflation
monetary policy rule. The key objective is to devise a way to move to such
a rule with the smallest possible costs to the economy. Here I explain how
it is possible, at least under ideal circumstances, to devise a transition path
with no loss of output. I focus on the United States and endeavor to make
the calculations as precise as possible by introducing more detailed wage-
setting equations than those used in either Chapter 2 (Equations [2.1] and
[2.2]) or Chapter 3 (equations [3.1] or [3.2]). This permits the "calibration"
of the equations by using micro data on long-term union labor contracts.
Long-term labor contracts in the United States usually last for several years,
although some contracts are indexed and some multiyear contracts entail
deferred wage increases in the second and third year of the contract. This
requires some modification of the contract equations that I first must explain.

Calibration of the Wage-Setting Equations

Let $x_j(t, s)$ be the log of the wage set in contracts of length j signed in
quarter t to prevail in the sth quarter following quarter t. I assume that j
equals either 4, 8, or 12 quarters, corresponding to one-, two-, and three-
year contracts. I also assume that wage changes occur at yearly intervals;
that is,

$$x_j(t, s) = x_j(t, 0), \quad s = 1, 2, 3, \quad j = 4, 8, 12 \qquad (7.1)$$

$$x_j(t, 4 + s) = x_j(t, 4), \quad s = 1, 2, 3, \quad j = 8, 12 \qquad (7.2)$$

$$x_{12}(t, 8 + s) = x_{12}(t, 8), \quad s = 1, 2, 3. \qquad (7.3)$$

Equation (7.1) states that the wage level is constant during the first year of
the one-, two-, and three-year contracts ($j = 4, 8, 12$) and equal to the value

determined in the first quarter $x_j(t, 0)$. Equation (7.2) states that the wage level is constant during the second year of the two- and three-year contracts ($j = 8, 12$) and equal to the value set in the first quarter of the second year $x_j(t, 4)$. Finally, Equation (7.3) states that the wage level is unchanged during the third year of three-year contracts ($j = 12$).

During each quarter, six wage levels are determined; three current levels: $x_4(t, 0)$, $x_8(t, 0)$, and $x_{12}(t, 0)$; and three deferred levels: $x_8(t, 4)$, $x_{12}(t, 4)$, and $x_{12}(t, 8)$. Note that there is no presumption that the deferred wage levels are equal to the current levels, so that deferred increases are possible according to this setup.

The aggregate wage is a weighted average of the contract wages and is given by the expression

$$w(t) = \frac{\sum_j \sum_{s=0}^{j-1} n_j(t-s) x_j(t-s, s)}{\sum_j \sum_{s=0}^{j-1} n_j(t-s)}, \tag{7.4}$$

where $n_j(t)$ is the number of workers in contracts of length j in quarter t. Equation (7.4) should be interpreted as the log of a geometrically weighted index of contract wages. It is analogous to the average wage defined in Chapter 2.

Wage determination is analogous to Equation (2.1) of Chapter 2 or to Equation (3.1) of Chapter 3. In particular, I assume that, in the absence of a need for a change in relative wages, workers and firms attempt to keep their own wages as close as possible to the prevailing level of wages during the period of the contract, with adjustments for skill and other differentials. If wage adjustments are thought to be necessary because of a shift in labor-market demand or supply conditions, then these adjustments will be made relative to this prevailing wage.

Consider first the case of nonindexed contracts. Assume that one-year contracts call for a wage adjustment to equal the average wage expected to prevail during the contract period. Similarly, the first year of two- and three-year contracts will have a wage adjustment equal to the prevailing wage during that same one-year period. Algebraically, the current settlements are then given by

$$x_j(t, 0) = \frac{1}{4} \sum_{s=0}^{3} \hat{w}(t + s), \qquad j = 4, 8, 12, \tag{7.5}$$

where $\hat{w}(t)$ is the expectation of $w(t)$, the average wage defined in Equation (7.4). For the deferred wage increases in the second year of two- and three-year contracts, assume that

$$x_j(t, 4) = \frac{1}{4} \sum_{s=4}^{7} \hat{w}(t + s), \qquad j = 8, 12 \tag{7.6}$$

and finally, for the deferred increase in the third year of three-year contracts,

$$x_{12}(t, 8) = \frac{1}{4} \sum_{s=8}^{11} \hat{w}(t + s). \tag{7.7}$$

Note that I do not add a measure of unemployment relative to the natural rate, or real output relative to potential output, to the right-hand side of these equations as was done in Chapters 2 and 3. By forcing these terms to equal zero, I ensure algebraically that the transition occurs in such a way that the pattern of wage settlements is consistent with full employment—disinflation without recession. Of course, it would be possible to modify the model by adding unemployment effects to the right-hand side of Equations (7.5) through (7.7) in order to examine how much unemployment might change for different transition paths.

When contracts are indexed, the contracted adjustment in wages will reflect the expected increase or decrease in wage rates that will arise because of changes in the price level. Consider the following example. In a steady inflation of 10 percent, the above contracting arrangements would imply that a three-year contract without indexing would have a 10-percent increase in the first year, followed by a 10-percent increase in each of the next two years $(10, 10, 10)$. Suppose, instead, that contracts are indexed at .3 in the second and third year, so that a 10-percent increase in the price level automatically adds 3 percent to the wage in the second and third year. Then, in a steady 10-percent inflation where prices and wages are increasing at the same rate, the set-wage increase would again be 10 percent in the first year but only 7 percent in the second and third years $(10, 7, 7)$. The remaining increase in wages of 3 percent in the second and third years would come from indexing; that is, $(10, 7, 7) + (0, 3, 3) = (10, 10, 10)$.

These effects are incorporated into the equations by adjusting down the set wage in Equations (7.6) and (7.7) by the amount of increase that is expected from indexing. The exact size of the indexing is assumed to be a constant fraction of the increase in the aggregate-price level during the previous four quarters. This constant is the same for all workers.[2] I assume that indexing reviews occur annually at the start of the second and third year of two- and three-year contracts. One-year contracts are not indexed. The real wage is assumed to be constant so that the indexing is assumed to be a fixed fraction of the increase in the aggregate wage. I will only simulate the model for paths for which the shocks to the equation system are equal to their expected values (zero) and for which real output is always equal to potential. The model, consisting of Equations (7.1) through (7.7) along

---

[2]Rather than assume that a fraction of workers have indexed contracts, I assume that all workers are indexed though at a lower rate. For example, if 50 percent of the workers have contracts indexed at .6, then this is treated in the model as if 100 percent of the workers have contracts indexed at .3.

with the full employment condition, is a linear (in the logarithms) rational expectations model. At each date, six wage levels are determined, and these depend on wage decisions made as far as eleven quarters in the past and on wage decisions to be made as far as eleven quarters in the future.

The model can be calibrated with data on the number of workers involved in contracts of different lengths, as shown in Table 7-1. For the calculations of the transition path, the number of workers was taken to follow the same pattern as for the three years from 1978 through 1980. To calculate the transition paths,[3] the model was solved by using the extended path algorithm discussed in Chapter 1. Deterministic simulations are appropriate for this transitional analysis, because a one-time move to a new policy is being investigated. In other words, we are not contemplating a megapolicy rule in which there is a probability of a switch to a new policy each period or a gradual move from one policy to another over time.

Consider a situation where the rate of wage inflation has been steady at about 10 percent per year. Then, according to the equations of the model, the current wage adjustment and deferred wage adjustments would all be equal to 10 percent per year. There would be a considerable overhang of deferred pay increases in future years. It is this overhang that makes it necessary for wage adjustments in other contracts to be gradual.

Suppose that, in the first quarter of a year, a general disinflation from 10 to 3 percent—measured in terms of wage inflation—begins and is thereafter expected to continue. With labor productivity growth of between 1 and 2 percent, wage inflation of 3 percent per year implies inflation in terms of the overall price level of between 1 and 2 percent per year. This is usually the range taken to be effectively zero inflation, recognizing various biases in measuring inflation. How such a disinflation is engineered through monetary policy depends greatly on how union wage settlements might develop. Table 7-2 shows the settlement pattern consistent with the equations of the model and therefore with full employment. The first six columns of Table 7-2 show the contract wage settlements in percentage terms. The column labeled "One-Year Contracts" shows the current settlement for workers signing one-year contracts in that quarter. Similarly the columns labeled "Year 1," in "Two-Year," and "Three-Year Contracts" show the percentage change in the current settlement for those cohorts. The columns labeled "Year 2" and "Year 3" show the deferred increase in the longer-term contracts. The effective wage change is simply the first difference of the log of the aggregate wage $w(t)$ from quarter to quarter ($w(t) - w(t-1)$). Because of the

---

[3]The details of the solution procedure can be explained as follows. I added a term $z(t) - w(t)$ to the right-hand side of the three contract equations and solved the model for a given $z(t)$ path. The variable $z(t)$ is defined so that actual output equals potential output when $z(t)$ equals $w(t)$. Such a $z(t)$ exists and is a function of the money supply for each country in the multicountry model (taking as given the money supplies of the other countries). I then summed up the squared differences in $[z(t) - w(t)]^2$ over the solution period and searched over $z(t)$ paths using a numerical algorithm to minimize the sum of these squares. The minimum value was always zero. By construction when $z(t) - w(t) = 0$, full-employment conditions hold.

TABLE 7-1   Number of Workers in Major Union Settlements by Contract Length, 1974:1–1987:4 (thousands of workers)

Quarter	Contract Length			Total
	1 Year	2 Years	3 Years	
1974:1	116	114	263	493
2	379	373	850	1,602
3	233	269	1,477	1,979
4	157	177	692	1,026
1975:1	67	86	395	548
2	172	326	264	762
3	325	215	529	1,069
4	77	84	231	392
1976:1	29	67	158	254
2	109	259	1,044	1,412
3	163	159	673	995
4	82	78	1,104	1,264
1977:1	43	98	226	367
2	215	138	950	1,303
3	125	121	1,325	1,571
4	52	60	400	512
1978:1	19	29	338	386
2	104	195	380	679
3	70	238	599	907
4	58	97	378	533
1979:1	45	31	186	262
2	107	164	836	1,107
3	39	49	1,166	1,254
4	29	135	667	831
1980:1	10	60	299	369
2	80	167	693	940
3	99	203	1,325	1,627
4	25	177	652	854

Source: Current Wage Developments (Washington, D.C.: Bureau of Labor Statistics). Major Settlements are those involving 1,000 or more workers. The numbers in the table are computed from cumulative totals published quarterly for each year. Before 1983:1, "1 Year" refers to contracts less than 18 months, "2 Years" refers to contracts between 18 and 30 months, and "3 Years" refers to contracts longer than 30 months. Starting in 1983:1, 1-year contracts are less than or equal to 12 months, 2-year contracts are between 12 and 24 months, and 3-year contracts are greater than 24 months. This change causes a break in the series in 1982:4.

seasonal pattern of workers negotiating each quarter, it is more informative to look at the change of $w(t)$ over four quarters.

The simulation begins in quarter 1 of year 1. Prior to this first quarter, the entries in Table 7-2 would have been 10 percent in all columns with the exception of the quarterly effective wage change that fluctuates seasonally.

TABLE 7-1   *(Continued)*

| | Contract Length | | | |
Quarter	1 Year	2 Years	3 Years	Total
1981:1	12	23	167	202
2	83	220	423	726
3	49	125	364	538
4	296	153	426	875
1982:1	34	79	530	643
2	94	651	491	1,236
3	119	146	564	829
4	—	—	—	—
1983:1	16	54	477	547
2	152	120	407	679
3	90	143	438	671
4	30	72	1,090	1,192
1984:1	20	73	229	322
2	92	138	282	512
3	61	141	410	612
4	43	42	776	861
1985:1	35	6	132	173
2	110	93	473	676
3	99	93	574	766
4	93	78	408	579
1986:1	35	49	199	283
2	46	122	521	689
3	36	44	795	875
4	28	86	525	639
1987:1	14	37	180	231
2	61	78	361	500
3	10	59	456	525
4	42	29	722	793

The entries in this last column were fluctuating seasonally according to the steady quarterly pattern 1.06, 2.66, 3.92, and 2.31, before the disinflation began.

What is most striking about Table 7-2 is the gradual decline in the inflation rate, especially in the early periods of the disinflation. The effective wage-change decline is barely noticeable for a full year. The decline is about 1 percentage point in the second year, a large 5 percentage points in the third year, and about 1 more percentage point in the fourth year. It is only after the new negotiations are well beyond the overhang of past deferred wage increases that noticeable declines in the inflation rate occur. Note, however, that in long-term contracts there is a definite sign that disinflation is underway: the third-year deferred increases in three-year contracts

TABLE 7-2   Current and Deferred Wage Changes during Disinflation (No indexing)

Year/ Quarter	One-Year Contracts	Two-Year Contracts		Three-Year Contracts			Effective Wage Change	
		Year 1	Year 2	Year 1	Year 2	Year 3	Quarter	Year
1:1	10.0	10.0	9.6	10.0	9.6	6.4	1.06	10.00
1:2	10.0	10.0	9.3	10.0	9.3	5.1	2.66	10.00
1:3	9.9	9.9	8.7	9.9	8.7	4.0	3.92	9.98
1:4	9.8	9.8	7.7	9.8	7.7	3.4	2.31	9.96
2:1	9.6	9.6	6.4	9.6	6.4	3.2	1.02	9.93
2:2	9.3	9.3	5.1	9.3	5.1	3.0	2.54	9.81
2:3	8.7	8.6	4.0	8.6	4.0	3.0	3.61	9.48
2:4	7.7	7.5	3.4	7.5	3.4	3.0	1.96	9.13
3:1	6.4	6.4	3.2	6.0	3.2	3.0	0.67	8.77
3:2	5.1	5.1	3.0	4.4	3.0	3.0	1.29	7.52
3:3	4.0	4.0	3.0	2.7	3.0	3.0	1.40	5.32
3:4	3.4	3.4	3.0	.9	3.0	3.0	0.60	3.97
4:1	3.2	3.2	3.0	3.2	3.0	3.0	0.34	3.64
4:2	3.0	3.0	3.0	3.0	3.0	3.0	0.81	3.15
4:3	3.0	3.0	3.0	3.0	3.0	3.0	1.18	2.93
4:4	3.0	3.0	3.0	3.0	3.0	3.0	0.70	3.02
5:1	3.0	3.0	3.0	3.0	3.0	3.0	0.32	3.00
5:2	3.0	3.0	3.0	3.0	3.0	3.0	0.80	3.00
5:3	3.0	3.0	3.0	3.0	3.0	3.0	1.18	3.00
5:4	3.0	3.0	3.0	3.0	3.0	3.0	0.70	3.00

are down substantially relative to the previous settlement. The third-year deferred increase in the settlement negotiated in quarter 2 is about half the previous third-year deferred increase.

Table 7-3 shows the results of a similar disinflation in the case where the contracts are indexed according to the assumptions of the model. It is assumed that on average, contracts have a 30-percent escalation. As one would expect, the actual effective wage change occurs more rapidly in this case as the indexing formulas permit some change in the wage levels determined in previous contracts. However, the difference is very small. Recall that there is no indexing in the first year and that indexing reviews occur only annually.

The transition is considerably slower than what is implied by rational expectations models with perfectly flexible prices. The simulations of this model indicate in quantitative terms how large the difference in speed might be if the U.S. union wage contracting is the source of stickiness. On the other hand, the speed of disinflation is faster than what is implied by conventional expectations-augmented Phillips curve models that imply that the rate of inflation cannot be reduced at all by aggregate-demand policy without an increase in unemployment. These models predict that inflation

TABLE 7-3   Current and Deferred Wage Changes during Disinflation
(30-percent indexing)

Year/ Quarter	One-Year Contracts	Two-Year Contracts		Three-Year Contracts			Effective Wage Change	
		Year 1	Year 2	Year 1	Year 2	Year 3	Quarter	Year
1:1	10.0	10.0	6.6	10.0	6.6	3.6	1.06	10.00
1:2	10.0	10.0	6.3	10.0	6.3	2.5	2.66	10.00
1:3	9.9	9.9	5.7	9.9	5.7	1.8	3.93	9.98
1:4	9.8	9.8	4.8	9.8	4.8	1.8	2.31	9.96
2:1	9.6	9.5	3.6	9.5	3.6	2.0	1.02	9.92
2:2	9.3	9.2	2.5	9.2	2.5	1.9	2.53	9.79
2:3	8.7	8.6	1.8	8.6	1.8	2.0	3.58	9.44
2:4	7.6	7.4	1.8	7.4	1.8	2.1	1.93	9.07
3:1	6.3	6.3	2.0	5.9	2.0	2.1	0.66	8.71
3:2	5.1	5.1	2.0	4.3	1.9	2.1	1.28	7.46
3:3	4.0	4.0	2.0	2.6	2.0	2.1	1.40	5.27
3:4	3.4	3.4	2.1	1.0	2.1	2.1	0.61	3.94
4:1	3.2	3.2	2.1	3.2	2.1	2.1	0.34	3.62
4:2	3.0	3.0	2.1	3.0	2.1	2.1	0.81	3.15
4:3	3.0	3.0	2.1	3.0	2.1	2.1	1.18	2.93
4:4	3.0	3.0	2.1	3.0	2.1	2.1	0.70	3.02
5:1	3.0	3.0	2.1	3.0	2.1	2.1	0.32	3.00
5:2	3.0	3.0	2.1	3.0	2.1	2.1	0.80	3.00
5:3	3.0	3.0	2.1	3.0	2.1	2.1	1.18	3.00
5:4	3.0	3.0	2.1	3.0	2.1	2.1	0.70	3.00

would remain at 10 percent if unemployment does not rise above the natural rate.

For these calculations, the rational expectations assumption is essential. Not only do people have to act as if they know the model, they have to know about the change in policy and about the exact transition path. In other words, the learning problems discussed are very real. However, it is not clear that a simple passive model of Bayesian or least-squares learning would be very helpful here. The difficulty is that wage negotiators have to be convinced that a deceleration of inflation will come later even though it is not occurring today. People who use a Bayesian analysis to adjust their expectations depending on what happened in the past will not change their priors much at all for the first two years of disinflation. This credibility problem is perhaps the central source of difficulty encountered during a period of disinflation.

At the heart of this credibility problem is a time-inconsistency problem that takes a particularly explicit form in this model on union wage settlements: if policymakers argue that it is optimal to ratify the overhang of past deferred wage increases with high-money growth, they will find it difficult to convince wage setters that it is not optimal to ratify the deferred wage increases in the future if such increases take place.

7.3 Transition to a New Fiscal Policy

In this section I consider the transition of fiscal policy from structural budget deficit to structural budget balance. In particular I examine the effects of a change in fiscal policy in the United States, in which the growth of government purchases is cut so as to reduce the structural government budget deficit. It was this type of change that was the purpose of the 1990 budget summit agreement in the United States—although taxes were also changed in the agreement. The rationale for budget-deficit reduction was that this would increase national saving, raise domestic investment, and lower the trade deficit.

In 1990 policymakers aimed to reduce the structural budget deficit gradually over a five-year period. One of the reasons for gradual reduction was the type of transitional issue discussed in this chapter. Trying to make the budget-deficit reductions gradual and credible, the aim was that future budget-deficit reductions would have favorable effects on long-term interest rates and thereby reduce the negative short-run impacts that a decline in government spending might otherwise have. Credibility was to be enhanced by placing various new rules on the budget that I will describe in the discussion of policy operation in Chapter 8. These rules allowed the budget deficit to expand if a recession occurred (which it did) and focused on reducing the structural deficit.

The appropriate transition path for budget-deficit reduction can be calculated quantitatively. Because of the multiyear aspects of the strategy, it is important to use a rational expectations approach. This is the only formal way to estimate the effects on interest rates of expected future declines in the deficit. To illustrate how such an estimation might be done, I consider several transition paths in this section. They differ in the stance of monetary policy in the United States and of fiscal policy abroad, differences that are quite relevant to the question of transition.

Credible Multiyear Budget-Deficit Reduction

Suppose that real U.S. government purchases of goods and services grow less rapidly for a five-year period starting in the first quarter of 1991.[4] In

---

[4]The following calculations are performed using the multicountry model of Chapter 3. As already mentioned, for that model the size of the percentage impacts of policy changes does not depend much on the level of the variables or the period of the simulation. The estimates reported here are therefore essentially time-invariant. To focus on a particular example, I report them as if they apply to the 1991–1995 period to which the 1990 budget summit agreement applied. In fact, they were simulated for a period four years earlier.

particular, I assume that by the first quarter of 1996, this cut results in real government purchases lower than in reality by an amount equal to 3 percent of real output. However, the full amount of the cut does not occur immediately. It is phased in gradually from the first quarter of 1991 through the fourth quarter of 1996 in equal percentage increments: 0.6 percent of real output in the first year, another 0.6 in the second year, and so on adding up to 3 percent by the end of five years. The gradual phase-in is meant to mitigate the real output effects of a cut in government purchases. No changes in tax rates or in other components of government expenditure are assumed.

With a forward-looking model, it is important to describe the expectations assumption that underlies the change in government spending. The implicit assumption made here is that, as of the first quarter of the simulation, people become aware of the planned cut in government spending. They know, starting in that quarter, that real government spending will be eventually lowered by 3 percent of real GDP, and they know that the cut will be phased in gradually. As we will see, this expectation begins to have immediate and large effects on interest rates and exchange rates as soon as the cut is announced and before most of the cut takes place.

The simulation results are reported in Table 7-4. This is a single deterministic simulation, which is appropriate given that a one-time shift to a balanced structural deficit is being investigated. As in the case of a transition to zero inflation, we are not contemplating a megarule in which such shifts in policy occur randomly from year to year.

Of a very large amount of information that can be obtained from a simulation of the multicountry model, only the most relevant facts are shown in Table 7-4. For example, only the first quarter of each of the years is reported. The first quarter is more relevant than the yearly average for assessing the impacts of changes in expectations. Moreover, the table looks at a limited set of key variables in three of the seven countries: the United States, Germany, and Japan.

Recall first the long-run effects of a cut in government purchases of 3 percent of real output. The multicountry model satisfies the natural-rate property so that there are no long-run demand effects on output; that is, output returns to potential output, even if potential output is higher as a result of the "crowding-in" of investment. Hence, the decreased share of government purchases leads to an increased share of the sum of everything else: consumption, investment, net exports (recall that durable consumption depends on interest rates in this model). In the long run, prices and exchange rates will have settled down to new equilibrium paths so that real interest rates in all countries must be equal. Thus, the amount by which investment, consumption, and net exports change depends on how much the world real rate of interest declines, on the interest-rate elasticities of investment and consumption, and on the elasticities of import and export demand. In theory, real net exports could rise by the full amount of the cut in government expenditures (3 percent of real output), domestic

TABLE 7-4   Effects of a Reduction in U.S. Government Purchases, 1991–1996

The counterfactual decline in real government purchases is equal to 3 percent of real GNP. The decline is phased in gradually in equal percentage increments each quarter starting in 1991:1 and finishing in 1996:1. Figures are in percentage differences from historical values (or percentage point differences for interest rates and ratios).

	91:1	92:1	93:1	94:1	95:1	96:1
Short-Term Rates						
U.S.—federal funds	−.45	−1.67	−2.12	−2.40	−2.48	−2.35
Germany—call money	.15	−.65	−.79	−.80	−.70	−.58
Japan—call money	−.05	−.55	−.99	−1.19	−1.10	−.84
Exchange Rates						
D-mark	13.10	12.50	11.20	9.61	7.80	5.92
Yen	11.10	10.30	9.08	7.85	6.48	4.96
Long-Term Rates						
U.S.—government bonds	−1.10	−1.93	−2.26	−2.43	−2.41	−2.31
Germany—government bonds	−.38	−.71	−.79	−.77	−.66	−.54
Japan—government bonds	−.34	−.80	−1.09	−1.12	−.94	−.69
Real Spending						
U.S. consumption	−0.05	−0.21	−0.38	−0.54	−0.57	−0.51
U.S. investment	0.00	0.48	1.00	1.56	2.38	3.89
German investment	−0.19	0.10	0.98	2.10	2.86	2.88
Japan investment	−0.13	−0.43	0.05	1.18	2.38	3.42
U.S. exports	0.13	1.58	3.61	5.47	6.87	7.73
U.S. imports	−0.47	−3.86	−6.27	−8.13	−9.34	−8.77
U.S. real GNP	0.03	−0.26	−0.39	−0.72	−0.97	−0.58
German real GNP	−0.20	−0.44	−0.39	−0.25	−0.06	0.07
Japan real GNP	−0.10	−0.48	−0.51	−0.24	0.16	0.38
Prices						
U.S. GNP deflator	−0.10	−1.12	−2.50	−3.85	−5.02	−5.95
German GNP deflator	−0.02	−0.51	−0.95	−1.24	−1.37	−1.35
Japan GNP deflator	−0.01	−0.42	−1.10	−1.72	−2.02	−1.93
U.S. import price	1.21	4.72	6.38	6.73	6.24	5.26
U.S. export price	−0.04	−0.78	−2.06	−3.41	−4.65	−5.65
Ratios to Real GNP						
U.S. real national saving	0.06	0.67	1.42	2.01	2.58	2.85
U.S. real investment	−0.00	0.10	0.26	0.42	0.63	0.78
U.S. real exports	0.06	0.57	1.16	1.59	1.94	2.07
Ratio to GNP						
U.S. net exports	−0.07	0.03	0.15	0.35	0.48	0.46

saving could rise by 3 percent of real output (if the interest-rate elasticity of consumption was zero), and investment could remain unchanged (if the interest-rate elasticity of investment was zero). With high interest-rate elasticities, there might be a very small increase in net exports. Hence, even in the long run, the theoretical implications are ambiguous and quantitative estimates are needed.

Table 7-4 shows how real output and prices would fall in the United States relative to their baseline values. Note that the negative effects of the government spending cut on real output are very small. The government spending multiplier is at the most one-third. This small effect is a result of the spending cut being largely anticipated: it is known to be phased in gradually. In fact, the simulation in Chapter 5 shows that the output effects of a fully *unanticipated* 3-percent decrease in government spending would be very much larger. In this simulation, long-term interest rates fall immediately with the start of the budget cuts, and this begins to stimulate investment and consumer durable purchases. Note how long-term rates drop more than short-term rates in the first years of the simulation. This is due to the forward-looking term structure assumptions of the model. In addition, the dollar exchange rate depreciates by a fairly large amount in the first quarter, and this stimulates net exports. After its initial fall, the dollar appreciates, slowly permitting a differential to exist between U.S. interest rates and foreign interest rates. Prices fall relative to the baseline—that is, inflation declines—throughout the simulation, forcing nominal interest rates to fall. Because of rigidities, due largely to the staggered wage contracts, however, wages and prices do not adjust instantaneously and real output falls as described. This rigidity is the main reason for considering a gradual transition.

The output effects in Germany and Japan are larger than in the United States in the first few years of the simulation. Again, this is because of the anticipated aspects of the policy change: the exchange rates in Japan and Germany appreciate by a large amount, and this reduces exports and increases imports in these countries. The trade deficit falls in the United States as does the surplus in Japan and Germany. Moreover, with the dollar expected to appreciate after the initial fall, interest rates do not fall as much abroad as in the United States. Recall from Chapter 5 that an *unanticipated* increase in government spending in the United States has much larger effects on U.S. output than on foreign output.

Consider briefly the long-run effects. Five years after the start of the cut in government purchases, real net exports have risen by 2.1 percentage points as a fraction of real GNP. This improvement in the real trade deficit has resulted in an increase in saving (real output less real consumption less real government purchases—$Y - C - G$) of 2.9 percentage points and a rise in real investment of .8 percentage points. Stated differently, the cut in government purchases results in a nearly equal rise in saving, and about three-fourths of this rise in saving has been an increase in net exports. The government spending cut has crowded in much more real net exports than real investment. Note, however, that the long-run effects of the government-spending change have not fully been reached in five years. The real long-term interest rate in the United States is still lower than the real long-term interest rate in Japan and Germany, because the real dollar exchange rate is still appreciating. In real terms, the U.S. long-term interest rate is about 1.5 percentage points below what it would otherwise have been, and the long-term yen interest rate is about .8 percentage points below what it otherwise would have been, leaving a differential of about .7 percent. After a further period of time, the U.S. interest rate will rise a bit, and the Japanese interest rate will fall a bit, until they reach equality (in terms of deviations from the baseline). This will tend to raise the measured saving rate (as consumption falls) and to lower the investment ratio.

The Role of Monetary Policy in the Transition

In the months preceding the 1990 budget summit agreement in the United States, there was considerable discussion about the role of the Federal Reserve. In principle monetary policy could be used to help cushion any real output effects associated with a reduction in the budget deficit. Monetary ease brought about by an increase in the money supply could stimulate output in the short run so as to offset the decline in output brought about by the cutback in government spending. With a credible agreement to reduce the budget deficit in the future, people would figure that interest rates in the future would decline, and this would cause a decline in long-term rates that would increase the demand for investment and thereby offset the contractionary effects of fiscal policy right away. The decline in short-term interest rates brought on by the Federal Reserve would be smaller than if the contractionary fiscal policy were unanticipated. In fact, the Federal Reserve has indicated that an adjustment of monetary policy would be appropriate if such an agreement on fiscal policy could be worked out and was credible. But what was the "right amount" of adjustment of monetary policy?

To answer this question, consider what happens if the simulated change in government purchases is matched by an increase in the money supply in the United States. Suppose, for example, that the increase in the money supply is approximately of the same order of magnitude as the decline in prices in Table 7-4. The results are shown in Table 7-5.

With such a monetary policy, relative to baseline, real output in the United States expands rather than contracts. The main channel of monetary policy is the real interest rate. According to the simulations, the nominal interest rates—both short- and long-term—are about 1 percentage point higher with the easier monetary policy. Real rates, however, are lower. Prices are expected to rise by 1 percent over the first year relative to the baseline rather than fall by 1 percent, and this raises the expected rate of inflation by about 2 percentage points. On net, therefore, the real rate of interest falls by 1 percent, and this stimulates investment demand and durable-consumption demand.

TABLE 7-5 Effects of a Reduction in Government Purchases with an Increase in the Money Supply, 1991–1996

The decline in purchases is 3 percent of real output and is phased in gradually starting in 1991:1 and ending in 1996:1. The money increase is 8 percent, phased in the same way. Figures are in percentage differences from historical values (or percentage point differences for interest rates and ratios).

	91:1	92:1	93:1	94:1	95:1	96:1
Short-Term Rates						
U.S.—federal funds	0.63	−0.30	−1.19	−0.23	−3.41	−1.79
Germany—call money	−0.11	−0.52	−0.61	−0.61	−0.55	−0.49
Japan—call money	−0.05	−0.54	−0.87	−1.01	−0.90	−0.01
Exchange Rates						
D-mark	19.80	19.90	19.90	18.70	16.20	14.40
Yen	17.50	17.60	17.70	16.90	14.80	13.40
Long-Term Rates						
U.S.—government bonds	−0.27	−0.80	−1.84	−2.54	−2.17	−1.90
Germany—government bonds	−3.19	−0.56	−0.61	−0.59	−0.53	−0.46
Japan—government bonds	0.00	−0.01	−0.01	−0.01	−0.01	−0.01
Real Spending						
U.S. consumption	0.55	1.53	1.56	1.21	0.74	0.42
U.S. investment	4.96	13.30	9.77	9.85	7.45	6.22
German investment	−0.23	0.07	0.87	1.80	2.41	2.39
Japan investment	−0.13	−0.35	0.17	1.19	2.17	2.96
U.S. exports	0.22	2.14	4.15	5.69	6.72	7.24
U.S. imports	0.80	1.43	−0.50	−2.79	−5.43	−6.46
U.S. real GNP	1.02	2.12	1.84	1.25	0.29	0.05
German real GNP	−0.16	−0.25	−0.21	−0.12	−0.03	0.01
Japan real GNP	−0.10	−0.43	−0.40	−0.14	0.18	0.30
Prices						
U.S. GNP deflator	0.10	1.40	2.48	2.83	2.60	2.06
German GNP deflator	−0.01	−0.52	−0.86	−1.06	−1.12	−1.08
Japan GNP deflator	−0.01	−0.43	−1.03	−1.53	−1.72	−1.61
U.S. import price	1.83	7.49	11.10	13.00	13.50	13.00
U.S. export price	1.03	1.05	1.08	1.14	1.18	1.18
Ratios to Real GNP						
U.S. real national saving	0.50	1.54	1.99	2.49	2.76	2.76
U.S. real investment	0.57	1.47	1.47	1.53	1.34	1.06
U.S. real net exports	−0.07	0.07	0.53	0.96	1.42	1.70
Ratio to GNP						
U.S. net exports	−0.27	−0.56	−0.47	−0.19	0.10	0.25

In this case, the dollar depreciates by about 20 percent against the deutsche mark and by 18 percent against the yen. The reason is that the rise in prices in the United States requires a depreciation of the dollar. The increase in net exports in the short run is much smaller than without the money increase because the expansionary effects of money on U.S. demand increase imports more than the depreciation of the dollar decreases imports. Note that this is an example where a depreciation of the dollar is associated with a short-term worsening of the trade deficit. Eventually the short-run output effects wear off, however, and the effects on the trade deficit are much like in the earlier case. In the very long run the effects should be the same because money is completely neutral in the long run in this model.

Can we say which of the two scenarios is better on policy grounds? In terms of domestic price stability, the monetary expansion is better in that the price level does not fluctuate as much. Moreover, in terms of output, the monetary expansion seems better. The decline in output is less in Germany and Japan, and there is no output decline in the United States. In terms of nominal exchange-rate stability, the second scenario is worse, however, in that the nominal exchange rate has fluctuated more. However, this fluctuation in the nominal exchange rate has relatively small effects on the economy. This seems to be a case where one would prefer to see the nominal exchange rate, rather than the domestic price level, absorb the burden of adjusting the composition of output when the government spending share declines.

Internationally Coordinated Transitions

Table 7-6 attempts to look at the transition to a lower budget deficit in the United States when fiscal policy expands abroad. This situation is similar to what the United States and Japan endeavored to accomplish as part of the Structural Impediments talks in 1990 and 1991. By reducing government spending in the United States, the U.S. trade deficit would be expected to come down. By increasing government spending in Japan, the Japanese trade surplus would be expected to come down. It was hoped that this would reduce trade frictions between the two countries.

Table 7-6 shows the effects of a simultaneous reduction in government spending in the United States and an increase in foreign government spending, not only in Japan but also in Germany. The foreign expansion is gradually phased in just as in the United States. The increase in government spending in these two countries is 2 percent of their real output.

The gradual increase in government spending in Japan and Germany has very small effects on real output in these two countries. The depreciation of the dollar is larger than in the case where the United States alone contracts, and this reduces net exports in both Germany and Japan—one of the purposes of a coordinated change. Eventually, long-term interest rates in both Germany and Japan rise relative to the baseline so that there is some crowding-out of net investment in those countries, but most of the

TABLE 7-6 Effects of a Simultaneous Reduction in U.S. Government Purchases and a Rise in German and Japanese Government Purchases, 1991–1996

The decline in U.S. purchases is 3 percent of real output. The increase in Germany and Japan is 2 percent of output. All are phased in gradually starting in 1991:1 and ending in 1996:1. Figures are in percentage differences from historical values (or percentage point differences for interest rates and ratios).

	91:1	92:1	93:1	94:1	95:1	96:1
Short-Term Rates						
U.S.—federal funds	−0.30	−1.02	−1.37	−1.63	−1.73	−1.66
Germany—call money	−0.09	−0.24	0.00	0.25	0.52	0.54
Japan—call money	−0.04	−0.41	−0.37	−0.05	0.42	0.57
Exchange Rates						
D-mark	19.40	19.00	17.80	16.00	13.60	11.10
Yen	18.60	18.20	17.30	15.90	13.80	11.30
Long-Term Rates						
U.S.—government bonds	−0.67	−1.22	−1.51	−1.68	−1.69	−1.67
Germany—government bonds	−0.20	−0.14	0.11	0.35	0.52	0.53
Japan—government bonds	−0.24	−0.37	−0.17	0.20	0.50	0.54
Real Spending						
U.S. consumption	−0.01	−0.09	−0.22	−0.35	−0.36	−0.30
U.S. investment	0.16	0.40	0.67	0.94	1.56	2.80
German investment	−0.16	0.37	0.82	0.80	0.13	−0.58
Japan investment	−0.11	−0.07	0.56	1.19	1.18	0.59
U.S. exports	0.20	2.21	4.80	7.09	8.78	9.69
U.S. imports	−0.49	−4.04	−6.58	−8.58	−9.93	−9.48
U.S. real GNP	0.09	−0.11	−0.19	−0.49	−0.71	−0.32
German real GNP	−0.18	−0.05	0.14	0.27	0.44	0.27
Japan real GNP	−0.14	−0.26	−0.04	0.32	0.69	0.25
Prices						
U.S. GNP deflator	−0.07	−0.68	−1.58	−2.51	−3.37	−4.07
German GNP deflator	0.01	−0.35	−0.29	−0.01	0.33	0.64
Japan GNP deflator	0.00	−0.36	−0.58	−0.44	0.05	0.59
U.S. import price	1.51	6.10	8.77	10.00	10.20	9.70
U.S. export price	−0.03	−0.47	−1.29	−2.21	−3.09	−3.84
Ratios to Real GNP						
U.S. real national saving	0.08	0.72	1.48	2.08	2.65	2.93
U.S. real investment	0.01	0.07	0.16	0.26	0.43	0.54
U.S. real net exports	0.07	0.65	1.32	1.82	2.22	2.39
Ratio to GNP						
U.S. net exports	−0.09	0.01	0.15	0.37	0.50	0.47

adjustment in the composition of output is in net exports. As is clear in Table 7-6, the direct impact of the fiscal contraction in these two countries on U.S. net exports is very small. Comparing Tables 7-4 and 7-5 shows how a fiscal expansion of this magnitude in Japan and Germany improves the U.S. trade balance by only a few tenths of a percentage point and that it does cause a significant reduction on the trade surplus in those countries.

I have focused entirely on real net exports. Also shown in the tables are the changes in nominal net exports, as well as changes in export prices and import prices, which are the source of the difference between real and current dollar measures of net exports. As is clear in the tables, the change in current dollar net exports (measured as a fraction of nominal GNP) is very small for all the scenarios when compared with real net exports. The reason for this is that for all scenarios, import prices rise more than export prices. The fall in the ratio of export prices to import prices is about 11 percent after five years. The fall in the terms of trade is, of course, what stimulates real net exports, but this same fall offsets this increase when computing current dollar net exports. The offset is made worse in this scenario by the fact that for the historical values, imports are much larger than exports.

7.4 Conclusion

The purpose of this chapter has been to explore the problems associated with the transition from one policy rule to a new and, it is hoped, better policy rule. The problem of transition is frequently encountered but has been given relatively less emphasis in research than policy design as defined in this book. In this chapter I focused on two specific transition problems in macroeconomics: disinflation and structural budget-deficit reduction.

Transition problems arise because it takes time for people to learn about a new policy and how it works. Credibility on the part of the policymakers will reduce learning time and will frequently reduce the cost of a transition to a new policy. Bayesian or least-squares learning models are at best rough approximations of this learning process and present the disadvantage of not modeling the analysis of policymakers' credibility. This is an area where more research would be very useful.

Transition problems also arise because of rigidities in the economy, such as wage contracts, loan contracts, or other long-term commitments. These rigidities suggest a gradual implementation of new policies. By simulating estimated rational expectations models in a deterministic mode, one can estimate the appropriate speed of implementation of policy during a transition.

This chapter showed how these calculations can be made for two important policy-implementation problems, disinflation and budget-deficit reduction. In both examples, the new policy is different from the old policy only in the intercept coefficients of the policy rule. The same approach could be applied to more general transition problems.

Reference Notes

The literature on learning in rational expectations models expanded greatly in the 1980s. Bray (1983) and Frydman (1983), Marcet and Sargent (1989), for example, have considered the problem of convergence to a rational expectations equilibrium. Usually, learning is modeled by a Bayesian or least-squares mechanism. The problem of learning during a transition, as discussed in Section 7.1, pertains to the specific case where people must learn about a new policy, as presented in the paper on learning by Taylor (1975), which also assumed Bayesian learning.

The discussion of a transition to zero inflation discussed in Section 7.2 is drawn directly from Taylor (1983a). A refinement of those calculations that includes many one-year contracts in addition to the union labor contracts is reported in Taylor (1982). Phelps (1978) and Ball (1990) have studied analytically the problem of transition to a low inflation rule (disinflation) in staggered contract models.

The discussion of the transition to a lower budget deficit in Section 7.3 is based on simulations of the multicountry model reported in Taylor (1988) that pertained to simulations in the late 1980s. That paper focused on the trade deficit, the subject of the conference where it was presented.

McKinnon (1991) has considered the problem of transition to a market economy, addressing a broad range of economic issues beyond the macro-economic transition questions that are the focus of this chapter. Lucas (1980) has briefly considered the problem of transitions to new policy rules in a paper on policy advising and policy rules, arguing that built-in institutional inertia and legislative lags would provide for a sufficiently gradual transition.

8

Policy Systems in Operation

The quantitative analysis of policy rules in the preceding two chapters is representative of a fundamentally new development in macroeconomics. That analysis could not have been done ten years ago—before the invention of new solution and estimation techniques for economywide equilibrium models with rational expectations, before the refinement of expectations-consistent wage and price theories that would fit actual data, or before the development of an empirical framework to handle international capital flows in efficient world markets.

Few would even have thought about doing such an analysis more than fifteen years ago—before the Lucas critique, before the recognition that rational expectations did not imply that policy was ineffective, before credibility was seen as an empirically significant virtue, or before the time-inconsistency rationale for policy rules was developed. Traditional econometric models were fine for directing policy.

It would be incomplete and misleading, however, to finish this book by pointing smugly to new policy methods and their advantages, looking disparagingly at old methods and mistakes, and omitting perhaps the most difficult element of macroeconomic policy, the operational step between policy analyzing and policy making. This chapter focuses on what new policy research implies for practical policy making. Put more formally, having studied the design of policy rules and the transition between rules in Chapters 6 and 7, this chapter looks at the operation of policy rules.

8.1   From Policy Rules to Credible and Systematic Policies

The policy rules investigated in Chapter 6—for example, the formula for the price rule in Equation (6.1) or the formula for the nominal income rule in Equation (6.3)—do not involve fixed settings for the instruments of monetary policy. This is a substantial difference from rules with fixed settings for the instruments such as the constant-growth rate rule for the money supply originally advocated by Milton Friedman. The rules of Chapter 6 are responsive, calling for changes in the short-term interest rate in response to deviations of the price level or real income from a target. They are quite precise about this response—the coefficients in the algebraic formulas provide exact instructions about how much the Fed should adjust the federal funds rate.

Despite the responsiveness and specificity of the algebraic formulas, however, policymakers are unlikely to start following them mechanically. And, at least with the current state of economic knowledge and technique, they may have good reasons. For example, the quarterly time period is probably too short to average out blips in the price level that are due to temporary changes in commodity prices. And although it is essential that interest-rate targeting pay attention to what is happening to real interest rates, the one-year-ahead rational forecast of the inflation rate from a multicountry model may not be measuring inflation expectations as accurately as surveys or evidence from futures markets. On the other hand, a quarter is too long to hold the federal funds rate fixed between adjustments. For example, when the economy starts into recession, sharp and rapid interest-rate declines might be appropriate.

Many of these problems could be corrected by straightforward generalizations of these policy rules. A moving average of price level deviations from a target over a number of quarters, for example, would be a way to smooth out temporary price fluctuations. Averaging real output deviations—or nominal output deviations—from target could also be considered. Measuring the expected inflation rate over a number of different horizons might also be desirable. Going to a monthly model (not a straightforward exercise)—and taking even longer moving averages—would be a way to make the interest rate more responsive in the very short term. Such generalizations are an important task for future research.

However, these modifications would make the policy rule more complex and more difficult to understand. And even with many such generalizations, it is difficult to see how such an algebraic rule could be sufficiently encompassing. For example, interpreting whether a rise in the price level is temporary or permanent is likely to require looking at other measures of prices (such as the consumer price index, the producer price index, or the employment cost index). Looking at expectations of inflation as measured by bond prices, surveys, or forecasts from other analysts is also likely to be helpful. Interpreting the level and the growth rate of potential output—the target Y^* in the policy rule—involves other factors such as productivity, labor force participation and demographic effects on unemployment. While the analysis of these issues can be aided by quantitative methods like the ones examined in this book, it is difficult to formulate them into a precise algebraic formula. Moreover, there will be episodes where the funds rate target will need to be adjusted to deal with special factors. For example, the

Federal Reserve provided additional reserves to the banking system after the stock market break of October 19, 1987, and it helped prevent a contraction of liquidity and restored confidence. Although liquidity shocks and confidence shocks are part of the analytical framework of the multicountry model, the Fed would need more than the interest-rate rule as a policy guide in such cases.

But where does this leave us? Should we give up on policy rules and return to discretion? In fact, arguments like the one in the preceding paragraph sound suspiciously like those used by advocates of discretion rather than rules. But if there is anything about which modern macroeconomics is clear—and on which there is substantial consensus—it is that policy rules offer major advantages in improving economic performance, as explained in Chapter 1 and elsewhere. Hence, it is important to seek a way to preserve the concept of a policy rule in a world where it is still unlikely that to follow mechanically a policy rule is advisable.

One such approach is described here. It was developed by the Council of Economic Advisers in 1989 and 1990 and was incorporated in the *Economic Report of the President*[1] in a way that was generally accepted in government policy-making agencies.[2] The approach consists of three parts that I illustrate in the context of monetary policy.

A New Look for Policy Rules

The first part is purely a semantic one. It simply involves introducing some new language as a proxy for potentially misleading academic jargon. In the first chapter of this book I emphasized that the term "policy rule" does not necessarily mean either a fixed setting for the policy instruments or a mechanical formula. My saying so, however, does not change common usage. The term "policy rule" sometimes connotes a fixed setting for the policy instruments, and it usually connotes a simplistic mechanical procedure. It would help if there were an alternative terminology.

One terminology was adopted in the 1990 *Economic Report of the President*. "Policy *rule*" was replaced by "*systematic* policy" or sometimes by "policy *system*" when a noun seemed more appropriate. Thus, in describing his economic policy principles in his 1990 economic message to Congress, President Bush stated, "My Administration will . . . support a credible, *systematic*

---

[1] The term "Economic Report of the President" conventionally refers to both a short economic message from the president to Congress (technically called the "Economic Report of the President") and the Annual Report of the Council of Economic Advisers. Both are printed in the same bound volume. Unless otherwise stated, I will use the conventional terminology.

[2] Drafts of the *Economic Report of the President* are circulated for comment throughout the White House, the Cabinet agencies, and the Federal Reserve. Major areas of disagreement are usually worked out so that the *Report* could legitimately be said to represent the Administration's economic-policy principles. Hence, the language from the *Report*, which I will refer to, is much more than the thinking of several economic advisers. It is something the line agencies could accept as well.

monetary policy program that sustains maximum economic growth while controlling and reducing inflation." (p. 4, italics added)

The adjective "systematic" is defined in the *Oxford American Dictionary* as "methodical, according to a plan, and not casually or at random." This connotes the important properties of a policy rule, without focusing on the more mechanical details. In any case, this was the intention.

Drawing the Line between Fundamentals and Details

The second part is to give a characterization of the fundamental properties of a systematic policy, stopping short of specifying less important details. Perhaps it is best to start with an analogy. Consider patent laws, for example, which are frequently compared with macropolicy rules in time-consistency literature. Patent laws establish the principle that inventors who register have the rights to market their invention for a given number of years. The details—whether the invention is novel, who invented it first, new licensing agreements—are left to patent office officials and to the court system. The question of where one draws the line between the fundamentals and the details will depend on many factors and is a good subject for future research. Clearly the line will be drawn at a different place for different types of policies—monetary policy, fiscal policy, or exchange-rate policy.

Some of the fundamental features of a monetary policy rule—like Equation (6.4) of Chapter 6—were given in the 1990 *Annual Report of the Council of Economic Advisers*:

> The Federal Reserve generally increases interest rates when inflationary pressures appear to be rising and lowers interest rates when inflationary pressures are abating and recession appears to be more of a threat.... Assessing just how much the policy instrument needs to be changed as circumstances evolve requires judgment. Thus, a policy approach that relies on the expertise of the FOMC members is appropriate and should be preserved. If the operating stance of policy is ... measured by interest rates, appropriate settings vary with the interest sensitivity of aggregate demand. (p. 85)

Note that this characterization gives the *signs* of the response coefficients of the policy rule: in terms of Equation (6.4), it says that the coefficients g_1 and g_2 should be positive. Rather than specifying the magnitudes of the coefficients, however, it states that the magnitudes should depend on the sensitivity of aggregate demand to interest rates. Put differently, the response coefficients should depend on the empirical relationship between interest rates and aggregate demand—the sum of consumption demand, of investment demand, and of the demand for net exports. That certainly is the implication of the design analysis of Chapter 6, but it is considerably less specific than stating the magnitudes of the responses as one could with an estimated model. However, given that there is no consensus on a single econometric model of the economy and given the well-founded suspicion that even structural models change over time, this is probably as far in the direction of specificity as one can draw the line at this time.

This characterization by itself, however, is not specific about the target for inflation or for real output. It only states that the federal funds rate should be adjusted when inflation rises or falls and when output rises or falls. By omitting a target for inflation, it draws the line well short of some of the fundamental properties of a good policy rule. Certainly, more is needed if the characterization is to effectively convey the fundamental properties of a policy rule such as Equation (6.4).

How can we include some of these fundamentals? Since the mid-1970s monetary targets have been used in many countries to state targets for inflation. If money velocity were stable, then, given an estimate of potential output growth, money targets would imply a target for the price level; given velocity and a real output target, the target price level would obviously fall out algebraically from the money-supply target. But the 1980s have shown that money velocity is not stable in the short run; this is why the discussion focuses on interest-rate rules. Nevertheless, the long-run stability of the velocity of some monetary measures allows one to state targets for the price level and to keep the tradition of focusing Federal Reserve policy on long-run targets on the money supply. The 1990 *Economic Report of the President* put it this way referring to the $M2$ measure of the money supply:

> Despite problems with the monetary aggregates, the Federal Reserve has not adopted a purely discretionary approach to policy.... In particular, research at the Federal Reserve and elsewhere shows that the velocity of M2 has been essentially stable over the long run. M2 could serve therefore as an anchor for price stability and as a basis for a credible, systematic long-run monetary policy. That is, as long as there are no signs of *permanent* shifts of M2 velocity, the Federal Reserve would do well to commit to eventually maintaining *long-run* growth of M2 consistent with expansion of the economy's potential to produce, while allowing higher or lower growth rates over shorter periods of time to offset shifts in velocity. Such an approach would be consistent with the Federal Reserve Act's requirements for monetary policy. (p. 86)

For example, with an estimated secular growth of real output of 2.5 percent, and steady velocity, a money growth range of 2.5 percent to 6.5 percent—the Fed's targets for 1991—would imply that the price level target grows at the rate of 0 to 4 percent per year. Given biases such as index-number problems in measuring prices, the average 2 per year implicit target inflation rate is probably very close to price stability or "zero" inflation.

A Consensus Rationale for Systematic Policies: Credibility

The third part is to give an easily understood rationale for sticking to a given systematic policy. Given the wide consensus about its importance, credibility should be at the heart of this rationale, as the simulations with the models in this book have shown that credibility does improve economic performance. The 1990 *Economic Report of the President* put it this way:

> Economic research and the lessons of the past two decades suggest a macro-economic strategy for meeting the challenges of the 1990s and beyond. If fiscal and monetary policies are systematic and credible, rather than characterized by the frequent exercise of short-sighted discretion, strong sustainable noninflationary growth can be achieved.
>
> Popular accounts of economic ideas typically focus on controversies and areas of disagreement. This focus is particularly common in discussions of macro-economics, where monetarists, supply-siders, Keynesians, new classical macro-economists, and others are often paired off against each other. While such controversies exist and have been important in the development of economic thinking, they mask two key areas of consensus concerning macroeconomic policy.
>
> First, agreement is now widespread on the detrimental effects of a short-sighted discretionary approach to macroeconomic policy that attempts neither to lay out policy plans nor to maintain a commitment to such plans. Because policymakers are regularly praised and criticized for short-run developments, they experience pressures to approach economic policy from a short-run viewpoint. Stating a plan or program as clearly as possible tends to counteract such pressures.
>
> Second, research and experience have demonstrated the great advantages of establishing a credible commitment to a policy plan. Improved credibility, which is enhanced by achieving stated policy goals and consistently following stated policy principles, can favorably affect expectations. It can help resolve the uncertainty that arises when changes in the structure of the economy complicate the interpretation of policy actions. It also enables households and businesses to plan for the future, thereby promoting saving, investment, and economic growth.

These three parts—(1) introducing the notion of "systematic" policies in place of the more mechanical-sounding policy "rules," (2) defining systematic policy in particular applications by drawing a line between essential fundamentals and details that are either less important or less amenable to formulation, and (3) stressing credibility as a key rationale for sticking with a policy rule—constitute one approach to the operation of policy rules in practice. The second part requires the most analysis and could benefit greatly from additional research. Given this operational approach, I now consider three case studies to illustrate its use.

8.2   The Oil-Price Shock of 1990

Operating a systematic monetary policy in the face of an oil-price shock is difficult and deserves particular study. It is even more difficult if the shock occurs during a transition to a new policy. I focus here on the events that followed the Iraq invasion of Kuwait on August 2, 1990, roughly six months after the principles of a systematic policy, summarized above, were published in the 1990 *Economic Report of the President.*

The oil-price shock occurred as the U.S. economy was growing slowly following the 1988–1989 monetary tightening—increases in the federal funds rate that had been aimed at containing and reducing the rate of inflation. If one characterizes the Fed actions in terms of the systematic policy described in the preceding section, then the increase in the federal funds rate can be interpreted as occurring for two reasons. First, economic growth in 1987 and 1988 was very strong, and inflation was rising; both factors would call for an increase in the federal funds rate according to a policy rule like that in Equation (6.4). Moreover, the Fed had indicated that its intention was to move the economy toward price stability. In other words, the Fed had been attempting to gradually disinflate—to make a *transition* to price stability, in the terminology of Chapter 7. In fact, the mean of the target growth rate ranges for the $M2$ money supply had been reduced from 7 percent in 1987 to 5 percent in 1990 and was reduced to $4\frac{1}{2}$ percent in 1991. The explicit intention of reducing the growth-rate targets was to reduce the rate of inflation by an equivalent amount.

Iraq invaded Kuwait on August 2, 1990. Iraq and Kuwait together had been producing 4.3 million barrels of oil a day, and there was a threat to the supply of oil from Saudi Arabia. Not surprisingly the price of oil rose sharply from $21 per barrel at the end of July to $28 on August 6 and eventually to a peak of $46 in mid-October. The monthly average price rose from $17 in July to $36 in October. The effect that this increase in oil prices might have on the economy was of great concern, and major efforts were put in place to estimate the economic impacts. Task forces were assembled, and many models—both traditional and forward-looking—were simulated to obtain estimates. The Council of Economic Advisers published a consensus estimate that a one-year temporary increase in oil prices of 50 percent could temporarily raise the overall price level (output deflator) by about 1 percent and, with a longer lag, cause real output to fall by about the same amount.

Policy Response

What should be the monetary and fiscal policy reaction to these changes? Suppose that a systematic monetary policy like the one described in the preceding section were in place. Taken literally, Equation (6.4) would say that an increase in the central bank's interest rate target—relative to what it otherwise would be—was in order: in the short run the price level would rise more than real output would fall. However, such an interest-rate increase would be inappropriate if the price level rise was temporary and would soon disappear.

In fact, much analysis suggested that the increase would be temporary. The futures market for oil was helpful in making this assessment. Although the spot price for oil doubled by mid-October, the one-year-ahead futures price changed very little. The December 1991 futures price rose by only about $4 per barrel while the spot price rose by $25. Moreover, oil-supply analyses suggested that increased oil production elsewhere could eventually make up most of the lost production in Iraq and Kuwait if the embargo continued. The main uncertainty was whether additional oil-production facilities would be destroyed before the conflict ended. This uncertainty was dramatically resolved with the successful start of Desert Storm in mid-January 1991.

For these reasons, an increase in interest rates to counteract the increase in the price level brought about by the oil shock would be inappropriate— despite the literal interpretation of Equation (6.4). However, not adjusting interest rates in the face of a rising price level requires an increase in the rate of money growth (again compared with what it otherwise would be), as well as an increase in nominal income. As the 1991 *Economic Report of the President* put it, "Depending on the size of the shock, a temporary increase in money-supply growth might be necessary . . . increasing it somewhat may result in a temporary increase in nominal GNP growth. But eventually, nominal GNP growth should return to a path consistent with low and stable inflation. Given credible monetary policy, an increase in nominal GNP growth need not cause an increase in long-run inflationary expectations." (p. 94)

In order to emphasize the importance of maintaining a credible policy in the face of a price shock, the experience of the 1970s was reviewed carefully. The oil-price shocks that occurred in the 1970s, it was argued, occurred at a time when monetary policy had little credibility. In fact, inflation was rising at a rapid pace before both the 1973 and the 1979 oil shocks. With little credibility, monetary policymakers could not permit the oil shocks to pass through completely into the price level without causing fear that they were continuing to tolerate even higher inflation.

The experience in Japan in the first and second oil shocks provided a useful example of the payoff from a credible monetary policy stance. The 1973 oil-price shock occurred in Japan while inflation was rising rapidly. However, the 1979 oil-price shock occurred after the Bank of Japan had adopted a more credible monetary policy with a much lower rate of money growth and a much lower rate of inflation. It turned out that the 1979 oil-price shock had much less effect on inflation and real output in Japan than the 1973 oil shock and a remarkably smaller effect than in the United States and other countries. Figure 8-1, which is a replica of two charts prepared by the staff of the OECD in August 1990 soon after the Iraq invasion of Kuwait, nicely illustrates the difference in Japanese policies toward the two oil-price shocks of the 1970s. The Japanese policies also make a striking contrast with the U.S. policies in the late 1970s.

International Macroeconomic Policy

What was the analysis in other countries? How did other countries respond to the 1990 oil-price shock, and how did it affect international

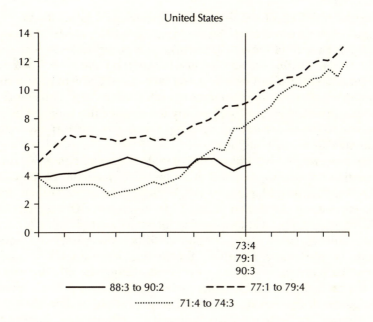

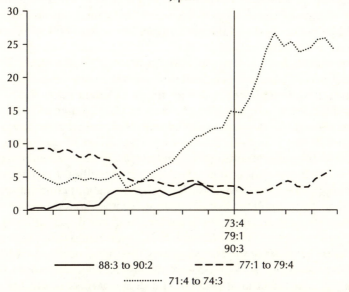

FIGURE 8-1   Current Inflation and Inflation at the Time of the Oil-Price Rises of the 1970s (percentage change in CPI from year before). The vertical line indicates the oil shock.

coordination? One of the first regular meetings of international finance officials that occurred after the Iraq invasion of Kuwait was the so-called "Working Party 3" of the OECD in Paris. This group includes senior policy officials from the finance ministry and the central bank in each of ten large industrial countries and usually meets four times a year to discuss macro-economic policy and developments in each country.[3] The September 1990 meeting provided a good opportunity to consider the appropriate policy response to the oil-price shock that began in August and was still occurring at the time of the meeting.

That meeting ended with a considerable degree of consensus that was to continue throughout the fall at a number of meetings of the G-7 and of the International Monetary Fund. Perhaps most important was that the oil-price rise was not viewed as requiring short-term changes in monetary policies. With central banks following monetary strategies that focused on adjustment of interest rates, this position is best interpreted as a policy response like the one discussed for the United States: interest rates should follow the path that would have occurred without the oil-price shock. In other words, the course that was correct before the oil shock should be maintained. If that meant that interest rates were to decline, then the decline should not be delayed; the "systematic" interest-rate policy should be maintained as closely as possible. There was also a broad consensus that the credibility of economic policies, which had been built up in the 1980s, should be maintained and that a clear message should be sent that this was the intention of policymakers.

The role of fiscal policy was also discussed. The automatic stabilizers of fiscal policy provide some built-in response to any negative effects on real output and employment that an oil shock might have, and it was certainly the intention in the United States in the summer of 1990 to allow this response to work to mitigate the impact of the oil-price shock on the economy. Some policy officials raised the possibility of overriding the automatic stabilizers—offsetting them by increasing taxes or reducing expenditures elsewhere—but others raised strong opposition to such overrides. Surprisingly, therefore, there was less consensus about continuing to keep "systematic" fiscal policies in place than there was about monetary policy.

The Gramm-Rudman-Hollings budget law, which was still in force in the United States in the summer of 1990, did not allow for the automatic stabilizers. Increases in the budget deficit, whether caused by new programs or by the automatic stabilizers, were against this law and would result in across-the-board cuts in spending. The deficit targets would not change even if an oil-price shock worsened economic conditions. Hence, changes

---

[3]The United States is the only country with three representatives at the table, the extra place traditionally reserved for a member of the Council of Economic Advisers. The chief economist from the International Monetary Fund and the Bank for International Settlements also attend these meetings and present forecast and policy analysis.

in this law were needed if the automatic stabilizers were to be allowed to help stabilize the economy. The revisions in the budget law worked out in the weeks following the oil-price shock required that the budget targets be adjusted for changes in the economy. The next section describes how these changes were put into the law and provides another illustration of the operation of policy rules.

8.3 Automatic Stabilizers and the Revision to the Budget Law

As part of the 1990 Budget Summit agreement, several legislative changes were made that altered the responsiveness of fiscal policy to the state of the economy. The changes were made at a time when it was recognized that the economy might be negatively affected by the oil-price shock and that the likelihood that the slowdown would turn into a recession was increasing. In fact the economy did enter a recession, and events that occurred during that recession illustrate some of the difficulties of operating a systematic fiscal policy in practice.

The new budget procedures distinguished between two types of government spending: (1) "discretionary" spending, which consists primarily of military purchases, foreign aid, and domestic purchases of goods and services, and (2) "entitlement" spending, which consists largely of transfer payments such as welfare, medicare, medicaid, and unemployment insurance. The budget law put explicit dollar "limits" on discretionary spending for five years and required that any *new* entitlement program be matched either by reductions in other entitlement programs or by increases in taxes; the latter was called the "pay-as-you-go" rule. Any legislation that violated either the "limit" rule or the "pay-as-you-go" rule would bring about an automatic "sequester"—an automatic across-the-board cut in the category of government spending where the violation occurred. If effective, the procedures would prevent *new* government programs from increasing the budget deficit.

Increasing budget deficits would be allowed if caused by the automatic stabilizers, however. For example, if unemployment compensation were to rise as the economy slowed down, then this would be allowed to increase the deficit. But legislated changes in entitlement programs would not be allowed unless they could be offset elsewhere in the budget or unless an emergency was declared by the president.

In effect, the 1990 budget agreement attempted to both reduce the structural deficit through the "limit" and "pay-as-you-go" rules and allow the automatic stabilizers to increase the budget deficit in a recession. Although the new budget law has such features, there is still significant room for improvement. The growth of "entitlement" spending, even on existing programs, began to rise rapidly. Legislative changes will be required simply to restrain this growth.

8.4   The Bond Market and Inflation

Assessing whether an increase in long-term interest rates is due to an increase in expected inflation or to an increase in the real interest rate is part of the task of operating a systematic monetary policy. For example, if the policy is to raise interest rates when inflation picks up, then a rise in long-term interest rates might suggest an incipient rise in inflation and might make policymakers less willing to keep the short-term interest rate steady, even if actual inflation does not change. But that increase in long-term interest rates could be due to other factors, such as a shift in the demand for investment or saving.

Such a situation arose in early 1990. After declining in the latter part of 1989, long-term interest rates rose sharply in early 1990. Ten-year Treasury-bond yields rose by 75 basis points. Concern about a rise in inflation could have caused this increase and, if so, could have called for a postponement of declines in interest rates that the systematic monetary policy would have called for. However, considerable evidence suggested that other factors were responsible for the increase in long-term rates.

The United States was not the only country to experience an increase in long-term interest rates. Germany had even larger increases, suggesting the possibility that real factors were behind the increase in interest rates. The German and U.S. interest rate increase is shown in Figure 8-2. In an integrated world capital market, an increase in interest rates in Germany could be transmitted to U.S. interest rates. That is the implication of the multicountry model used in this book.

In fact, there was a major change in Germany at this time that could have had such an impact on German long-term rates—anticipations that East Germany and West Germany would be unified and that the unification would increase the demand for capital in Germany and lead to an increase in the government budget deficit in Germany. Greater investment demand would be expected to raise real interest rates in Germany later in 1990 and in 1991 and, with forward-looking expectations, to raise long-term interest rates immediately. Again this is the implication of the multicountry model used in this book. In fact, the anticipated increase in demand for investment and reduction in national saving occurred in 1990 as the unification took place. In 1989 the West German budget was essentially in balance, with a surplus of .2 percent of GDP. That surplus turned dramatically in 1990 into a deficit of 3 percent of GDP. Hence, the timing turned out to be correct and consistent with this explanation.

But monetary policy decisions in early 1990 could not wait until 1991 when evidence was available about unification and its impact. In early 1990 the analysis had to rely on forecasts and model simulations to see if the magnitudes were plausible. In other words, would an increase in the demand for capital in Germany of plausible magnitudes cause an increase in interest rates of the magnitudes observed? Was it a quantitatively sufficient explanation? Calculations were made with forward-looking empirical

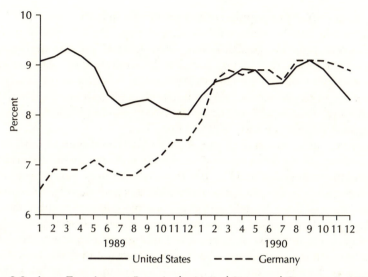

FIGURE 8-2 Long-Term Interest Rates in the United States and Germany in 1989 and 1990

models. The simulations suggested that increases in interest rates of about 1 percentage point were consistent with reasonably plausible increases in the demand for capital. Hence, an increase in expected inflation was not needed to explain the increase in long-term interest rates and gave some indication that the Fed's interest-rate policy need not be adjusted. It was necessary to use quantitative models to make this calculation, but a simple algebraic formula could not have captured the monetary actions.

8.5 Assessment: A Continuing Revolution?

Keynesian economics was born in the 1930s with the publication of Keynes's *The General Theory of Employment, Interest, and Money* (1936), popularized in the 1940s with the first edition of Paul Samuelson's principles text, and put into a specific econometric form in the 1950s with Lawrence Klein's Model I and follow-up models. But, as Walter W. Heller put it, Keynesian economics "came of age in the 1960s" when it was "pressed into public service." Commenting on this public service in the 1960s, Heller wrote, "These are profound changes. What they have wrought is not the creation of a 'new economics,' but the completion of the Keynesian Revolution— thirty years after John Maynard Keynes fired the opening salvo."[4]

The 1970s saw another revolution in macroeconomics—represented by the research papers collected in 1981 by Robert Lucas and Thomas Sargent.[5]

[4]Heller (1966), pp. 1, 2, and 59.
[5]Lucas and Sargent (1981).

One can see efforts to popularize this revolution in textbooks in the 1980s, at least at the intermediate level. And, as I hope the first seven chapters of this book make clear, efforts have been made to put the new ideas in econometric form—now perhaps beyond the equivalent of Klein's Model I.

This chapter touches on issues closer to the "coming-of-age" stage, the "pressing-into-public-service" stage, of the revolution. Does what I have written about in this chapter constitute the completion, in Heller's sense, of a revolution? I don't think so. At least I hope not.

Progress has been made on the semantics of rules, systems, and discretion and on the incorporation of credibility and systematic features into certain aspects of policy making. But there is still a huge gap between technical work, such as the stochastic simulation of algebraic rules in estimated rational expectations models, and the front-line conduct of monetary and fiscal policy. In a way, the focus on rules rather than discretion, which is inherent in modern research, has made filling that gap much more difficult and much less appealing to both researchers and policymakers than in the case of the Keynesian revolution. Heller began his 1966 book stating that the new economics of the 1960s was a source of "presidential power." Today's macroeconomic research—with its focus on limiting the discretion of policymakers, on designing institutions that will help ensure that policy rules are not changed for time-inconsistency reasons—cannot be advertised as a source of power in the same sense. Perhaps the increased recognition that limiting discretion with better institutional design is the way and the promise of the future will accelerate the completion of the current macroeconomic revolution. In any case, the "coming-of-age" pace set by the Keynesian revolution was thirty years. By the standard of that pace, we still have another ten years before the macroeconomic revolution of the 1970s could be viewed as immature for its age. There is no reason to be disappointed yet.

Reference Notes

The interpretation in Section 8.1 of policy rules as something less than mechanical formulas but more than discretion is still somewhat controversial. For example, Laidler (1991), who has been an advocate of monetary policy rules concludes, "We are left, then, with relying on discretionary policy in order to maintain price stability." McCallum (1988) is concerned with finding a specific formula that can be followed mechanically. Lucas's (1980) analysis of practical policy focused more on making additional legislative changes to enforce the policy rule.

The patent example is discussed in Kydland and Prescott (1977) and used by Taylor (1983b) to support the view that time inconsistency is not likely to be a good positive theory of inflation, even though its normative implication is profound. The translation of monetary targets into price-level targets, as discussed in Section 8.1, is behind the concept of P^* used at the

Fed. This concept is an attempt to specify the targets for a "systematic" monetary policy.

A good summary of international macroeconomic policy discussions in various fora including the OECD is found in Crocket (1989) and Dobson (1991).

One calculation of the impact of German unification on long-term interest rates, using a multicountry rational expectations model as discussed in Section 8.4, is published in Adams, Alexander, and Gagnon (1991). The *MX*3 model that was used for these calculations at the Fed is published in Gagnon (1991).

Appendix 1:
Data

This appendix describes the entire data series used to estimate the multicountry model described in Chapter 3. The model was estimated with seasonally adjusted quarterly national-income account data from 1971 to 1986. The exact starting and ending quarters vary slightly among the equations because of differences in estimation methods, differences in numbers of lags or leads in each equation, and differences in data availability in each country at the time of estimation.

The data were obtained from readily available sources. For all countries except the United States, most of the data were obtained from international agencies. The financial data on interest rates, exchange rates, and money supply are from the OECD's *Main Economic Indicators* (MEI) and the Federal Reserve Bank of St. Louis's *International Economic Conditions* (IEC). The national income account data are from the OECD's *Quarterly National Accounts* (QNA). The wage data are from the OECD's *Main Economic Indicators* and from the IMF's *International Financial Statistics* (IFS). The U.S. data were obtained directly from *Citibase* data diskettes. Some Japanese data were obtained from the Economic Planning Agency's *Annual Report on National Accounts.*

The degree of detail in the breakdown of GNP by spending component differs from country to country in the OECD's *Quarterly National Accounts*, and the differences in disaggregation in the model for some of the countries reflect this. There is no consumption breakdown for Germany or Italy. Nor is there a breakdown for fixed investment for Germany and Italy. For Japan, nonresidential investment is not broken down into structures and equipment.

Most of the national-income account data are published in seasonally adjusted form, but only seasonally unadjusted data are available for the German national account data and for Japanese disaggregated consumption. These seasonally unadjusted data series were seasonally adjusted, using the computer program microTSP, before they were used for estimation.

All the national income data is in constant dollars. The base years for real GNP, the price deflators, and the wage index are different in each country.

Some of the auxiliary series used to compute the series in the model are also included in the data description. The conversion description records the transformations that have been made on the original series before estimation or model simulation. Note that the series description refers to the original data; the conversion generates the model data from the original data. Most of the conversions are simply changes in units or frequencies. For example, a series originally with quarterly values in millions of francs must be multiplied by 0.004 to be converted to an annual value in billions of francs.

For Canada, France, Japan, and the United Kingdom, consumption expenditures on nondurable goods includes semi-durable expenditures as defined in the QNA (the series creation is defined accordingly). For Canada and Japan, net direct purchases abroad of gifts, a very small number, is simply added to services consumption. Other conversions involve seasonal adjustment as described above.

Diskettes containing a data bank of both the original and converted data are available from the author.

The following abbreviations are used:

MEI   OECD, *Main Economic Indicators*

IEC   Federal Reserve Bank of St. Louis, *International Economic Conditions*

QNA   OECD, *Quarterly National Accounts*

IFS   International Monetary Fund, *International Financial Statistics*

EPA   Japanese Economic Planning Agency, *Annual Report on National Accounts*

SA   Seasonally adjusted

NSA   Not seasonally adjusted

AR   Annual rate

QR   Quarterly Rate

QA   Quarterly average (transformed to quarterly frequency by averaging the monthly observations)

Series listed with the source QNA were collected from three different issues: 1986(4), 1986(3), and 1985(3). These were used to obtain observations for (1) 1973:1 onward; (2) 1972:1 to 1972:4; and (3) 1971:1 to 1971:4, respectively. For some series, the data in the 1985(3) issue differed from the data in the later issues because of revisions. In order to prevent jumps in these time series, the observations for 1971:1 to 1971:4 appearing in the 1985(3) issue were multiplied by the ratio 1972:1 observation from 1986(3)/1972:1 observation from 1985(3).

The series and the names of each series are listed below in alphabetical order:

C3: Private Consumption Expenditures—Germany (mil. 1980 marks)
NSA, QR, QNA
Quarterly: 1971:1–1986:3
Conversion: ×0.004, SA

C4: Private Consumption Expenditures—Italy (bil. 1970 lire)
SA, QR, QNA
Quarterly: 1971:1–1986:3
Conversion: ×4

C5: Private Consumption Expenditures—Japan (bil. 1980 yen)
SA, AR, Economic Planning Agency of Japan, *Annual Report*
Quarterly: 1971:1–1986:3
Conversion: None

C6: Private Consumption Expenditures—U.K. (mil. 1980 pounds)
(C6 series is CD6 + CN6 + CS6)
SA, QR, QNA
Quarterly: 1971:1–1986:3
Conversion: None

CD: Private Consumption Expenditures on Durable Goods—U.S. (bil. 1982 dollars)
SA, AR, CITIBASE 1986, Series: GCD82
Quarterly: 1971:1–1986:4
Conversion: None

CD1: Private Consumption Expenditures on Durable Goods—Canada (mil. 1981 Canadian dollars)
SA, AR, QNA
Quarterly: 1971:1–1986:3
Conversion: ×0.001

CD2: Private Consumption Expenditures on Durable Goods—France (bil. 1970 francs)
SA, QR, QNA
Quarterly: 1971:1–1986:2
Conversion: ×4

CD5: Private Consumption Expenditures on Durable Goods—Japan (bil. 1980 yen)
NSA, AR, EPA, *Annual Report*
Quarterly: 1971:1–1986:1
Conversion: SA

CD6: Private Consumption Expenditures on Durable Goods—U.K. (mil. 1980 pounds)
SA, QR, QNA
Quarterly: 1971:1–1986:3
Conversion: ×0.004

CN: Private Consumption Expenditures on Nondurable Goods—U.S. (bil. 1982 dollars)
SA, AR, CITIBASE 1986, Series: GCN82
Quarterly: 1971:1–1986:4
Conversion: None

CN1: Private Consumption Expenditures on Nondurable Goods—Canada (mil. 1981 Canadian dollars)
SA, AR, QNA
Quarterly: 1971:1–1986:3
Conversion: (CSD1 + CND1) × 0.001

CN2: Private Consumption Expenditures on Nondurable Goods—France (bil. 1970 francs)
SA, QR, QNA
Quarterly: 1971:1–1986:2
Conversion: CN2 = (CSD2 + CND2) × 4

CN5: Private Consumption Expenditures on Nondurable Goods—Japan (bil. 1980 yen)
NSA, AR, EPA of Japan, *Annual Report*
Quarterly: 1971:1–1986:1
Conversion: CN5 = CSD5 + CND5, SA

CN6: Private Consumption Expenditures on Nondurable Goods—U.K. (mil. 1980 pounds)
SA, QR, QNA
Quarterly: 1971:1–1986:3
Conversion: CN6 = (CSD6 + CND6) × 0.004

CND1: Private Consumption Expenditures on Nondurable Goods, Excluding Semi-durables—Canada (mil. 1981 Canadian dollars)
SA, AR, QNA
Quarterly: 1971:1–1986:3
Conversion: None, used to compute CN1

CND2: Private Consumption Expenditures on Nondurable Goods, Excluding Semi-durables—France (bil. 1970 francs)
SA, QR, QNA
Quarterly: 1971:1–1986:2
Conversion: None, used to compute CN2

CND5: Private Consumption Expenditures on Nondurable Goods, Excluding Semi-durables—Japan (bil. 1980 yen)
NSA, AR, EPA of Japan, *Annual Report*
Quarterly: 1971:1–1986:1
Conversion: None, used to compute CN3

CND6: Private Consumption Expenditures on Nondurable Goods, Excluding Semi-durables—U.K. (mil. 1980 pounds)
SA, QR, QNA
Quarterly: 1971:1–1986:3
Conversion: None, used to compute CN4

CPG1: Net Direct Purchases Abroad and Gifts—Canada (mil. 1981 Canadian dollars)
SA, AR, QNA
Quarterly: 1971:1–1986:3
Conversion: None

CPG5: Net Purchases Abroad and Gifts—Japan (bil. 1980 yen)
NSA, AR, EPA of Japan, *Annual Report*
Quarterly: 1971:1–1986:1
Conversion: None

CS: Private Consumption Expenditures on Services—U.S. (bil. 1982 dollars)
SA, AR, CITIBASE 1986, Series: GCS82
Quarterly: 1971:1–1986:4
Conversion: None

CS1: Private Consumption Expenditures on Services—Canada (mil. 1981 Canadian dollars)
SA, AR, QNA
Quarterly: 1971:1–1986:3
Conversion: CPG1 is added to the QNA series

CS2: Private Consumption Expenditures on Services—France (bil. 1970 francs)
SA, QR, QNA
Quarterly: 1971:1–1986:2
Conversion: ×4

CS5: Private Consumption Expenditures on Services—Japan (bil. 1980 yen)
NSA, AR, EPA of Japan, *Annual Report*
Quarterly: 1971:1–1986:1
Conversion: SA, CPG1 is added to the QNA series

CS6: Private Consumption Expenditures on Services—U.K. (mil. 1980 pounds)
SA, QR, QNA
Quarterly: 1971:1–1986:3
Conversion: ×0.004

CSD1: Private Consumption Expenditures on Semi-durable Goods—Canada (mil. 1981 Canadian dollars)
SA, AR, QNA
Quarterly: 1971:1–1986:3
Conversion: ×0.001, used to compute CN1

CSD2: Private Consumption Expenditures on Semi-durable Goods—France (bil. 1970 francs)
SA, QR, QNA
Quarterly: 1971:1–1986:2
Conversion: None, used to compute CN2

CSD5: Private Consumption Expenditures on Semi-durable Goods—Japan (bil. 1980 yen)
NSA, AR, EPA of Japan, *Annual Report*
Quarterly: 1971:1–1986:1
Conversion: None, used only to compute CN5

CSD6: Private Consumption Expenditures on Semi-durable Goods—U.K. (mil. 1980 pounds)
SA, QR, QNA
Quarterly: 1971:1–1986:3
Conversion: None, used only to compute CN6

E1: Foreign Exchange Rate—Canada (Canadian dollars per U.S. dollar)
NSA, CITIBASE, Series: EXRCAN
Monthly: 1947:01–1986:12
Conversion: QA, (1/original series) × 100

E2: Foreign Exchange Rate—France (francs per U.S. dollar)
NSA, CITIBASE, Series: EXRFR
Monthly: 1950:01–1986:12
Conversion: QA, (1/original series) × 100

E3: Foreign Exchange Rate—Germany (marks per U.S. dollar)
NSA, CITIBASE, Series: EXRGER
Monthly: 1951:01–1986:12
Conversion: QA, (1/original series) × 100

E4: Foreign Exchange Rate—Italy (lire per U.S. dollar)
NSA, CITIBASE, Series: EXRITL
Monthly: 1947:01–1986:12
Conversion: QA, (1/original series) × 100

E5: Foreign Exchange Rate—Japan (yen per U.S. dollar)
NSA, CITIBASE, Series: EXRJAN
Monthly: 1957:01–1986:12
Conversion: QA, (1/original series) × 100

E6: Foreign Exchange Rate—U.K. (U.S. dollars per pound)
NSA, CITIBASE, Series: EXRUK
Monthly: 1947:01–1986:12
Conversion: QA, ×100

EX: Exports of Goods and Services—U.S. (bil. 1982 dollars)
SA, AR, CITIBASE 1986, Series: GEX82
Quarterly: 1971:1–1986:4
Conversion: None

EX1: Exports of Goods and Services—Canada (mil. 1981 Canadian dollars)
SA, AR, QNA
Quarterly: 1971:1–1986:3
Conversion: ×0.001

EX2: Exports of Goods and Services—France (bil. 1970 francs)
SA, QR, QNA
Quarterly: 1971:1–1986:2
Conversion: ×4

EX3: Exports of Goods and Services—Germany (mil. 1980 marks)
NSA, QR, QNA
Quarterly: 1971:1–1986:3
Conversion: ×0.004, SA

EX4: Exports of Goods and Services—Italy (bil. 1970 lire)
SA, QR, QNA
Quarterly: 1971:1–1986:3
Conversion: ×4

EX5: Exports of Goods and Services—Japan (bil. 1980 yen)
SA, AR, EPA of Japan, *Annual Report*
Quarterly: 1971:1–1986:3
Conversion: None

EX6: Exports of Goods and Services—U.K. (mil. 1980 pounds)
SA, QR, QNA
Quarterly: 1971:1–1986:3
Conversion: ×0.004

G: Government Expenditures—U.S. (bil. 1982 dollars)
SA, AR, CITIBASE 1986, Series: GGE82
Quarterly: 1971:1–1986:4
Conversion: None

G1: Government-Consumption Expenditure—Canada (mil. 1981 Canadian dollars)
SA, AR, QNA
Quarterly: 1971:1–1986:3
Conversion: ×0.001

G2: Government-Consumption Expenditure—France (bil. 1970 francs)
SA, QR, QNA
Quarterly: 1971:1–1986:2
Conversion: ×4

G3: Government-Consumption Expenditure—Germany (mil. 1980 marks)
NSA, QR, QNA
Quarterly: 1971:1–1986:3
Conversion: ×0.004, SA

G4: Government-Consumption Expenditure—Italy (bil. 1970 lire)
SA, QR, QNA
Quarterly: 1971:1–1986:3
Conversion: ×4

G5: Government Expenditures—Japan (bil. 1980 yen)
SA, AR, EPA of Japan, *Annual Report*
Quarterly: 1971:1–1986:3
Conversion: G5 = GC5 + GI5

G6: Government Consumption Expenditures—U.K. (mil. 1980 pounds)
SA, QR, QNA
Quarterly: 1971:1–1986:3
Conversion: ×0.004

GC5: General Government-Consumption Expenditures—Japan (bil. 1980 yen)
SA, AR, QNA
Quarterly: 1971:1–1986:3
Conversion: None

GI5: General Government-Investment Expenditures—Japan (bil. 1980 yen)
SA, AR, EPA of Japan, *Annual Report*
Quarterly: 1971:1–1986:3
Conversion: None

IBS2: Breeding Stocks, etc.—France (bil. 1970 francs)
SA, QR, QNA
Quarterly: 1971:1–1986:2
Conversion: None, used to compute INE2

IF3: Gross Fixed Capital Formation—Germany (mil. 1980 marks)
NSA, QR, QNA
Quarterly: 1971:1–1986:3
Conversion: ×0.004, SA

IF4: Gross Fixed Capital Formation—Italy (bil. 1970 lire)
SA, QR, QNA
Quarterly: 1971:1–1986:3
Conversion: ×4

IF6: Gross Fixed Capital Formation—U.K. (mil. 1980 pounds)
Computed from IF6 = IR6 + INS6 + INE6
SA, QR, QNA
Quarterly: 1971:1–1986:3
Conversion: None

II: Inventory Investment—U.S. (bil. 1982 dollars)
SA, AR, CITIBASE 1986, Series: GV82
Quarterly: 1971:1–1986:4
Conversion: None

II1: Inventory Investment—Canada (mil. 1981 Canadian dollars)
SA, AR, QNA
Quarterly: 1971:1–1986:3
Conversion: ×0.001

II2: Inventory Investment—France (bil. 1970 francs)
SA, QR, QNA
Quarterly: 1971:1–1986:2
Conversion: ×4

II3: Inventory Investment—Germany (mil. 1980 marks)
NSA, QR, QNA
Quarterly: 1971:1–1986:3
Conversion: ×0.004, SA

II4: Inventory Investment—Italy (bil. 1970 lire)
SA, QR, QNA
Quarterly: 1971:1–1986:3
Conversion: ×4

II5: Inventory Investment—Japan (bil. 1980 yen)
SA, AR, EPA of Japan, *Annual Report*
Quarterly: 1971:1–1986:3
Conversion: None

II6: Inventory Investment—U.K. (mil. 1980 pounds)
SA, QR, QNA
Quarterly: 1971:1–1986:3
Conversion: ×0.004

IM: Imports of Goods and Services—U.S. (bil. 1982 dollars)
SA, AR, CITIBASE 1986, Series: GIM82
Quarterly: 1971:1–1986:4
Conversion: None

IM1: Imports of Goods and Services—Canada (mil. 1981 Canadian dollars)
SA, AR, QNA
Quarterly: 1971:1–1986:3
Conversion: ×0.001

IM2: Imports of Goods and Services—France (bil. 1970 francs)
SA, QR, QNA
Quarterly: 1971:1–1986:2
Conversion: ×4

IM3: Imports of Goods and Services—Germany (mil. 1980 marks)
NSA, QR, QNA
Quarterly: 1971:1–1986:3
Conversion: ×0.004, SA

IM4: Imports of Goods and Services—Italy (bil. 1970 lire)
SA, QR, QNA
Quarterly: 1971:1–1986:3
Conversion: ×4

IM5: Imports of Goods and Services—Japan (bil. 1980 yen)
SA, AR, EPA of Japan, *Annual Report*
Quarterly: 1971:1–1986:3
Conversion: None

IM6: Imports of Goods and Services—U.K. (mil. 1980 pounds)
SA, QR, QNA
Quarterly: 1971:1–1986:3
Conversion: ×0.004

IN5: Nonresidential Investment—Japan (bil. 1980 yen)
SA, AR, QNA
Quarterly: 1971:1–1986:3
Conversion: None

INE: Nonresidential Equipment Investment—U.S. (bil. 1982 dollars)
SA, AR, CITIBASE 1986, Series: GIPD82
Quarterly: 1971:1–1986:4
Conversion: None

INE1: Nonresidential Equipment Investment—Canada (mil. 1981 Canadian dollars)
SA, AR, QNA
Quarterly: 1971:1–1986:3
Conversion: ×0.001

INE2: Nonresidential Equipment Investment—France (bil. 1970 francs)
SA, QR, QNA
Quarterly: 1971:1–1986:2
Conversion: ×4, IBS2 is included in INE2

INE6: Nonresidential Equipment Investment—U.K. (mil. 1980 pounds)
SA, QR, QNA
Quarterly: 1971:1–1986:3
Conversion: ×0.004

INS: Nonresidential Structures Investment—U.S. (bil. 1982 dollars)
SA, AR, CITIBASE 1986, Series: GIS82
Quarterly: 1971:1–1986:4
Conversion: none

INS1: Nonresidential Structures Investment—Canada (mil. 1981 Canadian dollars)
SA, AR, QNA
Quarterly: 1971:1–1986:3
Conversion: ×0.001

INS2: Nonresidential Structures Investment—France (bil. 1970 francs)
SA, QR, QNA
Quarterly: 1971:1–1986:2
Conversion: ×4

INS6: Nonresidential Structures Investment—U.K. (mil. 1980 pounds)
SA, QR, QNA
Quarterly: 1971:1–1986:3
Conversion: ×0.004

IR: Residential Investment—U.S. (bil. 1982 dollars)
SA, AR, CITIBASE 1986, Series: GIR82
Quarterly: 1971:1–1986:4
Conversion: None

IR1: Residential Investment—Canada (mil. 1981 Canadian dollars)
SA, AR, QNA
Quarterly: 1971:1–1986:3
Conversion: ×0.001

IR2: Residential Investment—France (bil. 1970 francs)
SA, QR, QNA
Quarterly: 1971:1–1986:2
Conversion: ×4

IR5: Residential Investment—Japan (bil. 1980 yen)
SA, EPA of Japan, *Annual Report*
Quarterly: 1971:1–1986:3
Conversion: None

IR6: Residential Investment—U.K. (mil. 1980 pounds)
SA, QR, QNA
Quarterly: 1971:1–1986:3
Conversion: ×0.004

M: Money Supply (M1)—U.S. (bil. of dollars)
SA, CITIBASE, Series: FM1
Monthly: 1959:01–1986:12
Conversion: QA

M1: Money Supply (M1)—Canada (bil. of Canadian dollars)
SA, FRB St. Louis, IEC 1987(4)
Quarterly: 1971:1–1986:4
Conversion: None

M2: Money Supply (M1)—France (bil. of francs)
SA, FRB St. Louis, IEC 1987(4)
Quarterly: 1971:1–1986:3
Conversion: None

M3: Money Supply (M1)—Germany (bil. of marks)
SA, FRB St. Louis, IEC 1987(4)
Quarterly: 1971:1–1986:4
Conversion: None

M4: Money Supply (M1)—Italy (tril. of lire)
SA, FRB of St. Louis, IEC 1987(4)
Quarterly: 1971:1–1986:4
Conversion: ×1000

M5: Money Supply (M1)—Japan (tril. of yen)
SA, FRB of St. Louis, IEC 1987(4)
Quarterly: 1971:1–1986:4
Conversion: ×1000

M6: Money Supply (M1)—U.K. (bil. of pounds)
SA, FRB of St. Louis, IEC 1987(4)
Quarterly: 1971:1–1986:2
Conversion: None

P: GNP Deflator—U.S. (1982 = 100)
SA, CITIBASE 1986, Series: GD
Quarterly: 1971:1–1986:4
Conversion: ×0.01

P1: GDP Deflator—Canada (1981 = 100)
SA, QNA
Quarterly: 1971:1–1986:3
Conversion: ×0.01

P2: GDP Deflator—France (1970 = 100)
SA, QNA
Quarterly: 1971:1–1986:2
Conversion: ×0.01

P3: GDP Deflator—Germany (1980 = 100)
NSA, QNA
Quarterly: 1971:1–1986:3
Conversion: ×0.01, SA

P4: GDP Deflator—Italy (1970 = 100)
SA, QNA
Quarterly: 1971:1–1986:3
Conversion: ×0.01

P5: GDP Deflator—Japan (1980 = 100)
SA, QNA
Quarterly: 1971:1–1986:3
Conversion: ×0.01

P6: GDP Deflator—U.K. (1980 = 100)
SA, QNA
Quarterly: 1971:1–1986:3
Conversion: ×0.01

PEX: Exports Deflator—U.S. (1982 = 100)
SA, CITIBASE 1986, Series: GDEX
Quarterly: 1971:1–1986:4
Conversion: ×0.01

PEX1: Exports Deflator—Canada (1981 = 100)
SA, QNA
Quarterly: 1971:1–1986:3
Conversion: ×0.01

PEX2: Exports Deflator—France (1970 = 100)
SA, QNA
Quarterly: 1971:1–1986:2
Conversion: ×0.01

PEX3: Exports Deflator—Germany (1980 = 100)
NSA, QNA
Quarterly: 1971:1–1986:3
Conversion: ×0.01, SA

PEX4: Exports Deflator—Italy (1970 = 100)
SA, QNA
Quarterly: 1971:1–1986:3
Conversion: ×0.01

PEX5: Exports Deflator—Japan (1980 = 100)
SA, EPA of Japan, *Annual Report*
Quarterly: 1971:1–1986:3
Conversion: ×0.01

PEX6: Exports Deflator—U.K. (1980 = 100)
SA, QNA
Quarterly: 1971:1–1986:3
Conversion: ×0.01

PIM: Imports Deflator—U.S. (1982 = 100)
SA, CITIBASE 1986, Series: GDIM
Quarterly: 1971:1–1986:4
Conversion: ×0.01

PIM1: Imports Deflator—Canada (1981 = 100)
SA, QNA
Quarterly: 1971:1–1986:3
Conversion: ×0.01

PIM2: Imports Deflator—France (1970 = 100)
SA, QNA
Quarterly: 1971:1–1986:2
Conversion: ×0.01

PIM3: Imports Deflator—Germany (1980 = 100)
NSA, QNA
Quarterly: 1971:1–1986:3
Conversion: ×0.01, SA

PIM4: Imports Deflator—Italy (1970 = 100)
SA, QNA
Quarterly: 1971:1–1986:3
Conversion: ×0.01

PIM5: Imports Deflator—Japan (1980 = 100)
SA, QNA
Quarterly: 1971:1–1986:3
Conversion: ×0.01

PIM6: Imports Deflator—U.K. (1980 = 100)
SA, QNA
Quarterly: 1971:1–1986:3
Conversion: ×0.01

RL: Interest Rate—U.S. Treasury Composite, 10 Years+ (Long Term), % per annum
NSA, AR, CITIBASE, Series: FYGL
Quarterly: 1971:1–1986:4
Conversion: ×0.01

RL1: Interest Rate—Canada, Long Term, Government
AR, MEI
Quarterly: 1971:1–1986:4
Conversion: ×0.01

RL2: Interest Rate—France, Long Term, Government Guaranteed
AR, MEI
Quarterly: 1971:1–1987:1
Conversion: ×0.01

RL3: Interest Rate—Germany, Long Term, Government
AR, MEI
Quarterly: 1971:1–1987:1
Conversion: ×0.01

RL4: Interest Rate—Italy, Long Term, Government
AR, MEI
Quarterly: 1971:1–1987:1
Conversion: ×0.01

RL5: Interest Rate—Japan, Long Term, Government
AR, MEI
Quarterly: 1971:1–1987:1
Conversion: ×0.01

RL6: Interest Rate—U.K., Long Term, Government
AR, MEI
Quarterly: 1971:1–1987:1
Conversion: ×0.01

RS: Federal Funds Rate—U.S.
AR, CITIBASE, Series: FYFF
Quarterly: 1971:1–1986:4
Conversion: ×0.01

RS1: Call-Money Rate—Canada
AR, MEI
Quarterly: 1971:1–1986:4
Conversion: ×0.01

RS2: Call-Money Rate—France
AR, MEI
Quarterly: 1971:1–1987:1
Conversion: ×0.01

RS3: Call-Money Rate—Germany
AR, MEI
Quarterly: 1971:1–1987:1
Conversion: ×0.01

RS4: Six-Month Treasury Bill Rate—Italy
AR, MEI
Quarterly: 1971:1–1987:1
Conversion: ×0.01

RS5: Call-Money Rate—Japan
AR, MEI
Quarterly: 1971:1–1987:1
Conversion: ×0.01

RS6: Call-Money Rate—U.K.
AR, MEI
Quarterly: 1971:1–1987:1
Conversion: ×0.01

W: Wage Index—U.S. (Adjusted for Overtime and Industry Shifts, 1977 = 100)
SA, CITIBASE, Series: LEHX
Quarterly: 1971:1–1986:4
Conversion: ×0.01

W1: Wage Index—Canada (Hourly Earnings in Manufacturing, 1980 = 100)
SA, MEI
Quarterly: 1971:1–1986:4
Conversion: ×0.01

W2: Wage Index—France (Hourly Rates, Manufacturing, 1980 = 100)
MEI
Quarterly: 1971:1–1986:4
Conversion: ×0.01

W3: Wage Index—Germany (Hourly Earnings, Industry, 1980 = 100)
NSA, IMF IFS
Quarterly: 1971:1–1986:4
Conversion: ×0.01, SA

W4: Wage Index—Italy (Hourly Rates, Industry, 1980 = 100)
MEI, pre-1983 data adjusted from manufacturing
Quarterly: 1971:1–1986:4
Conversion: ×0.01

W5: Wage Index—Japan (Contractual Cash Earnings, All Industries, 1980 = 100)
NSA, IMF IFS
Quarterly: 1971:1–1986:4
Conversion: ×0.01

W6: Wage Index—U.K. (Average Monthly Earnings, All Industries, 1980 = 100)
SA, IMF IFS
Quarterly: 1971:1–1986:3
Conversion: ×0.01

Y: Gross National Product—U.S. (bil. 1982 dollars)
Computed from $Y = CD + CS + CN + II + INE + INS + IR + G + EX - IM$

Y1: Gross Domestic Product—Canada (bil. 1981 Canadian dollars)
Computed from $Y1 = CD1 + CS1 + CN1 + II1 + INE1 + INS1 + IR1 + G1 + EX1 - IM1$

Y2: Gross Domestic Product—France (bil. 1970 francs)
Computed from $Y2 = CD2 + CS2 + CN2 + II2 + INE2 + INS2 + IR2 + G2 + EX2 - IM2$

Y3: Gross Domestic Product—Germany (bil. 1980 marks)
Computed from $Y3 = C3 + II3 + IF3 + G3 + EX3 - IM3$

Y4: Gross Domestic Product—Italy (bil. 1970 lire)
Computed from $Y4 = C4 + G4 + IF4 + II4 + EX4 - IM4$

Y5: Gross Domestic Product—Japan (bil. 1980 yen)
Computed from $Y5 = C5 + G5 + IR5 + IN5 + II5 + EX5 - IM5$

Y6: Gross Domestic Product—U.K. (bil. 1980 pounds)
Computed from $Y6 = C6 + G6 + IF6 + II6 + EX6 - IM6$

For each of the model variables, the first quarter of 1986 value is given below.

Name	Value	Name	Value	Name	Value
Y	3656.000	CN	860.600	W3	1.240
Y1	400.000	CN1	86.500	W4	2.190
Y2	1197.000	CN2	397.600	W5	1.270
Y3	1578.000	CN5	70234.300	W6	1.700
Y4	89756.000	CN6	79.300	INE	309.700
Y5	294484.000	CS	1166.600	INS	148.100
Y6	257.000	CS1	97.400	IR	186.300
P	1.140	CS2	322.400	II	39.900
P1	1.240	CS5	81925.400	IF1	83.500
P2	4.000	CS6	58.300	II1	6.780
P3	1.190	RS	0.078	IN2	196.400
P4	8.060	RS1	0.104	IR2	49.200
P5	1.100	RS2	0.085	II2	0.400
P6	1.430	RS3	0.049	IF3	293.500
EX	369.200	RS4	0.132	II3	15.120
EX1	129.000	RS5	0.055	IF4	14812.000
EX2	302.000	RS6	0.118	II4	1112.000
EX3	532.100	RL	0.089	IN5	54983.000
EX4	4508.000	RL1	0.095	IR5	14341.000
EX5	52209.000	RL2	0.099	II5	1766.000
EX6	71.800	RL3	0.059	IN6	38.830
IM	495.100	RL4	0.134	IR6	8.412
IM1	114.300	RL5	0.047	II6	2.272
IM2	311.600	RL6	0.087	M	632.200
IM3	464.800	PIM	0.950	M1	30.550
IM4	22328.000	PIM1	1.180	M2	1283.700
IM5	41568.000	PIM2	3.260	M3	314.090
IM6	71.200	PIM3	1.160	M4	285250.000
E1	71.225	PIM4	8.190	M5	84417.000
E2	13.866	PIM5	0.800	M6	64.450
E3	42.583	PIM6	1.370	G	725.200
E4	0.063	PEX	1.020	G1	74.500
E5	0.532	PEX1	1.080	G2	159.600
E6	144.050	PEX2	3.470	G3	315.700
C3	886.000	PEX3	1.180	G4	14016.000
C4	57636.000	PEX4	6.900	G5	48629.000
CD	345.400	PEX5	0.880	G6	51.300
CD1	36.600	PEX6	1.350		
CD2	81.200	W	1.680		
CD5	11964.200	W1	1.450		
CD6	18.000	W2	1.710		

Appendix 2:
Computer Programs

This appendix briefly describes the computer software used for the estimations and model solutions discussed in the book. The main workhorse is the program to simulate nonlinear rational expectations models.

Solution of Rational Expectations Models

The simulations of the multicountry model discussed in the book were conducted using a program written in Fortran 77 that implements the Fair-Taylor extended path algorithm described in Chapter 1. This program and instructions for its use are available from the author. The program is written so that one with access to a UNIX-based workstation or mainframe with a Fortran compiler can recreate the simulations discussed in the book along with variants thereof. Knowledge of the Fortran language and the internal workings of the algorithm are not required.

The files for running the program include Fortran source code files with an "f" extension and data files with a "dat" extension. The file "extpath.f" contains the extended path algorithm program. In a sense, this file does all the work. The file "files.f" tells the program where the data files are located on the computer's hard disk. The default settings assume that all the files are located in the same directory. The data file "bl.dat" contains the baseline variable values used by the simulations. The files "coefs.dat," "ratio.dat," and "wage.dat" contain the estimated coefficients for the equations making up the model. The file "vcov.dat" contains the estimated variance-covariance matrix for the residuals from the estimated equations making up the model. The files "dlist.dat" and "print.dat" provide information to the program regarding the ordering of variables in the equations and for the printout. An additional file "job.dat" can be used to supply the program with simulation specifications when the user wishes to dispense with the interactive part of the program.

In order to use the program, the files "extpath.f" and "files.f" must be compiled and linked using a Fortran compiler. This need only be done once. When the program is run, the user only needs to respond to a number of prompted questions regarding the type of simulation and then the program runs automatically until completion. Among the options the user can choose from are whether the simulation is deterministic or stochastic, the type of instrument change or the type of policy rule simulated, and the nature of the shocks to the economy. These choices are made from a list provided with the program and include all the simulations presented in the book and variants on these simulations. In addition, the response coefficients in the policy rules can easily be adjusted. Thus, it is possible to investigate how sensitive the results of the simulations are to changes in the parameters or policy regime. Other changes—such as modifying the estimated coefficients of the equations of the model—require that the Fortran code of the program be changed.

The program requires approximately 4 Mb of RAM to operate. Successful completion of a single deterministic simulation on a Sun Sparcstation 1 workstation takes approximately 4 minutes and 15 seconds.

The output of the program consists of time series for all the variables in the model. This output is written to a file that can be read by commercial spreadsheet or plotting programs. The user can then analyze the data using available software.

The single-country model of Chapter 2 was solved using the Dagli-Taylor factorization method programmed in the VARMA computer software program by C. Ates Dagli. It could also be solved using the extended path method.

Estimation of Rational Expectations Model

1. Limited-Information Estimation

The estimation of all equations of the multicountry model, with the exception of the wage equations, was performed using the TSP program. In estimating the equations of the multicountry model, a subroutine was written to implement Hansen's generalized method of moments (GMM) estimation procedure within TSP. The subroutine also calculates the Sargan test statistic for overidentifying restrictions.

2. Maximum-Likelihood Estimation

The single-country model of Chapter 2 and the wage equations of the multicountry model were estimated using maximum likelihood. In order to evaluate the likelihood function at each function evaluation, the single-country model was solved using the Dagli-Taylor factorization method in the VARMA program written by C. Ates Dagli. The estimation of the wage equations was performed using a program written by Andrew Levin that also used the Dagli-Taylor method.

Stochastic Simulation

The variance-covariance matrix was factored using a modified Choleski method implemented in the TSP routine YLDFAC. A vector of standard normal variables is then constructed using a random-number generating algorithm. Multiplication of the triangular matrix resulting from the factorization by the vector of standard normals yields a vector of random variables with a variance-covariance matrix equal to the variance-covariance matrix of the structural residuals. This vector of residuals is then added to the equations of the multicountry model each quarter.

References

Adams, Gwyn, Lewis Alexander, and Joseph Gagnon. (1991). "German Unification and the European Monetary System: A Quantitative Analysis." Washington, D.C.: Federal Reserve Working Paper.

Anderson, Theodore W. (1971). *The Statistical Analysis of Time Series*. New York: Wiley.

Ball, Lawrence. (1990). "Credible Disinflation with Staggered Price Setting." Cambridge, Mass.: National Bureau of Economic Research Working Paper #3555.

Barro, Robert J., and David B. Gordon. (1983). "Rules, Discretion and Reputation in a Model of Monetary Policy." *Journal of Monetary Economics* 12: 101–22.

Baumol, William J. (1970). *Economic Dynamics*. New York: MacMillan.

Blanchard, Olivier, and Stanley Fischer. (1989). *Lectures in Macroeconomics*. Cambridge, Mass.: MIT Press.

Bray, Margaret. (1983). "Convergence to Rational Expectations Equilibrium." In *Individual Forecasting and Aggregate Outcomes*, edited by R. Frydman and E. S. Phelps. Cambridge, Eng.: Cambridge University Press.

Brayton, Flint, and Jaime Marquez. (1990). "The Behavior of Monetary Sectors and Monetary Policy: Evidence from Multicountry Models." In *Financial Sectors in Open Economies: Empirical Analysis and Policy Issues*, edited by Peter Hooper, et al. Washington, D.C.: Board of Governors of the Federal Reserve Board.

Bryant, Ralph, David Currie, Jacob Frenkel, Paul Masson, and Richard Portes, eds. (1989). *Macroeconomic Policies in an Interdependent World*. Washington, D.C.: The Brookings Institution.

Bryant, Ralph, Dale Henderson, Gerald Holtham, Peter Hooper, and Steven Symansky, eds. (1988a). *Empirical Macroeconomics for Interdependent Economies*. Washington, D.C.: The Brookings Institution.

Bryant, Ralph, Gerald Holtham, and Peter Hooper, eds. (1988b). *External Deficits and the Dollar*. Washington, D.C.: The Brookings Institution.

Bryant, Ralph, Peter Hooper, and Catherine Mann, eds. (1992). *Evaluating Policy Regimes: New Research in Empirical Macroeconomics*. Washington, D.C.: The Brookings Institution.

Calvo, Guillermo. (1978). "On the Time Inconsistency of Optimal Policy in a Monetary Economy." *Econometrica* 46: 1411–28.

Carlozzi, Nicholas, and John B. Taylor. (1985). "International Capital Mobility and the Coordination of Monetary Rules." In *Exchange Rate Dynamics under Uncertainty*, edited by J. Bhandari. Cambridge, Mass.: MIT Press.

Chow, Gregory C. (1975). *Analysis and Control of Dynamic Economic Systems.* New York: Wiley.

Cooper, J. P., and Stanley Fischer. (1974). "Monetary and Fiscal Policy in a Fully Stochastic St. Louis Econometric Model." *Journal of Money Credit and Banking* 6: 1–22.

Crocket, Andrew. (1989). "The Role of International Institutions in Surveillance and Policy Coordination." In *Macroeconomic Policies in an Interdependent World*, edited by Ralph Bryant, et al. Washington, D.C.: The Brookings Institution.

Dagli, C. Ates, and John B. Taylor. (1984). "Estimation and Solution of Linear Rational Expectations Models Using a Polynomial Matrix Factorization." *Journal of Economic Dynamics and Control* 8: 341–48.

Davidon, W. C. (1959). "Variable Metric Method for Minimization." A.E.C. Research and Development Report ANL 5990.

Dobson, Wendy. (1991). *Economic Policy Coordination: Requiem or Prologue.* Washington, D.C.: Institute for International Economics.

Dornbusch, Rudiger. (1976). "Expectations and Exchange Rate Dynamics." *Journal of Political Economy* 84: 1161–71.

Economic Report of the President, 1990, Washington, D.C.: U.S. Government Printing Office.

Economic Report of the President, 1991, Washington, D.C.: U.S. Government Printing Office.

Fadeeva, V. N. (1959). *Computational Methods of Linear Algebra.* New York: Dover Publications.

Fair, Ray C. (1984). *Specification, Estimation, and Analysis of Macroeconometric Models.* Cambridge, Mass.: Harvard University Press.

Fair, Ray C., and John B. Taylor. (1983). "Solution and Maximum Likelihood Estimation of Dynamic Nonlinear Rational Expectations Models." *Econometrica* 51: 1169–85.

Fair, Ray C., and John B. Taylor. (1990). "Full Information Estimation and Stochastic Simulation of Models with Rational Expectations." *Journal of Applied Econometrics* 5: 381–92.

Fischer, Stanley. (1977). "Long-Term Contracts, Rational Expectations, and the Optimal Money Supply Rule." *Journal of Political Economy* 85: 191–206.

Fischer, Stanley. (1990). "Rules versus Discretion in Monetary Policy." In *Handbook of Monetary Economics*, edited by B. Friedman and F. Hahn. Amsterdam: North-Holland.

Fleming, J. Marcus. (1962). "Domestic Financial Policies under Fixed and under Flexible Exchange Rates." *IMF Staff Papers* 9: 369–79.

Fletcher, R., and M. J. D. Powell. (1963). "A Rapidly Converging Decent Method for Minimization." *Computer Journal* 6: 163–68.

Frenkel, Jacob A., Morris Goldstein, and Paul Masson. (1989). "Simulating the Effects of Some Simple Coordinated versus Uncoordinated Policy Rules." In *Macroeconomic Policies in an Interdependent World*, edited by Ralph Bryant, et al. Washington, D.C.: The Brookings Institution.

Friedman, Milton. (1948). "A Monetary and Fiscal Framework for Economic Stability." *American Economic Review* 38: 245–64.

Frydman, Roman. (1983). "A Distinction between the Unconditional Expectational Equilibrium and the Rational Expectations Equilibrium." In *Individual Forecasting and Aggregate Outcomes*, edited by Roman Frydman and Edmund S. Phelps. Cambridge, Eng.: Cambridge University Press.

Fukuda, Shin-Ichi, and Koichi Hamada. (1987). "Toward the Implementation of Desirable Rules of Monetary Coordination and Intervention." In *Toward a World of Economic Stability*, edited by Y. Suzuki and M. Okabe. Tokyo: University of Tokyo Press.

Gagnon, Joseph. (1991). "A Forward-Looking Multicountry Model for Policy Analysis: MX3." *Economic and Financial Computing*, forthcoming.

Goldfeld, Stephen M., and Richard Quandt. (1972). *Nonlinear Methods in Econometrics*. Amsterdam: North-Holland.

Hall, Robert E. (1978). "Stochastic Implications of the Life Cycle–Permanent Income Hypothesis: Theory and Evidence." *Journal of Political Economy* 86: 971–88.

Hall, Robert E., and John B. Taylor. (1993). *Macroeconomics: Theory, Performance, and Policy.* 4th Ed. New York: Norton.

Hansen, Lars Peter. (1982). "Large Sample Properties of Generalized Methods of Moments Estimators." *Econometrica* 50: 1029–54.

Hansen, Lars Peter, Dennis Epple, and W. Roberds. (1985). "Linear Quadratic Methods of Resource Depletion." In *Energy, Foresight and Strategy*, edited by Thomas J. Sargent. Washington, D.C.: Resources for the Future.

Hansen, Lars Peter, and Thomas J. Sargent. (1980). "Formulating and Estimating Dynamic Linear Rational Expectations Models." *Journal of Economic Dynamics and Control* 2: 7–46.

Heller, Walter W. (1966). *New Dimensions in Political Economy.* New York: Norton

Helliwell, John F., Jon Cockerline, and Robert Lafrance. (1990). "Multicountry Modeling of Financial Markets." In *Financial Sectors in Open Economies: Empirical Analysis and Policy Issues*, edited by Peter Hooper, et al. Washington, D.C.: Board of Governors of the Federal Reserve Board.

Hickman, Bert. (1988). "The U.S. Economy and the International Transmission Mechanism." In *Empirical Macroeconomics for Interdependent Economies*, edited by Ralph Bryant, et al. Washington, D.C.: The Brookings Institution.

Keynes, John Maynard. (1936). *The General Theory of Employment, Interest and Money.* London: MacMillan.

Klein, Lawrence, ed. (1991). *Comparative Performance of U.S. Econometric Models.* Oxford, Eng.: Oxford University Press.

Kydland, Finn, and E. C. Prescott. (1977). "Rules Rather than Discretion: The Inconsistency of Optimal Plans." *Journal of Political Economy* 85: 473–92.

Laidler, David. (1991). "Price Stability and the Monetary Order." Fifth Bank of Japan Conference Proceedings. Tokyo: University of Tokyo.

Lucas, Robert E., Jr. (1976). "Econometric Policy Evaluation: A Critique." *Carnegie Rochester Conference Series on Public Policy* 1. Amsterdam: North-Holland.

Lucas, Robert E., Jr. (1980). "Rules, Discretion and the Role of the Economic Advisor." In *Rational Expectations and Economic Policy,* edited by Stanley Fischer. Chicago: Chicago University Press.

Lucas, Robert E., Jr. (1981). "Tobin and Monetarism: A Review Article." *Journal of Economic Literature* 19: 558–67.

Lucas, Robert E., Jr., and Thomas J. Sargent, eds. (1981). *Rational Expectations and Econometric Practice.* Minneapolis: University of Minnesota Press.

McCallum, Bennett. (1983). "On Non-Uniqueness in Rational Expectations: An Attempt at Perspective." *Journal of Monetary Economics* 11: 139–68.

McCallum, Bennett. (1988). "Robustness Properties of a Rule for Monetary Policy." *Carnegie Rochester Conference Series on Public Policy* 29: 173–203. Amsterdam: North-Holland.

McCallum, Bennett. (1989). "Real Business Cycle Models." In *Modern Business Cycle Theory,* edited by R. J. Barro. Cambridge, Mass.: Harvard University Press.

McKibbin, Warrick, and Jeffrey Sachs. (1989). "Implications of Policy Rules for the World Economy." In *Macroeconomic Policies in an Interdependent World,* edited by Ralph Bryant, et al. Washington, D.C.: The Brookings Institution.

McKinnon, Ronald. (1988). "Monetary and Exchange Rate Policies for International Financial Stability." *Journal of Economic Perspectives* 2: 83–103.

McKinnon, Ronald. (1991). *The Order of Economic Liberalization.* Baltimore: The Johns Hopkins University Press.

Mankiw, N. Gregory, and David Romer, eds. (1991). *New Keynesian Economics.* Cambridge, Mass.: MIT Press.

Marcet, Albert, and Thomas J. Sargent. (1989). "Convergence of Least Squares Learning Mechanisms in Self Referential Stochastic Models." *Journal of Economic Theory* 48: 337–68.

Marschak, Jacob. (1953). "Economic Measurements for Policy and Prediction." *Studies in Econometric Method,* Cowles Foundation Monograph 14. New Haven, Conn.: Yale University Press.

Miller, Marcus, and John Williamson. (1988). "The International Monetary System: An Analysis of Alternative Regimes." *European Economic Review* 32: 1031–48.

Mundell, Robert. (1962). "Capital Mobility and Stabilization Policy under Fixed and Flexible Exchange Rates." *Canadian Journal of Economics and Political Science* 29: 475–87.

Muth, J. F. (1961). "Rational Expectations and the Theory of Price Movements." *Econometrica* 29: 315–35.

Newey, Whitney M., and Kenneth West. (1987). "A Simple Positive Definite, Heteroscedasticity and Autocorrelation Consistent Covariance Matrix." *Econometrica* 55: 703–8.

Okun, Arthur M. (1978). "Efficient Disinflationary Policies." *American Economic Review* 68: 348–52.

Phelps, Edmund S. (1978). "Disinflation without Recession: Adaptive Guideposts and Monetary Policy." *Weltwirtschaftliches Archiv* 100: 783–809.

Phelps, Edmund S. (1990). *Seven Schools of Thought in Macroeconomics.* Oxford, Eng.: Oxford University Press.

Phelps, Edmund S., and John B. Taylor. (1977). "Stabilizing Powers of Monetary Policy under Rational Expectations." *Journal of Political Economy* 85: 163–90.

Phillips, A. W. (1954). "Stabilization Policies in a Closed Economy." *Economic Journal* 64: 290–323.

Poole, William. (1970). "The Optimal Choice of Instruments in a Simple Stochastic Macro Model." *Quarterly Journal of Economics* 84: 197–216.

Rehm, Dawn. (1982). *Staggered Contracts, Capital Flows and Macroeconomic Stability in the United States.* Ph.D. dissertation. Columbia University.

Sargent, Thomas J. (1987a). *Macroeconomic Theory.* 2nd ed. New York: Academic Press.

Sargent, Thomas J. (1987b). *Dynamic Macroeconomic Theory.* Cambridge, Mass.: Harvard University Press.

Shiller, Robert J. (1979). "The Volatility of Long-Term Interest Rates and Expectations Models of the Term Structure." *Journal of Political Economy* 87: 1190–1219.

Shiller, Robert J. (1991). "Comment." In *Comparative Performance of U.S. Econometric Models,* edited by Lawrence R. Klein. Oxford, Eng.: Oxford University Press.

Sims, Christopher. (1982). "Policy Analysis with Econometric Models." *Brookings Papers on Economic Activity* 1: 107–64.

Stiglitz, Joseph E. (1984). "Price Rigidities and Market Structure." *American Economic Review* 74: 350–55.

Taylor, John B. (1975). "Monetary Policy During a Transition to Rational Expectations." *Journal of Political Economy* 83: 1009–21.

Taylor, John B. (1977). "Conditions for the Unique Solutions in Stochastic Macroeconomic Models with Rational Expectations." *Econometrica* 45: 1377–85.

Taylor, John B. (1979). "Estimation and Control of a Macroeconomic Model with Rational Expectations." *Econometrica* 47: 1267–86.

Taylor, John B. (1980). "Aggregate Dynamics and Staggered Contracts." *Journal of Political Economy* 88: 1–24.

Taylor, John B. (1981). "Stabilization, Accommodation, and Monetary Rules." *American Economic Review, Papers and Proceedings* 71: 145–49.

Taylor, John B. (1982). "The Role of Expectations in the Choice of Monetary Policy." In *Monetary Policy Issues for the 1980s.* Kansas City: Federal Reserve Bank of Kansas City.

Taylor, John B. (1983a). "Comments on 'Rules Discretion and Reputation in a Model of Monetary Policy' by R. J. Barro and D. B. Gordon." *Journal of Monetary Economics* 12: 123–25.

Taylor, John B. (1983b). "Union Wage Settlements During a Disinflation." *American Economic Review* 73: 981–93.

Taylor, John B. (1985). "International Coordination in the Design of Macroeconomic Policy Rules." *European Economic Review* 28: 53–81.

Taylor, John B. (1986). "New Econometric Approaches to Stabilization Policy in Stochastic Models of Macroeconomic Fluctuations." In *Handbook of Econometrics,* edited by M. Intriligator and Z. Griliches. Amsterdam: North-Holland.

Taylor, John B. (1988). "The Current Account and Macroeconomic Policy: An Econometric Analysis." In *The U.S. Trade Deficit: Causes, Consequences, and Cures,* edited by Albert E. Burger. 12th Annual Economic Policy Conference Proceedings, Federal Reserve Bank of St. Louis. Boston, Mass.: Kluwer Academic Publishing.

Taylor, John B. (1989a). "Monetary Policy and the Stability of Macroeconomic Relationships." *Journal of Applied Econometrics* 4: S161–78.

Taylor, John B. (1989b). "Policy Analysis with a Multicountry Model." In *Macroeconomic Policies in an Interdependent World,* edited by Ralph Bryant, et al., pp. 122–41. Washington, D.C.: The Brookings Institution.

Visco, Ignazio. (1991). "A New Round of U.S. Model Comparisons: A Limited Appraisal." In *Comparative Performance of U.S. Econometric Models,* edited by Lawrence R. Klein. Oxford, Eng.: Oxford University Press.

Wallis, K. (1980). "Econometric Implications of the Rational Expectations Hypothesis." *Econometrica* 48: 49–73.

Whiteman, Charles H. (1983). *Linear Rational Expectations Models: A Users Guide.* Minneapolis: University of Minnesota Press.

Index